FROM DIRECT ACTION
TO AFFIRMATIVE ACTION

FROM DIRECT ACTION
TO AFFIRMATIVE ACTION

Fair Employment Law and Policy in America, 1933–1972

PAUL D. MORENO

LOUISIANA STATE UNIVERSITY PRESS
Baton Rouge and London

06 05 04 03 02 01 00 99 98 97   5 4 3 2 1
Designer: Michele Myatt
Typefaces: Stone Sans, Stone Serif
Typesetter: Impressions Book and Journal Services, Inc.
Printer and binder: Thomson-Shore, Inc.

Library of Congress Cataloging-in-Publication Data

Moreno, Paul D., 1965–
    From direct action to affirmative action : fair employment law and
policy in America, 1933–1972 / Paul D. Moreno.
        p.   cm.
    Includes bibliographical references and index.
    ISBN 0-8071-2138-X (alk. paper)
    1. Discrimination in employment—Law and legislation—United
States—History.   I. Title.
    KF3464.M665   1997
    344.7301'133—dc21   96-50168
                                                                  CIP

Chapters 2, 3, and 4 make use of material from the author's article "Racial Proportionalism and the Origin of Employment Discrimination Policy, 1933–50," *Journal
of Policy History,* VIII (Fall, 1996), copyright 1996 by Pennsylvania State Univeristy.
Reproduced by permission of Pennsylvania State University Press. Chapter 4 was
first published in somewhat different form as "Direct Action and Fair Employment:
The *Hughes* Case," *Western Legal History,* VIII (Winter–Spring, 1995), 1–34.

To Joe and Connie
with Love

CONTENTS

ACKNOWLEDGMENTS

I wish to thank the workers and taxpayers of the United States, particularly those of New York and Maryland, for their support of my college education. I would like to thank my teachers at the State University of New York at Albany, particularly Richard Kendall and Warren Roberts, for instilling in me a love of history and inspiring me to research and write. Alfred A. Moss, Jr., of the University of Maryland, and Jennifer Roback of the George Mason Center for the Study of Public Choice read the manuscript and offered much valuable criticism. Above all, I am grateful to Herman Belz for his friendship, advice, criticism, and encouragement. I would like to thank the staff of the Library of Congress, the New York, Maryland, and California state archives, and the New York State Division for Human Rights for their help. My wife, Lisa, read, edited, and improved the manuscript, and made the whole enterprise worthwhile. I dedicate the work to my parents who made it all possible.

FROM DIRECT ACTION
TO AFFIRMATIVE ACTION

INTRODUCTION

A generation after the Civil Rights Act of 1964 outlawed racial discrimination in employment, the dominant interpretation of equality was that racial minorities and women should be represented at every level in the work force in some proportion to their representation in the labor market. Statistical differences are the measure of discrimination.[1] In legal terms, this concept of discrimination is known as the "disparate-impact" theory of discrimination. The disparate-impact theory assumes that a statistically significant deviation between the proportion of minority group members in an employer's work force and the proportion of minority group members in the population constitutes prima facie proof of discrimination which, absent justification by the employer, establishes a violation of any or all of a number of federal, state, and local antidiscrimination laws.

Throughout most of the history of the twentieth-century civil rights movement, the main argument for equality was made on other grounds. Discrimination was understood to be "unequal treatment based on race." By this theory, members of minority groups were denied employment opportunities for no other reason than their race. Discrimination consisted of discrete, identifiable, individual acts of

---

1. Robert A. Sedler, "Employment Equality, Affirmative Action, and the Constitutional Political Consensus," *Michigan Law Review,* XC (1992), 1336; Ronald J. Fiscus, *The Constitutional Logic of Affirmative Action,* ed. Stephen L. Wasby (Durham, 1992); Thomas Sowell, *Civil Rights: Rhetoric or Reality?* (New York, 1984), 13–35.

different treatment. These two visions of discrimination and equality differ in several fundamental ways. The disparate-treatment vision is color-blind, insisting that if race were unknown, racial discrimination would be impossible; the disparate-impact vision is color-conscious, arguing that racial discrimination is institutional, subtle, and unconscious, and that only race-based preferential treatment can overcome its lingering effects. The disparate-treatment vision favors individual rights and merit-based personnel decisions; the disparate-impact vision is group-based, arguing that institutional racism is so pervasive as to render individual merit meaningless, and regards group representation as the safest guarantee of individual rights. The disparate-treatment theory calls for equality of opportunity, making no assumptions about the outcomes among racial groups; the disparate-impact theory calls for equality of outcome, maintaining that the proof of fair employment is proportional results, and that any imbalance is the result of discrimination.

Usually the transformation of the color-blind, individual rights, equality of opportunity formula into the color-conscious, group rights, equality of result one is attributed to courts and bureaucrats in the exigent circumstances of the 1960s. Hugh Davis Graham, in his authoritative treatment of the development of civil rights law and policy since 1960, notes, "Few if any of the serious arguments that would later be deployed to rationalize and sustain a doctrine of preferential discrimination were raised in its defense in 1963 and 1964."[2] While it is true that proponents of preferential treatment muted their ideas during the congressional debate on the Civil Rights Act, there was significant discussion of the issue, in its philosophical and practical aspects, decades earlier. Previous attempts to deal with the problem of employment discrimination show an articulation of the disparate-impact theory as early as the 1930s, often endorsed by mainstream organizations, administrators, and jurists.

This period also revealed a vexing antinomy in antidiscrimination efforts. Guaranteeing equal treatment and addressing individual cases of disparate treatment did not result in dramatic strides

2. Hugh Davis Graham, *The Civil Rights Era: Origins of National Policy, 1960–72* (New York, 1990), 120.

toward proportional group equality. Attempts to move beyond exhortation to enforcement, on the other hand, seemed to lead inevitably to the use of color-conscious, statistical group measures of employment, compelling employers to resort to preferential quota hiring and promotion, leaving the goal of equal treatment unsatisfied. In short, unless antidiscrimination laws were enforced, discrimination would go unchecked, but if antidiscrimination laws were enforced, quotas would result. Politically, in the twenty-five years before the Civil Rights Act of 1964, the nation was willing to sacrifice black economic advancement for the sake of the color-blind principle; in the twenty-five years since the Civil Rights Act of 1964, the nation has sacrificed the color-blind principle for the sake of preferential policies. This history suggests that this antinomy is inherent in legal attempts to combat racial discrimination in employment.

Many historians have noted the rapid transformation of the civil rights movement's goals in the mid-1960s, identifying deep-seated divisions within black organizations that became explicit in the 1960s, but have not explained how American law and policy adapted so quickly to the new civil rights agenda.[3] Scholarly treatments of employment policy were common in the postwar years, and reached a peak around the time of the enactment of the Civil Rights Act of 1964. Few have been written since 1965, and few of these works have been by historians.[4] Historians have only recently turned attention to the issue of employment discrimination in the modern era, where attention has usually focused on public accommodations and school desegregation, voting rights, or other civil rights issues.

3. See Harvard Sitkoff, *The Struggle for Black Equality, 1954–80* (New York, 1981), 208–22; William Chafe, *The Unfinished Journey: America Since World War II* (2nd ed.; New York, 1991), 302–20; Richard Polenberg, *One Nation Divisible: Class, Race, and Ethnicity in the United States Since 1938* (New York, 1980), 231–43.

4. Morroe Berger, *Equality By Statute: The Revolution in Civil Rights*, rev. ed. (New York, 1967); Paul H. Norgren and Samuel E. Hill, *Toward Fair Employment* (New York, 1964); Michael Sovern, *Legal Restraints on Racial Discrimination in Employment* (New York, 1966); Paul Burstein, *Discrimination, Jobs, and Politics: The Struggle for Equal Employment Opportunity in the United States Since the New Deal* (Chicago, 1985); Merl E. Reed, *Seedtime for the Modern Civil Rights Movement: The President's Committee on Fair Employment Practice, 1941–1946* (Baton Rouge, 1991); William H. Harris, *The Harder We Run: Black Workers Since the Civil War* (New York, 1982).

However, these recent histories of law and policy do not treat the years before 1960.[5] This work, covering the period from the New Deal to the rise of affirmative action, attempts to do so and to cast the development of modern national policy in a broader historical context.

The law of employment discrimination evolved at both the national and state levels, as the main efforts against racial discrimination in employment changed depending on time and circumstances. Law and policy were articulated in federal and state legal records, primarily in litigation. Appellate decisions are the foundation for the legal doctrines governing the law of employment discrimination, and lower courts of original jurisdiction provide the details of particular cases and help to reveal the social context of the law. Legislative history and the records of state and federal fair employment practice commissions are another principal source. Leading law reviews followed the development of antidiscrimination, and often contributed to it, and demonstrate both the development of the law and the opinion of the increasingly important academic legal community. Both national and local civil rights organizations were among the principal agents shaping law and public policy, and were aware of the tensions and conflicting tendencies at the heart of the effort. Finally, much recent work has been done in the field of law-and-economics and public choice theory which has provided valuable theoretical underpinnings for this history.[6]

The development of antidiscrimination law from 1933 to 1972 can be roughly divided into three periods. The first, from the onset of the Great Depression until World War II, concerns attempts of local black organizations to use the tactics of organized labor to gain jobs. The effort known as the "Don't Buy Where You Can't Work" movement led to the first legal decisions concerning discrimination in employment. This endeavor, clearly race-conscious and demanding quotas and proportional employment of various kinds, was largely unsuccessful and ineffective, but it articulated a nondis-

5. Graham, *Civil Rights Era;* Herman Belz, *Equality Transformed: A Quarter-Century of Affirmative Action* (New Brunswick, 1991).

6. See Werner Z. Hirsch, *Law and Economics: An Introductory Analysis* (2nd ed.; Boston, 1988), 1–22, 355–400.

crimination standard in employment for the first time, one that was remarkably prescient. The efforts of New Deal agencies in the 1930s to promote black employment evinced similar racialist tendencies. Like the "Don't Buy" movement, these efforts were tentative—justified and limited by the acute economic circumstances of the depression.

The second period extends from World War II to the enactment of the Civil Rights Act of 1964. In this period the color-blind, disparate-treatment definition of discrimination was favored. The improved economic conditions brought on by World War II and the postwar expansion made the preferential quota schemes of the 1930s seem inappropriate. The President's Committee on Fair Employment Practice insisted on color-blind equality of opportunity and scrupulously avoided any insistence on preferential treatment. This model was followed by the state fair employment practice commissions created in the postwar years, and (though less assiduously) by the successors to the President's Committee in the 1950s and 1960s. Although civil rights groups often criticized these committees, black economic gains in both absolute and relative terms in the postwar decade made the administration of these agencies seem effective enough. The quickening of the civil rights movement in the 1955–65 period combined with the halting of relative economic progress of black Americans to bring about a crisis in the color-blind antidiscrimination effort.

The third period covers the enactment and administration of Title VII of the Civil Rights Act of 1964. In this period the disparate-treatment definition of discrimination, written into the act, gave way to the disparate-impact definition advocated by civil rights groups, federal bureaucrats, and ultimately accepted by the federal courts. The disparate-impact theory was hammered out in the attack on a series of employment problems (proof of discrimination, the present effects of past discrimination, preferential treatment), many of which had been addressed more fully by the state fair employment practice commissions and the presidential committees since the war than was evident in the Civil Rights Act debates. The disparate-impact theory seemed to arise overnight in the late 1960s, but it had long antecedents and might have been anticipated.

1   The Color-Blind Aspiration, 1865–1933

Although the law of employment discrimination developed in the twentieth-century industrial economy, its roots lie in the nineteenth-century questions of civil rights, racial classifications in law, and the nature of discrimination. We may take Reconstruction as a proximate starting point, when Americans began to address the fundamental questions of law and race relations in the aftermath of slavery. Following wartime emancipation, Congress began to fashion policy regarding the status of the freedmen. It passed the Thirteenth Amendment, abolishing slavery, and then nationalized American citizenship in the Civil Rights Act of 1866 and the Fourteenth Amendment. Section one of the Fourteenth Amendment, the centerpiece of constitutional law of racial equality, reads, "All persons born or naturalized in the United States, and subject to the jurisdiction thereof, are citizens of the United States and of the State wherein they reside. No State shall make or enforce any law which shall abridge the privileges or immunities of citizens of the United States; nor shall any State deprive any person of life, liberty, or property, without due process of law; nor deny to any person within its jurisdiction the equal protection of the laws." The significance of race in American citizenship remained an issue. Were the freedmen (and other non-white Americans) to enjoy equal rights, privileges, and responsibilities as individuals, without regard to race, or were black Americans to constitute a distinct legal group—either as inferior, "second class" citizens or as a specially protected and favored class of citizens? In short, was American citizenship, constitutionally and legally defined, to be color-blind or color-conscious? Congress addressed this question in the Freedmen's Bureau acts, the Civil Rights Act of 1866, and the Fourteenth Amendment.

Historians and lawyers have long analyzed the implications of the Reconstruction amendments for race-conscious legislation. The standard argument of civil rights groups in their assault on segregation was that the Reconstruction amendments established a rule of strict color-blindness. The color-blind interpretation of the Constitution was embodied in Justice John Marshall Harlan's famous dissenting opinion in *Plessy* v. *Ferguson,* that "our Constitution is color-blind, and neither knows nor tolerates classes among citizens." Civil rights lawyers advanced this argument as part of their appeal in the historic desegregation case of *Brown* v. *Board of Education,* although the Court did not unequivocally accept it. Historians generally agree that it is difficult to sustain the argument that the framers of the Reconstruction amendments intended to apply a color-blind rule that would outlaw segregation in public education and public accommodations. In particular, when the Reconstruction Congress rejected the terminology of "nondiscrimination" for the Fourteenth Amendment, and used "equal protection" instead, it weakened the color-blind principle, and allowed judges to determine if racial classifications were "reasonable." Nevertheless, the Reconstruction Congress did establish a rule of "limited absolute equality," or of strict color-blindness in certain fundamental civil rights. Thus the Reconstruction period can be said to have established a color-blind tendency or aspiration that left room for its extension into areas beyond these certain cases. The Supreme Court ultimately departed from text and original intent but followed this aspiration.[1]

After *Brown,* advocates of affirmative action and race-based preferences for black Americans have taken the failure of the Reconstruction amendments to establish a strict color-blind rule as a justification for race-conscious policies. Denying that the Constitution

1. Andrew Kull, *The Color-Blind Constitution* (Cambridge, Mass., 1992); Earl Maltz, *Civil Rights, the Constitution, and Congress, 1863–69* (Lawrence, Kan., 1990); Alexander Bickel, "The Original Understanding and the Segregation Decision," *Harvard Law Review,* LXIX (1955).

is strictly color-blind, they argue that the use of racial classifications in social policy has always been constitutionally permissible. In this interpretation, the framers of the Reconstruction amendments envisioned and actually implemented "benign" racial classifications as compensation for slavery, primarily in the Freedmen's Bureau. Justice Thurgood Marshall applied this novel interpretation to defend racial quotas in higher education admissions in his 1977 *Bakke* opinion. But this view is untenable. Pro-slavery, border-state Democrats imputed the intent of preferential racial classifications in the Reconstruction debate while the proponents of the measures vehemently denied it. Neither the legislation establishing the Freedmen's Bureau nor its performance indicates an exclusive, pro-black racial consciousness. Bureau officials consistently affirmed the ideal of a racially neutral, common American citizenship. Moreover, the Freedmen's Bureau Act was a war-related emergency measure, and cannot be considered as the principal guide to the Civil Rights Act of 1866 and the Fourteenth Amendment. Reconstruction legislation and its proponents evinced no support for benign racial classification in their effort to eradicate invidious racial classifications.[2]

Before slavery had been completely abolished during the Civil War, Congress sometimes treated ex-slaves with racially specific legislation. After Congress passed the Thirteenth Amendment and began to deal with the freedmen as citizens, most racial classifications disappeared. The original version of the Freedmen's Bureau Act of 1864, for example, was limited to the assistance of freedmen. Moderate Republicans removed the bill's racial classification and applied it to all "refugees and freedmen," with "no distinction of color." If some radical Republicans believed that racial classifications used before

---

2. Charles Abrams *et al., Equality* (New York, 1965), 160; Gary Elden, "'Forty Acres and a Mule,' with Interest: The Constitutionality of Black Capitalism, Benign School Quotas, and Other Statutory Racial Classifications," *Journal of Urban Law,* XLVII (1969): 591–652; Eric Schnapper, "Affirmative Action and the Legislative History of the Fourteenth Amendment," *Virginia Law Review,* LXXI (1985), 753–98; *Regents of California v. Bakke,* 438 U.S. 265 (1978), 397; Paul Moreno, "Racial Classifications and Reconstruction Legislation," *Journal of Southern History,* LXI (1995), 271–304. Schnapper's article was a version of his brief for the NAACP Legal Defense and Education Fund, which Justice Marshall cited in his opinion.

the war to subordinate blacks should now be used to benefit them, and that to ignore race would confirm existing patterns of racial discrimination, they were defeated by the majority of Republicans who believed that continuing to use race, even for benevolent purposes, was inconsistent with the principle of equal citizenship. All subsequent Freedmen's Bureau and civil rights legislation employed language that was scrupulously color-blind.[3]

Despite this racially neutral language, pro-slavery, border-state Democrats repeatedly argued that Republican Reconstruction legislation discriminated against whites. Ignoring the plain language of the Freedmen's Bureau and Civil Rights bills, they maintained that the Republicans desired not to give equal rights to the freedmen, but to grant them special favors and promote social integration and miscegenation. The Republican sponsors of Reconstruction legislation, more reliable witnesses to congressional intent, denied the charges of preferential treatment as often as they were made. Lyman Trumbull, Republican leader in the Senate, argued that the very purpose of the legislation was to put an end to racial favoritism and distinction in the law. Others noted that the legislation was intended to fulfill the principle of the Declaration of Independence, that all men are created equal, removing any doubt that it had a racial qualification. At no time did any Republican assert or articulate the principle of racial preference. It was the opponents of legal equality who for racist reasons argued that the bill created a "benign classification" on behalf of black Americans.

The Freedmen's Bureau's reports show that it adhered faithfully to the racially impartial rules laid down by Congress. It provided food, clothing, and transportation to black freedmen and white refugees alike. In statistical terms the freedmen derived more benefit from bureau operations, but it is equally clear that the bureau operated on a racially impartial basis. The bureau's courts usually stepped in only when race-based state laws were in effect, and let state courts operate when states enacted race-neutral laws. Bureau schools were open to white and black children. The bureau did treat

3. Herman Belz, *A New Birth of Freedom* (Westport, Conn., 1976), 149–50; Belz, "The Freedmen's Bureau Act of 1865 and the Principle of No Discrimination According to Color," *Civil War History,* XXI (1975), 197–217.

the freedmen as less than equal, with a paternal regard for their welfare, in labor relations. It made special labor contracts for them that functioned as a sort of apprenticeship in free wage labor. This system was not specified in the Freedmen's Bureau Act, and some officials realized that it violated congressional policy. The bureau believed that racial distinctions, even seemingly "benign" ones, were a "recognition of the spirit of slavery," at odds with their mission, and moved quickly to end them.[4]

The language of the Civil Rights Act of 1866 and the Fourteenth Amendment was cast completely in terms of equal rights regardless of color. The same Democrats who opposed the Freedmen's Bureau bills because they saw racial preference in them also saw racial preference in these proposals. Again, congressional proponents asserted the color-blind principle. Lyman Trumbull could not understand how the border-state Democrats could argue that the Civil Rights Bill evinced preferential treatment for blacks "when the very object of the bill is to break down all discrimination between black men and white men." When President Andrew Johnson vetoed the bill on similar grounds, Trumbull replied, "The very object and effect of [section 1] is to prevent discrimination and language, it seems to me, could not more plainly express that object and intent."[5]

Congress took further steps to define citizenship and equality in the Civil Rights Act and the Fourteenth Amendment. An earlier version of the Civil Rights Act stated that "there shall be no discrimination in civil rights and immunities" among citizens, but Republicans who considered this language too sweeping removed it from the bill. Likewise, Congress considered a version of the Fourteenth Amendment, written by abolitionist Wendell Phillips and introduced by Thaddeus Stevens, which forbade states to make any legal classifications based on race or color. Congress also rejected this language in favor of "equal protection of the laws." Republican concern to limit the scope of the rights to be protected caused them to alter clear, strict, color-blind language. Congress maintained seg-

---

4. George R. Bentley, *A History of the Freedmen's Bureau* (Philadelphia, 1955), 140; Donald G. Nieman, *To Set the Law in Motion: The Freedmen's Bureau and the Legal Rights of Blacks, 1865–68* (Millwood, N.Y., 1979), 53, 91, 110, 136.

5. *Congressional Globe*, 39th Cong., 1st Sess. (1866), 599, 1758.

regated schools in the District of Columbia, and Republicans were still unsure if states would be required to extend voting rights without regard to race or color. Thus the Reconstruction Congress countenanced racial classifications in public education and public accommodations. While the tendency of Reconstruction legislation was clearly toward a color-blind rule of law in America, it did not uproot all racial classifications. It is not unreasonable to conclude, then, that the Reconstruction Congress *might have* allowed race-conscious remedial legislation with preference for blacks, since it permitted the anti-black variety. But in fact it did not, and it let stand some race-based legislation that was inimical to blacks regarding what were not considered fundamental rights.[6]

The Freedmen's Bureau, Civil Rights Act, and Fourteenth Amendment all established a racially neutral standard of American citizenship. Congress' overriding concern was to establish color-blind equality in fundamental rights. Any deviations from this principle, such as in the administration of the Freedmen's Bureau, were temporary concessions to the exigent circumstances of postwar disorder. While a legalistic, intentionalist case can be made to support the constitutionality of race-based legislation, it was Congress' attempt to write a color-blind definition of American citizenship into the Constitution that is most significant. While the authors of the Reconstruction amendments did not write a complete color-blindness into the Constitution, they gave scope for and encouraged what might be called a color-blind aspiration in the American Constitution.

The freed people shared the color-blind aspiration of the Republicans, and expressed the desire to eliminate racial classification from American citizenship. The free blacks of the North knew racial classifications and were determined to eliminate them. Appealing to the principles of the Declaration of Independence, the freed people insisted on nothing less and nothing more than equality in individual rights. "At their most utopian," historian Eric Foner remarks, "blacks in Reconstruction envisioned a society purged of all racial distinctions," and in public life "those who had so long been proscribed because of color defined equality as color-blind." The

6. Kull, *The Color-Blind Constitution*, 55–87; William E. Nelson, *The Fourteenth Amendment: From Political Principle to Judicial Doctrine* (Cambridge, Mass., 1988), 89, 124.

freedmen made their appeal as Americans, and sought the removal of racial classifications as consistent with America's republican principles. They did not seek special classification that would be a temporary, expedient abrogation of those principles in order ultimately to confirm them.[7]

During Reconstruction the federal judiciary did not go far in fulfilling the color-blind aspirations of Congress or the freed people. The Supreme Court of the 1870s and 1880s adhered to a moderate state-centered nationalism, preserved federalism, and struck a pose of relative judicial restraint. It achieved mixed results in the effort to realize a color-blind Constitution, or at least in making real the promise of fundamental equality in civil rights. The earliest judicial interpretation of civil rights legislation supported a broad view of national power to legislate directly against private civil rights offenders. The first Supreme Court interpretation of the Fourteenth Amendment, however, in the *Slaughterhouse Cases,* reveals conflicting tendencies. It took a narrow view of the Fourteenth Amendment, but made the rights of the freed people the central concern within it. Its five-to-four decision indicated room for future growth, especially in the area of non-racial property rights.[8]

The first test of the Fourteenth Amendment involved not the civil rights of the freed people, but a challenge to a New Orleans butchering monopoly. The argument pressed by the plaintiffs in the case was that the amendment, in its declaration that "no state shall make or enforce any law which shall abridge the privileges or immunities of citizens of the United States," prohibited all "class legislation"—any legislation that interfered in the right to pursue a

7. Eric Foner, *Reconstruction: America's Unfinished Revolution* (New York, 1988), 286–88, 372; Donald G. Nieman, "The Language of Liberation: African Americans and Equalitarian Constitutionalism, 1830–1950," in *The Constitution, Law, and American Life: Critical Aspects of the Nineteenth Century Experience,* ed. Donald G. Nieman (Athens, Ga., 1992), 67–90; Memorial, *Senate Miscellaneous Documents,* 40th Cong., 3rd Sess., No. 44.

8. Alfred H. Kelly, Winfred A. Harbison, and Herman Belz, *The American Constitution: Its Origins and Development* (7th ed., New York, 1992), II, 352–61; Charles Fairman, *Reconstruction and Reunion, 1864–88: Part One* (New York, 1971), 1308–1309.

lawful vocation. This argument challenged the idea of the state "police power" to legislate generally on matters of public health, safety, welfare, and morals. The *Slaughterhouse Cases* are often regarded as a judicial evisceration of the privileges and immunities clause of the Fourteenth Amendment, but historians have come to see Justice Samuel Miller's opinion as a careful, moderate construction of the amendment that kept the privileges and immunities clause alive for future cases, but was misread in subsequent decisions. However, Miller's decision on the privileges and immunities clause was obscure enough to allow easy misapplication.[9]

Miller noted that the main purpose of the Fourteenth Amendment was to protect the rights of the freed people, doubting "whether any action of a state not directed by way of discrimination against the Negroes as a class, or on account of their race, will ever be held to come within the purview of this provision." Miller's regard for federalism compelled him to hold that the rights claimed in the case were not a national concern, but he was careful to insist that equality in civil rights was. The principal dissenters in the case, Joseph Bradley and Stephen J. Field, were willing to transform federalism, but were not particularly concerned with the rights of the freed people. Bradley noted: "It is futile to argue that none but persons of the African race are intended to be benefited by this amendment. They may have been the primary cause of the Amendment, but its language is general, embracing all citizens." Miller had not made quite the argument Bradley here attacked, but Bradley's critique indicated the larger purposes he imagined for the Fourteenth Amendment.[10]

Either the majority or the minority opinion might have vindicated the rights of the freed people in the economic sphere.[11] Miller's opinion was race-conscious in a way similar to the Freedmen's Bureau, advocating not special consideration for blacks but insisting on due consideration of the context in which the Recon-

9. Robert C. Palmer, "The Parameters of Constitutional Reconstruction: *Slaughter-House, Cruikshank,* and the Fourteenth Amendment," *University of Illinois Law Review* (1984), 739–70.

10. Nelson, *The Fourteenth Amendment,* 163.

11. But see Donald E. Lively, *The Constitution and Race* (New York, 1992), 67–73.

struction amendments emerged. Miller kept the principal purpose of the Fourteenth Amendment in mind in order to restrict it to a smaller field of rights. However, it might have been better for minorities to enjoy economic liberty, if the market worked against discrimination. Bradley's opinion, more expansive and color-blind, implied protection for blacks as citizens in all walks of life, but no special consideration. However, as the restricted interpretation of the Fourteenth Amendment expanded into other economic concerns by the end of the century, the special racial concern of the amendment vanished.[12]

Civil rights advocates disregarded the almost uniformly negative thrust of late-nineteenth-century decisions while emphasizing some positive things that had been said along the way.[13] The 1880 case of *Strauder* v. *West Virginia,* one of a series of jury discrimination cases decided in the 1879–80 term, was a principal support for the color-blind interpretation of the Reconstruction amendments. A West Virginia statute excluded blacks from jury service, and a black man convicted by an all-white jury appealed in federal court. The Supreme Court overturned the conviction, holding that a state could not exclude jurors otherwise qualified for service solely because of race.[14] The decision in *Strauder* demonstrated a realistic understanding of the nature of discrimination and the special needs of blacks as a minority group. While Justice William Strong made reference to the abject condition of the freed people and the fact that this condition prompted the Reconstruction civil rights legislation, his paternalism was limited. He was careful to note that the Constitution required only that "the law in the States shall be the same for the black as for the white; that all persons, whether colored or white, shall stand equal before the laws of the States, and, in regard

12. Robert Higgs, *Competition and Coercion: Blacks in the American Economy, 1865–1914* (Cambridge, Mass., 1977); Jennifer Roback, "Southern Labor Law in the Jim Crow Era: Exploitative or Competitive?" *University of Chicago Law Review,* LI (1984), 1161–92; Gavin Wright, *Old South, New South: Revolutions in the Southern Economy Since the Civil War* (New York, 1986), 12–13.

13. Kull, *The Color-Blind Constitution,* 89.

14. In the same term the Court also held that the state exclusion need not be declared in statute to run afoul of the Civil Rights Act. *Neal* v. *Delaware* (103 U.S. 370 [1880]) overturned a conviction in which a state judge excluded blacks from the jury pool although no Delaware law contained an explicit racial exclusion.

to the colored race, for whose protection the amendment was primarily designed, that no discrimination shall be made against them by law because of their color." Moreover, Strong emphasized that civil rights equality did not countenance preferential treatment for the freed people—the law would be equally invalid if blacks controlled the legislature and excluded whites from jury service. But the Court refused to construe equality in jury service as requiring that a black defendant have an all-black jury or a jury with a certain proportion of jurors of his own race, a point made explicit in later jury discrimination cases. Discrimination based solely on race had to be proved; mere racial imbalance or disproportion did not suffice as such proof.[15]

Thus *Strauder* shows the color-blind aspiration at work in a majority opinion of the Supreme Court. It dealt with a fundamental right, and so did not present the problem of "social equality" in the public accommodations and public schools cases. It condemned a formal statutory exclusion, and its companion cases also condemned de facto exclusion under a nominally race-neutral law. At the same time, it did not insist that states take "affirmative action" to include blacks on all juries. States could still prescribe the qualifications of jurors, and in so doing make non-racial discriminations. The decision indicated a strict insistence on color-blind equality in fundamental rights. Indeed, southern Democrats were alarmed at the Court's strong stand, and viewed it as an announcement that the Republicans meant to use the judiciary as a redoubt now that they had been chased from the national legislature and executive. The contrary, restrictive tendencies of the Court, however, soon revealed themselves, and the color-blind aspiration found expression only in dissenting opinions.[16]

The 1883 *Civil Rights Cases* indicated that *Strauder* would stand as the high point of nineteenth-century, color-blind constitutionalism. Justice Bradley, who advocated a broader reading of the privileges and immunities clause in *Slaughterhouse,* struck down most of the Civil Rights Act of 1875, which provided for prosecution in federal courts of public accommodations operators who discriminated

15. Lively, *The Constitution and Race,* 75; *Strauder* v. *West Virginia,* 100 U.S. 303 (1880), 307; *Virginia* v. *Rives,* 100 U.S. 313 (1880).

16. *Strauder* v. *West Virginia,* 310; Fairman, *Reconstruction and Reunion,* 1374.

against anyone on the basis of race. Bradley based his decision on what would later be called the "state action theory" of the Fourteenth Amendment. The amendment prohibited states from violating civil rights; it did not grant Congress plenary power to legislate or to "create a code of municipal law for the regulation of private rights." Technically, private individuals could not deprive persons of their civil rights. They might murder or assault, but only officers acting under the authority of the state could deprive persons of civil rights. The civil rights protected by the Constitution were not "the social rights of men and races in the community," but only "those fundamental rights which appertain to the essence of citizenship."[17]

Bradley's opinion seemed to leave room for federal protection against discriminatory state law in public accommodations. "If the laws themselves make any unjust discrimination, amenable to the prohibitions of the Fourteenth Amendment," he wrote, "Congress has full power to afford a remedy under that amendment and in accordance with it." Bradley explicitly noted that the Court was not deciding whether the rights prayed for in the case were constitutionally protected, but the *Civil Rights Cases* implied that the Fourteenth Amendment "forbade states from depriving persons of equality of access on public conveyances." Bradley seemed to mean that if states enacted laws requiring segregation, the federal courts would void them under the Fourteenth Amendment. This type of legislation, enacting private, customary discrimination into statute, was not common before 1887. When it did appear, it took the form of "separate but equal," thereby introducing a wrinkle that Bradley had not anticipated. By then the Court had changed considerably, and did not follow Bradley's lead. Congress and the nation, too, had largely given up on the issue of civil rights. So while the *Civil Rights Cases,* as other 1870–1880s Court decisions, may not have subverted Republican congressional intent, the timing and effect of the decisions nullified their potential for the next eighty years.[18]

Bradley's opinion reflected the waning of national concern for

17. *The Civil Rights Cases,* 109 U.S. 3 (1883), 11, 17, 22.

18. *Ibid.,* 25; Charles A. Lofgren, *The Plessy Case: A Legal-Historical Interpretation* (New York, 1987), 26; C. Vann Woodward, *The Strange Career of Jim Crow* (3d ed., New York, 1974); Michael Les Benedict, "Preserving Federalism: Reconstruction and the Waite Court," *Supreme Court Review* (1979), 77.

civil rights. He wrote, "When a man has emerged from slavery, and by the aid of beneficent legislation has shaken off the inseparable concomitants of that state, there must be some stage in the progress of his elevation when he takes the rank of a mere citizen, and ceases to be the special favorite of the laws, and when his rights as a citizen, or a man, are to be protected in the ordinary modes by which other men's rights are protected." While likely an expression of disapproval of overzealous congressional enforcement acts, Bradley implied that the Civil Rights Act of 1875 was enacted solely on behalf of blacks.[19]

Justice John Marshall Harlan's dissent in the *Civil Rights Cases* became a major piece of color-blind constitutionalism. He interpreted the Thirteenth and Fourteenth Amendments together as prohibiting any governmental racial classifications. The Thirteenth Amendment not only abolished slavery, but protected the freed people from racial discrimination in civil rights. "The Thirteenth Amendment alone obliterated the race line, so far as all the rights fundamental in a state of freedom are concerned." Harlan further believed that Congress need not leave enforcement to the federal judiciary, but could act directly on the states and individual citizens by municipal legislation. Finally, completing his color-blind argument, Harlan responded to the "special favorites" argument: "It is, I submit, scarcely just to say that the colored race has been the special favorite of the laws. The statute of 1875, now adjudged to be unconstitutional, is for the benefit of citizens of every race and color."[20]

The remedial potential of the *Civil Rights Cases* was annulled and its restrictive tendency confirmed in the 1896 case of *Plessy* v. *Ferguson*. Addressing the southern movement for explicit statutory segregation in public places, the Court in *Plessy* ruled that "reasonable" racial classifications in state legislation were valid under the Constitution. Homer Plessy challenged Louisiana's separate-but-equal railroad statute of 1890, using *Strauder* and Harlan's dissent in the *Civil Rights Cases* to support his claim that the Fourteenth Amendment prohibited all racial classifications. Plessy also offered

19. *Civil Rights Cases,* 22.
20. *Ibid.,* 36–46, 61.

the germ of a sociological argument against segregation but did not develop it because of his insistence on the irrelevance of race. All told, Plessy's case was not strong and found sympathy only from Harlan.[21]

The Court in *Plessy* insisted that racial classification in social policy did not violate the Fourteenth Amendment's command of civil equality. Public school segregation served as an example, which Congress required in the District of Columbia and to which no one, including Harlan, objected on constitutional grounds. The Court repeated the *Civil Rights Cases* statement that the Fourteenth Amendment "does not authorize Congress to create a code of municipal law for the regulation of private rights; but to provide modes of redress against the operation of state laws." The key to the Court holding was that the classification must be "reasonable, and extend only to such laws as are enacted in good faith for the promotion of the public good, and not for the annoyance or oppression of a particular class." The Court denied that the Louisiana segregation statute was a measure signifying the inferiority of the black race. "We consider the underlying fallacy of the plaintiff's argument to consist in the assumption that the enforced separation of the races stamps the colored race with a badge of inferiority. If this be so, it is not by reason of anything found in the act, but solely because the colored race chooses to put that construction on it." Racial differences were real, and racial prejudice could not be overcome by legal enactment. Segregation was a reasonable legislative response to inevitable antipathy.[22]

John Marshall Harlan's dissent was the quintessential statement of color-blind constitutionalism: "In respect of civil rights, common to all citizens, the Constitution of the United States does not, I think, permit any public authority to know the race of those entitled to be protected in the enjoyment of such rights." In his most oft-quoted expression Harlan said, "Our Constitution is color-blind, and neither knows nor tolerates classes among citizens. In respect of civil rights, all citizens are equal before the law." Harlan repeated

21. Lofgren, *The Plessy Case,* 66, 158, 163, 166, 173.
22. *Plessy* v. *Ferguson,* 163 U.S. 537 (1896), 544–51.

the view of the Thirteenth and Fourteenth Amendments that he had enunciated in the *Civil Rights Cases*. He dismissed the majority's opinion that the law did not necessarily imply inferiority. "Every one knows that the statute in question had its origin in the purpose, not so much to exclude white persons from railroad cars occupied by blacks, as to exclude colored people from coaches occupied by or assigned to white persons." The act therefore was not a valid police regulation, but used the police power as a pretext to discriminate. Moreover, the test of "reasonableness" was no surety against further legal degradation of the black race, especially since Harlan denied that courts should judge "the policy or expediency of legislation."[23]

Notwithstanding the opprobrium with which *Plessy* is still regarded, it remains valid constitutional law. Although the Court in *Brown* held that separate is inherently unequal in education and other public institutions, it never explicitly overruled *Plessy*, and continues to regard racial classifications as valid if reasonable.[24] Harlan's dissent made the color-blind idea "one of the available meanings of the Fourteenth Amendment," but not one that was ever adopted by the Court. *Plessy* itself did not induce segregation, since the common law allowed common carriers to make their own "reasonable" classifications. Indeed, civil rights groups were able to attack segregation by insisting on substantial equality, and the Court never again held separate to be equal in a particular case. Civil rights groups throughout the twentieth century usually advanced the color-blind theory while attacking the inferiority of the separate accommodations. At the nadir of race relations the question arose: Could "segregation without discrimination" provide an alternative principle to color-blindness?[25]

Indeed, it is significant that it was during the 1890s, the waxing years of Jim Crow, that Congress itself began to use racial classifications as a way of equalizing racial benefits. Florida enacted the first Jim Crow law in 1887, the same year in which Congress passed the

23. *Ibid.*, 554–58.

24. Kull, *The Color-Blind Constitution*, and Lofgren, *The Plessy Case*, make this point.

25. Kull, *The Color-Blind Constitution*, 121, 132; Lofgren, *The Plessy Case*, 200.

Interstate Commerce Act. Principally concerned with the economic discrimination of railroad rates, Congress did not address racial classifications in the act, but in subsequent years the Interstate Commerce Commission held that separate-but-equal accommodations were acceptable. When the Republican Party regained control of Congress in 1890, in addition to introducing Reconstruction-type "Force Acts," Republican legislators introduced bills to provide reparations to Negro ex-slaves. The Second Morrill Land Grant College Act of 1890 wrote racial classification into law. In providing federal land and money for education, the act stated, "No money shall be paid out under this Act to a State or Territory for the support and maintenance of a college where a distinction of race or color is made in the admission of students but the establishment and maintenance of such colleges separately for white and colored students shall be held to be a compliance with the provisions of this Act if the funds received in such State or Territory be equitably divided." The act paid homage to the virtue of color-blindness with its recognition that proportional segregation was a second-best solution. Proponents of race-conscious programs in the 1930s argued that "this development in the field of public education illustrated that objective criteria of nondiscrimination could be developed, and that such criteria are effective in securing equitable benefits for minority groups." The origin of race-conscious legislation meant to benefit black Americans, or "benign discrimination," apparently lies in the 1890s, as a pragmatic response to the failure of Reconstruction and the rise of malignant racial classification.[26]

Supreme Court decisions in education, public accommodations, jury service, and voting may appear only marginally related to the

26. Lofgren, *The Plessy Case*, 145; Alexander M. Bickel and Benno C. Schmidt, *The Judiciary and Responsible Government: 1910–21* (New York, 1984), 750; Robert G. Dixon, Jr., "Transportation: Desegregation and Government Initiative, 1887–1955," in *Legal Aspects of the Civil Rights Movement*, eds. Donald B. King and Charles W. Quick (Detroit, 1965), 103–28; Mary Frances Berry, "Reparations for the Freedmen, 1890–1916: Fraudulent Practices or Justice Deferred?" *Journal of Negro History*, LVII (1972), 219–30; 26, *Statutes at Large* 417 (1890), sec. 1; Senate Committee on Education and Labor, *Fair Employment Practices Act: Hearings Before a Subcommittee of the Committee on Education and Labor*, 78th Cong., 2nd sess., September 8, 1944, p. 174; Foner, *Reconstruction*, 539.

issues of labor and employment, but are in fact more relevant than at first glance. The Court's failure to vindicate the rights of black citizens with regard to equal protection of the law had clear economic consequences, often preventing blacks from competing in the American market economy. Lack of equal protection manifested itself in segregated and inferior education, and in political disfranchisement which made inferior education possible. Inferior education in turn made black labor less productive. The inability of blacks to enforce contracts in court or to have their lives and property protected by the state had economic consequences. Direct statutory limitations on black employment were uncommon (South Carolina's 1915 law requiring segregation in cotton textile factories is one instance), but the incidental economic effects of civil rights deprivation was significant.[27]

So it was unlikely that a Supreme Court that used the Fourteenth Amendment sparingly in economic cases and refused to apply it to public education and public accommodation segregation would attack economic discrimination. Still there were laissez-faire, free-market answers to racial discrimination, even if the Court did not often apply them. There was more potential here than might appear at first, considering the Court's regard for "liberty of contract," and its understanding that the core values of the Civil Rights Act of 1866 and the Fourteenth Amendment were basically economic. Moreover, workplace integration has been easier than integration in housing, schools, and places of public accommodation. Notable pro–civil rights decisions of the 1890–1937 period came in property rights cases, and the National Association for the Advancement of Colored People (NAACP) and other civil rights organizations argued from this standpoint.

The Supreme Court decided the case of *Yick Wo* v. *Hopkins* in 1886, between the *Civil Rights Cases* and *Plessy*. This case involved a municipal ordinance by the city of San Francisco which required that operators of all laundries located in buildings constructed of wood secure a permit from the Board of Supervisors. Of 320 laun-

27. Richard Epstein, *Forbidden Grounds: The Case Against Antidiscrimination Laws* (Cambridge, Mass., 1992), 244–54; Higgs, *Competition and Coercion*, 124–25.

dries in San Francisco, some 240 were operated by subjects of the Emperor of China, and of these, 210 were in buildings constructed of wood. With one exception, all petitions by Caucasian operators were granted, while all Chinese applications, with one exception, were denied. This ordinance was a clear instance of discrimination against minorities in ostensibly progressive social regulation. Challenges in the Supreme Court of California and the federal circuit court rejected the Chinese operators' petitions, although the federal circuit court noted that the law was obviously discriminatory.[28]

Here was a law that involved no explicit racial classification, but was obviously directed against a particular racial group. The Supreme Court noted that the state had not enacted a valid police regulation, equally applicable to persons similarly situated. Instead, it gave power to a local body to make arbitrary and unreasonable discriminations. The Court regarded this arbitrary deprivation of the means of livelihood not as the inescapable consequence of state sovereignty and the police power, but as an execrable violation of minority rights and "the essence of slavery itself." This case, like *Strauder* and *Neal*, might have raised the question of disparate racial impact—whether any law that placed more of a burden on a particular minority group was for that reason suspect. However, the Court considered the actual operation of the law and the treatment of groups under it. Justice Stanley Matthews wrote that the ordinances operated against a particular class of persons. Regardless of the intent of the ordinance's authors, they were applied by the board in a manner that denied equal protection. "Though the law itself be fair on its face and impartial in appearance, yet, if it is applied and administered by public authority with an evil eye and an unequal hand, so as practically to make unjust and illegal discriminations between persons in similar circumstances, material to their rights, the denial of equal justice is still within the protection of the Constitution," Matthews concluded.[29]

Like *Neal*, *Yick Wo* is often cited as an example of how the Court could see through color-blind form to discriminatory substance, as it would fail to do in the 1890s. *Yick Wo* also illustrates the disparate-

---

28. *Yick Wo* v. *Hopkins,* 118 U.S. 356 (1886).
29. *Ibid.,* 370, 373–74.

treatment theory of discrimination. The court did not simply consult the racial disproportion of the ordinance; its impact on wooden
laundries was not the equivalent of a racial classification. Instead
the Court noted that the petitions of whites were routinely granted
and those of the Chinese denied—the groups, similarly situated or
qualified, were treated differently. It compared the situations of the
two groups, and found no reason for the disparate treatment except
race. The circuit court also noted "the notorious public and municipal history of the times" as further evidence of racial animus as the
basis for this behavior. But the potential of this decision for an antidiscrimination constitutionalism in America went unrealized for
the same reasons that the Reconstruction decisions did—the changing composition of the Supreme Court and congressional and popular disinclination to deal with the issue of civil rights.[30]

In 1915 the Supreme Court displayed the potential for economic
liberty to defend the rights of minorities. In *Truax* v. *Raich* it struck
down an Arizona statute, called "An act to protect the citizens of
the United States in their employment against non-citizens," which
declared that any employer of five or more workers "shall employ
not less than eighty percent qualified electors or native-born citizens." Although this majority set-aside was probably aimed at Mexican aliens, a native of Austria brought suit against it. The Court
confirmed the fundamental economic content of the civil rights secured by the Reconstruction amendments. "The right to work for a
living in the common occupations of the community is of the
essence of that personal freedom and opportunity which it was the
purpose of the Fourteenth Amendment to secure." Where the privileges and immunities clause was unable to protect butchers against
a monopoly, the equal protection clause was able to protect aliens
from state-mandated limits in private employment.[31]

The Court confirmed the doctrine of "liberty of contract" that it
had used in other contexts to strike down what it considered unreasonable regulations of wages, hours, and working conditions.

30. *Ibid.,* 363.

31. *Truax* v. *Raich,* 239 U.S. 33 (1915), 34. Justice McReynolds dissented because
he saw the case as a suit against a state in violation of the Eleventh Amendment. He
added, however, "That the challenged act is invalid I think admits of no serious argument."

While effective against state-mandated quotas in private employment, it would seem that a doctrine of "employment at will," regarding employment as a contract between equal parties, would make it all but impossible to combat discrimination based on race in private employment.[32] Indeed, the state of Arizona pleaded that, whatever the requirement of the law, the alien employee may have been terminated for any reason at any time, and so had no standing to sue in an employment-at-will situation. The Court noted: "The fact that the employment is at the will of the parties, respectively, does not make it at the will of others. The employee has manifest interest in the freedom of the employer to exercise his judgment without illegal interference or compulsion and by the weight of authority, the unjustified interference of third parties is actionable although the employment is at will." The Court implied that employers who desired to make employment decisions without regard to race had some protection against state-mandated restrictions and also against the customary prejudice of fellow workers. If employers were free to respond to unfettered labor market forces, this would limit employment discrimination based on race. But the state-mandated restriction in support of segregation limited the operation of a free market in labor.[33]

The Arizona law was no better as an exercise of the police power or as a "reasonable classification." No state could "deny to the lawful inhabitants, because of their race or nationality, the ordinary means of earning a livelihood." No legitimate public interest was served by the act, which made discrimination against aliens an end in itself. The 20 percent ceiling on alien employment and the limit of the act to employers of five or more did not make it more reasonable. While the state claimed that this was not a total deprivation of the right of the alien to work, the Court found the limits to be arbitrary and, if the principle were granted, without any basis to prevent the state from making them even more stringent.[34]

32. The Court noted that "the act is not limited to persons who are engaged on public work or receive the benefit of public moneys," without indicating if such public works quotas might be valid (*ibid.*, 40).

33. *Ibid.*, 38; Epstein, *Forbidden Grounds,* 28–40.

34. *Truax v. Raich,* 41, 42.

Yick Wo and *Truax* were among the few Supreme Court decisions between 1890 and 1937 that favored racial equality in civil rights. Although they dealt with the fundamental freedom to labor, and so had potential to ameliorate racial discrimination in employment, their laissez-faire assumptions tied them to some of the most infamous decisions of the Court, and so they usually have been overlooked. They also did not deal directly with black Americans, the largest oppressed minority group in America. The 1917 case of *Buchanan v. Warley* did deal directly with black Americans, and has received more attention as a successful laissez-faire assault on racial discrimination.[35]

The *Buchanan* case arose out of the movement for residential segregation in response to the "Great Migration" of rural southern blacks into border-state cities. Baltimore enacted the first municipal segregation ordinance in 1910, and other cities followed. Louisville's ordinance virtually created the local NAACP, which organized a challenge to the act. The ordinance held that blacks could not move into a block that was predominantly white and, to maintain a superficial equality, prohibited whites from moving into black-majority blocks. Louisville justified the measure as a police-power regulation to prevent racial conflict. The NAACP created a case where a white man, Buchanan, sold a lot on a white-majority block to a black man, Warley. When Warley refused to execute the contract due to the segregation statute, Buchanan sued to compel him. Since the lot was situated between the only two black lots on the block, Buchanan argued, no white man would buy it, and the ordinance, compelling him to offer it only to whites, rendered his property valueless. Moorfield Storey for the NAACP likened blacks to employers whose property rights were vulnerable to abuse of the state police power in economic and social regulatory legislation. The plaintiff argued that there was no legitimate state purpose served by the law, and that it was enacted solely out of racial animus.[36]

Expressing a unanimous opinion, Justice William R. Day held for

35. *Buchanan v. Warley*, 245 U.S. 60 (1917).

36. Bickel and Schmidt, *The Judiciary and Responsible Government*, 797; *Buchanan v. Warley*, 63.

the plaintiffs and struck down the ordinance. The decision could not be squared with *Plessy,* which Day tried to avoid. The idea that real property, unlike public schools or public accommodations, could not in its nature be separate but equal, was broached but never fully explicated. Day relied mostly on individual property rights, but also gave a firm endorsement to the antidiscrimination principles of *Slaughterhouse* and *Strauder.* The decision contained Jim Crow if it did not roll it back.

Historians have frequently commented on the irony of this defense of racial minority rights in the context of a property rights decision.[37] The Court's unanimity suggests that justices like Day, who had a good record in civil rights decisions, and were tolerant of the police power, grasped the minority rights aspect of the case while justices like James C. McReynolds, hostile to both minority group rights and the regulation of property, fastened onto the property rights element. It is interesting to note that the one justice who almost dissented was Oliver Wendell Holmes, who actually prepared an opinion which he did not deliver.[38] Holmes's main concern was the obviously collusive nature of the suit. "The contract sounds so very like a wager upon the constitutionality of the ordinance that I cannot but feel a doubt whether the suit should be entertained without some evidence that this is not a manufactured case," he noted. Holmes could not believe that the ordinance harmed the rights of whites. It was possible that it harmed the rights of blacks, he said, but that case was not before the Court. The plaintiffs in the case argued that "the Constitution cannot be satisfied by any such offsetting of inequalities," and Day held that, while the Fourteenth Amendment's principal purpose was to protect blacks, "the broad language used was deemed sufficient to protect all persons, white or black, against discriminatory legislation by the States."[39]

Holmes did not deliver his opinion, probably because he believed the case of insufficient moment to justify a lone dissent. Holmes's discomfort with the collusive nature of the suit is curious, as collusive suits to test the constitutionality of a law were not un-

37. See Bickel and Schmidt, *The Judiciary and Responsible Government,* 811.
38. Reproduced *ibid.,* 592.
39. *Buchanan* v. *Warley,* 63, 76.

common. It is difficult to understand why Holmes did not see through to the real point the participants were trying to make. It is not unlikely that, had the case been brought on the real issue of deprivation of black property rights, Holmes still would have upheld the state police power. The movement for residential segregation was considered a progressive reform, and many legal scholars objected to *both* the decision's defense of property rights *and* its condemnation of apartheid.[40]

The dichotomy with which most commentators have approached *Buchanan*—that the decision either vindicated property rights principally and minority rights only incidentally, or that the decision used property rights as a stalking horse to assert racial equality—is an artificial one.[41] The symbiosis of individual property rights and racial justice marked the Reconstruction period and many of the cases that supported civil rights: "To see *Buchanan* as an opinion about property rights, rather than about the rights of blacks, separates a seamless concept of baseline constitutional protection against racial discrimination and misjudges the thrust of the Court's action."[42]

While the *Buchanan* decision was able to curb the police power in its attempt to mandate segregation by statute, the Court did not upset other methods of segregation, such as zoning and the restrictive covenant. Thus the Supreme Court in 1926 upheld a covenant in a property contract which stipulated that the purchasing party would not sell the property to a black buyer for a period of twenty-one years. This rule (overturned in 1948) shows the ability of racism to assert itself in a private property system, but it required the cooperation of all the white parties involved and enforcement by state power.[43]

The Progressive Era did not hold out many hopes for improvement in black economic fortunes. If there was any chance that the

40. Bickel and Schmidt, *The Judiciary and Responsible Government,* 805.

41. Lively, *The Constitution and Race,* 95, presents the former view; Kull, *The Color-Blind Constitution,* 139, presents the latter.

42. Bickel and Schmidt, *The Judiciary and Responsible Government,* 816.

43. *Corrigan v. Buckley,* 271 U.S. 323 (1926); Epstein, *Forbidden Grounds,* 112–15; Higgs, *Competition and Coercion,* 116.

progressives' willingness to use state power to reform the political economy might work to the advantage of black Americans, it was lost in a general indifference or outright hostility to black interests. Disenfranchisement and segregation were the cornerstones of southern progressivism, and northern progressives were not inclined to object. The Progressive Era was perhaps the low point in American race relations, and the exclusion of blacks from the progressive agenda contributed to new forms of black organization and protest, in the Niagara movement and the formation of the NAACP.[44]

It has been remarked that had the Court taken as activist a position on race issues as it did with state economic and social regulation of property, Jim Crow might never have taken root, or real equality in a separate-but-equal framework might have resulted. The 1890–1937 "laissez-faire" Court did not, however, routinely strike down state economic and social regulation, but sustained them in the vast majority of cases. In reality, the permissive attitude the Court took toward racial classifications in *Plessy* paralleled its attitude toward state economic regulation. The Court was as markedly reluctant to use the Fourteenth Amendment to overturn state police power in economic regulation as it was in race relations. "Laissez-faire" might as accurately describe the Court's attitude toward state police power as its attitude toward entrepreneurship. It may be that economic discrimination based on race would have been diminished had the Court taken a more activist role in defending individual rights of all kinds and allowed black Americans to compete in a market economy. As Richard Epstein remarks, "Mr. Herbert Spencer's *Social Statics* is just the right antidote to Jim Crow."[45]

The limits of the color-blind aspiration in the era of segregation, of course, need no recounting. Since employment was generally pri-

---

44. Dewey Grantham, *Southern Progressivism: The Reconciliation of Progress and Tradition* (Knoxville, 1983), 111–59; C. Vann Woodward, *Origins of the New South, 1877–1913* (Baton Rouge, 1951), chap. 14; August Meier, *Negro Thought in America, 1880–1915* (Ann Arbor, 1963), 164–65.

45. Lively, *The Constitution and Race*, 95; Kelly, Harbison, and Belz, *The American Constitution*, II, 405; Michael Les Benedict, "Laissez-Faire and Liberty: A Re-Evaluation of the Meaning and Origins of Laissez-Faire Constitutionalism," *Law and History Review*, III (1985), 296–97; Lofgren, *The Plessy Case*, 80–88; Epstein, *Forbidden Grounds*, 99, 115.

vate and governed by the common law doctrine of "employment at will," there was probably less chance for effective governmental anti-discrimination policy in this area than in voting, jury service, public education, or public accommodations. Free-market principles, however, contained their own set of antidiscrimination principles, and their effect is revealed in the cases where the Supreme Court applied them. The NAACP saw this and made its successful appeal in *Buchanan* accordingly. However, the future of antidiscrimination law in employment lay with the interventionism of the New Deal, with its support of organized labor, and its new view of property rights. Antidiscrimination efforts in employment began in earnest in the 1930s, when black Americans sought to follow the lead of organized labor in the New Deal.

2   Racial Proportionalism in the 1930s

The 1930s saw the beginning of a discussion of the problem of racial discrimination in employment. The Great Depression, the maturation of civil rights organizations, and the New Deal's change in American principles of property rights and labor policy helped launch this discussion. Campaigns undertaken by black organizations and federal agencies began to devise race-based strategies to combat discrimination in employment, and our modern concept of equal employment opportunity, which holds that an employer's work force should contain approximately the same proportion of minorities as are present in the population, first received expression in this period.[1]

The Great Depression brought employment discrimination to the fore as a civil rights issue, along with the more familiar problems of segregation, disfranchisement, and lynching. In the 1930s, local black organizations experimented in a new form of protest called "direct action." Applied against white businesses in black urban areas that did not employ blacks, the method consisted of organizing the community of black customers, publicizing their grievances, negotiating with white owners, and, when necessary,

---

1. A precursor of the 1930s campaign can be found in the response of the Ford Motor Company to the post–World War I depression. Ford's policy was "that Negroes should make up the same proportion of the workers as corresponded to their proportion in the population of Detroit." Gunnar Myrdal, *An American Dilemma: The Negro Problem and Modern Democracy* (New York, 1944), 1120–21.

coordinating boycotts and picketing against them. The essential demand was for an all-black employment policy, or some proportional policy based on the estimated racial composition of the employer's trade. These methods appear to have begun in Chicago before the depression, and when the economic collapse began in 1929, "Don't Buy Where You Can't Work" campaigns spread to almost every major black area in American cities.[2]

The direct action tactic was controversial. National black organizations like the NAACP and the Urban League were ambivalent about the confrontational course chosen by local organizations. Communist groups hoped to capitalize on racial unrest, but feared that race-consciousness would override class-consciousness. White business reaction was mixed as well. Many ghetto employers, especially large chain store retailers, came to terms with local black organizations. Others, principally small retailers, objected and sought relief in the courts. Initially the courts denied the right of black organizations to picket for the purpose of compelling race-based hiring, but the U.S. Supreme Court's 1938 *New Negro Alliance* decision seemed to endorse the activity. Together, these campaigns initiated a discussion of the nature of discrimination and the proper and most effective methods of combating it. The Baltimore campaign first addressed the question of a race-conscious strategy to combat discrimination in employment, and the New York campaign showed many of the complications inherent in such a strategy. The Washington, D.C., campaign was the most successful and provided tentative answers to some of these questions.

At the same time, New Deal agencies took steps toward applying a standard of racial proportionalism in federal employment policy. As in the direct-action campaign, considerable ambivalence and debate surrounded the effort, but its occasional acceptance indicated that by 1940 the idea of numerical standards as the proof and rem-

2. August Meier and Elliot Rudwick, "The Origins of Nonviolent Direct Action," in *Along the Color Line,* ed. August Maier and Elliot Rudwick (Urbana, 1976), 313–88; Edward Peeks, *The Long Struggle for Black Power* (New York, 1971), 268–89; Gary Jerome Hunter, "'Don't Buy From Where You Can't Work': Black Urban Boycott Movements during the Depression, 1929–41" (Ph. D. dissertation, University of Michigan, 1977), 256–68; Roi Ottley, *New World A-Coming* (New York, 1943), 113–21.

edy for racial discrimination might provide the guiding strategy for civil rights groups, government agencies, and courts. The 1930s provide a usually unrecognized experiment with the current concept of affirmative action, which lay dormant for the next generation.

The leader of the Baltimore campaign to win jobs for blacks was Kiowa Costonie, a mysterious figure who arrived in the city in 1933 after working in Sufi Abdul Hamid's "Don't Buy Where You Can't Work" campaign in Chicago. Costonie worked with local church and civic groups, forming a Citizens' Committee that picketed Baltimore A&P stores until they agreed to hire black clerks. The campaign then moved to small retailers on Pennsylvania Avenue, seeking black employment in proportion to the stores' black trade. Believing that Jewish control of the city's retail trade would enable the owners to relocate their white employees in downtown or suburban situations, the Citizens' Committee also expected Jewish retailers to sympathize with victims of racial discrimination. While many did, and agreed to their demands, merchant Aaron Samuelson refused, and others joined him. Costonie's group began to picket these stores on December 8, 1933.[3]

The pickets never numbered over two dozen, but attracted a great deal of public attention and curtailed trade on the entire block. The Citizens' Committee and merchants accused each other of intimidation, but the police treated the action as an ordinary labor union dispute and did not intervene. After a week, Samuelson and other merchants sought an injunction in Baltimore City Circuit Court. Depicting Costonie as a charlatan and denying that they discriminated against blacks, the plaintiffs complained that the committee insisted on summary discharge of white employees and their replacement by blacks chosen by the committee, harassed and

3. For general background see *Green* v. *Samuelson*, 99 A.L.R. 529 (1935); *Samuelson* v. *Green*, Transcript, Baltimore City Circuit Court, Equity Papers, Maryland State Archives, Annapolis; Henry J. McGuinn, "Race, Cultural Groups, and Social Differentiation," *Social Forces*, XVIII (1939), 256–68; Andor D. Skotnes, "The Black Freedom Movement and the Workers' Movement in Baltimore, 1930–39" (Ph. D. dissertation, Rutgers University, 1991); Baltimore *Afro-American*, December 23, 1933, p. 3; Pittsburgh *Courier*, December 23, 1933, p. 1.

intimidated their customers, and caused irreparable damage for which there was no legal remedy. Judge Albert Owens immediately issued a preliminary injunction. In January, the defendants answered that they never demanded the discharge of any white employees or a black-only policy, but merely "requested" employment of "a reasonable number of Negroes." They denied any intimidation, noting that many employers had voluntarily met their request, and insisted on their right to publicize their campaign.

Judge Owens conducted a trial in May, 1934. Since the plaintiffs sought the equitable remedy of a permanent injunction, there was no jury. Maryland law protected the right of labor organizations to picket in labor disputes, but Owens regarded the Citizens' Committee not as a labor organization but as "volunteer agitators." No employer-employee relationship existed, so picketing for employment of a reasonable number of Negroes was a criminal conspiracy to deprive the retailers of their lawful trade and use of their property. While Owens expressed a personal, paternalistic affection for blacks, he regarded picketing as inherently disorderly. Admitting that the case was unprecedented, he nevertheless would not consider the theory behind the picketing, or sociological evidence of the economic condition of Baltimore's Negro population. Owens insisted that employers were free to choose their workers, as opposed to the pickets who seemed to regard an employer as "a sort of public utility." This outlook doomed the defendants' case, and Owens made the injunction permanent.[4]

The leaders of the protest movement denounced the decision and called for an appeal. Juanita Jackson, leader of one of the organizations constituting the Citizens' Committee, persuaded the NAACP to pledge a one-hundred-dollar contribution for every four hundred dollars the local organizations raised to appeal the case, and solicited help from the American Civil Liberties Union (ACLU). Walter White, executive secretary of the NAACP, reported that Roger Baldwin of the ACLU was not interested, telling White, "We are unable to help in a case which does not set a useful precedent."

4. *Samuelson* v. *Green;* Felix Frankfurter and Nathan Green, *The Labor Injunction* (New York, 1930), 25–31.

Baldwin thus missed the opportunity to contribute to a case that was, by all other accounts, attempting to set a radically new precedent. Another Citizens' Committee member, Clarence Mitchell, while having caviled about Costonie's tactics, was dismayed at Owens' racial and class bias, and saw the decision as a threat to the entire labor movement. Failure to appeal the decision, he wrote in a weekly newspaper column, "means making ourselves liable to exploitation by every white scoundrel who dares to invade our neighborhood and set up business, carrying our resources off and giving nothing in return either economically or morally to our communities. This is the reptile which must be crushed and crushed now."[5]

The Maryland Court of Appeals heard the case in Annapolis on April 2, 1935. Attorneys for the Citizens' Committee argued that the issue should be considered a labor dispute, which they contended did not require the existence of an employer-employee relationship. Moreover, the trial court injunction was overly broad, prohibiting them from holding meetings or coordinating boycotts— lawful activity short of picketing. Samuelson's attorneys argued that public policy of Maryland and the United States forbade racial discrimination against all groups, not only blacks, and that demands for the discharge of white employees undermined the efforts of civil rights advocates to combat "racial discrimination of all kinds."[6]

The appeals court concluded that the picketing, if successful, must necessarily result in the discharge of white workers. The court sympathized with the plaintiffs' view that a white-owned store in a black neighborhood was exploitative, but insisted that illegal methods could not be used against such wrongs. While the court did modify the injunction to permit meetings and boycotts, its opinion

5. Mitchell letter in NAACP Papers, Series I, Group G, Box 85, Library of Congress; Mitchell testimony in Transcript; Denton L. Watson, *Lion in the Lobby: A Biography of Clarence Mitchell* (New York, 1990), 88–96; Juanita Jackson to Walter White, May 29, 1934, White to Jackson, June 1, 5, 11, 1934, in NAACP Papers, I-G-85; Walter White to Arthur B. Spingarn, June 1, 1934, in Arthur B. Spingarn Papers, Box 12, Library of Congress.

6. W. A. C. Hughes to Arthur B. Spingarn, June 11, 1934, in Spingarn Papers; *Green v. Samuelson*, Maryland Court of Appeals, *Records and Briefs*, vol. 574, January Term, 1935.

on picketing was in complete accord with Owens. The court characterized the dispute as "a racial or social question" to which the rules of labor disputes did not apply. As the court must apply the same rule to all groups, an extension of the plaintiffs' logic would lead to the expulsion of black workers from white areas, so the court forestalled such a possibility.[7]

This case raised several issues that would prove to be important in the subsequent development of the law of racial discrimination in employment. The most important of these, concerning the proof of discrimination, was raised only in passing because racial discrimination in private employment was nowhere legally proscribed in 1934.[8] Nevertheless, lawyers for the Citizens' Committee tried to impute discrimination in terms of the numbers of blacks employed by the retailers, and their treatment on the job. The employers claimed in response that all newly-hired clerks were treated the same, "regardless of color or creed." The retailers did not exclude blacks entirely from their work forces, but the few who were employed may have indicated "tokenism," the practice by which employers protected themselves against the appearance of unfair treatment of minorities by keeping a small number of blacks on hand, usually in menial positions. One of Samuelson's black clerks quit her job and joined the pickets to prevent Samuelson from pointing to her as his token black employee. Both sides broached the question of the proof of discrimination, but neither had enough to gain by it to pursue it.[9]

The question of the proof of discrimination turned out to be the most enduring and perplexing problem in the field of discrimination law. If the presence of a token number of minorities was enough to absolve an employer of the charge of discrimination, then discrimination would be all but impossible to prove. Conversely, if a

7. *Green* v. *Samuelson*, 99 A.L.R. 529.

8. A few northeastern states did prohibit racial discrimination in state employment, by utilities, and by labor unions. See Arthur Earl Bonfield, "The Origin and Development of American Fair Employment Legislation," *Iowa Law Review*, LII (1967), 1051; Will Maslow and Joseph B. Robison, "Civil Rights Legislation and the Fight for Equality, 1863–1952," *University of Chicago Law Review*, XX (1953), 393.

9. *Samuelson* v. *Green*.

disparity between the racial composition of the neighborhood and the employer's work force was accepted as prima facie proof of discrimination, employers would have to resort to hiring by racial quotas to avoid charges of discrimination. Since racial discrimination in private employment was not illegal, however, and because the Baltimore group had so many other hurdles to overcome, no one examined the full implications of this problem.

The question of displaced white workers had done much to foil the Baltimore effort, and other black organizations using direct-action tactics would have to grapple with it. The case also raised the issue of racial or ethnic proportionalism as the principle that underlay the demands of the protesters, and in particular the fear that the principle would gain momentum and "balkanize" the nation. The Baltimore protesters implied that blacks, already excluded from white areas and discriminated against in their own, could only gain from a system of racial proportionalism. The Citizens' Committee proposed not a general application of proportional representation, but its application where it would benefit their group. Disagreement over this policy would persist.

The immediate question raised by the Baltimore picketing case was whether the legal rules of labor disputes applied to cases of this nature. Maryland, like many states and the federal government, had extended to organized labor the right to strike and picket. In 1932, Congress passed the Norris–La Guardia Act, which prohibited federal courts from issuing injunctions in labor disputes. Several states followed suit, enacting "little Norris–La Guardia acts." The New Deal extended the protection of labor bargaining power still further in the National Labor Relations Act (NLRA). Black organizations sought to extend these privileges to the field of employment discrimination. Rebuffed in Maryland in 1934, they pursued this goal elsewhere.

Local black organizations in Harlem, New York, also waged a direct-action campaign leading to a notable debate and legal decision concerning employment discrimination. As the depression spurred calls for boycotts of white businesses that did not employ blacks in Harlem, the Reverend John H. Johnson of Saint Mark's Protestant Episcopal Church formed the Citizens League for Fair Play in 1933, whose elite leadership favored persuasion short of boycotts and picketing. The CLFP successfully boycotted a department store in June, 1934, to gain employment for several black clerks. The clerks selected for the jobs were too light-skinned and bourgeois for Sufi Abdul Hamid and other black nationalists, who broke off and formed the "Picket Committee of the Citizens League for Fair Play." Johnson's organization denied any association with or approval of the Picket Committee, which initiated a stepped-up campaign of picketing and was accused of intimidation and assaults on shoppers. Hamid, known as the "Black Hitler" for his rhetorical anti-semitism and admiration for Germany's anti-Jewish boycotts, exposed deep divisions in the black community over the "Don't Buy" movement.[10]

The NAACP organ, the *Crisis*, published a debate on the issue of boycotting tactics in September, 1934, just as the Picket Committee began its campaign. New York *Age* reporter Vere E. Johns supported the tactic as a desperate but necessary measure in the face of Harlem's acute economic plight. White workers would not be displaced, he noted, and white owners could expect more trade when they drew their work force from the community. Black journalist George S. Schuyler opposed the tactic as counter-productive, since most blacks worked outside of black areas and could face white retaliation. The tactic imitated the substitution of race for merit practiced by southern white supremacists, and would only encourage "professional Anglo-Saxons." He echoed the warning of the American Jewish Committee against Hitlerian racial separatism, and concluded that "unhealthy race-consciousness is growing among Aframericans like swine in a fattening pen."[11]

This debate over race-conscious employment efforts was part of

10. New York *Times,* September 26, 1934, p. 44, May 21, 1935, p. 15; Cheryl Lynn Greenberg, *"Or Does it Explode?" Black Harlem in the Great Depression* (New York, 1991), 114–39; William Muraskin, "The Harlem Boycott of 1934," *Labor History,* XIII (1972), 361–67; Meier and Rudwick, "Origins of Nonviolent Direct Action," 318–19; *A. S. Beck Shoe Corp.* v. *Johnson,* 274 N.Y.S. 946 (1934); Charles Lionel Franklin, *The Negro Labor Unionist of New York* (New York, 1936), 130–42; Claude McKay, *Harlem: Negro Metropolis* (New York, 1940), 194; *Crisis,* XLI (September, 1934), 258; New York *Age,* September 22, 1934, p. 1.

11. Vere E. Johns, "We Must Have Jobs," *The Crisis,* XLI (September, 1934), 258; George S. Schuyler, "A Dangerous Boomerang," *ibid.,* 259; Muraskin, "Harlem Boycott," 364.

a general debate within the NAACP over philosophy and tactics. W. E. B. Du Bois embraced "segregation without discrimination" and black nationalism in the early 1930s, drifting away from the organization that he had helped to found. Depression conditions also brought the issue of racialism to a head for communist groups, who were wary of any working-class movement they did not control. In theoretical terms, the movement evinced a petit-bourgeois consciousness and a race-consciousness that undercut the communists' own color-blind vision of proletarian solidarity. After initial opposition, communist groups often joined direct-action campaigns and sponsored their own later in the decade. But the internal conflict among black groups in Harlem confirmed their suspicions that racialism diverted attention from class consciousness.[12]

Within this context of intramural strategic controversy, the Picket Committee made its demand that the A. S. Beck Shoe Store on 125th Street employ 50 percent black help drawn from their organization. The district manager agreed to promote some black porters to sales positions, but refused to hire Picket Committee members. After two weeks of picketing, during which two Picket Committee members were convicted of assaulting a store patron, the owners sought an injunction in New York State Supreme Court in Manhattan. The owners presented affidavits from black employees who opposed the committee's demands, witnesses to committee intimidation, and black organizations opposed to its methods. Aware of the recent Baltimore decision, the owners denied that the Picket Committee was a labor organization and claimed it was rather a racial organization which, if placated, would contribute to further racial and ethnic discord. The committee denied that it had

---

12. Nancy J. Weiss, *Farewell to the Party of Lincoln: Black Politics in the Age of FDR* (Princeton, 1983), 97; August Meier and John H. Bracey, Jr., "The NAACP as a Reform Movement, 1909–1965: 'To Reach the Conscience of America,' " *Journal of Southern History,* LIX (1993), 17; Taylor Branch, *Parting the Waters: America in the King Years, 1954–63* (New York, 1988), 49–53; St. Clair Drake and Horace R. Cayton, *Black Metropolis: A Study of Negro Life in a Northern City* (New York, 1945), 85; Mark Naison, *Communists in Harlem During the Depression* (New York, 1983), 50–51, 100–103, 115–25; McKay, *Harlem,* 181–262; Meier and Rudwick, "Origins of Nonviolent Direct Action."

threatened anyone or made arbitrary demands, and dismissed criticism by other black organizations as a light-skinned conspiracy, branding its opponents as traitors to their race.[13]

State Supreme Court Justice Samuel I. Rosenman, a prominent liberal who had served as legal adviser to former governor Franklin D. Roosevelt, heard the case in October, 1934. Rosenman had a reputation for progressive labor decisions, and his decision was more muted than the conservative Owens', putting aside disputed questions of intimidation, violence, defamation, and the percentage of black help demanded.[14] But Rosenman too decided that the dispute warranted an injunction, "even if it be determined that the picketing is peaceful and truthful in its assertions." Like Owens, he called the picketing "solely a racial dispute, born of the understandable desire on the part of some of the Negroes in this community that the stores in the neighborhood where they spend their money should employ a percentage of Negro help." Rosenman concluded that other groups would have to be permitted the privilege of picketing against blacks, leading to racial tension and riots. The court granted the injunction to protect the entire community as well as Beck.[15]

Walter White responded angrily to Rosenman's decision, telling him it "smacks more of Hitler's Germany than of democratic America." White conceded that the motives and tactics of some of the groups

13. New York *Age,* October 13, 1934, p. 1; *Amsterdam News,* September 15, 1934, p. 1, October 20, 1934, p. 1; *A. S. Beck Shoe Corp.* v. *Johnson,* New York County Supreme Court, Index No. 33-689 (1934), New York City Hall of Records (hereafter cited as *Beck,* NYCSC); Muraskin, "Harlem Boycott," 363, 368; Memorandum in Support of Motion, in NAACP Papers, I-D-104. The Supreme Court in New York is a trial court of original jurisdiction. Its decisions can be appealed to the Appellate Division of the Supreme Court or to the New York State Court of Appeals, the state's highest tribunal. Beck did not distinguish among the various black organizations, so Johnson appeared as the principal defendant despite the fact that his organization was not involved in the picketing and disclaimed any association with the Picket Committee. The court ultimately dismissed the charges with regard to Johnson.

14. Rosenman edited a draft opinion to remove language referring to intimidation and defamation. *Beck,* NYCSC.

15. Samuel B. Hand, *Counsel and Advise: A Political Biography of Samuel I. Rosenman* (New York, 1979); *Beck,* NYCSC; *Beck* v. *Johnson.*

involved were questionable, but maintained that Rosenman should not have condemned the principle of direct action. White told NAACP Vice-President Arthur B. Spingarn that Hamid and others had attempted to turn the campaign into a personal racket, and that the Reverend Johnson had told White that Beck was right to seek an injunction. White spoke to Rosenman on November 14, and reported that the judge, now fearful of its unintended consequences, had second thoughts about his decision. While Rosenman hoped that it would be appealed, he expected that an appellate court would uphold his decision. Though Spingarn recommended attorneys to handle the case, White finally decided not to appeal.[16]

Although there was no trial testimony and Rosenman ruled out consideration of most of the disputed facts, and though Rosenman's opinion on the law was largely derived from the Baltimore case, *Beck* attracted more notice as a decision by a well-known judge with a liberal view of labor law in a significant northeastern jurisdiction.[17] Law reviews gave the *Beck* case a considerable amount of attention. While the benefit to society of labor union picketing outweighed the risk of violence, supporters of the decision noted, the risk of violence in racial disputes exceeded the potential benefit, and racial picketing would worsen already tense race relations in New York. Critics of the decision asserted that the labor organization–racial organization distinction was a spurious one. If the black organizations simply organized themselves formally as a labor union, they noted, they would achieve greater legitimacy, because there were many racially exclusive labor unions already in existence. (This is exactly what Arthur Reid of the Picket Committee did, securing a charter for the Harlem Labor Union in 1936.) Advocates of legal protection for racial organizations argued that black bargaining power against whites needed to be strengthened just as labor's power was being strengthened against capital. Critics of the decision suggested that it might kindle rather than forestall race riots,

16. Walter White to Samuel I. Rosenman, November 1, 1934, White to Arthur B. Spingarn, November 3, 1934, Spingarn to White, November 5, 1934, White to Spingarn, November 15, 1934, Spingarn to White, November 16, 1934, in Spingarn Papers.

17. The *University of Pennsylvania Law Review,* LXXXIV (1935), 105, was the only major review to note *Samuelson,* in one paragraph.

and that frustrations which Rosenman prevented from being expressed by other means might have added kindling to the Harlem Riot that broke out six months afterwards. One reviewer noted that any policy of group self-improvement must entail the risk of violence. Another reviewer advocated allowing racial groups to control employment in their neighborhoods in order to promote the "development of the negro in segregated districts," and hoped that future decisions would promote this policy.[18]

Legal academics thus exhibited the same ambivalence about race-based remedies to employment discrimination as seen among white employers, black organizations, and the courts. Some white employers responded to appeals to employ blacks in black areas, and negotiated when picketed rather than seek an injunction. Smaller retailers often objected and won relief in the courts. Black organizations were divided between new, racially exclusive local organizations that favored direct action, and older, interracial national organizations that either opposed it or offered only tepid support. The courts, facing a novel legal problem, focused on the narrow, technical question of the labor injunction, and denied that the privilege of picketing extended to pursuit of proportional racial employment. Applying the common law of torts, these courts tended to affirm a policy against legal recognition of racial classifications.[19]

While the Baltimore and New York campaigns failed to gain legal recognition for the racial jobs picket and soon collapsed, a Washington, D.C., organization persisted after several initial setbacks and in 1938 convinced the U.S. Supreme Court that its controversy with white employers, essentially the same as those in Baltimore and New York, was a labor dispute as defined by federal statute. The New Negro Alliance was formed in 1933 by young, college-educated blacks dissatisfied with the listless performance of the established civil rights groups during the depression. Able leadership, superior organization, and persistent legal appeals helped the New Negro Al-

18. *Harvard Law Review,* XLVIII (1935), 691; *Columbia Law Review,* XXXV (1935), 121; *New York University Law Quarterly Review,* XII (1935), 485.

19. Albon L. Holsey, "A Harlem Shoe Store," *Southern Workman,* LX (1931), 395–97.

liance succeed where the Baltimore and New York groups failed. The alliance had the legal services of law professor William Hastie, who later became a federal judge and governor of the Virgin Islands. With these resources the New Negro Alliance went farther toward articulating a justification for race-conscious remedies to the problem of black employment than the Baltimore or New York groups, and presented the first sociological explanation of employment discrimination.[20]

The alliance initially set out to protect Negro workers under the National Industrial Recovery Act (NIRA), the first piece of New Deal industrial planning. The minimum wage provisions of the National Recovery Administration (NRA) codes permitted white employers to replace their black workers, who had been paid less than the new rate, with whites. Minimum wage levels enabled prejudiced employers to "indulge their taste for discrimination" without having to pay for it. After the alliance won the reinstatement of three black workers by picketing a small restaurant, it went after larger employers, including the A&P chain. Hastie secured the acquittal of two picketers who were arrested on disorderly conduct charges during the action, and the A&P ultimately came to terms that included the employment of thirty Negro clerks. The alliance's efforts against High's Ice Cream Stores and Kaufman's Department Store brought the first actions for injunctions against them in December, 1933. Harry Kaufman, in the federal district court for Washington, D.C., alleged that the alliance demanded that he discharge "many" of his white employees to make room for alliance-chosen Negroes, but letters from the alliance to Kaufman show that he exaggerated the extent of the alliance's demands. The alliance's letters noted that Kaufman employed no Negroes in responsible positions, and that his store did not return in employment to the black community what it took out in revenue. The alliance never sought a specific percentage or quota for black employment, avoiding the contentious tactics of 50 to 100 percent demands and the displacement of in-

20. Gilbert Ware, *William Hastie: Grace Under Pressure* (New York, 1984), 66–80; Meier and Rudwick, "Origins of Nonviolent Direct Action," 321; John Aubrey Davis, "We Win the Right to Fight for Jobs," *Opportunity*, XVI (August, 1938), 230–37; Franklin, *Negro Labor Unionist,* 128.

cumbent white workers which had confounded the Baltimore and New York groups.[21]

Kaufman also made an appeal to segregation part of his complaint. He pointed out that "the demands of the defendant go to the extent of requiring the plaintiff to place behind its sales counters colored and white employees working side by side, without regard to the natural and inevitable result of such a situation." Like Baltimore, Washington was a segregated city in the 1930s, and Kaufman's appeal to the social policy of racial separation might be of considerable effect in the courts. The alliance neither denied that its demands would result in an integrated work force nor attacked the principle of segregation, but simply denied the pertinence of the complaint. This indicated the complicated nature of the alliance's race-conscious tactics.

The alliance insisted that there was a place for "intelligently controlled racialism" in the effort to improve black economic conditions. William Hastie based this view on his belief that for blacks "a special racial disadvantage was superimposed upon the common difficulties of workers generally." W. E. B. Du Bois, arguing that segregation was not inherently harmful to blacks, was heartened by the alliance's approach. Du Bois suggested that "segregation without discrimination" could benefit black Americans, and saw the work of the New Negro Alliance as a practical application of this idea. Hastie, however, was quick to dissociate the alliance's efforts from Du Bois' approval of segregation. While "in theory there can be segregation without unequal treatment," he said, "any negro who uses this theoretical possibility as a justification for segregation is either dumb, or mentally dishonest, or else he has, like Esau, chosen a mess of pottage." Du Bois responded that the alliance was in fact "fighting segregation with segregation," even if it was afraid to

21. Wright, *Old South, New South,* 223; Gary S. Becker, *The Economics of Discrimination* (2nd ed., Chicago, 1971); Walter Williams, *The State Against Blacks* (New York, 1982); Washington *Tribune,* August 31, 1933, p. 1, October 12, 1933, p. 1, December 7, 1933, p. 1; *Kaufman, Inc.* v. *New Negro Alliance,* United States District Court for the District of Columbia, Equity no. 56586, National Federal Records Center, Suitland, Md.; Washington *Tribune,* December 21, 1933; Sketch of New Negro Alliance History, in William Hastie Papers, Reel 38, Manuscript Division, Library of Congress.

admit it. Pointing out that the alliance's demands extended only as far as jobs in black neighborhoods, Du Bois said, "They were transmuting segregation into power that would bring an end to racial segregation someday." This was what Du Bois meant by fighting segregation with segregation. "Whatever they call it," he said, "that is what we both mean."

The organ of the alliance, the *New Negro Opinion*, tried to strike a moderate chord. "Uncontrolled and fanatic racialism is undoubtedly bad. But worse even than that is lack of unity. . . . We believe in intelligently controlled racialism as an approach to the eradication of racial lines." The Washington New Negro Alliance exhibited the same uncertainty about race-consciousness that black organizations demonstrated in Baltimore and New York. But the alliance became more deeply involved in the issue, and arrived at a tentative answer. Anticipating Justice Harry Blackmun's statement some forty years later that "in order to get beyond racism, we must first take account of race," the alliance reasoned that race-conscious separatism was acceptable if it avoided discrimination, and was used as a means to accomplish the ultimate goal of a society without racial lines.[22]

Political scientist Ralph Bunche criticized the alliance, complaining that its race-consciousness would split the ranks of organized labor and thereby harm black workers. Bunche's position was informed by the Marxist vision of working-class solidarity, similar to that of the Baltimore and New York communists. According to Bunche, "Despite its protestations to the contrary, it is clear that the New Negro Alliance pursues a narrowly racial policy—one that has no orientation in terms of labor unity or organization—and one that definitely opposed Negro against white workers. Its membership is middle class and so is its ideology." Its efforts were devoted to obtaining white-collar clerical jobs, ignoring blue-collar workers. The New Negro Alliance exhibited a business rather than a labor ethos, which would be of marginal economic consequence to the black community.[23]

22. Ware, *William Hastie,* 67–71; Meier and Rudwick, "Origins of Nonviolent Direct Action," 323–24; Blackmun statement in *Regents of California* v. *Bakke.*

23. Ralph Bunche, "The New Negro Alliance: 'We Must Organize Our Purchasing Power,'" in *Black Nationalism in America*, eds. John H. Bracey, Jr., August Meier, and Elliott Rudwick (New York, 1970), 377–86.

Hastie, arguing in court against the issue of a restraining order, claimed that the Norris–La Guardia Act of 1932 prohibited federal courts from issuing such an order. This statute defined a "labor dispute" as any controversy concerning terms or conditions of employment and collective bargaining, "regardless of whether or not the disputants stand in the proximate relation of employer and employee." A case grew out of a labor dispute when "persons participating or interested in" a labor dispute were parties in a case.[24] The federal district court granted an injunction without opinion on this point, and the Washington, D.C., Court of Appeals declined to review the decision. The alliance continued to picket other stores in 1934 and 1935, occasionally winning jobs. It went back to court when the Sanitary Grocery Company sought an injunction in April, 1936.[25]

The facts presented by Sanitary in the spring of 1936 were similar to previous racial picketing cases. District of Columbia District Judge Joseph W. Cox addressed the broader implications of the case, framing it in the context of recent conflict between capital and labor which the Norris–La Guardia Act was intended to ameliorate. "Here it is suggested that it is proper and lawful for this kind of contest to be adopted by other groups not directly interested in any way in industry or business itself," Cox wrote. He concluded that the alliance's tactics would only add to sectional, religious, and racial disorder, as much as if Methodists or southerners threatened any establishment that did not employ members of their groups. "So I think it would be extended from the economic zone in which we are already having so much trouble," he reasoned, "into the sectional or religious or racial zones." Congress enacted the Norris–La Guardia Act to contain rather than expand conflict. A Virginia Democrat, Cox was unlikely to endorse the broad reading of the Norris–La Guardia Act proffered by the New Negro Alliance. Cox in-

24. 47 Stat.L. 70 (1932).
25. Washington *Tribune*, October 12, 1933, p. 1, December 21, 1993, p. 1, December 28, 1933, p. 1, January 11, 1934, p. 1, January 18, 1934, p. 1, April 26, 1934, p. 1; Pittsburgh *Courier*, January 27, 1934, p. 1, April 25, 1936, p. 1, May 9, 1936, p. 1, *New Negro Alliance v. Kaufman, Inc.*, U.S. Court of Appeals, District of Columbia, *Records and Briefs*, vol. 483, no. 6187 (1934); Ware, *William Hastie*, 76.

vited the alliance to appeal the decision, hoping to gain a clearer interpretation from a higher court.[26]

The alliance did appeal the decision, contending that its picketing was peaceful, orderly, and lawful. It noted that the Maryland Court of Appeals had allowed the Citizens' Committee to organize, boycott, and publicize, and insisted that it had greater privileges as a labor organization under the Norris–La Guardia Act. Racial discrimination, the alliance argued, was equivalent to discrimination against organized labor generally. Sanitary's attorneys were in a more favorable position, invoking *Beck, Green,* and the court of appeals' own decision against the alliance two years earlier in Kaufman's case. The composition of the Washington, D.C., Court of Appeals was also in their favor. All but one of the judges were sixty-five or older, two of them having been appointed by Theodore Roosevelt, and were likely to agree with Cox.[27]

In a major setback for the alliance, Judge Josiah Alexander Van Orsdel followed *Beck* and *Green* in his four-man majority opinion, handed down in July, 1937. Strongly disapproving the New Negro Alliance's tactics, he said its purpose was "to interfere with the business of [Sanitary] as to compel it to surrender its free right to choose its employees and conduct its business in whatever lawful manner it may elect." A labor dispute could only come into existence, Van Orsdel reasoned, after an employer had chosen an employee. Since the entire case turned on the definition of a "labor dispute" under the Norris–La Guardia Act, this point disposed of the case. "However commendable the purposes of the appellants may be in attempting to improve the condition of their race," Van Orsdel concluded, they could not deprive Sanitary of its rights. "To sustain such action on the part of an organization established merely to advance the social standing of its race would be in complete disregard

---

26. *Sanitary Grocery Co.* v. *New Negro Alliance,* Supreme Court of the District of Columbia, Equity no. 61165, Washington National Records Center, Suitland, Md.; *New Negro Alliance* v. *Sanitary Grocery Co.,* U.S. Court of Appeals for the District of Columbia, *Records and Briefs,* vol. 549, no. 6836 (1936); Harold Chase *et al.,* eds., *Biographical Dictionary of the Federal Judiciary* (Detroit, 1976), *s.v.* Cox, Joseph W.

27. Chase *et al.,* eds., *Biographical Dictionary, s.v.* Cox; *New Negro Alliance* v. *Sanitary Grocery Co.*

of fundamental principles of public policy, and cannot be supported upon any principle of law, equity, or justice."[28]

Associate Justice Harold M. Stephens' partial dissent provided little solace for the alliance. He regarded the injunction's prohibition of boycotting as too broad, noting that the trial court in effect ordered blacks to trade with Sanitary. He also objected to the majority's excessively narrow reading of the Norris–La Guardia Act, in particular its idea that an employer-employee relationship was the *sine qua non* of a "labor dispute." Stephens cautioned the court against using this definition carelessly, suggesting that peaceful picketing might be allowed in other than labor disputes, depending on the particular case. Nevertheless, Stephens agreed that the controversy was not a labor dispute, even under the most liberal construction of the Norris–La Guardia Act. He concluded that, despite the economic issues at stake, the dispute was essentially a racial dispute. The main judicial consideration in picketing, he argued, was the likelihood of violence. In a labor dispute, the benefit derived from protecting labor in the pursuit of its goals outweighed the risk of violence. In a racial case the probability of violence was high, and sound public policy required the court to enjoin even peaceful picketing in racial disputes.[29]

Undeterred by the adverse ruling of the court of appeals, the New Negro Alliance petitioned the Supreme Court in October, 1937. It added an important sociological foundation to its previous arguments. Blacks were the group hardest hit by the depression, and their plight was a function of "the general social and economic structure of this country," it argued. Blacks could wield economic influence only as consumers, so the courts must permit picketing to bring that influence to bear. Moreover, it was sound public policy to allow this method of improving black employment, because it helped prevent blacks from becoming public charges. The alliance appealed to the Supreme Court to advance the cause of social justice for blacks as it had done for labor in cases that protected picketing from injunction. "There appears to be no difference between

28. *New Negro Alliance* v. *Sanitary Grocery Co.,* in *Records and Briefs.*

29. Stephens, incidentally, was a young (fifty-two), recently appointed Catholic Democrat.

these situations and the dispute involved in this case other than in this case those seeking to arrange conditions of employment happened to be identified as members of the Negro race," it pointed out. "In the equation of justice there is no element of color." This appeared to be a plea for separate-but-equal status that was substantially equal, or "segregation without discrimination." The Supreme Court agreed to hear the appeal.[30]

Having succeeded in getting its case before the Supreme Court, the alliance expanded its sociological argument. The task of the Court, as the alliance saw it, was to help equalize the relative advantage of groups—racial as much as economic—competing in the economy. "In the fierce conflict and 'free struggle for life,'" it said, "the chief concern of courts should be to equalize those economic weapons at the command of both parties in the struggle and if the law interferes at all with the operation of the 'natural' economic forces, its purpose would be to prevent one side from having too great an advantage over the other." Concrete social facts revealing the relative weights of the contestants were relevant to this purpose. Thus the alliance presented statistics showing the disproportionate number of Negroes on relief in Washington. This situation was due to a number of factors, including overt discrimination, the mechanization of agriculture, and black social instability. Discrimination could be seen in government employment. While blacks were 27.1 percent of the city's population, they composed only 2.8 percent of police officers and 1.9 percent of firemen. The alliance expanded this profile by using E. Franklin Frazier's profile of race and occupational groups showing blacks concentrated in the lowest occupational categories. All of these conditions necessitated the use of boycotting and picketing as a means of turning black purchasing power into jobs. It was especially appropriate to the Sanitary case, since the store being picketed was located in a census tract that was 96.6 percent black.[31]

The idea that the racial composition of an employer's work force

30. U.S. Supreme Court, Petition for Writ of Certiorari, *Transcripts of Records and File Copies of Briefs, New Negro Alliance v. Sanitary Grocery Co.*, 1937, vol. 106, no. 511; hereafter cited as *New Negro Alliance, Transcripts of Records*.

31. Brief of Petitioners, *ibid.*

should approximate the racial composition of the area of its operations was the newest part of the alliance's appeal. While the alliance carefully eschewed any particular percentage demands, the justification for their tactics indicated that they did have a particular percentage in mind. The alliance used social science to convince the court of the logic of its approach. It was well established that judicial activists would take these facts into account in their attempt to shape public policy. This was the underlying strategy of judicial liberalism since the famous 1908 case of *Muller* v. *Oregon,* based on the "Brandeis brief." The use of social science before the court in racial matters certainly smacked of *Plessy* and "separate but equal," although in this case the alliance tried to use social science not to combat segregation, but to insist that segregation truly be equal. Here were the elements for a formula of "intelligently controlled racialism." The alliance made more than just the simple assumption that since almost all of Sanitary's patrons were black, its work force ought to be similarly constituted. They based their calculation on census information, extending it to the public employment picture of the entire city. Composing 27.1 percent of the city's population meant that blacks should constitute just such a percentage of public employment. The larger implications of the alliance's pattern of thought were considerable. The idea presented by the alliance of racial proportionalism in employment became the touchstone of employment under the disparate-impact theory some thirty years later.[32]

The defendant, Sanitary, relied on what had heretofore been a winning strategy, stressing the idea that the New Negro Alliance was neither a labor union nor the representative of potential black unionists. Sanitary claimed that it employed a number of black workers, who were neither dissatisfied with their situations nor in any way represented by the New Negro Alliance. Relying heavily on the opinions of *Green, Beck,* and the previous *New Negro Alliance* cases, Sanitary responded to the new, sociological argument of the alliance by noting that its work force was now completely unionized.[33]

32. Lofgren, *The Plessy Case,* 204–207.
33. Briefs for Respondent, *New Negro Alliance, Transcripts of Records.*

The Supreme Court reversed the court of appeals and upheld the New Negro Alliance's right to picket on March 28, 1938. Justice Owen Roberts' six-to-two majority decision accepted the facts as the alliance presented them, that their pickets were orderly, peaceful, made no untrue statements, and did not physically obstruct Sanitary's business. The most important part of Roberts' decision was that the lower court's "conclusion that the dispute was not a labor dispute within the meaning of the [Norris–La Guardia] Act, because it did not involve terms and conditions of employment in the sense of wages, hours, unionization, or betterment of working conditions is erroneous." Reviewing the text of the act, Roberts declared that its terms "plainly embrace the controversy . . . and classify it as one arising out of a dispute defined as a labor dispute. They leave no doubt that the New Negro Alliance and the individual petitioners are, in contemplation of the Act, persons interested in the dispute." Beyond the plain words of the text, the legislative history of the act showed that Congress intended to broaden the privileges of organized labor under the Clayton Act, which had been nullified by federal courts in the 1920s. Roberts implied that the lower courts in this case were attempting similarly to thwart the will of Congress.[34]

Equating formal labor unions and broader groups like the New Negro Alliance, Roberts held that Congress intended to prevent discrimination against racial and religious minorities as much as it meant to prevent discrimination against organized labor. In the case's most memorable statement, Roberts declared, "Race discrimination by an employer may reasonably be deemed more unfair and less excusable than discrimination against workers on the ground of union affiliation." This, however, begged the question of whether Sanitary's employment policy was discriminatory.

The *New Negro Alliance* decision occurred during the first term of the Supreme Court following the "court-packing crisis" of 1937. The Court was now decidedly more friendly to New Deal legislation and labor unions, and would become more so as President Roosevelt made appointments to the Court in his second term. The

34. *New Negro Alliance* v. *Sanitary Grocery Co.,* 303 U.S. 552 (1938).

Supreme Court's turn away from the defense of property rights in favor of deference to government regulation of property undermined the judicial framework that had supported state judges' decisions against racial picketing in Maryland and New York. It is notable that Owen Roberts, whose "switch" from conservative to liberal in 1937–1938 averted the court-packing crisis and determined the new direction of American constitutional law, was the one who wrote the *New Negro Alliance* opinion. Two of the conservatives who provoked Roosevelt's plan, Willis Van Devanter and George Sutherland, had been replaced by New Dealers Hugo Black and Stanley Reed. The two remaining conservatives, James McReynolds and Pierce Butler, dissented. McReynolds wrote that Congress could not have intended to "encourage mobbish interference with the individual's liberty of action." Any dissatisfied group could now claim the right to picket to obtain preference for its members with any employer. "The ultimate result of the view now approved by the very people whom present petitioners claim to represent, it may be, is prefigured by the grievous plight of minorities in lands where the law has become a mere political instrument."[35]

The principal concern of the Court in the *New Negro Alliance* case was to uphold the Norris–La Guardia Act and to prevent the lower federal courts from interpreting it too narrowly. While there is no doubt that Congress meant to prohibit injunctions in labor disputes which did not involve an employer-employee relationship, it is doubtful that Congress anticipated or intended to protect the right of organizations like the New Negro Alliance to picket for jobs. The alliance did not represent people engaged in any common craft or occupation, and did not negotiate the terms or conditions of employment, as common labor organizations did. As Justice Stephens noted, the lower federal courts had construed the act too narrowly by insisting that an employer-employee relationship define a labor dispute, but Congress did not seek to protect organizations that so remotely resembled labor organizations.

The *New Negro Alliance* case was seen at the time and subsequently as a major breakthrough in the pursuit of civil rights. Its

35. *Ibid.*

long-term implications may have been great, but the Court had focused on the technical question of the applicability of the Norris–La Guardia Act, without venturing into the larger social policy questions of racial picketing. It is worth noting that the New Negro Alliance was protesting discrimination rather than making any specific numerical demands. Forbidding federal courts to issue injunctions in peaceful racial picketing cases protected the New Negro Alliance in the federal jurisdiction of Washington, D.C., but the response of state courts could vary. Several states had enacted statutes similar to that involved in the *New Negro Alliance* case ("little Norris–La Guardia acts"), but most had not. More important, even in states which had done so, the courts did not always follow the U.S. Supreme Court.[36]

The New Negro Alliance had achieved a remarkable organizational and legal breakthrough in the late 1930s. It successfully melded the cautious, patient legalism of the national black organizations and the innovative direct-action tactics of the local groups. It avoided some of the problems that blocked other groups, such as explaining the fate of incumbent white employees, deciding who the beneficiaries of the jobs campaign should be, and insisting on specific quotas. Facing the dilemma of race-consciousness in the pursuit of racial equality and attempting to justify it, the alliance strategy showed the influence of sociological jurisprudence and legal realism that would be of vital importance to the civil rights movement.[37]

There was a revival of direct action activity in the spring of 1938, immediately following the *New Negro Alliance* decision and the severe depression of 1937–1938. The national black organizations were becoming more favorable to the tactic because of the New Negro Alliance's example. But some state courts continued to enjoin

36. NAACP, *29th Annual Report for 1938* (New York, 1939), 15; Meier and Rudwick, "Origins of Nonviolent Direct Action," 326; Ware, *William Hastie,* 79; "Labor Law—When a Dispute Exists Within the Meaning of the Norris–La Guardia Act," *Michigan Law Review* XXXVI (1938), 1146–76; Pauli Murray, "The Right to Equal Opportunity in Employment," *California Law Review,* XXXIII (1945), 396.

37. Genna Rae McNeil, *Groundwork: Charles Hamilton Houston and the Struggle for Civil Rights* (Philadelphia, 1983), 84, 133, 216–17.

picketing by racial groups. A Pennsylvania court denied an injunction sought by an employee discharged after an employer capitulated to such picketing, and a New Jersey court denied an injunction in a case where store owners could not show that the picketing caused irreparable damage. A rare case from the South ignored the *New Negro Alliance* decision, and an injunction there was upheld by the state appellate court. In Cleveland, pickets were able to win jobs from employers.[38]

New York courts were more likely to apply the ruling of the *New Negro Alliance* case, under the state's version of the Norris–La Guardia Act which protected picketing in a labor dispute. A Queens supreme court denied an injunction, holding that *New Negro Alliance* effectively overturned *Beck*. In Brooklyn, however, a judge stopped disorderly picketing involving unreasonable demands and anti-semitic appeals. Cases involving the Harlem Labor Union (HLU), created by Ira Kemp of the African Patriotic League after *Beck,* showed the limits of the *New Negro Alliance* decision. Local observers notified the national office of the NAACP that the HLU was turning the jobs-for-Negroes campaign into a racket, and New York courts repeatedly enjoined this organization. However, the HLU was able to convince a New York appellate court that trial courts must at least hold hearings and make specific findings of fact before an injunction issued.[39]

38. "Suggestions for Consideration by the Committee for General Welfare and Bill of Rights of the Unofficial Committee on the Constitutional Convention, New York State," September 23, 1937, in National Urban League Papers, Series XII, Box 6, Manuscript Division, Library of Congress; Meier and Rudwick, "Origins of Nonviolent Direct Action," 331; *Stevens* v. *West Philadelphia Youth Civic League,* 3 L.R.R.M. 792 (1939); 34 *Pennsylvania District and County Reports,* 612 (1939); *Siegell et al.* v. *Newark National Negro Congress,* 2 L.R.R.M. 859 (1938); Newark *Evening News,* April 20, 1938, p. 1; Newark *Star-Eagle,* April 20, 1938, p. 1; New York *Times,* April 21, 1938, p. 4; *Texas Motion Picture and Vitaphone Operators* v. *Galveston Motion Picture Operators,* 132 S.W.2d 299 (1939); Cleveland *PlainDealer,* May 1, p. 32, May 5, 1938, p. 3.

39. "Labor—Norris–La Guardia Act," *St. John's Law Review,* XIII (1938), 171; *Anora Amusement Corp.* v. *Doe,* 12 N.Y.S.2d 400 (1939); *Stoller* v. *Citizens Civic Affairs Committee,* File no. 3858 (1940), Kings County Supreme Court, Clerk's Office, Brooklyn, N.Y.; *Stoller* v. *Citizens Civic Affairs Committee,* 19 N.Y.S.2d 597 (1940); Citizens Civic Affairs Committee to National Negro Congress, April 16, 1938, in National Negro Congress Papers, Microfilm Collection, Group I, Reel 12, Manuscript Division, Library of Congress; Muraskin, "Harlem Boycott," 370; Meier and Rudwick, "Origins of

Mainstream labor groups were better able to take advantage of the *New Negro Alliance* decision and make substantial employment gains for blacks. One month after the decision, Adam Clayton Powell, Jr.'s Greater New York Coordinating Committee for Employment threatened to boycott and picket Consolidated Edison, and the utility agreed to hire black clerks in Harlem and an "appreciable percentage" of Negroes in the future. Later that year the committee and the Uptown Chamber of Commerce agreed to give one-third of Harlem jobs to Negroes. This agreement would not displace any white incumbents, and provided a joint arbitration committee to settle grievances. Mayor Fiorello La Guardia hailed the agreement as "a tribute to common sense and justice." Powell considered the plan a model for the rest of New York and other cities. Finally, in 1941 Powell's committee agreed to boycott the Eighth Avenue Bus Company in support of a Transport Workers Union strike in exchange for a TWU promise to negotiate for the hiring of blacks and whites on a one-to-one quota basis until blacks reached 17 percent of the skilled blue-collar work force.[40]

Black self-help efforts of the 1930s opened the discussion of racial preference as an antidiscrimination method, and blacks in particu-

---

Nonviolent Direct Action," 328; Memorandum for Walter White, November 1, 1939, in NAACP Papers, I-C-323; *Pappas v. Straughn*, 7 L.R.R.M. 693 (1940); *Stolper v. Straughn*, 23 N.Y.S.2d 604 (1940), *Stolper v. Straughn*, File no. 11021 (1940), *Solomon v. Straughn*, File no. 9705 (1940), *Hillary Theater v. Straughn*, File no. 16694 (1940), Kings County Supreme Court, Clerk's Office, Brooklyn, N.Y.; *Parkshire Ridge Amusements v. Miller*, File no. 15873 (1937), Kings County Supreme Court, Clerk's Office, Brooklyn, N.Y.; *Lifschitz v. Straughn*, File no. 14917 (1940), Kings County Supreme Court, Clerk's Office, Brooklyn, N.Y.; *Lifschitz v. Straughn*, 27 N.Y.S.2d 193 (1940); *Smith v. Citizens Federation of Labor*, File no. 12729 (1941), Kings County Supreme Court, Clerk's Office, Brooklyn, N.Y.

40. New York *Times*, April 29, 1938, p. 8, August 8, 1938, p. 1, August 10, 1938, p. 21; Charles V. Hamilton, *Adam Clayton Powell, Jr.* (New York, 1992), 89–104; Meier and Rudwick, "Origins of Nonviolent Direct Action," 329; Dominic J. Capeci, Jr., "From Harlem to Montgomery: The Bus Boycotts and Leadership of Adam Clayton Powell, Jr. and Martin Luther King, Jr.," *Historian*, XLI (1979), 721–37; Greenberg, "*Or Does It Explode*," 204–205; Joshua B. Freeman, *In Transit: The Transport Workers Union in New York City, 1933–66* (New York, 1989), 255–56.

lar would benefit from any active government attempt to provide employment and relief. The New Deal liberals, however, were torn between their commitment to racial minorities and their political alliance with southern Democrats. The New Deal thus included a considerable amount of deference to local custom in the administration of its programs and left segregation in the South undisturbed. Yet to a surprising degree the New Deal faced the problem of racial discrimination in public employment. In the Public Works Administration (PWA) construction program it ultimately formulated the nation's first openly race-conscious attempt to improve black employment, through the use of racial job quotas.

Both racially liberal, white New Dealers and leaders of black organizations were ambivalent about securing equal treatment for Negroes through special consideration of any kind, especially through strict numerical quota representation. In the early years of Roosevelt's first administration, the National Urban League (NUL) was generally more vocal in support of quota representation and the NAACP more cautious. In relief and public works employment, the NUL argued for explicit preferential treatment clauses, taking veteran preferences as its model. The NAACP cited the absence of Negroes as evidence for complaints of discrimination, and Walter White called on President Herbert Hoover to ensure that "a just proportion" of public works funds be spent on black labor. However, the NAACP denied that it demanded proportional representation, and told a local group pursuing such representation that "we are not sure that the quota system is the best safeguard because it may be used in such a way, in some circumstances, to restrict the opportunities of Negro workers."[41]

Harold Ickes, as secretary of the interior and administrator of the Public Works Administration, engineered the principal effort to aid

41. Weiss, *Farewell to the Party of Lincoln*, 37–39; Frances Perkins to Eugene Kinkle Jones, April 17, 1933, in NAACP Papers, I-C-223; William N. Markoe to Bernard Dickman, July 8, 1933, in NUL Papers, VI-E-84; C. C. Spaulding to State Chairmen, July 25, 1935, "Erection of Low-Cost Housing Under the Recovery Act," n.d., in NUL Papers, IV-A-4; New York *Times,* September 11, 1932, p. 14; Unsigned to Frances Perkins, May 18, 1933, in NAACP Papers, I-C-223; Unsigned to George Drayton, October 11, 1938, in NAACP Papers, I-C-323.

black employment in the 1930s. Ickes had been president of the Chicago NAACP from 1922 to 1924, and considered the inclusion of Negroes in New Deal relief programs an important priority. One of Ickes' most important steps in developing a racial policy was the appointment of Clark Foreman, a southern white liberal, and Robert C. Weaver, a black economist, to his staff. Foreman and Weaver proposed a National Advisory Board on Negro Welfare, but Ickes dissuaded them from pursuing this project. Though eager to include minorities in government programs, Ickes considered it a bad precedent to establish a government agency representing a specific minority group. Instead Ickes had each government agency choose one of its members to ensure that it gave fair consideration to Negroes in program administration. These staff members together formed the "Interdepartmental Group Concerned with the Special Problems of the Negro Population," led by Foreman and Weaver of the Interior Department.[42]

Ickes' first step to end discrimination in federal employment was a simple one. On September 1, 1933, he issued an order prohibiting discrimination based on race or religion in all PWA projects. Ickes immediately faced the problem of making this prohibition effective. Contractors had no objective definition of "discrimination," so token compliance—the presence of one member of a racial or religious minority group—might satisfy their definition of nondiscrimination. More important, the New Deal's commitment to organized labor meant that local building trades unions, and not the contractor per se, made employment decisions. Contractors thus could exculpate themselves from charges of violating the PWA nondiscrimination clause by blaming the exclusionary practices of

42. John B. Kirby, *Black Americans in the Roosevelt Era: Liberalism and Race* (Knoxville, 1980), Chap. 2; Marc W. Kruman, "Quotas for Blacks: The PWA and the Black Construction Worker," *Labor History*, XVI (1975), 37–49; Raymond Wolters, *Negroes and the Great Depression* (Westport, Conn., 1970), 196–209; U.S. Commission on Civil Rights, *1961 Report, Part III: Employment* (Washington, 1961), 88–91; Allen Francis Kifer, "The Negro Under the New Deal, 1933–41" (Ph. D. dissertation, University of Wisconsin, 1961), 218–32; Harold Ickes to Clark Foreman, January 2, 1934, in U.S. Department of the Interior, Records of the Secretary, General Subject File, Box 10, Record Group (RG) 48, National Archives (NA).

labor unions. Representatives of black technical workers complained to Ickes in early 1934 that trained and qualified Negro workers were not being given a fair proportion of work in federal projects, despite the nondiscrimination order. As Robert Weaver noted in 1936, "It was humanly impossible to define discrimination in a situation where a borrower, a contractor, and a labor union were involved." Walter White of the NAACP, while praising Ickes' order as an excellent first step, asked the secretary to keep in mind more drastic action if the order should prove ineffective.[43]

The first meeting of the Interdepartmental Group, in February, 1934, considered the means of making Ickes' order more effective. Almost all of the departmental representatives expressed a belief that fair treatment of Negroes by their departments would be evidenced by a work force profile that roughly approximated the racial composition of the country. Clark Foreman told the group that the nondiscrimination order precluded "special attention to Negroes as such," but it was obvious that prejudice against Negroes excluded them from many government jobs. The Interdepartmental Group was as yet unable to formulate an answer to the problem of enforcing nondiscrimination in government employment, and Foreman was beginning to despair that even New Deal organizations that desired to treat Negroes fairly continued to discriminate.[44]

By the summer of 1934 the Interdepartmental Group had arrived at more concrete answers to the problem of racial discrimination in PWA projects. Isador Lubin of the Bureau of Labor Statistics disclosed a confidential plan by which the Labor Department would negotiate for projects that would use 50 percent Negro labor. The opposition of predominantly white labor unions would make this goal difficult to attain, Lubin noted, and he doubted that the plan would be legally enforceable. Robert Weaver pointed out that such

43. John A. Lankford to Ickes, January 11, 1934, Ickes to Lankford, January 25, 1934, in Office of the Interior Secretary, General Classified File 1–280, Box 506, Walter White to Ickes, October 14, 1933, in Records of Ickes, Box 10, RG 48; Robert C. Weaver, "An Experiment in Negro Labor," *Opportunity*, XIV (1936), 295–98.

44. Minutes of the First Meeting of the Interdepartmental Group, February 7, 1934, Foreman to Ickes, February 20, 1934, in Office of the Interior Secretary, File 1–280, Box 506, RG 48.

a quota would be easy to fill in certain jobs—unskilled laborers and some of the older skilled construction jobs like carpentry and masonry—but almost impossible to fill in more modern jobs like plumbing and electrical work. The 50-percent quota seemed not inherently wrong, but arbitrary.

Clark Foreman suggested basing the proportion of Negroes in each job category upon the occupational census of 1930. The government could demand that contractors employ, at a minimum, the same percentage of Negroes in various skilled trades in a city as was found in each of these trades in 1930. Foreman proposed that "any variation in the various trades from that of the 1930 census can be considered prima facie discrimination unless a good reason is given for it." Such a proportion was fairer than a fixed one of 50 percent, which Foreman thought would be an injustice to both white and black labor.[45]

The PWA put Foreman's plan into effect. The legal division of the Bureau of Employment Security assured the Interdepartmental Group that the PWA could take whatever steps necessary to carry out Ickes' nondiscrimination order, "even going so far as to fix quotas for the employment of Negroes for each class of work on a particular project." (No quotas were devised for other racial or religious groups.) If the job involved organized labor, the unions could be required to fill the quotas by their own membership or issue work permits to Negro non-members. Harold Ickes sent a message to the NAACP's 1935 annual conference explaining this program. The contract for the first federal housing project, in Atlanta, specified that 12 percent of the skilled labor payroll must go to Negro employees. Ickes hoped that such provisions would induce contractors to adopt voluntary quotas. The Atlanta builders, Ickes reported, exceeded the quota for skilled payrolls and employed substantial Negro unskilled labor. Ickes also promised that he would consider other means if this program failed to end discrimination.[46]

45. Minutes of the Fourth Meeting of the Interdepartmental Group, June 1, 1934, in Office of the Interior Secretary, General Classified File 1–280, Box 506, RG 48.

46. Lawrence Oxley to Isador Lubin, August 17, 1935, in Lawrence Oxley Records, Box 12, RG 183, NA: Message of Harold Ickes to Annual NAACP Conference, 1935, in Office of the Interior Secretary, General Classified File 1–280, Box 506, RG 48.

National Urban League representatives thought that the level of unemployment rather than the proportion by the 1930 occupational census should determine the quota. The NUL supported the PWA racial quota in public housing projects and wanted it extended to all PWA projects, but advised that the contractual clauses be given "teeth," including fines and back pay awards for victims of discrimination. Robert Weaver was at pains to explain to black organizations that the PWA quotas were considered minimums, not maximums, and that a filled quota was not prima facie evidence of nondiscrimination, although he was not consistent on this point. Other officials discussed related legal complications associated with expansion and enforcement of the program. The PWA hesitated to put "teeth" into its racial quota system, a PWA administrator explained, because it doubted that the system could survive a legal challenge.[47]

The PWA quotas, even if rigidly enforced, did not completely solve the problem of black employment in the building trades. If Negroes were excluded from building trades unions in 1930, that exclusion would be perpetuated by basing quotas on the 1930 occupational census. Changes in the local population made some local quotas impossible to fill. Chicago contractors knew that they would be unable to fill a 12 percent skilled quota with qualified Negroes, and so hesitated to agree to such a provision. In Newark there were not enough Negroes to fill a 5 percent quota for skilled workers. Negroes from outside of the city demanded that they be allowed to take the jobs, but this ran afoul of the PWA's policy of giving preference to local labor in its projects. In Miami, the local custom of segregating black mechanics to work in black districts deprived them of the opportunity to work on white projects, and so the Miami quota of 6 percent went unfilled.[48]

The PWA quota system can be seen as an experimental program to compensate for harm done to black labor by earlier labor legisla-

47. "Resume of Conference on Employment Difficulties faced by Negroes on PWA Projects," in Oxley Records, Box 12, RG 183.

48. Howard Gould to Lawrence Oxley, January 26, 1935, Harry Scheck to H. L. Kerwin, February 27, 1935, in Oxley Papers, Box 12, RG 183; Brooklyn Urban League–Lincoln Settlement, "Report of the Industrial Department," in NUL Papers, IV-D-28; L. E. Thomas to NAACP, August 29, 1939, in NAACP Papers, I-C-400.

tion, similar to the New Negro Alliance's response to the minimum wage provisions of the NIRA. With the onset of the Great Depression, cities were deluged with unemployed workers who threatened to drive down wage rates. For example, organized construction craftsmen were threatened by competition from lower-wage migrant labor. Congress responded with the Davis-Bacon Act of 1931, requiring the payment of "prevailing wage rates" to labor in federal construction projects, to reduce the incentive for builders to employ non-union labor. Many of these migrant workers were black, and the Davis-Bacon Act was motivated in part by racial animus. In this light, the PWA quota system can be seen as the first of many government attempts to impose fair employment standards after having facilitated discrimination by earlier regulation.[49]

The PWA system was a small effort to improve black employment, and was overwhelmed by other New Deal policies which harmed black labor. The PWA strategy itself reflected the "scarcity economy" mentality of the 1930s and was aggravated by federal intervention that inhibited economic growth and full employment. Lending its aid to cartelization in its piecemeal economic planning, the New Deal fostered precisely the sort of anti-competitive economic structure that facilitated discrimination. Among the most important policies of the New Deal to do so was the National Labor Relations Act (NLRA). While the NLRA encouraged less restrictive unions, such as the Congress of Industrial Organizations (CIO), its overall effect was to strengthen an interest group that had strong economic incentives to exclude blacks or other unpopular minorities. As had been the case since the 1920s, government and industry commitment to high wages for those employed meant unemployment for newcomers. As the most important interest group in

49. Armand J. Thieblot, Jr., *The Davis-Bacon Act* (Philadelphia, 1975), 6–10; Epstein, *Forbidden Grounds,* 46. For a general discussion see Herbert Hill, *Black Labor and the American Legal System* (Washington, D.C., 1977), 22, 98; William A. Sundstrom, "Last Hired, First Fired? Unemployment and Urban Black Workers During the Great Depression," *Journal of Economic History,* LII (1992), 415–29; Owen M. Fiss, "A Theory of Fair Employment Laws," *University of Chicago Law Review,* XXXVIII (1971), 235–314; Williams, *The State Against Blacks;* James J. Hoey, radio address, printed in *Congressional Record* 78 (January 11, 1934), 432.

the Democratic Party in the mid-twentieth century, organized labor profoundly complicated progress toward fair employment.[50]

Although there were few objections in principle to the PWA experiment, some groups did disagree with the quota plan. The U.S. Reemployment Service refused to cooperate with the PWA plan because it considered the plan to be discrimination in favor of Negroes, and would leave the way open for later discrimination against them. Roy Wilkins of the NAACP continued to maintain that "this Association does not subscribe to the belief that employment of colored people should be in strict proportion to the population ratio," but, all else being equal, believed that qualified blacks should be given preference, especially where black clients were concerned. The NAACP raised no objection to the population ratio adopted by the PWA. R. W. Stone of the University of Chicago Business School argued that laborers should be chosen on the basis of their fitness for work and on their economic need, "irrespective of color, religion, politics, or union affiliation," rather than by a quota system, but was unable to suggest an effective nondiscrimination method that did not resort to quotas. A group called the City and State Federation of Colored Women's Clubs advocated the expansion of the PWA quota system to all government agencies, urging "that in each and every department where federal funds are expended Negroes be given fair representation in proportion to their ratio of the population." Ickes' office rejected this idea, arguing that "at least in theory . . . true democracy finds no place for dual setups based upon race, religion, or creed." Complete integration was the answer to racial discrimination, the Interior Department advised, despite its own experiment in quota hiring. Doubt persisted even among those who devised and administered the PWA plan.[51]

50. Ellis Hawley, *The New Deal and the Problem of Monopoly: A Study in Economic Ambivalence* (Princeton, 1966), 277; Gary Becker, "Union Restrictions on Entry," in *The Public Stake in Union Power,* ed. Philip D. Bradley (Charlottesville, 1959), 209–24; Richard Posner, "Some Economics of Labor Law," *University of Chicago Law Review,* LI (1984), 988–1011; Wright, *Old South, New South,* 206, 223.

51. "Resume," R. W. Stone to Lawrence Oxley, January 25, 1935, in Oxley Records, Box 12, RG 183; Roy Wilkins to Federal Emergency Relief Agency, January 21, 1935, in Works Progress Administration, FERA Central Files, Interracial Relations,

Established black organizations generally approved of the PWA plan. In New York City the Reverend John Johnson, organizer of the Harlem boycott of 1934, called it "what we have been asking the Government to do for many years." James H. Hubert, New York Urban League director, called the policy "precisely what those of us in the NYUL have been advocating as the proper procedure." The quota plan also won the support of the district Democratic party leader. The New York *Amsterdam News,* a black newspaper, approved the 1936 announcement of a 3-percent quota in a Harlem project, but cautioned that black nationalists were likely to call for the majority of the jobs rather than a mere 3 percent, since the project was in a predominantly black area. As in the Harlem boycott of 1934, however, the *News* warned that this kind of logic would exclude blacks from far greater opportunities for jobs in white construction areas.[52]

The PWA quotas were successfully instituted in most cases, and met no legal challenge. The government was able to wield great influence on construction contractors during the 1930s because private construction spending had dried up; this was the main source of "teeth" in the program. Builders often had no choice but to accept the PWA's terms. Moreover, most contractors met the quotas fairly easily. As Robert Weaver later wrote, "Since these were the first projects and there was doubt in the minds of those in the PWA, who were uncertain of the possibilities of enforcement, the percentages were purposely placed low." The main purposes of the program were to help regain some of the ground lost by Negro construction workers in the 1930s, and to provide a model for other government agencies.[53]

Box 31, RG 69; J. F. Pierce to Ickes, September 3, 1935, Ickes to Pierce, September 17, 1935, in Office of the Interior Secretary, General Classified File 1–280, Box 506, RG 48.

52. Oxley to Lubin, January 23, 1936, in Oxley Records, Box 12, RG 183; *Amsterdam News,* April 11, 1936.

53. John P. Davis, "A Brief Note on the Negro and the New Deal," in National Negro Congress Papers, I, Reel 1; Kruman, "Quotas for Blacks," 37–49; Weaver, "Experiment in Negro Labor," 295–98; Robert C. Weaver, *Negro Labor: A National Problem* (Port Washington, N.Y., 1946), 13. According to the U.S. Commission on Civil Rights, the Public Housing Administration maintained its enforcement of contractor quotas until 1958. See U.S. Commission on Civil Rights, *1961 Report,* 90.

Although the PWA quota system in construction did not expand into all government employment, other New Deal programs used racial proportionalism as their standard of fair employment policy. The Tennessee Valley Authority (TVA) attempted to approximate the Negro population of its construction sites in its work force, about 11 percent black. While some in the TVA believed that this policy was a step toward a color-blind employment policy, others advocated a merit system that did not take race into account. One historian of TVA policy has noted, "Paradoxically, although TVA acknowledged having a racial quota for unskilled employment, it denied having an overall racial policy and insisted that it followed a policy of nondiscrimination in regard to race." The NAACP argued that quotas should be based on need rather than population proportion, and that population quotas denied black Americans their fair share of jobs.[54]

Other New Deal agencies followed the PWA and TVA pattern. Harold Ickes was particularly conscious of maintaining a proper proportion of blacks in the Civilian Conservation Corps, the Armed Forces, and in his own office. When Robert Weaver moved to the U.S. Housing Authority in 1937, he established a policy in which the public housing projects built on a quota system of employment were also tenanted according to a racial proportion system, and these labor and tenant quotas continued into the 1950s. The National Youth Administration, part of the Works Progress Administration, decided that "the number of young men and women of any racial group given assistance shall not represent a smaller percentage of the total number aided than the proportion their racial group represents to the total proportion of the school districts." As Mary McLeod Bethune explained, the application of a quota system here could be defended because it was preferable to the complete absence of educational facilities for blacks, especially in the South.[55]

54. Nancy L. Grant, *TVA and Black Americans: Planning for the Status Quo* (Philadelphia, 1990), 19–24; Walter White to Robert Fechner, December 28, 1937, Fechner to White, December 29, 1937, in NAACP Papers, I-C-223; Kifer, "The Negro Under the New Deal," 280.

55. Kifer, "The Negro Under the New Deal," 66; Diary of Harold Ickes, September 15, 1940, May 17, 1941, March 6, 1943, August 15, 1943, September 5, 1943, Manuscript Division, Library of Congress; Weiss, *Farewell to the Party of Lincoln*, 53; Ickes to

Whether PWA quotas were ceilings or floors on black employment remains uncertain. The contracts stipulated that failure to meet the quota was prima facie proof of discrimination, but did not specify if a filled quota provided prima facie proof of nondiscrimination. Quota employment of blacks was necessary, but was it sufficient? This important point brought to light the matter of whether quotas were a sound public policy generally or merely an expedient tactic in particular circumstances. Some black groups appear to have believed that the quotas merely represented a minimum percentage, a floor that did not immunize the contractor from charges of discrimination. The weight of evidence indicates that the quotas were grants of immunity—and this may explain why they were never challenged by contractors. Usually the quotas were exceeded, so black groups did not try to sue for enforcement.[56] Robert C. Weaver maintained in private that the quotas were floors.[57] But in public he wrote that quota employment was considered prima facie evidence that the contractor had *not* discriminated against Negro labor.[58]

The PWA was unusual as a New Deal agency that formulated a policy of nondiscrimination and tried to enforce it. What is especially remarkable is the means by which it did so—a job quota system. Considering the southern pattern of legal segregation, and the New Deal's policy of deferring to local custom in its programs, a

McKeough, July 6, 1935, in Office of the Interior Secretary, General Classified File 1–280, Box 506, RG 48; Neil J. Convey to John A. Jones, November 27, 1939, in NAACP Papers, I-C-400; National Youth Administration "Information," September 10, 1935, in Oxley Records, Box 12, RG 183; Kirby, *Black Americans*, 22; Ralph Bunche, *The Political Status of the Negro in the Age of FDR* (Chicago, 1940), 623.

56. "The New Deal Era," in National Negro Congress Papers, I, Reel 21; Harlem River Houses Advisory Committee to Langdon Post, April 23, 1936, in NAACP Papers, I-C-401; Isador Lubin to Roy Copeland, January 13, 1936, in Oxley Records, Box 12, RG 183; "Employment in USHA–Aided Projects in New York City," September 22, 1939, in NAACP Papers, I-C-401; John M. Carmody, "Jobs for American Workers: The Negro in the Government's Work Program" (1940?), in National Negro Congress Papers, I, Reel 22.

57. See note 47, above.

58. Robert C. Weaver, "Federal Aid, Local Control, and Negro Participation," *Journal of Negro Education* XI (1942), 53.

quota system may have been the most logical and equitable manner of distributing government favors. Black organizations concerned about black participation in New Deal programs must have found it difficult to defend a color-blind principle in the midst of the color-conscious segregation system. Even those who had misgivings about the PWA quota system must have preferred it to a futile and unenforceable declaration of policy—the equivalent of no policy at all. Robert C. Weaver discovered this firsthand. He considered the quota system to be an acceptable solution because it was concrete, practical, and preemptive rather than merely reactive, and provided a formula for the proof of discrimination. "Instead of the Government's having to establish the existence of discrimination, it is the contractor's obligation to establish the absence of discrimination," he wrote of the PWA program. The national black organizations largely agreed. Their opposition to the ad hoc, 50- or 100-percent quotas of Kiowa Costonie and Sufi Abdul Hamid disappeared in the more refined quota system of Foreman and Weaver. This system went beyond the "segregation without discrimination" of the New Negro Alliance, as it rejected gross population as a formula. The PWA antidiscrimination system consisted of establishing a definition of discrimination that placed the burden of proof on the employer, and based that definition on occupational statistics.[59]

On the eve of World War II, the idea of proportionalism as the means to combat racial discrimination in employment appeared to have considerable potential. In the acute conditions of the depression, alternatives to the color-blind aspiration of civil rights were devised and applied to new situations. But as the depression-era job scarcity that gave rise to the first significant expression of the proportionalist idea changed, the strategies used to combat racial discrimination in employment changed as well.

59. Weiss, *Farewell to the Party of Lincoln,* 51.

Establishing a National
Antidiscrimination Policy

World War II brought an end to the massive unemployment in the United States. Black Americans, however, were the first to be fired during the depression and were the last to be hired during the defense industry job boom of the 1940s. In response to political pressure brought by black organizations, principally A. Philip Randolph's March on Washington movement, President Roosevelt promulgated executive orders that forbade racial discrimination by all government contractors. The President's Committee on Fair Employment Practices, commonly known as the FEPC, monitored defense contractor compliance with the order. Although it did not survive the war, and could not compel recalcitrant employers and unions to end their discriminatory practices, the FEPC publicized a national antidiscrimination policy. It exposed and ended some of the worst discrimination in defense industries, and opened employment opportunities for American minority groups. Most important, it served as the model that equal employment advocates would pursue for the next twenty years—an administrative agency specifically designed to combat discrimination in employment. Moreover, the wartime FEPC attempted to do what the PWA thought was impossible—to enforce a nondiscrimination policy without resorting to race-conscious quota policies. At the same time, federal and state courts confirmed the antidiscrimination policy expounded by the national government during the war and applied it to cases in the last years of the war and in the early postwar period. These decisions suggested that the judiciary might pursue an active antidiscrimination policy in conjunction with, or even instead of, the legislative and executive branches.

As the United States began to react to the European war in 1940, the question of the role of the black American in the armed forces and in defense industries presented itself. In the 1930s black Americans, although devastated by the economic disaster, gained influence in national politics by means of a more mature Negro press, national organizations like the NAACP, a greater labor union presence, and a measure of voting power in northern cities. The government could not ignore their concerns as easily as it had during World War I. Accordingly, when Franklin D. Roosevelt established the Defense Advisory Commission in May, 1940, to advise him on manpower use, he appointed Robert C. Weaver to its staff, but the board only "recommended" nondiscrimination in defense industries. Congress prohibited discrimination in its October, 1940, Selective Service Act. Nevertheless, black Americans were left out of the burgeoning defense boom and job training programs, and remained segregated and held the most menial positions in the armed forces.[1]

In response to this exclusion in defense preparation, A. Philip Randolph, president of the Brotherhood of Sleeping Car Porters, organized the March on Washington movement. This all-black movement threatened a massive direct-action campaign to bring a large number of Negroes to Washington to seek redress of their grievances. In particular, Randolph demanded presidential action to end discrimination in defense industries and the armed forces. Although Roosevelt delayed as long as he could, the specter of racial conflict and disunity finally led him to agree in part to the movement's demands. Roosevelt issued Executive Order 8802 on July 25, 1941, prohibiting discrimination in defense work, but not the armed forces, and Randolph postponed the march.[2]

1. Herbert Garfinkel, *When Negroes March: The Organizational Politics of FEPC* (New York, 1969); Louis Ruchames, *Race, Jobs, and Politics: The Story of FEPC* (New York, 1952); Reed, *Seedtime;* G. James Fleming, "Historical Roots of Fair Employment Practice," *Phylon* VII (1946), 32–40.

2. Code of Federal Regulations 3 (1938–43), 957; hereafter cited as CFR.

The premise of Executive Order 8802 was that national defense depended on national unity and the utilization of all American manpower, "regardless of race, creed, color, or national origin." The order noted that discrimination based solely on these considerations continued despite the national emergency, to the detriment of morale. Roosevelt reaffirmed the government's nondiscrimination policy and directed agencies involved in defense training to "take special measures" to implement it. Roosevelt ordered that a nondiscrimination clause be placed in all defense contracts and, to put "teeth" in the order, established a five-member Committee on Fair Employment Practice within the Office of Production Management. The committee received and investigated complaints of violation of the order, and recommended appropriate remedies to government agencies and the president.

Civil rights groups greeted the executive order enthusiastically. Although its first chairman was Mark Ethridge, a liberal white Mississippian who assured southerners that the order was defense policy and not social policy, the committee included two black members, Earl Dickerson and Milton Webster. This "first FEPC" operated under Executive Order 8802 until May, 1943. Based on emergency wartime executive power, the FEPC enforced no congressional statutes and relied on no specific appropriation from Congress. It functioned as a fact-finding, investigative administrative body, but could not subpoena witnesses or evidence, issue orders of its own, nor sue in courts to enforce the nondiscrimination policy. It relied almost entirely on good will and cooperation of employers and unions, backed only by the vague threat of cancellation of federal contracts and the usually uncertain support of President Roosevelt.[3]

It might have been simplest to apply a proportional requirement from the outset, using the ideas developed and applied in direct-action campaigns, New York City labor relations, and the Public Works Administration. Indeed, as the executive order was being drafted, a quota system appears to have been President Roosevelt's initial idea of ensuring nondiscrimination. Walter D. Fuller, president of the National Association of Manufacturers and FEPC sup-

3. Ruchames, *Race, Jobs, and Politics,* 25.

porter, advocated racial hiring quotas. Robert Weaver warned against the application of the previous decade's tactics to the new situation. Quota measures, designed not to break new ground but to preserve old ground, were entirely inappropriate in a period of full employment. "Fortunately," he wrote, "the proposals to apply minimum percentage clauses in such a period were not heeded, and other more realistic devices were adopted."[4]

The FEPC began its work in the summer of 1941, and soon attracted attention with a series of hearings in Los Angeles, Chicago, and Birmingham. These hearings were designed to estimate the nature and extent of discrimination in American defense industries as well as to make employers and labor unions aware of the presidential order forbidding such discrimination. None was held in the Southwest, at the request of the State Department, which did not want publicity about discrimination against Mexican-Americans to sour relations with Mexico.[5]

The first FEPC revealed and eliminated many of the grossest manifestations of discrimination, such as racially marked applications, the assignment of minorities to menial jobs regardless of skill, discriminatory job advertisements, and recruitment from discriminatory schools or unions. It eschewed "minimum percentages," but did take notice of statistical disparities, stating that "the fact that a particular defense contractor does not employ members of certain minority groups or employs them only in insignificant numbers as compared with the total number of employees, while explainable in part as resulting from the scarcity of applications from individuals in those minority groups, lends support to the conviction that members of minorities are discriminated against in their effort to secure employment." A low percentage of minorities was not prima facie proof of discrimination, but one among a number of factors that suggested discrimination. At the same time, the committee informed employers that quota employment did not satisfy the nondiscrimination order. Equal treatment, not special treatment, was the

---

4. Doris Kearns Goodwin, *No Ordinary Time: Franklin and Eleanor Roosevelt; The Home Front in World War II* (New York, 1994), 249; Reed, *Seedtime*, 27; Weaver, *Negro Labor*, 14.

5. Reed, *Seedtime*, 46; Clete Daniel, *Chicano Workers and the Politics of Fairness: The FEPC in the Southwest, 1941–45* (Austin, 1991), 38–44.

standard they must apply. Any consideration of race rather than merit, even if it worked to the advantage of minority group members, was discriminatory. This condemnation of racial quotas was reiterated by the War Production Board and War Department.[6]

These policies may have reflected a principled adherence to a truly color-blind definition of nondiscrimination, or timidity based on the weakness of the committee's mandate and powers. The PWA in the 1930s was doing building contractors a favor in a weak market, and was therefore able to demand quotas. By contrast, during World War II defense contractors had little to fear from the FEPC. Ironically, the same wartime emergency that enabled the president to establish the FEPC also worked to limit the committee's effectiveness. War production could not be disrupted by an insistence on compliance with the executive order. The FEPC straddled its color-blind principles in its Birmingham, Alabama, hearings in June, 1942. A controversy arose between committee chairman Mark Ethridge and committee member Earl Dickerson. Ethridge had assured southerners that the fair employment order in no way imperiled the social system of segregation, but Dickerson used the Birmingham hearings to condemn the segregation system that he saw as the root of unfair employment practice in the South. The dispute was settled when the committee decided that segregation itself was not forbidden by the executive order and could only be a cause for complaint if it resulted in employment discrimination. Similarly in May, 1943, a riot broke out at the Alabama Shipbuilding and Drydock Company after the company promoted Negroes as recommended by the FEPC. The committee had to abandon its plan to eliminate discrimination everywhere in the yard. It allowed the Alabama company to set aside four shipways for Negroes in which jobs

6. Ruchames, *Race, Jobs, and Politics*, 32–45; "A Summary of the Hearings of the President's Committee on Fair Employment Practice," October 20–21, 1941, in NAACP Papers, II-B-11; United States Committee on Fair Employment Practice, *First Report* (Washington, 1945), 55, 58; "Summary;" Ruchames, *Race, Jobs, and Politics*, 31; United States Committee on Fair Employment Practice, *Final Report* (Washington, 1947), 16–19, 56–57; House Committee on Labor, *To Prohibit Discrimination in Employment:* Hearings before the Committee on Labor, 78th Cong., 2nd Sess., 1944, p. 209; Martin Reese to WPB, March 21, 1942, Minutes of the Meeting Held at the Hotel Commodore, June 25, 1942, P. Thomas to Walter White, June 26, 1942, in NAACP Papers, II-A-260; War Department Memo, September 10, 1942, in Hastie Papers, Reel 36.

previously closed to Negroes would be open to them, but also excluded them from other yard jobs. The committee here adopted the "segregation without discrimination" position of the New Negro Alliance and the 1930s racialists.[7]

The first committee was widely hailed for its efforts, and anticipated a larger budget and the establishment of regional offices in its second year. When President Roosevelt announced on July 30, 1942, that the committee would be moved into the War Manpower Commission, friends of the FEPC were flabbergasted. This move would put the FEPC budget under direct congressional control and place it under the authority of Paul V. McNutt, considered to be an opponent of the nondiscrimination effort. While Roosevelt assured FEPC supporters that the change was intended to strengthen rather than weaken the committee, McNutt confirmed his opponents' suspicions when he postponed the committee's hearings on the railroad industry in January, 1943. The outcry among civil rights groups compelled Roosevelt to issue another executive order, creating a new, independent FEPC. Executive Order 9346 expanded the size of the committee to seven members, abolished the old committee, and described in more explicit terms the role of the FEPC. Significantly, the president rejected a proposal by Attorney General Francis Biddle that the committee be given the power to issue court-enforceable cease-and-desist orders. The order authorized the FEPC to "conduct hearings, make findings of fact, and take appropriate steps to obtain the elimination of such discrimination." In language that appeared to give the committee more power, President Roosevelt authorized the FEPC "to promulgate such rules and regulations as may be appropriate or necessary to carry out the provisions of this order." Despite these differences, the new or second FEPC, which operated from July, 1943, to the spring of 1946, generally followed the pattern set by the first committee.[8]

7. Ruchames, *Race, Jobs, and Politics*, 25, 41, 58, 147; Bruce Nelson, "Organized Labor and the Struggle for Black Equality in Mobile during World War II," *Journal of American History*, LXXX (1993), 952–88; Malcolm Ross, *All Manner of Men* (New York, 1948), 50.

8. Ruchames, *Race, Jobs, and Politics*, chap. 3; CFR 3 (1938–43), 1280; James A. Nuechterlein, "The Politics of Civil Rights: The FEPC, 1941–46," *Prologue* (Fall, 1978), 179.

The FEPC successfully adjusted almost five thousand cases by peaceful negotiation, though it regretted that the few difficult cases involving recalcitrant employers and unions received greater attention than the more numerous peacefully settled ones. Having brought employment discrimination to national attention, its policies had an enduring influence after the war. Its supporters claimed that the committee had been effective, and that discrimination would return in its absence. The "mere existence" of the committee made the fight against discrimination easier, with most cases settled by informal negotiation and conciliation. Education had proved to be a vital part of the committee's program, but peaceful, cooperative methods needed reliable legal force in order to work. The FEPC was successful enough for all liberal groups to call for a permanent peacetime commission by statute, but also successful enough to provoke the hostility of powerful southern Democrats who would kill liberal FEPC proposals.[9]

The second FEPC operated for the remainder of the war until its funds were cut following a fierce congressional debate, in July, 1945. The House of Representatives had established a Special Committee to Investigate Executive Agencies in February, 1943, chaired by Virginia Democrat Howard Smith. The special committee looked into FEPC activity in its winter, 1944, hearings, but ultimately let the FEPC alone and issued no report. The hearings, however, provided ammunition for FEPC opponents like Senator Richard Russell of Georgia, who took up the increasingly popular cause of congressional resistance to executive expansion and federal bureaucratic aggrandizement. Attacking the FEPC as a particularly egregious instance of these tendencies, Russell called it a threat to free enterprise, and predicted that racial violence would ensue if it continued its activities. Believing that the agency was an employment program for blacks, he introduced a bill providing that no group that comprised less than 15 percent of the population of the United States could receive more than 25 percent of the FEPC's payroll.

9. FEPC *Final Report*, viii, xv, 12, 19; Reed, *Seedtime*, 147; Ruchames, *Race, Jobs, and Politics*, 151, 162; Ross, *All Manner of Men*, 39; Robert Morrison MacIver, *The More Perfect Union: A Program for the Control of Inter-Group Discrimination in the United States* (New York, 1948), 160.

This bill failed to pass, but Russell succeeded in passing a statute (called the "Russell Amendment") that prohibited federal funding for any agency which had existed for more than one year without a specific congressional appropriation. When a southern filibuster of a defense appropriations act threatened the conduct of the war, Congress limited the funding of the committee to the first half of 1946.[10]

While Congress balked at FEPC funding, the federal judiciary followed up FEPC action in a way that helped establish a national policy against employment discrimination. The constitution of the Brotherhood of Locomotive Firemen and Enginemen excluded blacks from membership. A large number of blacks served as railroad firemen on southern railroads, but were considered "unpromotable" to the position of engineer in collective bargaining agreements. Negro firemen on southern railroads remained in the arduous, dirty position of fireman and accumulated considerable seniority in this position while white firemen were quickly promoted to engineers. Technological advances, however, made the fireman's job much easier, and no longer disdained as "Negro work." During World War I, the Brotherhood negotiated an agreement with the railroads not to exceed a 50 percent quota of Negro firemen. During the depression, shortage of work made the fireman's position still more attractive to whites and the white brotherhood sought to eliminate the black firemen altogether, by any means necessary. There were at least twenty-one shootings of Negro firemen from to 1931 to 1934. Finally, in 1940, the brotherhood amended its collective bargaining agreement with the railroads to ensure that only "promotable" (white) firemen were used on new jobs.[11]

It was not surprising that the railway brotherhoods were among

10. Ruchames, *Race, Jobs, and Politics,* chaps. 5 and 6; Reed, *Seedtime,* 157–59; Graham, *Civil Rights,* 13; Ross, *All Manner of Men,* 249.

11. George Louis Creamer, "Collective Bargaining and Racial Discrimination," *Rocky Mountain Law Review,* XVII (1945), 163–96; *Steele* v. *Louisville & Nashville Railroad,* 323 U.S. 192 (1944); FEPC *Final Report,* 12–14; McNeil, *Charles Hamilton Houston,* 156–71; Ross, *All Manner of Men,* 119–21.

the most egregious discriminators. The FEPC noted that labor unions were the most difficult obstacle to their efforts, and the railroad brotherhoods were among the oldest and most powerful unions in the country. They possessed all of the characteristics of strong and exclusive organizations; the locomotive engineers provided a vital service in an industry which could ill-afford labor interruptions. As with any labor union, the brotherhoods had an interest in keeping their wages high by keeping their numbers low, and so racial exclusion was in their interest.[12]

Bester William Steele and Tom Tunstall were among the black firemen who complained to the FEPC about the agreement to curtail their employment. The southern railroads defied FEPC orders, so they brought suit in state and federal court. Their cases progressed along separate tracks, in southern state and lower federal courts, reaching the U.S. Supreme Court in 1944. Tunstall claimed that the national Railway Labor Act (RLA) imposed a duty on the railroad unions to represent all their members in good faith. The U.S. district court and the Fourth Circuit Court of Appeals in Virginia dismissed the suit for lack of jurisdiction, concluding that the RLA meant to stabilize labor-management relations and not to regulate the membership policies or bargaining practices of the unions. Since the courts could not decide disputes between rival unions claiming to represent railroad workers, the circuit court concluded that still less could they decide disputes within a union.[13]

While the federal court in *Tunstall* made its decision on the narrow grounds of the Railway Labor Act, the Alabama Supreme Court considered the broader question of racial discrimination in employment brought about by labor agreements. It may have been true that the brotherhood was not treating the Negroes it represented fairly, but this was of no legal importance. Congress, the Alabama court held, did not require fair representation, and the act

---

12. Herbert Northrup, "Discrimination and the Trade Unions," in *Discrimination and National Welfare,* ed. R. M. MacIver (Port Washington, N.Y., 1949), 69; Hill, *Black Labor and the American Legal System,* 183; G. Warren Nutter, "The Limits of Union Power," in *The Public Stake in Union Power,* ed. Bradley, 299.

13. *Tunstall* v. *Brotherhood,* 140 F.2d 35 (1944); Ruchames, *Race, Jobs, and Politics,* 70; FEPC *Final Report,* 12–14.

compelled the employer, the Louisville & Nashville Railroad, to negotiate with the brotherhood exclusively. The custom of Negro exclusion was a long-standing one which the railroads judged wise and proper, and one with which Steele, who worked for the L&N for over thirty years, was well acquainted. Therefore Steele must have consented to such discriminatory custom as a part of his employment contract.[14] The court cited *Plessy* v. *Ferguson* as an example of legal recognition of such traditional policies of racial separation deemed proper by the railroad. "Certainly the management of the road has as much right to take into consideration this delicate problem as does the law-making body of any state in passing a law looking to the peace and good order of society," the court declared. Congress could have no objection to this, since the principal purpose of the RLA was "to provide for the public safety an uninterrupted transportation system."[15]

The decision by the Alabama Supreme Court has been called "peculiarly illustrative of the rationalizations by which courts have sought to protect the peculiar racial structure of the South." Yet its reasoning is not altogether contrived. It affirmed the independence of labor unions and the obligation of the employer to bargain exclusively with them. Beyond this generally liberal recognition of labor union privileges, the court preserved as much as it could of the liberty of contract (Steele's rights were contractual only) and of an employer's freedom to manage its enterprise as it saw fit. The crucial element lay in the Railway Labor Act. According to the Alabama court, the broadest purpose of the act was to provide a smoothly operating railroad system, not to promote a social policy contrary to that defended in *Plessy* v. *Ferguson*. The Alabama Supreme Court did not recognize any national policy against discrimination. Absent this recognition, the decision may have been "nothing more than an attempt to place a foundation of precedent and rationality beneath, and screen with a facade of respectability, a conclusion arrived at on wholly other and highly emotional grounds." Neverthe-

14. Although Steele sued only to retain his seniority rights as a fireman and not for promotability into the engineers, the court reasoned that "a recognition of the principles for which he contends here must ultimately lead to that end."

15. *Steele* v. *Louisville & Nashville Railroad*, 16 So.2d 416 (1944).

less, the U.S. Supreme Court did not have an easy time asserting the national nondiscrimination policy against the Alabama court's reasoning.[16]

The Supreme Court reversed the Alabama Supreme Court and the Fourth Circuit Court of Appeals in December, 1944. The unanimous decision, written by Chief Justice Harlan F. Stone, relied upon a novel interpretation of the RLA. Stone noted that, along with the privileges extended to the railroad unions, Congress imposed the duty of equal protection of its minority members. The plenary power granted to the labor unions, the Court reasoned, was akin to the grant of power given to a legislature. Justice Stone asserted, "Unless the labor union representing a craft owes some duty to represent non-union members of the craft, at least to the extent of not discriminating against them as such in the contracts which it makes as their representative, the minority would be left with no means of protecting their interests or, indeed, their right to earn a livelihood by pursuing the occupation in which they are employed." Fair representation was the price the unions had to pay for the benefit of the Railway Labor Act.[17]

But the Court did not go so far as to demand that Negroes be granted full membership in the union. The unions could not discriminate in collective bargaining agreements based on "such irrelevant differences" as race, but those same irrelevant and invidious discriminations could still bar blacks from membership in these unions. Justice Frank Murphy wrote a separate concurring opinion attacking this exemption in the judicial construction of a national policy of nondiscrimination. Stone's opinion was based on statutory interpretation rather than the constitutional issue, and Murphy argued that the union could not ignore rights guaranteed by the Constitution when it exercised congressionally granted powers. Murphy observed, "The cloak of racism surrounding the actions of the Brotherhood in refusing membership to Negroes and in entering into and enforcing agreements discriminating against them, all under the guise of congressional authority, still remains." This was the logical extension of the doctrine put forth in the majority opin-

16. Creamer, "Collective Bargaining," 174.

17. *Steele* v. *Louisville & Nashville Railroad*, 323 U.S. 192; *Tunstall* v. *Brotherhood of Locomotive Firemen and Enginemen*, 323 U.S. 210 (1944); Ross, *All Manner of Men*, 135.

ion, namely, that "the Constitution voices its disapproval whenever economic discrimination is applied under authority of law against any race, creed, or color."

Political and social considerations, and a solicitous regard for the prerogatives of labor unions, no less than a cautious approach toward racial equality, prevented the majority from going as far as Murphy. The Court's disposition of *Steele* and *Tunstall* allowed the railroad unions to keep their most important privilege, that of controlling their membership. The Court was loath to strike at the generally exclusionary practices, inherent in labor organization, which encouraged specifically racial exclusion. "Fair representation" was thus a pragmatic way of balancing New Deal interest groups and deferring a showdown between the essentially irreconcilable interests of exclusionary labor unions and fair employment.[18]

The International Brotherhood of Boilermakers (IBB) was another union that excluded Negroes and used its collective bargaining powers to exploit black craftsmen. In the context of strong demand for boilermakers and associated shipwrights during World War II, the white IBB wanted to limit the use of black boilermakers in West Coast shipyards to the lowest occupational category of laborer. Eventually the union relaxed its opposition and established separate auxiliary lodges for blacks, which conferred all of the responsibilities but few of the advantages of the parent union. When black shipyard workers refused to pay dues to this "Jim Crow" union, the IBB insisted that they be fired under their closed shop agreement with the yards, and the operators felt bound to comply.[19] The FEPC ordered an end to this practice, but only two of the five yards involved complied. Consequently, several individual boilermakers pursued suits in state courts.[20]

---

18. Epstein, *Forbidden Grounds,* 118–25.

19. The FEPC probably committed a serious blunder in attacking the yards, which often tried to pursue fair employment, as much as the unions, which frustrated their efforts. This again reveals the general problem of New Deal affinity for organized labor running into its desire for racial equality. See Reed, *Seedtime,* 277.

20. *Ibid.,* chap. 9; FEPC *Final Report,* 19–21; *James* v. *Marinship Corp.,* 155 P.2d 329 (1945); Albert S. Broussard, *Black San Francisco: The Struggle for Equality in the West, 1900–1954* (Lawrence, Kan., 1993), 143–65; Charles Wollenberg, "*James* v. *Marinship:* Trouble on the New Black Frontier," *California History,* LX (1981), 262–79.

Joseph James, a shipyard worker and president of the San Francisco Committee Against Segregation and Discrimination, brought suit in the Marin County Superior Court for an injunction against the union and the Marinship Corporation which operated the yards for the United States. In February, 1944, the court granted the injunction against Marinship, forbidding it to refuse to hire, or to discharge, or to discriminate against any employee for refusing to join an auxiliary union. The court issued no order affecting the union. James and others also brought suit under the Fifth and Fourteenth Amendments in federal district court, but the actions were dismissed for lack of jurisdiction.[21]

Marinship appealed to the California Supreme Court, but the injunction was affirmed in December, 1944. The shipyard operators pleaded, like the railroads in *Steele,* that they were bound by their agreement with the boilermakers union. The California Supreme Court held that labor union agreements could not be enforced for illegal purposes. The United States Supreme Court had recently upheld the state power to restrict the abuse of labor union privileges, limiting the holding of *Thornhill* v. *Alabama,* that picketing was free speech. The court held that an arbitrarily closed union that excluded persons from membership based on race was incompatible with a closed-shop agreement. It concluded that the monopoly on labor that a union enjoyed by such an agreement entailed responsibilities, and that a labor union with a closed-shop agreement was no longer a private, fraternal, voluntary association.

The procedural question was whether a labor union could refuse to enforce a collective bargaining agreement or strike for goals contrary to public policy. The substantive one was whether racial discrimination was an illegitimate goal. According to the court, the record disclosed that Negro auxiliary members were practically excluded from union benefits and the court suggested that such exclusion was contrary to the duty of fair representation imposed on the unions by the National Labor Relations Act and the Railway Labor Act. "It is difficult to see how a union can fairly represent *all* the employees of a bargaining unit unless it is willing to admit all

21. 54 F.Supp. 94 (1944).

to membership." The court reluctantly admitted that no precedent existed for such an interpretation of the NLRA, and that the Supreme Court had stopped short of such a doctrine in *Steele* and *Tunstall*. Instead the Court consulted "the public policy of the United States and this state." Government action discriminating against Negroes was forbidden by the Fifth, Fourteenth, and Fifteenth Amendments; political parties and labor unions had recently been held to a standard similar to those of legislatures in *Smith* v. *Allright*[22] and *Steele*. The California court reasoned that "although the constitutional provisions have been said to apply to state action rather than to private action, they nevertheless evidence a definite national policy against discrimination because of race or color." California civil rights laws prohibited discrimination in public accommodations, and these laws could be applied to labor unions.

The California Supreme Court found an express statement of a national antidiscrimination policy in Executive Order 9346. It also held that the provision of administrative remedies in the FEPC did not preempt enforcement of rights in ordinary courts. The boilermakers had the choice of continuing to exclude Negroes and giving up their closed shop monopoly, or of abandoning their exclusion policy and admitting Negroes to full membership. The California court denied Marinship's contention that this ruling gave Negroes a greater right to membership than that extended to other persons. Rather than contemplating preferential treatment as a remedy, the injunction was "clearly intended to do no more than eliminate discrimination upon the basis of race and color alone."

Extending the work of the FEPC, the judicial decisions in *Steele, Tunstall,* and *James* had great potential in the fight against employment discrimination. *James* was especially ambitious, because it asserted a general, constitutional principle of nondiscrimination at both the national and state levels that was enforceable both in courts and in administrative bodies like the FEPC. In private, Charles Hamilton Houston, an NAACP attorney working on the railroad

---

22. 321 U.S. 649 (1944), holding that the Texas Democratic party's exclusion of blacks from membership was state action prohibited by the Fourteenth Amendment.

cases, considered *Steele* and *Tunstall* the culmination of five years of effort, with the Supreme Court affirming every argument made by civil rights groups. Publicly, however, civil rights activists also emphasized the limitations of these holdings. They were limited to particular plaintiffs in particular industries, and further progress would have to proceed on an individual, case-by-case basis. The end of the war would terminate many of the jobs involved in these cases and almost all in the California shipyards. Moreover, the end of the war marked the demise of the FEPC. These cases demonstrated the need for a permanent, peacetime FEPC to coordinate the antidiscrimination effort, and to relieve individual plaintiffs of the time and expense of bringing individual suits. Impressive as vindications of nondiscriminatory legal principles, these cases also underscored the need for an administrative body to make these principles effective and avoid piecemeal remedies. While northern state fair employment practice committees did follow up on the railroad cases, labor union discrimination continued to be among the most significant economic barriers to black Americans.[23]

The significance of *Steele, Tunstall,* and *James* was the enunciation of the principles of a national policy of nondiscrimination. Moreover, these cases confirmed the wartime FEPC approach that eschewed the racial proportionalism of the depression era. Thus the FEPC rejected a proposal by the IBB to retain separate lodges but to divide work on a racial quota basis, because "an individual's opportunity to be dispatched for employment would be based upon the artificial criterion of race or color and not upon his individual qualifications or any other similarly pertinent objective factor." The committee based its ruling upon previous FEPC decisions that disapproved of proportional solutions to discriminatory practices. The FEPC was unable to reach a satisfactory agreement with the IBB before it went out of existence, but it concluded its work with a strong anti-quota stand supported by the courts. The illegitimacy of racial classifications in all but the most extreme cases was underscored by the Supreme Court in the Japanese relocation cases, in which the

23. Charles Hamilton Houston Memorandum, December 20, 1944, Edward R. Dudley to New York *Herald-Tribune,* April 11, 1945, in NAACP Papers, II-B-94; FEPC *Final Report,* 21.

extraordinary justification of a racial classification signaled that the Constitution was normally color-blind.[24]

As the war neared an end, the possibility arose that black wartime gains would be lost entirely in the reconversion. The most desirable industrial jobs were unionized, and these jobs claimed a higher proportion in the American economy than at any previous time due to the New Deal's pro-organized labor policies. However, one of the main principles for which the American Federation of Labor (AFL) and the CIO fought was that of seniority. Both management and labor valued the seniority system, giving job security to the most experienced workers, and providing employers with an experienced and stable work force. The disadvantage for black workers was that their newly-acquired places in the American labor force were the first to be sacrificed in a postwar downturn. The phrase "last hired, first fired," always resonant to the Negro worker, was never more so than after V-J Day.

There was an obvious solution to the problem of the seniority system in postwar reconversion: to give black workers added seniority to compensate for their prewar discriminatory exclusion. Employers and unions applied this system, known as "superseniority," to returning servicemen, calculating their seniority based on credit for time served in the armed forces. If superseniority served as a veteran's benefit to recognize their service to their country, why should Negroes not receive similar benefits in recognition of their past discriminatory treatment? At the very least, some suggested that black workers be laid off in proportion to their percentage of an employer's work force.[25]

The reasons against a race-based superseniority system were well rehearsed by 1945. According to the wartime fair employment prac-

24. Reed, *Seedtime*, 312–14; Ross, *All Manner of Men*, 151; "Statement of Basis for Committee's Decision . . . in re Boilermakers Proposal," in Records of the President's Committee on Fair Employment Practice, Legal Division, Box 327, Record Group 228, National Archives; Kull, *The Color-Blind Constitution*, 144; *Hirabayashi* v. *U.S.*, 320 U.S. 81 (1943); *Korematsu* v. *U.S.*, 323 U.S. 214 (1944).

25. Weaver, *Negro Labor*, 283–305; Charles S. Johnson and Preston Valien, "The Status of Negro Labor," in *Labor in Postwar America* (Brooklyn, 1949), 555.

tice model, equality was won not by giving black workers special treatment or by a guarantee of racially proportionate representation, but by a color-blind, merit-based, equality of opportunity standard. Black Americans wanted admittance into the organized labor movement, not preferential treatment by it. Moreover, organized labor—at least at the national level—was one of the Civil Rights movement's allies, and a black demand for special treatment in seniority would only strain that relationship. Indeed, one of the few FEPC–related wartime strikes, of the Philadelphia transit system, was largely attributed to fears that blacks promoted due to FEPC efforts would gain some sort of race-based superseniority. Both union leaders and civil rights groups agreed with the FEPC, considering reconversion problems in the summer of 1944, that superseniority was not an option. In early 1945 CIO president Philip Murray announced the labor movement's opposition to any such plans. Considering seniority as the main industrial relations bulwark against the kind of arbitrary favoritism and discrimination that affected the Negro worker, the labor movement favored its retention and urged a full employment guarantee instead to obviate the layoff problem. Industrial unions almost all rejected proposals to alter the seniority system. As Robert C. Weaver put it, "As a general rule, group-adjusted seniority is like hot ice cream; it is not consistent with the basic principles of the concept."[26]

The NAACP and CIO fought a proposal for a racial superseniority system by the communist-dominated United Electrical, Radio, and Machine Workers Union (UE) in Bridgeport, Connecticut. When the local, communist-infiltrated NAACP supported the idea, the national office denounced the local, saying that the association never endorsed "asking for special attention because we happen to be Negroes." As Thurgood Marshall noted, "It has long been a cardinal point in the program of the Association to strongly oppose any idea that would distinguish colored citizens as a unique or separate group apart from the rest of the American people." NAACP Labor Secretary Herbert Hill called quotas and preferential treatment "a

26. Ruchames, *Race, Jobs, and Politics*, 112; Reed, *Seedtime*, 323; Gloster B. Current Speech to NAACP Chicago Conference, July 13, 1944, in NAACP Microfilm, I, Reel 11, LC; Chicago *Defender*, January 27, 1945; Weaver, *Negro Labor*, 301.

sugar-coated form of segregation." The association called for equal treatment under Connecticut's fair employment practice law, not special treatment in violation of it.[27]

The revival of demands for quota hiring, layoffs, and proportional representation during the postwar reconversion period made sense if, as Robert Weaver argued, the race-conscious proportionalism of the 1930s was a product of the distressed economic condition of the decade while the color-blind, equal-opportunity, fair-employment model of the war years resulted from a full employment economy. The adamant resistance to the Bridgeport quota proposal shows that the NAACP sought no reversion to the 1930s model despite postwar economic retrenchment. The expanding employment opportunities of World War II provided the circumstances to devise a national policy of color-blind nondiscrimination, implemented with some success by an executive agency, and supported and forwarded by the highest courts in the country. Nevertheless, the tension between these two approaches to racial discrimination in employment would remain a salient feature in the postwar period.

27. Madison S. Jones, Jr., to William Winston, July 14, 1949, Thurgood Marshall to Winston, July 27, 1949, Herbert Hill to Jack Butler, July 19, 1949, in NAACP Papers, II-A-586.

4 Proportionalism in the Fair Employment Era: The *Hughes* Case

The economic situation for black Americans at the end of World War II was uncertain. Even if prosperity followed the war, at least some of the gains made by blacks during the wartime job glut were bound to be lost. If the nation lapsed back into depression, their situation would remain as parlous as during the 1930s. The end of the war also brought the demise of the FEPC. Attempts to secure a permanent, peacetime federal FEPC failed, but several states established FEPCs, and there was also a revival of direct action activities in the late 1940s. In the fair employment framework laid down by the FEPC and by the state FEPCs, the legal status of picketing to promote racial hiring remained undetermined. The California case of *Hughes* v. *Superior Court,* in the years between 1947 and 1950, provided the earliest and fullest legal argument over the place of race-based employment practices in modern America.

Lucky Stores, a chain of groceries, operated a store near the Canal Housing Project in Richmond, California. It was a union shop, and the union was open to blacks. In May, 1947, a shoplifting incident put in motion a long dispute between Lucky and several civic organizations. The manager of the store and another employee apprehended and had caused to be arrested McKinley Jackson, under suspicion of stealing six pounds of bacon. A group led by the Progressive Citizens of America (PCA), and including the Richmond NAACP branch, protested to Lucky's management that the employees used unnecessary force against Jackson, striking him while his hands were held, and recklessly firing a pistol outside the store. Their representatives insisted that the employees involved in the arrest be discharged, and that Lucky institute a new employment policy, whereby only blacks were hired until their proportion of the store's work force approximated the black proportion of Lucky's patronage.

Lucky refused to comply and the PCA picketed the store. Lucky obtained an injunction on June 5, 1947, from the Contra Costa County Superior Court, the trial judge basing his order squarely on the 1934 New York *Beck* case, which held that picketing for racial quotas, regardless of how truthful or orderly, was contrary to sound public policy. Judge Hugh H. Donovan noted, "I should very much like to see this position tested in the appellate courts." The picketing continued despite the injunction, and on June 23 John Hughes and Louis Richardson, members of the PCA and the Richmond NAACP, were cited for contempt of court, fined twenty dollars, and sentenced to two days in jail. They appealed the convictions to a California appeals court.[1]

NAACP branches usually coordinated their activities with the national office, but the Richmond branch of the NAACP had been under the control of a group of communists since the end of the war, who were using employment discrimination protests as a lure to attract black organizations to support party activities. Attempts by the national office to regain control from the communists in 1947 were unsuccessful, and as late as 1949 Roy Wilkins referred to it as "probably the most completely controlled NAACP branch in the country." Communist domination of the Richmond branch and the quota issue put the NAACP national office in an awkward position, but Special Counsel Thurgood Marshall told Noah W. Griffin, West Coast regional secretary of the NAACP, that the office was vitally interested in the case, and considered it one of the easiest types of cases to win due to the *New Negro Alliance* decision.[2]

1. Decision, *Lucky Stores v. Progressive Citizens of America,* May 26, 1947, in California State Archives (hereafter cited as *Lucky v. PCA*). I am grateful to the office of the Contra Costa County Clerk and the California State Archives for providing me with copies of the documents of this case.

2. Noah W. Griffin to Roy Wilkins, August 7, 1947, Griffin to Gloster B. Current, November 19, 1947, Irene Morgan to West Coast Regional Office, December 2, 1947, People of Richmond to NAACP Board of Directors, February 28, 1949, in NAACP

In his appeal, Hughes claimed that the Superior Court had exceeded its jurisdiction when it issued the preliminary injunction. He defended the goals of the PCA, arguing that the ten thousand Negroes of Richmond suffered unemployment "greatly disproportionate to the unemployed among the white persons of Richmond." Lucky was the real party in interest, rather than the superior court, and responded that Hughes called for only prospective hiring of Negroes, and alleged that "the demands made contemplate the discharge of some of the present personnel" of the store. The *New Negro Alliance* case had protected picketing to protest discrimination, but not picketing to compel racially proportionate hiring. Lucky also introduced affidavits to demonstrate that it did not discriminate on the basis of race, hiring on the basis of "physical cleanliness, mental alertness, moral integrity, and qualifications as to experience for a particular job sought to be filled." The Retail Clerks Union provided the employee pool for Lucky, and denied that it discriminated on the basis of color. Three black members of the union were currently employed in the store.[3]

From the technical questions of the privileges of picketing under the Fourteenth Amendment and California law, Lucky began to pry open the question of the proof of discrimination. Lucky argued that Hughes had not made any specific charges of discrimination in the trial court, and was asking the appellate court to assume that discrimination existed, but the court refused to consider any evidence not brought before the trial court. Although Lucky argued that the national FEPC policy and California policy in *Marinship* made it illegal to consider race at all in hiring decisions, it implied that the presence of Negroes in Lucky's employ proved a nondiscrimination policy. In the course of later litigation, Lucky's attorneys would de-

Papers, II-C-18; Griffin to Current, March 9, 1949, in NAACP Papers, II-C-234; Griffin to Walter White, November 8, 1946, White to Griffin, November 11, 1946, White to Committee on Administration, November 16, 1946, Griffin to White, November 18, 1946, Griffin to White, December 12, 1946, in NAACP Papers, II-A-201; Thurgood Marshall to Noah Griffin, June 13, 1947, in NAACP Papers, II-B-87.

3. Petition for Writ of Certiorari, June 23, 1947, *Transcript,* 36–43; Memorandum and Points of Authority, June 23, 1947, *Lucky* v. *PCA;* Answer and Return to Writ of Certiorari, August 15, 1947, *Transcript,* 43–52; Brief on Appeal, Brief of Amici Curiae in Support of Respondent, August 15, 1947, *Lucky* v. *PCA.*

velop a theory of the proof of discrimination that did more than rely on tokenism. Hughes defended proportional hiring as distinguishable from a quota system used to limit minority group entry into professional schools or highly skilled trades due to the presence of discrimination against Negroes. Hughes argued that percentages were always relevant in the determination of whether discrimination existed. Blacks were discriminated against most in the hiring phase of employment, he said, and "Discrimination in hiring is infinitely more difficult to prove than is discrimination after once having been employed." Proportional representation in grocery store employment was appropriate because this work did not require skills or training. However, it was not necessary to establish the fact of Lucky's discrimination in order to justify picketing for proportional representation, since picketing was protected regardless of its purpose.[4]

In November, 1947, Judge Raymond Peters, for a unanimous three-man appeals court, vacated the contempt order, applying the principles of *New Negro Alliance* rather than its New York predecessor, *Beck*. The court, having refused to consider the affidavits of nondiscrimination, declared that blacks were clearly "an economically discriminated-against group," exploited by white employers like Lucky. This fact gave the Negro population an economic interest and made their picketing a "labor dispute." The court dismissed the issue of fear of racial violence, declaring it a risk worth taking for the goal of reducing discrimination, with picketing for employment quotas being a legitimate means to this end. The court conceded that quota hiring would normally be contrary to public policy, but that Lucky's discriminatory employment policy justified it. Indeed, it was the discrimination practiced against blacks that permitted them, but not other groups, to make quota demands. "The right is granted not because the pickets are members of a minority group, but because that minority group is economically discriminated against, and is attempting to rectify that condition," the court concluded.[5]

4. Supplemental Brief of Respondent, September 24, 1947, Oral Argument on Petition for Writ of Certiorari, August 25, 1947, Supplemental Memorandum of Points and Authorities, September 4, 1947, *Lucky v. PCA.*

5. Opinion, November 20, 1947, *Transcript,* 61–83, *Lucky v. PCA; Hughes v. Superior Court,* 186 P.2d 756 (1947).

This resounding victory for the PCA, with implications clearly more substantial than those of the *New Negro Alliance* case, upheld the right to picket to promote racial hiring on every major point. It forcefully rejected the state law decisions of *Beck* and *Green* v. *Samuelson*, and justified such picketing as a matter of public policy. The court went so far as to dismiss the risk of racial violence to pursue the goal of economic equality, and by limiting its permission to victims of discrimination, determined the possibility that every racial or ethnic group might employ these methods.

Lucky persuaded the California Supreme Court to review the decision, moving a direct action case to the highest court in a state for the first time, and stirred the interest of the NAACP national office. Oakland attorney Allan Brotsky notified Robert L. Carter, NAACP assistant special counsel, that his office was preparing an *amicus* brief for the Richmond NAACP before the California Supreme Court. He requested economic data and legal materials from the national office and told them, "The appellants intend to rely upon the demagogic argument that demanding proportional hiring of Negroes constitutes discrimination against the white population." But Assistant Special Counsel Marian Wynn Perry did not think the argument was demagogic. "I am very disturbed at the object of the picketing," she wrote. "I can think of few things more dangerous than tying Negro employment to Negro patronage since it appears to condone a quota system of hiring and would be, of course, disastrous to any campaign to secure jobs for Negroes outside of Negro areas and Negro patronized stores." Perry suggested that the national office and the Richmond branch discuss their policies in this regard. The NAACP went ahead with its support of the issue in *Hughes*.[6]

In the state supreme court, Lucky continued to press its argument that although the appellate decision assumed that Lucky discriminated, discrimination had neither been alleged nor proved at trial. It added that in November, 1946, it hired two Negro clerks in re-

6. Allan Brotsky to Robert L. Carter, January 30, 1948, Marian Wynn Perry to Clarence Mitchell, February 18, 1948, in NAACP Papers, II-B-87.

sponse to an appeal from a black organization called the Knights' Political League. This information, along with the affidavits of Lucky's personnel managers, were meant to establish that Lucky did not discriminate in hiring. *Marinship* and California public policy, they noted, "precluded discrimination in favor of negroes and against whites. . . . The duty created by the rules in these cases is the general one of refraining from discrimination of any type, and not merely to refrain from discrimination against negroes." Lucky repeated that discrimination in employment was not difficult to prove, since one need show conduct, not racial prejudice. It admitted that scarcity of Negroes might establish a prima facie case of discrimination, but other reasons for the scarcity might overcome such a prima facie case. Heavy black employment in shipyards and other war-related industries might have accounted for their relative absence in retail establishments, Lucky suggested. Safeway, filing an *amicus* brief on Lucky's behalf, noted that token employment was not proof of fair employment. "Absent other facts, an experienced and fair trial judge or lawyer would give little or no weight to such token hirings," insisting that discrimination was a fact to be proved, refutable by employers, and not to be assumed by courts. Lucky denied that discrimination in ordinary employment was any different from discrimination in professional education or skilled trades. "In cases in which discrimination exists it is apparent that that discrimination can be readily established," it concluded, "and the battery of organizations and volunteer attorneys opposing us in this case makes it apparent that Negroes in making such a charge will not lack for champions in the Courts."[7]

Dismissing Lucky's claims as tokenism, Hughes maintained that discrimination against blacks was obvious, and that whether or not Lucky discriminated was irrelevant. The First Amendment protected the right to picket for any reason, and picketing for racial quota hiring was legitimate for groups that were victims of discrimination. Not that Lucky in particular discriminated, but the fact that blacks in general were victims of discrimination, justified this

7. Answer to Brief, May 3, 1948, Respondent's Petition for a Hearing by the Supreme Court, December 30, 1947, *Transcript,* 52–61, Brief of Safeway Stores, December 31, 1947, *Lucky* v. *PCA.*

action. Hughes was careful to deny that proportional hiring was preferential treatment or discrimination against non-blacks. Rather, it was "equality of opportunity," because, absent discrimination, it must be assumed that blacks would be found in the work force in rough approximation to their proportion of the general population. For low-level jobs like grocery clerks, without any objective test of qualification, proportionalism was a practical, concrete way to ensure fair employment for discriminated-against groups. Hughes argued that the pickets might have demanded an all-black employment policy, but that a 50-percent quota was a compromise. However, if non-victim groups picketed for quotas, an injunction would be a proper remedy. Finally, Hughes asked the court to consider the relative character of the parties in determining the charge of discrimination: The NAACP and the PCA, with their concern for the economic welfare of the Negro race, and Lucky Stores, which would not even discuss a program of employment on a fair and nondiscriminatory basis. Lucky responded that the character of the NAACP or PCA did not determine the charge of discrimination. "Courts, not volunteers, are established to determine the merits of litigation; and such determination must be on evidence, not on self-serving statements as to the respective characters of the parties," it noted. Moreover, Lucky's refusal to consider proportional employment was not a refusal to consider a nondiscrimination policy. Above all, the burden of proving discrimination lay on Hughes and Richardson, and they had not met it. Employment by racial quota was an inappropriate response even to proved discrimination "because it discriminates against individuals, not because it discriminates against the white race," Lucky concluded.[8]

The California Supreme Court reversed the appellate court, reinstating the injunction on November 1, 1948. Justice B. Rey Schauer for a four-man majority wrote a short decision which found that the picketing was intended to force Lucky to discriminate. As Schauer expressed it, "If Lucky had yielded to the demands of [Hughes], its

8. Petitioner's Answer to Petition for Hearing by the Supreme Court, January 9, 1948, *Transcript*, 83–90; Brief of Amici Curiae in Support of Petitioners, April 28, 1948, in NAACP Papers, II-B-87; Brief of Petitioners, May 19, 1948; Answer to Brief, June 4, 1948, *Lucky* v. *PCA*.

resultant hiring policy would have constituted, as to a proportion of its employees, the equivalent of both a closed shop and a closed union in favor of the Negro race." California policy, as stated in *Marinship,* was to prohibit consideration of race. "It was just such a situation—an arbitrary discrimination upon the basis of race and color alone, rather than a choice based solely upon individual quali- fication for the work to be done—which we condemned." Schauer skirted the question of the proof of discrimination. He suggested that, as in the *New Negro Alliance* case, picketing to protest discrimi- nation would be lawful, but noted that Hughes picketed not to protest a discriminatory hiring policy, but to institute one. Regard- less of Lucky's policy, picketing to compel a racial hiring quota was unlawful. Schauer derived California policy not from statute (Cali- fornia had no fair employment practice law) but from the judicial precedent of *Marinship.* While Schauer explicitly disregarded *New Negro Alliance* as a relevant precedent for a state jurisdiction, he did not fall back on *Beck,* as the trial court had, and his decision can be seen as consistent with *New Negro Alliance.* The decision announced, in effect, a judicial creation of a fair employment practice policy in- sofar as picketing, and perhaps other incidents of labor law, were concerned.[9]

Hughes received the support of two dissenting opinions. Justice Jesse W. Carter's dissent disputed the majority's interpretation of certain facts in the case, and was somewhat inchoate and diffuse. The dissenting opinion of Roger Traynor was more cogent. Traynor argued that *Marinship* was not a relevant precedent for this case, be- cause the Progressive Citizens did not wield the power that the closed union in *Marinship* did. "Rules developed to curb abuses of those already in control of the labor market have no application to situations where the moving party is seeking to gain a foothold in the struggle for economic equality," he said. Lack of formal labor union status had been the chief legal impediment of the New Negro Alliance and other black organizations before 1938. In an ironic twist, Traynor turned this into their main advantage. Traynor ac-

---

9. *Hughes* v. *Superior Court,* 198 P.2d 885 (1948); Opinion, November 1, 1948, *Transcript,* 90–97, *Lucky* v. *PCA.*

cepted Hughes' argument that ubiquitous discrimination against blacks, rather than discrimination in the case at hand, justified proportionalism as a guarantee of equality. "Those racial groups against whom discrimination is practiced may seek economic equality either by demanding that hiring be done without reference to race or color, or by demanding a certain number of jobs for members of their group," Traynor reasoned. Minority groups retained this option, and courts must preserve it, he said, in the absence of an antidiscrimination statute. "In arbitrating the conflicting interests of different groups in society courts should not impose ideal standards on one side when they are powerless to impose similar standards upon the other," he concluded. Racial discrimination by majority groups was properly condemned by the courts, but minority groups should not be held to this standard if they demanded racial discrimination in their favor.

Traynor insisted that the proportional scheme, and any sort of racial discrimination, was not illegal in California. "No law prohibits Lucky from discriminating in favor of or against Negroes. It may legally adopt a policy of proportionate hiring," he pointed out. In another state, with a fair employment practice law that outlawed racial considerations in hiring, it might be said that the demand for proportional hiring was a demand that Lucky violate the law. Traynor, noting the absence of such a law in California, denied that there was any equivalent in the common law. Accepting the fact of discrimination as obvious, he was in sympathy with both the means and ends of the PCA. Yet he suggested that such means and ends were lawful only in the absence of fair employment legislation, which most liberals sought in the fight against racial discrimination and which seemed to be the logical conclusion to which his sense of racial justice pointed. Moreover, Traynor appeared to deny the attempt of Schauer and the majority to erect the equivalent of a fair employment practice law based on judicial precedent (*Marinship*) and a general public policy against discrimination based on race. Traynor has been depicted as a precursor of Warren Court liberalism and judicial activism, and his sympathies for Hughes and his associates in this case seem to confirm that. His indifference to the means used to combat racial discrimination in employment, that minorities "may seek economic equality either by demanding that hiring be done without reference to race or color or by demanding a certain number of jobs for members of their group," is notable. It indicates an ambivalence on the part of liberals in the postwar period about the proper means to combat racial discrimination in employment.[10]

Hughes asked the California Supreme Court to reconsider the case. Its decision, Hughes claimed, would help to justify racial discrimination, since there was no way the court could determine what constituted an "arbitrary" demand upon Lucky. If the NAACP asked Lucky to employ *one* Negro, would that be arbitrary? Where was the point at which the line of arbitrariness was crossed? Hughes attempted to impress upon the court the rationality of the workforce–patronage ratio. It made sense because discrimination was not mathematically provable. Blacks were 10 percent of the American population, Hughes noted. "If there were no discrimination in the employ of Negroes, presumably the Negro population would find employment throughout the American economy in approximately the same ratio; that is, of one Negro in each industry to nine whites." Of course, this ratio would increase in localities that were more than 10 percent black. All that the PCA demanded of Lucky was that it "conform to the pattern that would undoubtedly exist if the admitted fact of economic discrimination against Negroes disappeared from America." Hughes inquired if the Court had, in effect, made fair employment the law in California. Hughes asked, "If [we] cannot seek to impose discriminatory hiring practices, does it not follow that employers, such as Lucky, cannot *maintain* discriminatory hiring practices?" Hughes should be able to obtain an injunction against Lucky to prevent its discriminatory hiring, he concluded, still assuming, rather than proving, that Lucky discriminated.

Lucky continued to insist that what Hughes demanded was "discrimination in favor of the Negro race" and "preferential treatment of a particular race." While they were free to pursue jobs for mem-

10. *Hughes* v. *Superior Court,* 198 P.2d 885; Dissenting Opinion, November 1, 1948, *Transcript,* 107–11, *Lucky* v. *PCA;* G. Edward White, *The American Judicial Tradition* (New York, 1988), 292–316.

bers of their race and to protest discrimination, they must do so in a lawful manner. Lucky placed the issue in the narrower context of picketing and labor law rather than exploring the question of a judge-made fair employment practice law. In the immediate setting of the case, Lucky continued to deny that it practiced discrimination. All of its personnel actions had been based "upon an individual, rather than a racial basis." This clearly denied the demographic model of proof of discrimination advanced by Hughes. The California Supreme Court denied the petition for a rehearing.[11]

The opinion of the legal community, as expressed in the law reviews, went against the California Supreme Court decision. A note in the *California Law Review* pointed to the discrepancy of outlawing picketing for discrimination in favor of Negroes in a state that did not prohibit employers from discriminating against them. California "evidently does not consider this discrimination, though against public policy, a serious enough evil to restrain Lucky Stores from practicing it. Yet it is held to be such an evil that picketing to attain it is unlawful." The author suggested that the U.S. Supreme Court could use this discrepancy to overturn the decision. While admitting that "a quota system is concededly discriminatory, and though the proportion of patronage is an arbitrary measure of fair hiring," it was not so unreasonable as to be struck down. It did not call for complete exclusion of whites, the note argued, and was "one objective standard that is reasonable in determining whether discrimination exists in the absence of legislation defining and controlling the practice." Until the problem of racial discrimination in employment was confronted by the state, the courts should not close off this avenue of redress. The *Syracuse Law Review* agreed, arguing that "it is doubtful whether the objective of the picketing . . . when viewed realistically, should be considered illegal, especially in the absence of a statute or rule of the common law proscribing proportional hiring of racial groups." Such hiring was probably illegal in New York under the 1945 Law Against Discrimination, and under state judicial decisions rendered before its enactment.[12]

11. Petition for Rehearing, November 16, 1948, *Transcript*, 111–21, *Lucky* v. *PCA*.
12. "Notes and Recent Decisions," *California Law Review*, XXXVII (1949), 296–301; "Recent Decisions," *Syracuse Law Review*, I (1949), 153.

George H. Grover, in the *Southern California Law Review,* recognized the uncertain position of racial quotas in the civil rights movement. He was troubled that the court had not considered the constitutional, free-speech aspect of the case, which might give the issue a fuller hearing. While the antidiscrimination principle expressed in *Marinship,* disregarding race altogether, was probably preferable, it was not the only antidiscrimination method available. He credited the court for defending the *"true* nondiscrimination" principle expressed in *Marinship,* but believed that the principle might actually perpetuate inequality. On the other hand, Hughes' compromise of the true principle, while perhaps expedient, "may actually delay the day when consideration of racial origin will be absent from the economic scene." The pickets were "too ready here to accept the fact of discrimination—perhaps their system of openly competing racial groups would even aggravate the situation." In the end, the court should have recognized the honest split of opinion on the subject and allowed the defendants to express their opinion by picketing.[13]

The split opinion in the California Supreme Court on the subject of proportional employment raised a strategic problem for the NAACP. San Francisco attorney Cecil F. Poole advised the national office not to join in the Richmond branch's appeal to the U.S. Supreme Court. He told Thurgood Marshall in early 1949 that the California Supreme Court decision prohibited only picketing that demanded proportional hiring, and that it left "general picketing for jobs" untouched. Poole condemned the goal of proportional hiring and advocated a jobs campaign based on "the democratic principle that we are entitled to equal opportunity based upon merit and ability to compete in the labor market without being prejudged on account of race or color." Hughes' goal, however, was "at variance with this great sustaining principle and in place of the criterion of equality and merit substitutes artificial criteria." The particular criteria chosen in Richmond could have the effect of exclud-

13. George G. Grover, "Comment," *Southern California Law Review,* XXII (1949), 442–54.

ing blacks from large national industries, and give many local firms license to discriminate. Poole agreed that the decision was a bad one in terms of labor law and free speech, but still advised that the NAACP drop it. In the future, he felt, there would be opportunities to "vindicate the general right of picketing without having also to defend the dubious principle of proportional picketing." Marian Wynn Perry, who had expressed reservations about the case a year earlier, supported Poole. Reiterating her objection to proportional employment, she raised the question of "whether we can support the right to picket for such an aim." Thurgood Marshall noted that "the NAACP is opposed to proportionate hiring and quotas in general. On the other hand, I believe that all of the legal staff is in favor of peaceful picketing."[14]

It occurred to Lucky's attorneys that the NAACP's opposition to quotas might induce them to file a brief on their behalf. Loren Miller, Los Angeles attorney and member of the NAACP's National Legal Committee, told Thurgood Marshall of such a request by Frank S. Richards, who was handling the appeal for Lucky, and said, "I explained to him that I had no authority to speak for the Association in this instance, but that I felt of course we could not assume his position, even in the face of our opposition to proportionate employment." Richards, disappointed, wrote Marshall, "We are unable, however, to understand how you can contend, as we feel you must support petitioners in this case, that the policy of the State of California against racial discrimination in employment is not sufficiently important to justify state interference with picketing, which might otherwise be protected under the doctrine of *Thornhill* v. *Alabama*."[15] Miller, too, advised the association to focus on the free

14. Loren Miller to Thurgood Marshall, November 12, 1948, Cecil F. Poole to Marshall, January 10, 1949, Memorandum of Marian Wynn Perry, January 27, 1949, Edises, Treuhaft, and Condon to Marshall, January 22, 1949, in NAACP Papers, II-B-87; Perry to W. Robert Ming, January 20, 1949, Ming to Perry, February 4, 1949, in NAACP Papers, II-B-71; Perry to Robert L. Carter, July 12, 1949, Marshall to Ming, Nabrit, and Johnson, October 26, 1949, in NAACP Papers, II-B-87.

15. In this 1940 case, the Supreme Court struck down an Alabama law prohibiting peaceful picketing and confirmed the idea that picketing was a form of free speech.

speech element of the case. "That position is rather admirably set forth in Traynor's dissent. I think that such a brief could dissociate the Association from any support of picketing for proportional employment, and at the same time affirm our stand in favor of free speech," he said. The NAACP decided to drop the issue of proportional racial hiring and proceed with the case on the more important, less controversial free speech and picketing grounds.[16]

The *Hughes* case was argued before the Supreme Court on November 8 and 9, 1949. Hughes' lawyers, Bertram Edises and Robert L. Condon, asked the justices to clarify their rulings on picketing as freedom of speech. The Court's apparently strong stand in *Thornhill* had been undermined, and they thought *Hughes* presented "the strongest factual justification for constitutional protection of any picketing considered by this court since the *Thornhill* decision." If the picketing here were not protected, the entire premise of First Amendment protection of picketing would need reconsideration. This case also gave the Court an opportunity to reinforce its position as "a firm champion of the oppressed Negro people" taken in the recent *Steele* case, when it imposed the duty of "fair representation" of racial minorities by labor unions.

Edises and Condon also defended proportional hiring as a proper, concrete solution to the economically depressed condition of black Americans. They reiterated the premise of their proportional idea, that "if there is no discrimination against Negroes, one would expect to find them gainfully employed in various pursuits in approximately the same proportion that their population bears to the nation as a whole." Thus Lucky's claim that Hughes called for race-based preference was spurious. Hughes did not demand "more jobs for Negroes as clerks than would have been the case if Lucky had followed a non-discriminatory hiring policy." The pickets demanded more than a nondiscriminatory policy. They demanded "not merely to compete on the open market for jobs, an equality shown by experience to be of dubious value to Negroes, but . . . a definite percentage of Negroes be hired as vacancies occurred."

16. Loren Miller to Marshall, October 27, 1949, Frank S. Richards to Marshall, October 28, 1949, in NAACP Papers, II-B-87.

The position of black Americans, similar to that of women and children in earlier social legislation, meant that preference for them did not constitute discrimination against any others. In this case, "Special consideration does not become 'discrimination' where its beneficiaries are a uniquely oppressed and exploited social group." Even if Negroes were given this consideration—turned into a "closed union," as Schauer put it—they would remain disadvantaged. "Indeed, it may legitimately be doubted whether there are many who seek the privilege of incorporation into the ranks of Negro, since that 'privilege' is accompanied by political, social, and economic disenfranchisement. To compare such 'exclusiveness' with that of a union having a deliberate policy of racial discrimination is to play with words and ignore realities," Edises and Condon argued. Finally, they appealed to judicial nationalism. If the U.S. Supreme Court accepted the California Supreme Court's decision, it would leave to the states the determination of which "public policy" could prohibit picketing—for racial hiring or any other goal. "An acceptance of such an interpretation will involve an abdication by this Court of its position as ultimate interpreter of the Constitution," they concluded.[17]

General Counsel Arthur J. Goldberg of the CIO filed a brief on behalf of Hughes, seeing in the California decision a threat to Negro organizations and organized labor in general. Picketing for any purpose must be presumed lawful, he argued, fearing that the Supreme Court was retreating from its picketing-as-speech doctrine. Goldberg defended the goal of proportional hiring while admitting that it was perhaps "not the ideal solution" to the problem of employment discrimination. The absence of either state or federal fair employment laws made it "the only practicable remedy available to negro organizations." The U.S. Supreme Court had recognized as much in the *New Negro Alliance* case, he said, while California's supreme court had "assumed the ideal and ignored the facts," applying a color-blind standard to a color-conscious world, and letting "its logic obscure the facts of life."[18]

17. Opening Brief for Petitioners, October 22, 1949, *Transcript, Lucky* v. *PCA.*

18. Brief for the Congress of Industrial Organizations as Amicus Curiae, November 3, 1949, *ibid.*

The ACLU also took an interest in the case, voiced by Arthur Garfield Hays and Osmond K. Fraenkel. Their concern was limited to the free speech implications of California's ruling. "At the outset we wish to state that we condemn the purpose of the picketing herein," they said. They were merely defending the legality of the picketing. "However misguided the theories of the petitioners, their picketing must fall of its own weight. That is the very essence of free speech," they told the Court. Embracing the "marketplace of ideas" principle of Oliver Wendell Holmes, the ACLU also had to come to terms with Holmes' "clear and present danger" dictum. They denied that the advocacy of unpopular ideas constituted such a danger. To affirm the California decision, they said, "would be to hold that the mere advocacy of a distasteful lawful objective represents a clear and present danger of a substantive evil to the State." They pointed out that discriminatory hiring practices were not deemed evil enough by the state of California to bring about a fair employment practice law, and that "the majority nowhere indicated that the common law policy of the State prevented discrimination." Thus *Hughes* was "merely an expression by the Courts of the State of California of disapproval of the objective sought by the picketing— the ideas advocated." Courts could not enjoin ideas, the ACLU concluded.[19]

Finally, the NAACP, through Robert L. Carter and Thurgood Marshall, filed a brief on behalf of Hughes. They, too, focused on the free speech aspect of the constitutional dispute, and cautiously evaded the issue of proportionalism. They stated that "we are opposed to what has been alleged to be the ultimate objective of the petitioners in this action—proportional or quota hiring of Negroes . . ." but agreed with the CIO and ACLU that the purpose, even if they did not approve of it, was lawful. Moreover, the NAACP doubted whether Hughes' aims in fact amounted to the advocacy of a quota system. The California Supreme Court misinterpreted the aims of Hughes, they suggested. "The Court, interpreting 'proportionate' as a mathematical word of art, concluded that petitioners were advocating

19. Brief for the American Civil Liberties Union as Amicus Curiae, November 7, 1949, *ibid.*

employment of Negro clerks in strict ratio to whites, probably determined by a census of Richmond's growing and variable population," they surmised. They suggested that the Court consider a more realistic, if less literal, interpretation of the demands. Hughes' signs, calling for "Negro clerks in proportion to Negro trade," should not be taken literally. Signs in labor disputes, the Court held in earlier cases, often used "loose language or undefined slogans." Hughes' demand, the NAACP contended, "takes on a meaning more hortatory and less artificial, which was the meaning undoubtedly conveyed to those living in the context of the controversy." Rather than seeking an unlawful policy, or even a lawful if undesirable one, the NAACP argued that "they were simply interested in increasing employment opportunities for Negroes and eliminating discrimination against them, something quite in accord with the public policy of the State of California, and of the United States." Except for the dubious determination of proportional demands, they concluded, *Hughes* was substantially the same as the *New Negro Alliance* case, and should be judged accordingly.[20]

The argument of Marshall and Carter, that Hughes did not demand a proportional policy at all, is all but impossible to square with the one made by Hughes' own lawyers, Edises and Condon, who explained and defended the proportional goal. It is not surprising, however, that the local initiators of the picketing and the NAACP national authorities should present such divergent arguments to the Supreme Court. The national office had been tardily informed of the situation in Richmond, and there was considerable internal debate on whether to support the *Hughes* case, and on what strategy to apply. The brief was unconvincing on this new point, and failed to reinforce or supplement Hughes' case before the Supreme Court.

The American Jewish Congress (AJC) had originally planned to support Hughes, but ultimately did not. Jack Pearlman of the AJC's Commission on Law and Social Action prepared a brief in support of Hughes in the summer of 1949, stating at the outset the organi-

---

20. Brief for the National Association for the Advancement of Colored People as Amicus Curiae, November 5, 1949, *ibid.*

zation's objection to proportional hiring. They considered it "another form of the quota system" that perpetuated the use of irrelevant considerations such as race and religion, instead of merit, in hiring decisions. The congress directed its efforts toward securing fair employment practice legislation at the national and state levels, which aimed at "equality of opportunity in employment and of necessity outlaws quotas."

But Pearlman defended Hughes' constitutional right to picket for the proportional system and the logic of the demand itself. The quota system constituted the most practical formula to achieve the goal of nondiscrimination. Mere exhortation of Lucky to hire on the basis of merit rather than color was "unenforceable and therefore futile." Pearlman also supported the assumption that, absent discrimination, the proportion of Negro workers would reflect the proportion of Negroes in the population. As Pearlman saw it, "The specific demand made herein indicates that the proportion of Negro clerks in the Canal Street store was lower than the proportion of Negro trade there. Such a situation could reasonably indicate a discrimination against Negroes." Although the AJC did not file this brief, the draft of this argument indicates that the logic of population–work force symmetry, advanced by Edises and Condon, had some appeal and was gaining currency.[21]

Hughes' advocates were trying to shift the focus from quotas to antidiscrimination and free speech, to pull Hughes back from explicit proportionalism to the ground of the *New Negro Alliance*. They were in favor of affirmative action but not quotas. But the *amici* were at odds with the appellants, who favored proportionalism as the definition of fair employment, not an expedient until fair employment was adopted.

Lucky's attorneys, Frank S. Richards and Hugh T. Fullerton, disputed several of the points made by Hughes and his supporters. Above all, they denied that Lucky operated a discriminatory hiring system. Hughes, in fact, never brought this allegation before the trial court. All that could be shown was that if Hughes' demands

21. Commission on Law and Social Action of the American Jewish Congress, Draft Brief in Hughes, Prepared by Jack Pearlman, August 7, 1949, in NAACP Papers, II-B-87.

were met, Lucky would operate a discriminatory policy, "a quota of jobs for Negroes based on skin coloration rather than on individual merit." Richards and Fullerton further contended that demands for a quota system did constitute a "clear and present danger" to a vitally important state policy. They disputed the analogy of Edises and Condon to special legislation for women and children that had been approved by the Court. "Petitioners contend . . . that preferential treatment for Negroes is not discrimination because they are a uniquely oppressed and exploited group. . . . But [they] overlook the fact that, while classifications based on sex may be reasonable for such purposes as minimum wage legislation, classifications based on race are seldom justifiable under our Constitution."

Lucky's attorneys accepted that Hughes' long-range goal might be that of nondiscrimination, but the short-term use of discrimination would do more harm than good, and actually encourage discrimination in non-black areas. Finally, Richards argued that the *New Negro Alliance* case did not apply here, since the alliance picketed in protest against discrimination, and did not demand a specific hiring quota. The injunction in that case had been very broad, while the injunction issued in California acted specifically against the quota demand. Thus the Supreme Court should respect the determination of the California courts that Hughes' demands constituted a clear and present danger to an important state policy.[22]

The Supreme Court decided the *Hughes* case on May 8, 1950. Felix Frankfurter wrote the decision for the unanimous court affirming the decision of the California Supreme Court. Frankfurter stated the main question of the case: "Does the Fourteenth Amendment . . . bar a State from use of the injunction to prohibit picketing of a place of business solely in order to secure compliance with a demand that its employees be in proportion to the racial origin of its then customers?" Frankfurter noted that California had been sensitive to the problem of discrimination in employment, and that in this case its supreme court decided "that it would encourage discriminatory hiring to give constitutional protection to [Hughes'] ef-

22. Brief for Respondent, October 26, 1949, *Transcript, Lucky* v. *PCA.*

forts to subject the opportunity of getting a job to a quota system." Frankfurter agreed that this decision was especially relevant to the American population, which was "made up of so many diverse groups." To allow Negroes in Richmond to picket for quota hiring would encourage every minority group to do so. "The differences in cultural traditions instead of adding flavor and variety to our common citizenry might well be hardened into hostilities by leave of law," he said. Implicit in this statement was a rejection of Edises' argument that the particular discrimination suffered by black Americans justified their picketing but not that of others.[23]

The Court went on to clarify the extent of the Constitution's protection of picketing as free speech. "It has been amply recognized that picketing, not being the equivalent of speech as a matter of fact, is not its inevitable legal equivalent," Frankfurter noted. California courts had made a legitimate distinction between picketing against discrimination and picketing to compel discrimination. While the Supreme Court did not interpret *Hughes* as tending to encourage discrimination, it could not overrule California's determination on this point. "We cannot construe the Due Process Clause as precluding California from securing respect for its policy against involuntary employment on racial lines by prohibiting systematic picketing that would subvert such a policy," he wrote. The relevant precedent here was the *Giboney* case, where the Court sustained an injunction of a labor union's attempt to compel an employer to violate a state anti-trust policy.

Frankfurter rejected the argument that California's lack of a fair employment statute indicated a weak policy, or no policy, against discrimination. "The fact that California's policy is expressed by the

23. *Hughes* v. *Superior Court,* 339 U.S. 460 (1950). Justices Black, Minton, and Reed concurred in Frankfurter's decision upon the precedent of *Giboney*. William O. Douglas was recovering from a riding accident and took no part in the consideration of the case. While it is impossible to say how he would have judged in 1950, twenty-four years later Douglas cited *Hughes* in his opposition to an affirmative action admissions program at the University of Washington Law School; see *DeFunis* v. *Odegaard,* 416 U.S. 312 (1974), 337–38. Justice Tom Clark prepared a dissent, but did not publish it. Mark Tushnet, "Change and Continuity in the Concept of Civil Rights: Thurgood Marshall and Affirmative Action," *Social Philosophy and Policy,* VIII (1991), 154.

judicial organ of the State rather than by the legislature we have repeatedly ruled to be immaterial." The Fourteenth Amendment drew no distinctions as to which branches of state government made the law. Frankfurter stated, "California chose to strike at the discrimination inherent in the quota system by means of the equitable remedy of injunction to protect against unwilling submission to such a system." Frankfurter nevertheless conceded something to the argument for quota hiring, regardless of the "discrimination inherent" in it. Frankfurter had been careful to focus on "involuntary" and "unwilling submission" to a quota system brought about by picketing. A state's prohibition of picketing to compel proportional hiring did not necessarily imply that the state also prohibited voluntary quota systems by employers. Frankfurter here recognized the point that California might permit Lucky to discriminate, in favor of as well as against, racial groups. His decision in this case was limited to the use of picketing to compel quota hiring.

Frankfurter gave some explanation for his judgment that "the discrimination inherent in the quota system" was permissible if private and voluntary, even in a state that had devised some policy against discrimination. "A State is not required to exercise its intervention on the basis of abstract reasoning," he said, and "the Constitution commands neither logical symmetry nor exhaustion of a principle." He quoted previous Supreme Court decisions that made room for this sort of flexibility: "The problems of government are practical ones and may justify, if they do not require, rough accommodation—illogical, it may be, and unscientific." A state may "direct its law against what it deems the evil as it actually exists without covering the whole field of possible abuses, and it may do so none the less that the forbidden act does not differ in kind from those that are allowed," Frankfurter noted, adding that "lawmaking is essentially empirical and tentative, and in adjudication as in legislation the Constitution does not forbid 'cautious advance, step by step, and the distrust of generalities.'" Frankfurter concluded by saying that he would not generalize or go beyond the circumstances of this particular case.[24]

24. Frankfurter citing *Metropolis Theatre Co.* v. *Chicago,* 228 U.S. 61 (1912); *Central Lumber Co.* v. *South Dakota,* 226 U.S. 157 (1912); *Carroll* v. *Greenwich Insurance Co.,* 199 U.S. 401 (1904).

The October, 1949, term had been a largely successful one for civil rights groups. The Court's decisions in *Henderson* v. *U.S., Sweatt* v. *Painter,* and *McLaurin* v. *Oklahoma State Regents,* although decided on narrow, technical issues, indicated that segregation rested on increasingly insecure constitutional ground. The Court at this time was probably closer than it ever had been to renouncing *Plessy* v. *Ferguson* and applying a strict color-blind constitutional standard. Although civil rights and civil liberties groups saw it as a defeat, *Hughes* may be seen as part of an emerging pattern of decisions by the Supreme Court which disapproved of racial classifications and culminated in the 1954 *Brown* decision. *Hughes* can also be seen as part of the Vinson Court's tendency toward more restrictive organized labor and picketing decisions but more liberal civil rights decisions.[25]

Although Frankfurter rejected most of Hughes' arguments, he also ignored several of them, and overall the opinion probably raised more questions than it answered. Frankfurter apparently wanted to leave great latitude to states to combat racial discrimination in employment. California, he reasoned, had expressed its disapproval of quota hiring and prohibited picketing to compel it. If California could permit quota hiring, as Frankfurter suggested, could a state by the same principle choose to *compel* quota hiring? What were the consequences for states that did have fair employment laws? Most commentators, like the American Jewish Congress and the *Syracuse Law Review,* believed that the fair employment approach precluded quota hiring. But if California, with its judge-made antidiscrimination policy, could permit quotas, could New York? In short, could the race-conscious approach of direct action, rejected by the courts, be pursued in the fair employment context? This question might become relevant if state fair employment laws failed to produce the naturally proportional work force envisioned by Hughes' supporters. Finally, Frankfurter chose not to enter into the question of proof of discrimination. Hughes claimed to have proved Lucky's discriminatory policy by the disparity between the black population and the number of black employees; Lucky

25. Kull, *The Color-Blind Constitution,* 147; Robert G. McCloskey, *The Modern Supreme Court* (Cambridge, Mass., 1972), 114–17.

claimed to have proved its nondiscrimination by its two or three black employees. Frankfurter left that determination where the California Supreme Court placed it—irrelevant beside the point of picketing to compel proportional hiring. This increasingly important question would be taken up outside the courts, in the administrative procedures of state fair employment practice commissions, in the next fifteen years.

5   Fair Employment in New York, 1945–1955

After Congress ended the wartime Fair Employment Practice Committee, the antidiscrimination effort shifted to state FEPCs. New York enacted the first FEPC in 1945, and by 1963 twenty-five states enacted laws modeled after the New York State Law Against Discrimination (LAD), covering 40 percent of the nation's nonwhite population. Commentators, frequently the architects of affirmative action, have given these agencies scant attention, usually dismissing them as timid attempts to apply an inadequate antidiscrimination standard. Historians have given them almost no treatment at all. Yet these agencies were the most important shapers of antidiscrimination law and policy between the wartime FEPC and the Civil Rights Act of 1964, and examining them in the context of the historical development of fair employment casts new light on the state FEPCs.[1]

Two approaches toward employment discrimination—the race-conscious model of the "Don't Buy Where You Can't Work" pickets and certain New Deal agencies and the color-blind model pursued by the wartime FEPC—were available to state fair employment administrators. The first postwar decade highlights the achievements and limitations of the state fair employment practice commissions' efforts to devise effective color-blind rules of fair employment. The state commissioners, believing that an overly aggressive enforce-

1. Alfred W. Blumrosen, *Modern Law: The Law Transmission System and Equal Employment Opportunity* (Madison, 1993), 42; Herbert Hill, "Twenty Years of State FEPCs: A Critical Analysis with Recommendations," *Buffalo Law Review,* XIV (1965), 22–69.

ment of antidiscrimination laws must lead to race-conscious employment decisions and racial quotas, adhered scrupulously to the fair employment model from their inception through the 1950s. This was the source of much of the criticism leveled at them. In the postwar decades the New York State Commission Against Discrimination was regarded as the standard in the field, leading the way in antidiscrimination efforts in employment and housing. While not without critics among civil rights groups, New York's effort was undoubtedly the most serious and systematic of any state's.

World War II and the federal FEPC provided the impetus for states to enact their own peacetime FEPCs after the war. Since the Civil War, many northern states had enacted civil rights laws first to prohibit segregation, and then to prohibit discrimination in public employment, labor unions, public utilities, and public works contracting. But enforcement of these laws was left to public prosecutors and private suits, and thus had little effect. Prosecutors would not bring cases, proof of discrimination beyond a reasonable doubt was difficult in criminal cases, and private suits were expensive. No attempts to enforce these primitive fair employment laws were reported before World War II. The wartime FEPC provided a more effective model for the states, especially since states could, through the police power, reach private, intrastate employment that was constitutionally beyond the reach of the federal government.[2]

New York had taken steps toward a fair employment law during World War II, providing for administrative agencies to enforce its civil rights laws. This culminated in the New York State War Council's Committee on Discrimination. In 1944 the New York State Temporary Commission Against Discrimination studied the problem of employment discrimination, held hearings, and recommended what became the New York State Law Against Discrimination. Also knows as the Ives-Quinn Law, after its sponsors, the New York LAD declared that the opportunity to obtain employment without regard to race, creed, color, or national origin was a civil

2. Marguerite Cartwright, "Legislation Against Discrimination in Employment in New York State" (Ph. D. dissertation, New York University, 1948), 93; Maslow and Robison, "Civil Rights Legislation," 363–413; Bonfield, "Origin and Development," 1043–92.

right. To enforce this right the law established a State Commission Against Discrimination (SCAD) consisting of five salaried, but not full-time, members. The law gave the commission the power to promulgate rules and policies to effectuate the purpose of the law, to receive and investigate allegations of employment discrimination, to conduct hearings, to issue subpoenas to produce testimony and documents, and to issue legally enforceable cease-and-desist orders. In short, it had the full range of powers available to New Deal agencies like the National Labor Relations Board (NLRB).[3]

The law declared it an unlawful employment practice for an employer or employment agency to refuse to hire, or to fire, or to discriminate against any person in compensation or other terms of employment because of race, creed, color, or national origin. It likewise forbade labor unions to deny membership to any person on these grounds. The statute covered all employers of six or more people, except for social, fraternal, religious, and other non-profit organizations. Employers and employment agencies could not make any pre-employment inquiries about an applicant or a prospective applicant's race, creed, color, or national origin, "unless based upon a bona fide occupational qualification." Finally, employers, unions, and employment agencies were forbidden to retaliate against anyone who brought a complaint or otherwise cooperated with the law.

The law authorized the commission to act upon an individual's verified complaint of discrimination, but the state industrial commissioner or attorney general could also bring complaints. An investigating commissioner then set out to determine if probable cause existed to sustain the allegation. If there was probable cause, the commissioner was to "endeavor to eliminate the unlawful employment practice complained of by conference, conciliation, and persuasion." This was a key provision of the law, establishing its

---

3. George L. Schaefer, "Current Legislation," *St. John's Law Review,* VI (1932), 422–28; Cartwright, "Legislation Against Discrimination," 297–336; State of New York, *Executive Department Laws,* Chapter 118, Article 12, March 2, 1945; Terry Lichtash, "Current Legislation," *St. John's Law Review,* XIX (1945), 170–76; "Statute," *New York University Law Quarterly Review,* XXI (1946), 134–41; Charles H. Tuttle, "The New Law Against Discrimination," *New York State Bar Association Bulletin,* XVII (1945), 76–83; W. Brooke Graves, *Fair Employment Practice Legislation in the United States, Federal—State—Municipal* (Washington, D.C., 1951).

general tone of peaceful education and resolution of disputes, rather than compulsion to eliminate discrimination. It was a lesson taken from the federal FEPC that most discrimination cases could be solved by moral suasion if it were known that the law had legal sanctions behind it. This also served as a safeguard to assuage employers' fears about an overzealous, inquisitorial enforcement of the law.

If conciliation failed, the law required the respondent to appear at a public hearing before the commission. The commission need not conduct the public hearing according to the strict procedures or rules of evidence of a criminal or civil trial, but could be flexible. If the commission sustained the charges in public hearing, it could then order remedies requiring the respondent "to cease and desist from such unlawful employment practice and to take such affirmative action, including (but not limited to) hiring, reinstatement or upgrading of employees, with or without back pay, or restoration to membership in any respondent labor organization." This provided the "teeth" that fair employment advocates long desired, and which had been the most glaring deficiency of the federal FEPC.

The law provided for judicial review of commission orders, and it allowed the commission to seek judicial enforcement of its orders. The findings of fact made by the commission were to be conclusive "if supported by sufficient evidence on the record considered as a whole." This was a much less stringent standard than "beyond a reasonable doubt" in criminal prosecution or "preponderance of the evidence" in civil suits, and provided vast administrative discretion. Moreover, the law directed that "the provisions of this article shall be construed liberally for the accomplishment of the purposes thereof." Since conciliation was meant to obviate the need for numerous public hearings, appeals to the courts were meant to be even less frequent. A disappointed complainant could appeal for judicial review of a commission decision, but could expect no more judicial scrutiny than a disappointed employer-respondent. Significantly, as in the NLRA, the individual worker had no right to bring a suit against a private employer if the administrative agency did not proceed on his behalf.[4]

4. Until 1952, an individual could proceed against a labor union or public utility under the older state civil rights laws, but no individual right against private employers existed. In 1952 the enforcement of these laws was given to the SCAD.

The law proved to be remarkably popular and durable. Its language satisfied religious, labor, and civil rights groups and assuaged the fears of most businessmen. Opponents believed that it would restrict free enterprise, institute an officious centralized bureaucracy, and drive businesses out of the state. Others objected to the laws on sociological grounds, arguing that laws could not change prejudice, and that any legal attempts to compel association would actually exacerbate racial, religious, and ethnic tensions. Groups like the NAACP preferred fewer exemptions in the law, and thought that "conciliation" was too ambiguous an expression of the law's purpose and an inappropriate response to violations of civil rights. They also desired stiffer penalties for willful noncompliance. These groups' first priority was to pass the law; enforcement methods could be perfected afterward. Without the bloc of southern senators present in Washington, it was easier to pass the New York state law than the federal FEPC. The Republicans controlled the legislature in New York, and Governor Thomas E. Dewey and the majority leaders of the legislature supported the bill. Although large numbers of conservative upstate Republicans defected, there was enough Democratic support to pass the bill before the end of World War II.[5]

The state FEPCs faced the formidable problem of defining discrimination and fair employment practices. At law, discrimination was considered an individual act of unequal treatment based on some forbidden category, and required that intent to discriminate be proved. The idea that discrimination could be measured by comparing an employer's proportion of minority workers to the proportion of minorities in the population was another available concept. The New Negro Alliance was among the first to articulate this idea, and it was expanded and detailed in the *Hughes* case. The concept had been anticipated in the PWA contractor quota system, and then self-consciously avoided by the federal FEPC. The FEPC had identified a racially unbalanced work force as something that indicated or suggested discrimination, without necessarily proving it. The state

5. New York *Times,* February 18, 1945, pt. IV, p. 10, February 22, 1945, p. 1; "Letter of the Executive Committee of the Massachusetts Bar Association on Pending Anti-Discrimination Legislation," *Massachusetts Law Quarterly,* XXX (1945), 10–13; Robert L. Carter to James A. Curtis, November 27, 1944, in NAACP Papers, II-A-250.

FEPCs were unwilling to define their mission or measure their success in statistical terms. Civil rights groups often criticized them for their caution in this regard, but they themselves were reluctant to resort to the equation of work force and population as a standard. State FEPCs in the postwar years established the administrative machinery of antidiscrimination law, arrived at a working definition of discrimination, and set the standards for its proof at law.

The best-developed body of law that might bear on the question of proving discrimination in employment was that of the jury discrimination cases. Proving discrimination in cases of complete exclusion was simple, but it became a problem in cases of token representation. The U.S. Supreme Court repeatedly held that "fairness in selection has never been held to require proportional representation of races upon a jury," but this did not solve the problem of "tokenism," or the use of maximum quotas to limit minority group participation. Although it always considered testimony of commissioners and other witnesses, the Court had relied primarily on statistical disparities and probabilities—one Negro on each grand jury was too probable, too close to proportional representation, to be the result of chance. Yet just how much disparity was significant the Court left unstated. Thus in later jury discrimination cases federal judges were faced with the difficult task of requiring commissioners to make sure that they considered qualified black jurors while forbidding them to take race into account when composing jury lists. The Court's difficulty in explaining the difference between the significance of statistical disparities and proportional representation adumbrated a key issue in employment discrimination law.[6]

The jury discrimination cases provided some background for tackling the problem of employment discrimination, but employment and jury service were not perfectly analogous. Proving discrimination in employment differed from proving discrimination in jury selection primarily in sample size and the range of qualifications. Apart from restrictions on female and child labor, the prohibition of discrimination based on labor union affiliation was the

6. Earl C. Dudley, Jr., "The Congress, the Court, and Jury Selection: A Critique of Titles I and II of the Civil Rights Bill of 1966," *Virginia Law Review*, LII (1966), 1104; David W. Barnes, "The Problem of Multiple Components or Divisions in Title VII Litigation: A Comment," *Law and Contemporary Problems*, XLVI (1983), 201–208.

only significant restraint on employer selection of employees, and provided one of the few sources for the problem of proving discrimination. Section 8 (3) of the National Labor Relations Act made it illegal for an employer to discriminate against employees based on labor union membership. Evidence of such discrimination was sometimes clear and not controverted, but usually the NLRB had to weigh conflicting evidence. It noted that it "frequently found persuasive evidence of discrimination in an unduly high percentage of union members or union leaders included among employees discharged, laid off, or refused reinstatement." The board attempted to determine whether disproportion was fortuitous or deliberate, and noted that disproportion itself was given considerable weight but was not itself conclusive. The board apparently never held that disproportion made a prima facie case of discrimination, but considered it with other evidence of disparate treatment of union members. Presented with a case in which an employer laid off a disproportionately large number of union members, the NLRB concluded,

> It would be expected that in a selection of employees to be laid off without regard to union affiliation the proportion of union members among those laid off would approximate the proportion existing in the group from which selection was made. . . . Of course any combination is a possible result on the basis of pure chance. Variation from the expected does not necessarily establish that the operation of chance has been frustrated by intelligent selection. When, however, the variation is marked or is manifested consistently in repeated samplings, the hypothesis that union membership was irrelevant to the selection gives way to the inference that the selection was made upon a discriminatory basis.

The federal courts sustained the NLRB's administrative discretion in these cases, permitting the board to make inferences from disproportion, especially when combined with other evidence of disparate treatment.[7]

7. National Labor Relations Board, *Third Annual Report* (Washington, D.C., 1939), 81–82; *U.S. Smelting, Refining and Mining Company,* 10 N.L.R.B. 1015 (1939), 1019; *Hilgartner Marble Company,* 13 N.L.R.B. 1200 (1939), 1206; *Ford Motor Company,* 29 N.L.R.B. 873 (1941), 891; *F. W. Woolworth Co.,* 25 N.L.R.B. 1362 (1940), 1373; *Montgomery Ward v. NLRB,* 107 F.2d 555 (1939), 563–64; *F. W. Woolworth Co. v. NLRB,* 121 F.2d 658 (1941), 660–62.

The establishment of the wartime FEPC and the many state FEPCs in the next decade was an important first step toward eliminating racial discrimination in employment. The next hurdle was the problem of enforcing these fair employment statutes. Legal scholars predicted that the evidentiary proof that these commissions used in individual cases would in large part determine their effectiveness. Although the commissions proceeded by individual cases, they were dealing with racial groups, and inevitably drew inferences from statistical patterns. The antidiscrimination effort, then, contained elements of both law and sociology. The sociologist dealt with groups and used inductive reasoning based on large patterns, statistical aggregations of individual acts. The lawyer, however, was confined to individual cases, and could not make the same inferences from larger social patterns that the sociologist could.[8]

Fair employment commissions faced the problem that, if they made sociological inferences in their administration of fair employment statutes, these would be liable to challenge in the courts, where a legal rather than a sociological standard obtained. Thus the commissions tended to rely on conciliation, persuasion, and voluntary compliance in order to keep out of court. As long as the commissioners remained in an informal administrative rather than formal legal setting, they could retain their flexibility.[9] While the commissioners might not require intent to discriminate to investigate charges and attempt conciliation, if the case went to court they would be required to demonstrate intent to discriminate, and mere statistics could not do this.[10] Indeed, commissioners often could not bring cases against employers who had large work forces with no minori-

8. "An American Legal Dilemma: Proof of Discrimination," *University of Chicago Law Review*, XIV (1949), 107. This unsigned note is among the most valuable and prescient treatments of this matter.

9. *Ibid.*, 119; William H. Lamb, "Proof of Discrimination at the Commission Level," *Temple Law Quarterly*, XXXIX (1966), 303.

10. The New York commissioners did not require intent for probable cause. SCAD Law Bulletin (LB) 37, January 1, 1950, LB 60, December 1, 1951, in New York State Commission Against Discrimination, Records, New York State Division for Human Rights Library (NYSDHR Library), New York.

ties if they did not have a qualified individual who charged discrimination.[11]

Commissioners would have a difficult time using the statistical assumptions of the jury discrimination cases, as the number of factors to be considered before arriving at an expected number of minority employees was so great as to make the inference extremely doubtful. The number of qualified Negro applicants would have to be considered, as well as recent personnel changes in the workplace, and any number of other factors. Qualifications for particular jobs were more complex than qualifications for jury service or voting, and the statistical sample of applicants was different and usually much smaller than the general population of a county used in the jury discrimination cases.[12]

As in the jury discrimination cases, statistical inference could be frustrated if an employer used a quota system to mask discrimination. It was almost impossible to distinguish a shrewdly operated quota system from the results of chance distribution, and the enforcement of fair employment statutes might have the ironic result of encouraging such artificial limitations on minority group employment. An employer could protect itself against charges of discrimination if it employed minorities in roughly the proportion that statistics would predict. In this way, a quota system acted as insurance for employers against discrimination charges. This suggested the basic dilemma in the administration of fair employment statutes: statistical inferences might be the easiest way for commissioners to begin to prove discrimination, but if statistical imbalance proved discrimination or shifted the burden of proof from the complainant to the respondent, employers would be tempted to resort to quota systems. Quota systems would limit the opportunities for some minority workers, even if they gave preferential treatment to some others. More important, they would defeat the animating purpose of antidiscrimination laws of eliminating irrelevant factors like race from employment decisions. The SCAD recognized that it had to shape its own standard of proof, and drew on the jury and

11. "The Right to Equal Treatment: Administrative Enforcement of Antidiscrimination Legislation," *Harvard Law Review,* LXXIV (1961), 553.

12. "An American Legal Dilemma," 121.

labor union analogies. It decided that a prima facie case of discrimination required not just statistical disproportion, but proof that the complainant was qualified for the job in question. When a prima facie case was made, the burden shifted to the respondent to explain, and legal proceedings might begin.[13]

During its first five years of operation, the State Commission Against Discrimination received almost all of its criticism from groups who vigorously supported the law's enactment. Despite reports from the commission that it was making substantial progress against discrimination, critics contended that the commission acted too slowly, was too conciliatory, and cared too little for the fate of the individual complainant. Within a few years of its inception, they argued, the minority groups it was meant to serve had lost faith in it. In these years the commission was steadfast in its refusal to adopt race-conscious statistical standards for proof of discrimination, following in the path established by the federal FEPC. Its choice of a disparate-treatment rather than a disparate-impact definition of discrimination seemed workable in its first ten years, but dissatisfaction with the commission after 1960 forced major changes that led finally to the adoption of aggressive affirmative action and quota measures.

Civil rights groups were frustrated in their attempt to apply the Ives-Quinn law retroactively, to gain seniority benefits for black workers who had been discriminated against by the Pennsylvania Railroad. Elmer Carter, the investigating commissioner, told the NAACP that resolution took so long because the commission wanted to keep the case open in order to change industry patterns beyond the individual complaints. The question of whether the commission should act first for the individual victim of discrimination or seek to alter larger patterns of discrimination was a fundamental issue in all subsequent antidiscrimination policy making. Carter ultimately dismissed the individual complaints, since the seniority

13. *Ibid.*, 123; Sovern, *Legal Restraints*, 124; Ralph K. Winter, Jr., "Improving the Economic Status of Negroes Through Laws Against Discrimination: A Reply to Professor Sovern," *University of Chicago Law Review*, XXXIV (1967), 834; SCAD Memorandum of Law (MOL) 54, October 31, 1950, NYSDHR Library.

system operated in a race-neutral manner and because the law could not be applied retroactively. At the same time, he attempted by informal negotiation to get the railroads to compensate black workers. Nevertheless, he drew back from any race-specific adjustments.[14]

Carter's interpretation of the LAD was probably a sound one and consistent with legislative intent. The act was meant to be prospective, and the impression that the law could reach acts of discrimination committed before its passage would have upset public support for the law and may not have survived judicial review. Carter meant to accomplish as much as possible without public hearings and court challenges. Though critics who favored affirmative action later complained that the commission failed to develop clear standards in court, it is more likely that by staying out of court, the SCAD left the door open for the disparate-impact standard of discrimination, since the disparate-treatment formula was not tested and articulated in case law.[15]

Critics of Carter's interpretation of the law organized the Committee to Support the Ives-Quinn Law, comprised of the NAACP, Urban League, and American Jewish Congress, to monitor the SCAD's work. Will Maslow of the American Jewish Congress recommended that the SCAD follow the NLRB pattern of using consent decrees to enable the agency and the defendant employer to agree on terms in court without going through full adversary proceedings. The commission could then enforce agreements against recalcitrant offenders through contempt-of-court proceedings. Maslow also recommended that employers file bimonthly statistical reports on Negro employment so that the commission could tell whether

14. Details of the case can be found in NAACP Papers, II-B-107, and the Records of the New York State Commission Against Discrimination, case C-1441–46, in Series 10409–89 A, Box 24, New York State Archives, Albany, N.Y.; New York *Times,* September 3, 1948; Henry Spitz, "Patterns of Conciliation Under the New York State Law Against Discrimination" (SCAD pamphlet, New York, 1952), 5; Report of the Conference on Employment of Negroes in Operating Crafts of Principal Railroads," September 9, 1953, General Subject File, Box 64, in Records of the President's Committee on Government Contracts (PCGC), RG 220, NA.

15. Alfred W. Blumrosen, *Black Employment and the Law* (New Brunswick, 1971), 19, 85.

opportunities were improving or declining. "In the last analysis," Maslow wrote, "only such statistical demonstrations of increased Negro employment will answer those critics of the Ives-Quinn law who say that legislation cannot eliminate discrimination." Maslow's suggestions ran counter to the commission's general policy of conciliation and voluntary compliance. Henry C. Turner, who helped draft the LAD, thought that the use of statistical summaries would contradict the law's provisions banning pre-employment inquiries and would also be ineffective. Charles Garside, chairman of the commission, rejected Maslow's plan, noting that the commission did not want to undermine its own policy against racial inquiries and did not want to compel employers to keep extensive employment records. The SCAD finally decided that such statistics would be of little use and that even if desirable, the commission would not have the means of collecting them.[16]

Maslow's suggestions reveal a determination on the part of civil rights advocates to establish a precise measurement of progress against discrimination. Without such data, they felt, the SCAD could not identify discrimination or define compliance. Behind this and other recommendations was the perception that the SCAD, without these definitions, was not enforcing the law vigorously enough. The commission, however, was not willing to accept statistical imbalance in the work force as proof of discrimination. Commentator Morroe Berger, in an early analysis of the SCAD's policies, argued that the counting of minorities in firms previously closed to them was the best gauge of the SCAD's progress. He criticized the commission for its refusal to do so, and attributed it to the SCAD's "rejection of the 'quota system of employment' of minority groups." The consequence, he wrote, was "spotty, generalized, and impressionistic statements," rather than "scientific self-evaluation."[17]

Anne Mather, director of the Committee to Support the Ives-Quinn Law, issued a report on the experiences of various civil rights

16. Will Maslow to Henry Spitz, March 13, 1947, Maslow to Henry C. Turner, March 27, 1947, Turner to Maslow, March 28, 1947, Maslow to Turner, April 3, 1947, in NAACP Papers, II-B-109.

17. Morroe Berger, "The New York Law Against Discrimination: Operation and Administration," *Cornell Law Quarterly*, XXXV (1950), 747–96.

groups under the LAD. She reported that the small number of complaints filed with the SCAD was not a reflection of decreased discrimination, but of ignorance of the law's operation. The commission took an unduly long time to process complaints, making cooperation of victims and their attorneys difficult. While the groups approved of the commission's policy of looking beyond the individual complaint into the overall employment picture of the employer, they complained that this was done at the expense of the individual victim. They accused the SCAD of accepting token employment of minorities as sufficient evidence of compliance with the law. In general, the SCAD seemed willing to settle for terms that were not too onerous on employers, with little regard for the satisfaction of the complainant.

Mather recommended publicity of the commission's existence and work, more attention to relief for individual complainants, increased involvement of civil rights groups in the operation of the law, industry-wide investigations, and greater tests of compliance. Large numbers of minorities could apply in particular industries to gauge compliance with the LAD. "Discrimination can rarely be proved against an individual because many pretexts are always available to reject an applicant," she argued, "but discrimination always shows up when a large number of hirings and rejections are examined statistically."[18]

Both the SCAD policies and Mather's recommendations revealed a conflict between individual and group concepts in the administration of antidiscrimination laws. While the Committee to Support the Ives-Quinn Law insisted on justice for the individual complainant, it also advocated statistical surveys of aggregate group employment. As a result, critics of the SCAD regarded statistical disparity as proof of discrimination, making a prima facie case of unlawful practice against an employer. Similarly, the commission was created to protect individuals against arbitrary discrimination in employment, but often concerned itself with opening opportuni-

18. Committee to Support the Ives-Quinn Law, "Report on the Experience of the UL, NAACP, and AJC with the SCAD with Conclusions and Recommendations," March 11, 1948, Memo to the SCAD from the Committee to Support the Ives-Quinn Law, April 20, 1948, "A Project to Promote Better Enforcement of the New York Ives-Quinn Law," in NAACP Papers, II-A-260.

ties for minority groups in entire industries. This confusion was perhaps inherent in the problem of protecting individuals from suffering discrimination based on their membership in a racial group. It may also have been inherent in the administrative method chosen to deal with the problem. Normally, individual rights were vindicated in courts of law, and the antidiscrimination commissions were established to avoid the courtroom. Underneath these differences about individual or group focus, and the appropriate administrative machinery, lay the fundamental question of the nature of discrimination. The individual complaint procedure was based on the idea that discrimination consisted of discrete, identifiable instances of unequal treatment, while the pattern-centered approach implicitly regarded discrimination as systemic, unintentional, and impersonal. Both Mather and Garside wanted parts of each of these definitions: Mather wanting the SCAD to give fast and effective relief to the individual victim but also to proceed without an individual complaint and on an industry-wide basis; Garside insisting on individual complaints but using them to pursue wider goals than individual relief.

The implications of these ambivalent approaches were profound, bringing into question the nature of discrimination. As in the *Hughes* case, the civil rights groups suggested that discrimination was not an act by particular employers against individuals, but a group phenomenon, with blacks as a group needing protection. They argued on the one hand that discrimination was categorically wrong, that the LAD should grant no exemptions to small businesses, and that the SCAD should work for justice in individual cases, and on the other hand that discrimination was a contingent wrong, punishable only if a group quota or proportion were not met. The commission likewise was confused on whether it should apply a legal standard to individual cases, or sociological approach to groups.[19]

The organizations comprising the Committee to Support the Ives-Quinn Law clashed repeatedly with commission administra-

19. Hadley Arkes, *First Things: An Inquiry into the First Principles of Morals and Justice* (Princeton, 1986), 93; Hadley Arkes, *Beyond the Constitution* (Princeton, 1990), 219.

tors, and sometimes advised complainants to reject the SCAD conciliation agreements as biased in favor of employers. The commission's focus on education and conciliation lost the confidence of minority group representatives. Particularly disappointing was the SCAD's refusal to let groups like the NAACP bring complaints, limiting complaints to "a person aggrieved by an act of discrimination." The civil rights groups sought more influence as monitors and brokers in the antidiscrimination effort, playing a role similar to the CIO in the development of the NLRB, to "capture" the SCAD. Frustrated, they believed the commission had been captured by employers.[20]

Charles Garside regarded the members of the Committee to Support the Ives-Quinn Act as interlopers. He insisted that the law was created for all the citizens of New York, not for particular minority groups. He accused the committee of drumming up complaints and encouraging minority group members to apply for jobs beyond their level of qualification. Garside resisted the committee's calls for statistical methods, denying that there was any correlation between fair employment and proportionalism. "A climate of equal opportunity and diversified recruitment is no guarantee of substantial minority group representation in the employment pattern," he cautioned. The SCAD believed it was avoiding interest group capture and building public support for fair employment.[21]

The case of the Brooklyn Borough Gas Company reveals the at-

20. Anne Mather to Committee, March 2, 1948, Conference on the NYLAD, Summary of Proceedings, May 11, 1948, in NAACP Papers, II-B-109; Memo of Anne Mather, November 24, 1948, Memo of Marian Wynn Perry, February 2, 1949, in NAACP Papers, II-B-106; "The NYSCAD: An Appraisal of Three and a Half Years under the Ives-Quinn Act," January, 1949, in NAACP Papers, II-A-264; New York *Times*, February 20, 1949, p. 48, July 2, 1949, p. 22; "SCAD Inaction Hit by NAACP," NAACP News Release, May 5, 1949, in NAACP Papers.

21. Memo of the SCAD, "Re: Recommendations of the Committee to Support the Ives-Quinn Law," November 5, 1948, in NAACP Papers, II-A-260; Senate Committee on Labor and Public Welfare, *Antidiscrimination in Employment: Hearings before the Senate Committee on Labor and Public Welfare*, 80th Cong., 1st sess., (1947), 344; Elmer Carter, "Policies and Practices of Discrimination Commissions," *Annals of the American Academy of Political and Social Science*, CCCIV (1956), 62–77; MacIver, *More Perfect Union*, 244.

tempt of civil rights groups to act as brokers in the enforcement of the LAD, and the conflicting conceptions of fair employment involved. In 1946 Will Maslow wrote a letter to the Brooklyn Borough Gas Company charging discrimination against Jews. The NAACP urged the SCAD to undertake an investigation of the company, and a communist group sent a petition to the governor charging that "the doors of the company have been completely barred to Jews, Negroes, and Italians." No formal complaint was made to the SCAD, but the gas company itself asked the SCAD to undertake an investigation of its employment practices.

The SCAD concluded that the charge of discrimination was completely baseless. Of 352 employees, eleven were Jewish and nine were Negro. While Jews were found in the highest occupational categories, "the company followed the almost universally accepted custom until the passage of the LAD in that Negroes were considered only for custodial jobs." This profile did not reflect the racial and ethnic composition of the area, although it had when the company was formed in 1898. There was limited turnover among employees, and the method of recruitment used by the company—recommendation by incumbent employees—helped maintain the original composition of the work force. There was no evidence that this was a deliberate effort to exclude Jews.

The gas company thus had not violated the LAD. The commission concluded, "The LAD does not contemplate the compulsory employment of the incompetent, nor the establishment of quotas for the Negro, the Jew, or the foreign-born employees. In the American democracy merit is the only attribute which is entitled to preferential consideration." The commission ruled out suggestions made by local groups that the company confine its hiring of new employees to Negroes and Jews until its work force was proportionally representative of the community. Instead, it approved the Brooklyn Borough Gas Company's policy of taking "affirmative steps to demonstrate that its employment practices are in keeping with the letter and the spirit of the laws of the state enacted for the purpose of insuring equal opportunity to all of its citizens." Thus the company agreed to abandon its "inbreeding" recruitment method, to centralize and standardize personnel decisions, and broaden its recruitment base. The SCAD, more concerned about the present and future than about the past, was satisfied with these steps.[22]

Despite the serious friction between the commission and the groups that had been among its main supporters, the SCAD claimed substantial progress in its fight against employment discrimination. Irving Ives, sponsor of the Law Against Discrimination and in 1947 a U.S. Senator, noted that employers in the state had been won over and now supported fair employment. Advocating a national FEPC, he added that conciliation had worked to reduce discrimination in the state, "and today the amount of discrimination in the State of New York is almost at the vanishing point." The commission reported in 1949 that it had been "forced to resist alike the pressure of those who would attain the objectives of the Law by the quick resort to its punitive features and those who stubbornly oppose any governmental intervention in the conduct of their business affairs." The commission stood by its policy of considering the total employment pattern of the respondent rather than just his treatment of the individual complainant. It insisted that the progress against discrimination was not quantifiable, and that "mere statistics alone cannot tell the complete story." The commission concluded, "Even to the casual observer it is evident that significant progress in employment opportunities has been made in the State of New York since the enactment of the Law Against Discrimination." A greater improvement in the minority occupational pattern, however, ran up against the fact that many minorities lacked necessary occupational skills "because of past discriminatory practices and the provisions of collective bargaining agreements that require the fulfilling of vacancies by re-employment." Finally the SCAD observed that it "attempted to administer the LAD in an atmosphere of cooperation. The alternative is to administer the Law in an atmosphere of conflict."[23]

22. "Summary of the Report of Investigation of Employment Practices of the Brooklyn Borough Gas Company," Mary Dillon to Elmer A. Carter, August 14, 1946, in NAACP Papers, II-B-106.

23. Senate Committee, *Antidiscrimination in Employment*, 12, 614; New York State Commission Against Discrimination (NYSCAD), *1948 Annual Report*, 7–12; Spitz, "Patterns of Conciliation," 16.

Yet the commission implied that there were substantial limits to what a successful anti-discrimination law could accomplish. Clearly the SCAD was not willing to risk pushing the LAD too hard. It had held that seniority systems, even those that perpetuated the effects of past discrimination, would not be disturbed. Committed to broader interests than the civil rights groups, it utilized tactics of conciliation and cooperation that bordered on voluntary compliance. Above all, the commission rejected any statistical standard for the proof of discrimination or as evidence of compliance with the law, turning a deaf ear to those who regarded proportionalism as the goal.

Civil rights organizations' criticism of the SCAD faded after 1950, as black Americans continued to close the economic gap. Black American incomes rose in absolute terms, and rose faster than white incomes. In 1953 the black unemployment rate was 4.5 percent, a historic low, and a rate only 1.7 times the white unemployment rate, near a historic low. From 1939 to 1953 nonwhite median family income rose from 37 percent to 56 percent of white income, increasing 382 percent while white income rose 217 percent in the same years. Of course, the rapid gain might have reflected the desperate economic position of blacks at the end of the depression, but the progress made it appear that discrimination was abating and minority group economic opportunity improving. The manufacturing sector of the American economy was still expanding, providing high-wage jobs for relatively low-skilled workers. Most of these gains took place in northern states with fair employment practice (FEP) laws, where migration of southern Negroes continued. Many observers concluded that state FEP policies were partly responsible for these gains. Whereas the economic crisis of the depression sometimes produced demands for quota employment, postwar prosperity muted such demands and permitted state FEPCs to proceed under a color-blind rule.[24]

Civil rights groups frequently pointed to the success of the state

24. U.S. Department of Commerce, Bureau of the Census, *Historical Statistics of the United States: Colonial Times to 1970* (Washington, D.C., 1975), I, 135, 303.

FEPCs as support for a national statute. Representatives and senators from FEP states and state commissioners sounded triumphant. Will Maslow of the American Jewish Congress, critic of the SCAD in the late 1940s, told a senate committee,

> While these statutes have not brought about the millennium, they have been enforced with effectiveness. They have opened employment opportunities principally for Negroes to a much larger extent than we had anticipated. . . . The statutes have received widespread public compliance. It has been necessary in only a few cases to go to court to obtain enforcement of these statutes. We have had quarrels with some of these agencies. We would have wanted them to move faster, to adopt a more diligent and perhaps a more militant attitude toward the law. But I think these are minor criticisms. On the whole my organization is content with these statutes, and would like to see them spread throughout the whole country and the federal government.

This statement is difficult to reconcile with those of the late 1940s. It may be that Maslow concealed his real opinion of the New York SCAD in order to support congressional FEP efforts. But if we take him at his word, civil rights groups had come to terms with the commission. While the law had not revolutionized employment patterns in New York, it had perhaps gotten down to the hard core of discrimination, eliminating as much discrimination as was possible under the mandate of the 1945 law.[25]

25. House, *Report on the Federal Fair Employment Practice Act,* 81st Cong., 1st sess., 1949, H. Rept. 1165, pp. 8, 27; Senate Committee on Labor and Public Welfare, *State and Municipal Fair Employment Practices Legislation,* Staff Report to the Subcommittee on Labor and Labor-Management Relations, 82nd Cong., 2nd sess., 1953, pp. 20–21; Louis Kesselman, *The Social Politics of FEPC: A Study in Reform Pressure Movements* (Chapel Hill, 1948), chap. 14; Senate Committee on Labor and Public Welfare, *Discrimination and Full Utilization of Manpower Resources: Hearings Before the Committee on Labor and Public Welfare,* 82nd Cong., 2nd sess., 1952, p. 97; Steven M. Gelber, *Black Men and Businessmen: The Growing Awareness of a Social Responsibility* (Port Washington, N.Y., 1974), 34, 82, 90, 111–12; Senate Committee, *Discrimination and Full Utilization of Manpower Resources,* 218; Morroe Berger, "Fair Employment Practice Legislation," *Annals of the American Academy of Political and Social Science,* CCLXXV (1951), 34–40; Herbert R. Northrup, "Progress Without Federal Compulsion," *Commentary,* XIV (1952), 206–11; MacIver, *More Perfect Union,* 167.

The state commissions continued to stress conciliation and non-compulsory persuasion, despite charges that they were too timid. Because prejudice and discrimination were so ingrained in American institutions, Elmer Carter of the SCAD noted, it was the commission's primary goal to educate employers, unions, employment agencies, and the public in the principles of equality of opportunity. The idea of systemic or "institutional" racism and discrimination, although not yet clearly articulated, was present in antidiscrimination thinking in the 1950s. In the 1960s this concept would become the theoretical source of aggressive affirmative action programs. In the 1940s and 1950s, however, the SCAD regarded systemic discrimination as an argument *against* aggressive and coercive policies. The long process of breaking down the color barrier in the railroad brotherhoods was not evidence of torpor, but, to those who recognized the long and bitter history of racial antagonism in the unions, a mark of progress. The fact that the SCAD was successful where the federal FEPC failed showed the value of enforcement as a last resort, not its routine application. The executive director of the Pennsylvania FEPC noted that a prudent administrator would use conciliation first even if the law did not require it.[26]

Fair employment officers argued that the New York law's effectiveness could not be gauged by the number of enforced orders or complaints. The small number of enforcement actions indicated the efficacy of the weapon as much as it indicated undue restraint by the commissioners. The best way the law could work was if employers and unions internalized it and complied on their own. As with the federal FEPC, no one could tell how much voluntary compliance the mere existence of the law prompted, but the SCAD thought it was considerable. Moreover, one complaint could open many jobs for minority group members, especially when the com-

26. Berger, "New York State Law Against Discrimination," 747–96; "The Operation of State FEPCs," *Harvard Law Review,* LXVIII (1955), 685–97; Elmer A. Carter, "Practical Considerations Under the New York Law Against Discrimination," *Cornell Law Quarterly,* XL (1954), 40–59; Jay Anders Higbee, *The Development and Administration of the New York Law Against Discrimination* (University, Ala., 1966), 74; House Committee on Education and Labor, *Federal Fair Employment Practices Act: Hearings Before the Committee on Education and Labor,* 81st Cong., 1st sess., 1949, p. 74; Elliott M. Shirk, "Cases Are People: An Interpretation of the Pennsylvania Fair Employment Practice Law," *Dickinson Law Review,* LXII (1958), 289–305.

mission used the individual complaint to launch a wider investigation.[27]

In its first ten years, the SCAD handled 2,772 complaints. One-quarter of these were sustained as probable cases of discrimination, and in another fifth the individual complaint was dismissed but the commission found other evidence of discrimination. The vast majority of charges (71 percent) were race-based. The commission resolved almost all of the sustained complaints by conciliation. Establishing a case of discrimination, a commissioner considered the qualifications for the job in question, compared the qualifications of the complainant and the person actually hired or promoted, as well as how long the job was open, and the recruitment sources. The investigator would also consider the overall pattern of employment of minorities, especially if there were few or none employed in an area where many were available.[28]

Thus, although the SCAD considered group statistics in its determination of discrimination, the main consideration remained fair treatment of the individual applicant. As frequently stressed, employers were required to hire only qualified minority group members. So the SCAD maintained its opposition to quota employment of the variety seen in the 1930s, "admitted by all students of this subject to be unsound and . . . unalterably opposed by the Commission." Henry Spitz, general counsel of the commission, noted that neither the SCAD nor any other state FEPC could insist on specific quotas such as those in Federal Housing Administration construction contracts, because the state FEPC statutes defined discrimination more narrowly than executive agencies might.[29]

27. Norgren and Hill, *Toward Fair Employment,* 108; Carter, "Practical Considerations," 42, 48; Higbee, *Development and Administration,* 19, 137, 147; Senate Committee, *Antidiscrimination in Employment,* 364; House, *Report on the Federal Fair Employment Practice Act,* 8; Berger, "New York State Law Against Discrimination," 772.

28. Carter, "Practical Considerations," 46–47. For cases illustrating these techniques in various states, see for New York, *Banks* v. *Capitol Airlines* 5 R.R.L.R. (1960), 263–80; for New Jersey, *Thompson* v. *Erie Railroad,* 2 R.R.L.R. (1957), 237–49; and for Connecticut, *Draper* v. *Clark Dairy,* 25 L.R.R.M. (1950), 79–83.

29. "The New York State Commission Against Discrimination: A New Technique for an Old Problem," *Yale Law Journal,* LVI (1947), 849; Higbee, *Development and Administration,* xiv; "The Operation of State FEPCs," 689; NYSCAD, *1948 Annual Report,* 11; SCAD LB 103, July 1, 1955, LB 109, January 1, 1956, LB 131, November 1, 1957,

Although some continued to advocate quotas as fair employment, the SCAD condemned them in several cases. It found the Harlem Labor Union guilty of violation of the LAD in its attempt to monopolize employment in Harlem for Negroes. The SCAD told the HLU that it would not condone the restriction of job opportunities in Harlem to Negroes any more than it would condone the restriction of job opportunities outside the Harlem area to white persons. Despite the legacy of segregation and discrimination, if Negroes asserted such a right it would ultimately work to their detriment. In a construction case, the SCAD found that a 10-percent quota that excluded a nonwhite carpenter was illegal. In a similar case, an insistence that a construction job in a black neighborhood utilize predominantly Negro labor was dismissed as a complaint by the SCAD. In 1955 the SCAD rejected the argument of a Teamster that a minimum number of Negroes be set in occupational categories for promotion purposes, declaring that "this Commission has been consistently opposed to a quota system both as a matter of Law and as a matter of policy." The SCAD maintained that "quotas may establish an apparent immediate gain; they almost invariably result in long-term loss so far as the purposes of the Law Against Discrimination are concerned. The history of so-called minimums becoming maximums is far too persuasive to be overlooked."[30]

The SCAD did not give detailed reports for these cases, but most of them followed the pattern of local civic groups engaged in sporadic direct-action projects.[31] The major civil rights groups did not

NYSDHR Library; Stenographic Transcript of the Proceedings Before the President's Committee on Government Contract Compliance, Washington, D.C., July 15, 1952, p. 182, in George B. Meany Archives, Collection 25, Box 7, Silver Spring, Md.

30. NYSCAD *1949 Annual Report,* 26; *1950 Annual Report,* 44–45; *1951 Annual Report,* 33; *1955 Annual Report,* 57; Cater, "Policies and Practices," 67; SCAD LB 17, May 1, 1948, LB 31, September 1, 1949, LB 39, March 1, 1950, LB 51, March 1, 1951, NYSDHR Library.

31. The fact that the SCAD did not publish detailed reports about successful cases, or issue statistical summaries, was a major criticism made by civil rights groups. The original SCAD case files from 1945–1950 were almost completely destroyed, and after 1950 only a random sample is preserved in the New York State Archives in Albany.

defend them; the NAACP support of the *Hughes* plaintiffs seems to be unusual. It was apparent that this style of "segregation without discrimination," preserving jobs in black areas for blacks only, was counterproductive. But the idea of a fair share or of racial proportionalism in the nation at large, a kind of extension of local direct action, was more appealing. Civil rights groups' desire to have the SCAD account for minority participation at all levels in industry-wide investigations shows that the national organizations, while eschewing local segregation-without-discrimination, were not adverse to race-conscious remedies to employment discrimination.

The SCAD disposition of the General Motors cases reveals the way it worked in the 1950s. In 1956, eight complaints regarding hiring and promotions were brought against General Motors plants in Tarrytown, New York. The absence of black foremen and clerical workers was the principal indication of discrimination. Complainants also charged that GM maintained a quota system to keep the ratio of black workers to a low level. The SCAD investigated the entire employment picture at the GM plants, explained the disproportion as based on valid, non-racial reasons, particularly union seniority over which the employer had no control. The SCAD recommended that the company broaden its recruitment base for white collar jobs. It found GM in substantial but not full compliance with the LAD, "certainly not the kind of compliance which one would hope for in a giant industrial organization which is so much the symbol of American genius and enterprise." As in the railroad cases, the SCAD was unable to interfere with the operation of a seniority system that perpetuated the effects of past discrimination, despite the desire of some commissioners to attack seniority, because state FEP laws did not define these practices as illegal. FEPCs often found more difficulty dealing with labor unions than with employers, especially since organized labor was one of the principal supporters of fair employment legislation while the business community usually opposed its enactment.[32]

32. *Johnson* v. *Fisher Body Division,* 2 R.R.L.R. (1957), 542–51; Transcript of the Proceedings Before the President's Committee on Government Contract Compliance, Meany Archives; Richard B. Couser, "The California FEPC: Stepchild of the State Agencies," *Stanford Law Review* XVIII (1965), 187–212.

The flexibility of the SCAD's powers, however, can be seen in the 1955 brewery cases. Black drivers brought complaints against the Teamsters and the brewery owners, claiming that they had not been given a fair share of referrals in delivery jobs and, as a result, had been unable to acquire a higher level of seniority. The SCAD found probable cause in their complaints, and brought the Teamsters to a public hearing in 1955, the first time in which a union had reached this stage. Before the commission went to court to enforce its order, the four local unions agreed to sign a consent decree. While the SCAD refused to implement a complainant's demand that a minimum number of Negroes be established in the Group II seniority category, it did secure this seniority benefit for nineteen black drivers who had been the victims of discriminatory referrals. While the commission could not redress the effects of seniority system discrimination that took place before 1945, it could order that victims of discrimination that took place after the enactment of the LAD be given the places they had been denied by discriminatory treatment.[33]

Defending the slow progress of the 1950s, Elmer Carter, the commissioner who handled the GM cases, noted, "It is not that change does not occur but that it is apt to occur so slowly as not to be readily observable. Acceleration of change depends to a great extent upon the vigor with which the Negro and other groups pursue their rights and seek the redress provided by the law when they are denied." He remarked privately,

> Speaking personally, I would like to point out that the GM cases and all of our cases support this thesis—that no real test of the opportunities which exist for Negroes can be made unless there are Negroes willing to make the sacrifice to attain the skills and be measured by the same unit of measurement that other men are measured by. This requires, for the most part, some sacrifices, but I have never known an individual or a race that was economically disadvantaged who attained stature and status without sacrifice. This, to my mind, is the ultimate test of character.

33. NYSCAD, *1955 Annual Report,* 57–58, 94–97; SCAD LB 86, February 1, 1954, LB 125, November 1, 1964, NYSDHR Library.

Carter concluded, "If there is not reason for exultation, there is reason for confidence and assurance that the ideal of equality of opportunity can be achieved in our country."[34]

Carter's approach to the problem of employment discrimination rested on two assumptions. First, the fact that racism and discrimination were endemic in American life called for a cautious, conciliatory effort to encourage compliance with the LAD. The second assumption was that the pace of progress depended upon the extent to which minorities strived and availed themselves of the services of the SCAD. These ideas, tenable at mid-decade, undergirded decisions like those in the railroad and GM cases. The civil rights groups' critique rested on two opposite assumptions. They held that endemic racism called for aggressive enforcement, and that the SCAD's failure to adopt such a program caused minorities to lose faith in the commission. This critique, in abeyance at mid-decade, had not been effectively answered and would return in the 1960s.

Carter's standard of equal treatment appears to have been the one applied by most state commissions in the postwar years. While the results of this approach are disputed, it is fairly certain that the state FEPCs opened opportunities for a substantial number of black Americans to rise to positions commensurate with their talents and merits. They were particularly effective at opening clerical and white-collar jobs to increase the ranks of the black middle class. While the state FEPCs and equal treatment helped enlarge the black middle class, and opened unskilled jobs to blacks, their very success may have whetted appetites for more, for increased demands that the commissions were unwilling to meet.[35]

When the powers of the SCAD were challenged in the New York courts, they were resoundingly affirmed. In the 1953 case of *Holland v. Edwards* Judge Francis Bergan of the New York Supreme Court, upheld by the court of appeals, confirmed the commission's finding

34. Carter, "Practical Considerations," 58; Carter to Dean Chamberlain, March 5, 1955, in 10409–84 A, Box 24, NYS Archives.

35. E. Franklin Frazier, *Black Bourgeoisie: The Rise of a New Middle Class in the United States* (New York, 1957), 47; Gelber, *Black Men and Businessmen*, 82, 90, 111; James Rorty, "FEPC in the States: A Progress Report," *Antioch Review*, XVIII (1958), 317–29.

of discrimination by an employment agency that inquired into an applicant's change of name. The court upheld the SCAD's investigatory powers and its administrative procedures, accepting its findings as "substantial evidence" which the court had to regard as conclusive. To the agency's contention that the name change inquiry was not intended to discriminate, the court answered, "Discrimination in selection for employment based on considerations of race, creed, or color is quite apt to be a matter of refined and elusive subtlety. Innocent components can add up to a sinister totality." The court gave the commission the widest possible latitude in administering the law, noting that the legislature delegated immense power to the commission, and that "in the field of discrimination as defined by the statute the jurisdiction of the Commission must be taken as plenary." Similarly, the law gave the courts extraordinary power to issue orders enforcing the commission's findings. The LAD had placed the courts in a position of unusual discretion, greater than that usually assumed by courts in administrative law, with "an unusual measure of judicial supervision and a shared judicial responsibility." The unanimous decision on the part of New York's highest court supporting Judge Bergan's judgment showed that there would be no legal impediments to the SCAD's operation.[36]

Two years later the appellate division of the New York Supreme Court narrowly upheld a SCAD decision to dismiss a complaint for lack of probable cause. In this case, Pan American Airlines rejected Wendell Jeanpierre, a black pilot, on the grounds of his work history—having held eighteen different jobs in the previous sixteen years. Jeanpierre argued that this was merely a pretext and that his race was the reason for the rejection. When the SCAD dismissed his complaint, he sued to compel it to pursue his case. The supreme court judge refused, holding that the courts had no jurisdiction until the SCAD issued an order after a public hearing. The appellate division affirmed this decision, three to two. The two dissenters argued that the court had the power to review the SCAD decisions at any point in its proceedings, and that it should reverse the SCAD's judgment in this case. The dissenters made much of the "suspicious" fact that Pan Am employed no Negroes in flight capacities.

---

36. *Holland v. Edwards*, 122 N.Y.S.2d 721 (1953); 119 N.E.2d 581 (1954).

The complete absence of minority group members was not itself proof of discrimination, they understood, but in this case there was more evidence than this disparity to suggest that discrimination took place—Pan Am attempted to dissuade Jeanpierre from seeking the job, citing the many southerners who worked as pilots and stewards and the personal difficulty Jeanpierre would face with his co-workers. Even if Jeanpierre's particular case was not sustainable, the overall pattern of Negro exclusion by Pan Am and other airlines merited closer scrutiny. The SCAD essentially admitted this, since it continued to engage in conference and negotiation with Pan Am after it dismissed Jeanpierre's complaint. Without a formal complaint, however, the commission could not resort to public hearings or court orders in these negotiations. In dismissing the complaint the commission had discarded its "teeth," and the dissenters regarded this as "an improvident exercise of discretion and was arbitrary, capricious, and unreasonable."[37]

The dissenters argued that the SCAD was willing to let Pan Am use the complainant's work history as a pretext for discrimination—in other words, the commission applied not an "equal treatment" but a "reasonable treatment" standard, in which any non-racial reason given would be acceptable. "By this reasoning, a complainant, in order to prevail, must be virtually perfect in all respects," one sociologist noted. "He must meet a theoretical rather than an actual standard," one to which white applicants or employees were not held. The SCAD may have applied a reasonable treatment standard in other cases, but the records of this case indicate that the commission made the comparisons requisite for an equal treatment standard. The effectiveness of the state FEPCs in the 1950s could be determined by the extent to which they applied the equal treatment standard required by law or lapsed into a reasonable treatment standard. A systematic study of this kind has never been undertaken, however, and sufficient evidence may not exist to do so.[38]

The dissenters in *Jeanpierre* wanted to push the SCAD beyond its

37. *Jeanpierre v. Arbury*, 1 R.R.L.R. 685 (1956); 162 N.Y.S.2d 506 (1957); Higbee, *Development and Administration*, 250.

38. Leon Mayhew, *Law and Equal Opportunity: A Study of the Massachusetts Commission Against Discrimination* (Cambridge, Mass., 1968), 200–201; SCAD MOL 85 (1955); LB 40, April 1, 1950, LB 52, April 1, 1951, NYSDHR Library.

self-imposed limits. The SCAD did not render findings of probable cause unless it was fairly certain that the case would be sustained in the courts based on evidence at a public hearing. This was the reason that so few legal appeals were made, and that the SCAD was so successful—it pursued only ironclad cases. In more ambiguous cases, which were the majority, the commission relied on informal negotiation and voluntary compliance. The dissenters in *Jeanpierre* felt that this was too lax an approach for the SCAD to take, and that the LAD required the commission to do more. Echoing the criticisms of the Committee to Support the Ives-Quinn Act, the dissenters charged that the commission attempted "to avoid the full discharge of the duty imposed upon it because compliance may prove embarrassing, distasteful, or even troublesome to an employer." While the majority confirmed the SCAD's procedures, the significant dissent suggested that far from acting as a bridle, judicial review might serve as a goad to the SCAD.

It was ironic that the courts might be more aggressive than the commission in enforcing the antidiscrimination laws. Ever since the New Deal, liberal reformers favored administrative agencies like the NLRB, which could investigate, prosecute, and decide cases with only limited judicial review. The New York SCAD had all the powers of such an agency. Individuals had no personal right to equal treatment, but could appeal unfavorable decisions of the commission. However, except in cases of arbitrary or capricious administration, the courts deferred to the administrators. The idea that courts were better able to protect individual rights than administrative bodies was implicit in the dissenters' opinion in *Jeanpierre*. Likewise, criticism of the substantive rules adopted by the state FEPCs, rather than the administrative structure of the statutes under which they operated, foreshadowed the main problem of the state agencies in their second decade.

6   Fair Employment in New York, 1955–1965

The legal strategy used to oppose racial discrimination in employment changed radically in the second decade of state FEPC operation, 1955–1965. The state FEPCs reacted to a changing social and economic environment, including important alterations in the outlook of the civil rights movement and a slowdown in the economic advancement of black Americans. After 1954 and the *Brown* case, the expectations of the civil rights movement expanded greatly. During this time, however, the economic advances that backs achieved in the period between 1940 and 1955 were not sustained. Consequently demands arose for a more aggressive, result-oriented fair employment policy. The New York state commission's strict, formal insistence on color-blind application of fair employment practices gave way to a strategy of social engineering that relied on benevolent color-consciousness to obtain equal outcomes.

The Supreme Court's decisions in *Brown* v. *Board of Education* in 1954 and 1955 marked a watershed in the modern civil rights movement. Although it appeared to repudiate *Plessy* v. *Ferguson* and to vindicate the idea of a color-blind Constitution, *Brown* was actually an ambiguous decision that did much to facilitate later experiments with "benevolent" racial classifications. The Court had the opportunity explicitly to overturn *Plessy* and forbid all racial classifications but did not, fearing political repercussions. Desiring to maintain unanimity and avoid unnecessary antagonism among southerners and those who must implement the decision, it handed down a decision that obscured more than it revealed. In addition, the Court provided little explanation or recommendation for implementation. As one jurist remarked: "If segregated schools were not constitutional, what kinds of schools were? Was the evil segregation itself or merely the state's imposition of it? Was a color-blind society or the betterment of an oppressed race the Court's chief objective?" It remained unclear whether racial classification was a categorical or a contingent wrong. Despite later elaboration and extension, the Court never held that racial classifications were per se unconstitutional. The Court's reluctance to lay down a color-blind rule avoided political conflict and also preserved "its power to pick and choose among racial classifications."[1]

The departure from a color-blind principle was even more evident in the second *Brown* decision of 1955. This decision, allowing state authorities to delay their desegregation of schools, held that black students who suffered from segregation had no individual rights apart from the right of their race to desegregated education. This was a marked departure from the professional school decisions of 1950, where the Court ordered immediate relief to individual plaintiffs. This aspect of the decision suggested that "Negroes (unlike whites) possess rights as a race rather than as individuals, so that a particular Negro can rightfully be delayed in the enjoyment of his established rights if progress is being made in improving the legal status of Negroes generally." State FEPCs had felt the tension between individual and group rights approaches to the problem of employment discrimination, and *Brown* tended to support group rights. This reluctance to declare and enforce a strict color-blind constitutional rule not only delayed the desegregation of southern schools for over a decade, but helped make possible the application of color-conscious remedies in education, voting, and employment after 1965.[2]

1. *Brown* v. *Board of Education,* 347 U.S. 483 (1954); 349 U.S. 294 (1955); Lofgren, *The Plessy Case,* 200–205; Kull, *The Color-Blind Constitution,* 155, 171; J. Harvie Wilkinson, III, *From "Brown" to "Bakke": The Supreme Court and School Integration, 1954–78* (New York, 1979), 29.

2. Louis Lusky, "The Stereotype: Hard Core of Racism," *Buffalo Law Review,* XIII (1963), 458; Diane Ravitch, *The Troubled Crusade: American Education, 1945–80* (New York, 1983), 129; Wilkinson, *From "Brown" to "Bakke,"* 66–67; Terry Eastland and William J. Bennett, *Counting by Race: Equality from the Founding Fathers to "Bakke"* (New York, 1979), 120–23.

The arguments in *Brown* revealed a conflict between color-blind legalism and color-conscious sociology. Civil rights lawyers in *Brown* argued for a color-blind rule under the Fourteenth Amendment, but the social science evidence they used to support their case suggested that this might not be possible. The constitutional argument that desegregation could be achieved by forbidding all state-imposed racial classifications in some ways clashed with the sociological argument that desegregation must be replaced by integration which might require racial classification. The failure of the Court to announce a comprehensive color-blind rule may not have disappointed some civil rights activists. It had been part of the assault on segregation to insist on substantial equality in segregated education, and thus make segregation too expensive for the South to maintain. Thurgood Marshall, who argued the *Brown* case before the Supreme Court, had shown his willingness to defend quota demands for employment in the Baltimore and Richmond picketing cases, and remained flexible on the issue of racial classifications. Marshall and many other civil rights lawyers had been trained in the theory of legal activism taught by Charles Hamilton Houston at Howard University Law School. Houston, himself trained in the school of sociological jurisprudence of Roscoe Pound, taught that black Americans could use the legal process to vindicate rights that were unattainable for a minority group through the political process. "Given an immoral America," Houston's biographer has written, "the NAACP campaign required that lawyer–social engineers use the Constitution, statutes, and 'whatever science demonstrates or imagination invents' both to foster and to order social change for a more humane society." While nothing in Houstonian jurisprudence required the choice of benevolent color-consciousness over color-blindness, the theory of social engineering facilitated the step of replacing the formalism of desegregation with the more ambitious task of integration. As Charles Abrams, chairman of the New York State Commission Against Discrimination from 1955 to 1959, said of *Brown*, "When the Supreme Court ordered desegregation, it not only shattered the unsavory separate but equal doctrine but also exposed the more savory doctrine of 'color blindness' to reexamination." *Brown* had the potential to move the antidiscrimination effort in employment past the color-blind procedural fairness doctrine applied by the state FEPCs in their first decade toward a race-conscious equal outcome plan of social engineering.[3]

Another development that fueled calls for new antidiscrimination approaches was the stalling of rapid black economic improvement since 1940. Much postwar progress resulted from the movement of the South's rural black population into industrial jobs in northern cities, but long-term changes in American economic and social structure made this route less helpful to black migrants of the 1950s. The American economy became less production-oriented, as service employment outnumbered production employment for the first time. Heavy industries like autos and steel were reducing their unskilled industrial work forces, and a larger proportion of the American civilian work force was organized in the mid-1950s than ever before or after. Union seniority rules meant that recently-hired black workers were the first to be laid off in economic downturns, causing blacks to bear a disproportionate burden of general economic distress. Moreover, American urbanization was also on the wane, with suburban population exceeding urban population for the first time in the mid-1950s. These changes resulted partly from policy choices made in Washington and the cities which aggravated urban social problems. From the standpoint of social policy, the migrants were moving to the city at the wrong point in history.[4]

Specific economic indicators demonstrated the problem. The black unemployment rate was at its historic low point in 1953 at 4.5 percent, and at an all-time low relative to the white unemployment rate at a ratio of 1.7 to 1. In 1955 the black unemployment rate jumped to 8.7 percent. This was lower than the previous year,

3. Ravitch, *Troubled Crusade,* 126; McNeil, *Groundwork,* 84, 116, 133, 216–17; Address of Charles Abrams before the Teachers Guild on the Occasion of the Presentation of the John Dewey Award to Thurgood Marshall, March 2, 1957, in NAACP Papers, III-J-6.

4. Polenberg, *One Nation Divisible,* 127–63; Edward C. Banfield, *The Unheavenly City Revisited* (Boston, 1974), 14; Joel Schwartz, *The New York Approach: Robert Moses, Urban Liberals, and Redevelopment of the Inner City* (Columbus, Ohio, 1993), 229; Timothy Bates, "Black Economic Well-Being Since the 1950s," *The Review of Black Political Economy,* XII (1984), 17.

but marked the first time in which the black unemployment rate was more than double the white rate, where it remained for the next ten years and, with some dips, has continued to the present. Black and white incomes were closest in 1954, with median non-white family income at over 56 percent of the white income level. By 1958 this had fallen to under 50 percent, and did not show any sustained improvement until the mid-1960s when it exceeded 60 percent regularly. Black migration out of the South continued, as the ratio of nonwhite to white income in the region collapsed from 46 percent to 33 percent between 1953 and 1959. While the ratio of nonwhite to white median income rose slightly in the north-central and western regions of the country in these years, it actually fell from 75 percent to 72 percent in the Northeast. The decline in relative economic improvement by the mid-1950s, and the inability of northern cities to renew it, was an important development leading to new demands on the northern FEPCs.[5]

The mid-1950s heralded a quickening of the civil rights movement. Dr. Martin Luther King, Jr.'s Montgomery, Alabama, bus boycott of 1955–1956 marked the arrival of a dynamic leader in the struggle against formal segregation. The Little Rock desegregation crisis in 1957 marked the first introduction of federal troops for civil rights enforcement since Reconstruction. Likewise the Civil Rights Act of 1957, which strengthened judicial protection of voting rights and created the Commission on Civil Rights, was the first congressional recognition of the civil rights issue in the twentieth century. While the federal government was slowly but surely taking steps to address racial problems in the South, race relations problems were becoming increasingly national. The civil rights issues of the North, within a framework of economic disparity, were employment discrimination and segregation in schools and housing.

5. U.S. Department of Commerce, *Historical Statistics*, I, 135, 303; Norval D. Glenn, "Some Changes in the Relative Status of American Nonwhites, 1940–60," *Phylon*, XXIV (1963), 109–22; James P. Smith and Finis Welch, "Black Economic Progress After Myrdal," *Journal of Economic Literature*, XXVII (1989), 519–64; Bates, "Black Economic Well-Being," 7, 11, 17; Richard B. Freeman, "Changes in the Labor Market for Black Americans, 1948–72," *Brookings Papers on Economic Activity* (Washington, D.C., 1973), 80.

New York expanded the scope of its Law Against Discrimination to include public accommodations in 1952, public housing in 1955, and age discrimination (workers aged forty-five to sixty-five) in 1958. New York's Democratic governor, Averell Harriman, endorsed a stronger civil rights program in his 1954 campaign, which included giving the SCAD the power to initiate a discrimination suit without an individual complaint. Harriman's first step toward strengthening the SCAD was to appoint Charles Abrams as chairman in 1955.[6]

Abrams was one of the foremost advocates of benevolent race-consciousness in the late 1950s, and a well-known expert on urban housing problems who believed that minority employment gains were being held back by their residential concentration in urban ghettoes. In particular, civil rights groups often supported racial set-asides in public housing as a means of maintaining integration. If housing places were allotted by need, and most of the needy were nonwhite, public housing would quickly become all nonwhite. In order to foster integration, minority group proportions had to be kept below the "tipping point"—the point beyond which "white flight" ensued. When accused of endorsing violations of civil rights principles for purposes of integration, Abrams warned against an overweening regard for individual rights and color-blindness. Instead, he stressed the need for the social engineer to be color-conscious, since "the public administrator like the painter cannot mix colors unless he looks at them first." He denounced "an atmosphere in which public officials loosely hurl words around like 'quota system' the minute anyone tries to desegregate." Quotas were "wicked catch-words," he warned, used by foes of desegregation. Abrams was not alone in trying to avoid the issue. "Organizations committed to fighting for minorities and/or civil rights in general," one commentator noted, "exhibit a carefully thought-out sort of schizophrenia: it's okay to use a quota—in fact, it's necessary—but you should never talk about it."[7]

6. Higbee, *Development and Administration,* xiv; New York *Times,* September 26, 1954, p. 58.

7. Victor Navasky, "The Benevolent Housing Quota," *Howard Law Journal,* VI (1960), 30–68 (quote, 45); Isaac N. Grover and David M. Helfeld, "Race Discrimination in Housing," *Yale Law Journal,* LVII (1948), 426–58; Jack Greenberg, *Race Relations*

In the early 1960s defenses of the benevolent housing quota became more common, and legal theorists began to articulate a defense of race-consciousness and group rights. They noted, accurately, that the Court had never outlawed racial classifications per
se, but only unreasonable, invidious ones. Racial classifications
could be used for benevolent purposes, to compensate for the effects of past discrimination. It would be tragic if the Fourteenth
Amendment, only recently turned to its true purpose of racial
equality in *Brown*, were now turned against practical plans for
integration. To freeze the Constitution in the rules of color-
blindness and individual rights would be the triumph of formal-
ist, mechanical jurisprudence. Quotas could be used as a temporary expedient, recognizing that the choice was between perpetual
segregation or integration by social control. The use of quotas recognized the reality of group rights; to insist on the individual
Negro's right to housing was tantamount to insisting on the individual worker's right to contract as a bar against labor organizations.
Alexander M. Bickel, one of the nation's leading constitutionalists,
concluded, "For the moment, unless and until experience should
belie the hope that may animate benevolent quota proposals or
demonstrate that, rather than a possibly progressive expedient,
they are a retrogressive one, benevolent quotas should be allowed
their season of leeway, without offense to principle." Yet the issue
embarrassed Abrams, who felt that a complicated subject was being
used as political slogan against him. He advised against a public
discussion of the issue, however, and sought a statement indicating that the SCAD did not approve of quotas. As the executive director of the Commission on Intergroup Relations put it, "Apparently there is a very real danger that the laws originally intended to
guard against the use of any public aids and powers to reinforce or
extend racial segregation may now actually become instruments to

---

in American Law (New York, 1959); Philip G. Auerbach and Murray C. Goldman,
"Racial Discrimination in Housing," *University of Pennsylvania Law Review*, CVII
(1959), 515–50; "Benign Quotas: A Plan for Integrated Private Housing," *Yale Law
Journal*, LXX (1960), 126–34; New York *Times*, May 14, 1956, March 3, 1957, p. 62,
January 27, 1964, p. 16; Address of Charles Abrams before the Teachers Guild,
NAACP Papers; Whitney Young, *To Be Equal* (New York, 1964), 147.

effect racial segregation in publicly aided housing developments."[8]

Abrams drew the fire of Oswald Heck, Schenectady Republican and speaker of the New York State Assembly. Heck and others regarded Abrams as a "political appointee" and unfit for the job. "He's too much of a zealot; he isn't balanced in such a sensitive job," Heck said. The legislature refused Abrams' request for additional funds for the SCAD and for the power to initiate complaints, instead cutting the SCAD's budget. Governor Harriman defended Abrams, declaring that he, too, was a "zealot" when it came to civil rights.[9]

Abrams' program for employment consisted of increased powers for the SCAD, especially the powers to initiate investigations without a complaint, to publicize successful cases, and to root out token compliance with the law. To deal with black economic stagnation in the late 1950s, civil rights advocates increasingly looked toward industry-wide, pattern-centered efforts that would focus on the overall minority-group participation rate. The success of the state FEPCs in their early years had made discrimination harder to detect, and they would have to rely more on inferences from statistical imbalances. A significant imbalance in a work force should constitute a prima facie case of discrimination and shift the burden of proof onto the respondent. Although cunning tokenism would remain difficult to combat, shifting the burden of proof onto the employer would be more effective than proceeding on an individual basis.[10]

Legal scholars at this time were articulating the concept of "group rights." Beginning with the idea of Roscoe Pound that the

8. Oscar Cohen, "The Case for Benign Quotas in Housing," *Phylon,* XXI (1960), 20–29; William E. Hellerstein, "The Benign Quota, Equal Protection, and the Rule in Shelley's Case," *Rutgers Law Review,* VII (1963), 531–61; Boris I. Bittker, "The Case of the Checker-Board Ordinance: An Experiment in Race Relations," *Yale Law Journal,* LXXI (1962), 1387–1423; Alexander M. Bickel, *The Least Dangerous Branch: The Supreme Court at the Bar of Politics* (New Haven, 1962), 71; Memorandum for Conference with Mayor, May 28, 1956, Frank S. Horne to Herbert Bayard Swope, May 24, 1956, in Charles Abrams Papers, Reel 16, John M. Olin Library, Cornell University; SCAD LB 201, September 1, 1963, NYSDHR Library.

9. Transcript of Heck Interview, April 29, 1956, in Abrams Papers, Reel 16; New York *Times,* March 2, 1956, p. 1; March 5, 1956, p. 16; March 8, 1956, p. 28; April 30, 1956, p. 15; May 13, 1956, p. 50.

10. Irving Kovarsky, "A Review of State FEPC Laws," *Labor Law Journal,* IX (1958), 478–94.

law should recognize and try to balance individual and societal interests, Thomas Cowan advocated the legal recognition of intermediary associations like labor unions. This extension of New Deal interest-group politics to legal principle could have significant consequences for racial and ethnic relations. Some civil rights advocates were wary of the embrace of group rights rather than the individual rights philosophy among their allies. Group rights had been the concept championed by segregationists and white supremacists, while liberals based their demands on individual rights and the idea that the state should not recognize racial group identity in the law. Applying "benign" or "benevolent" quotas was a retrogressive step which might become invidious, and should only be embraced as an intermediate step.[11]

In accord with the group-rights theory, and the suggestion of civil rights groups that redressing individual cases of discrimination "should not be considered the sole or indeed the most effective way of eliminating discriminatory practices," Abrams focused the SCAD on industry-wide investigations into New York airline, banking, and railroad operations. This was not an entirely new tactic, as the SCAD had since its inception used an individual complaint to review and reform larger employment practices. Abrams, telling the governor that the "SCAD is not a popular agency among minority groups, and is very unpopular in some," would have gone farther, but the commission's limited budget, personnel, and lack of power to initiate prosecution restricted him. In addition, the administration was cautious about "possible populist actions against antidiscrimination laws, and a possible concert of action in less enlightened areas of the state against expanding the agency's power and funds." Nevertheless, Abrams was the most popular SCAD chairman among civil rights groups, and Harriman often referred to this appointee as an indication of his earnest concern for civil rights.[12]

11. Robert A. Horn, *Groups and the Constitution* (New York, 1956); Thomas A. Cowan, "Group Interests," *Virginia Law Review,* XLIV (1958), 331–46; Blumrosen, *Modern Law,* 82; Jack Greenberg, "Race Relations and Group Interests in the Law," *Rutgers Law Review,* XIII (1959), 503–10.

12. Memorandum for the Governor's Statement before the NAACP, November 30, 1956, Averell Harriman to Charles Abrams, December 20, 1958, in Abrams Papers, Reel 4; Abrams to Harriman, January 4, 1956, Shad Polier to Abrams, December 20, 1955, April 14, 1958, in Abrams Papers, Reel 16.

The legislature proposed to spend an additional $100,000 to establish a civil rights bureau in the attorney general's office which would take over the SCAD's court enforcement work. Republicans were responding to the call for civil rights enforcement, claiming that the attorney general's office would give the commission more powerful legal sanction, while respecting their aversion to the SCAD acting as "judge, jury and prosecutor." Civil rights groups, Abrams, and Harriman opposed this plan, feeling that it would only divide and dilute antidiscrimination efforts, and "politicize" civil rights in the attorney general's office. The attorney general already had the power to bring complaints to the SCAD, a power which he had never exercised. Harriman ultimately vetoed the bill, and the NAACP expressed its support, commiserating that it was an awkward step to veto a bill increasing civil rights appropriations as a pro–civil rights measure.[13]

Nelson Rockefeller became governor of New York in 1959, and Charles Abrams resigned as SCAD chairman. Rockefeller appointed longtime SCAD commissioner Elmer Carter to the chairmanship. The contrast between the men was apparent, Carter seen as diligent, patient, and fair while Abrams was the confrontational, controversial zealot. Carter was associated with the relatively conservative National Urban League, having served as editor of *Opportunity,* its newspaper. But he had also led the New York picketing-for-jobs campaign with Adam Clayton Powell in the late 1930s. As a commissioner, he worked within the formal, legal confines of the LAD, but also worked informally to gain some consideration for past discrimination. His respect for individual self-reliance and merit employment, evinced in the General Motors cases, showed his traditional, bourgeois, Booker T. Washington style. Believing that equality would come but slowly, he was swimming against the tide of the civil rights movement.[14]

The early 1960s marked a turning point in the civil rights movement. The Greensboro, North Carolina, sit-ins protesting segrega-

13. "Appeal to Reaction Seen in Attack on New York Commission Officer," February 21, 1957, Roy Wilkins to Averell H. Harriman, May 2, 1957, in NAACP Papers, III-A-190; Charles Abrams to Herbert Hill, March 18, 1958, in NAACP Papers, III-A-191; Harriman to Udell Hicks and Grover Glenn, July 6, 1956, in Abrams Papers, Reel 4.

14. New York *Times,* January 28, 1959, p. 19.

tion in public accommodations continued the use of direct action begun in the 1950s by the Southern Christian Leadership Conference (SCLC). Charismatic new leaders like James Farmer at the Congress of Racial Equality (CORE) and Whitney Young at the NUL led the organizations in new directions. Civil rights groups turned to the North in the 1960s, and to the problems of housing and employment. Demanding equality of outcome rather than just equality of opportunity, the groups also became more race-conscious and racially exclusive.[15]

The civil rights organizations became increasingly responsive to the demands of the mass of black Americans. The new civil rights agenda put an emphasis on equality of outcome because of the emerging problem of the "underclass," the isolated, impoverished ghetto population in northern cities. Only a program of compensatory treatment, one that not only ended discrimination but made up for the effects of the discrimination of the past, could help this group. Merit employment and equality of opportunity, it was argued, would actually frustrate the necessary programs. The traditional civil rights insistence on color-blindness would have to be rejected in favor of a color-conscious obligation. Having achieved a measure of political power, black Americans began to demand preferential treatment and recognition of group entitlements, based on the assumption of proportionalism.[16]

Whitney Young was the most prominent civil rights leader advocating the new agenda. His public statements recognized that "if the United States drops legal, practical, and subtle racial barriers in employment, housing and education, public accommodations, health and welfare facilities, the American Negro still will not achieve full equality in our lifetime." Calling for an extraordinary effort, a

15. August Meier and Elliot Rudwick, *CORE: A Study in the Civil Rights Movement, 1942–68* (New York, 1973), 124, 183–88; Meier and Rudwick, *Along the Color Line,* 380; "The Negro Drive for Jobs," *Business Week,* August 17, 1963, p. 52.

16. Nat Hentoff, *The New Equality* (New York, 1965), 89–95; Joseph B. Robison, "Giving Reality to the Promise of Job Equality," *Law in Transition Quarterly,* I (1964), 104–17; Richard Lichtman, "The Ethics of Compensatory Justice," *Law in Transition Quarterly,* I (1964), 76–103; Samuel Krislov, *The Negro in Federal Employment: The Quest for Equal Opportunity* (Minneapolis, 1967), 144; Daniel Bell, "Reflections on the Negro and Labor," *The New Leader,* January 21, 1963, p. 18.

"Domestic Marshall Plan," to rescue the underclass, the Urban League recognized that this program appeared to conflict with the principle of equal treatment, but denied that this implied preferential treatment for minorities. Internally the NUL understood "that the traditional concept of equal opportunity is not sufficient. Our basic definition of equal opportunity must be broadened and deepened to include recognition of the need for special effort to overcome serious disabilities resulting from historic handicaps." Indemnification would have to be part of the program, to provide reparations to black Americans for past discrimination. The Urban League limited its language of compensation and reparation in public, but Young wrote, "This approach suggests that if a business has never hired Negroes in its offices or plants and two equally qualified people apply, it should hire the Negro to redress the injustice previously visited upon him." Business had "to place qualified Negroes—because they are Negroes—in entrance jobs in all types of employment and in positions of responsibility." But even conscientious employers would soon realize that there were not sufficient numbers of equally qualified black applicants, and then they would have to take on added efforts of making them qualified.[17]

Young noted that "America's prime mover corporations, those businesses and industrial giants noted for progressive policies, have adopted or will soon adopt affirmative action programs to integrate their work forces." In 1963, General Motors took up Young's suggestion of preference for equally qualified blacks, the Dallas Post Office gave preferential treatment for supervisory positions to black workers who had scored lower on civil service exams, and Pitney-Bowes announced a plan for preferential hiring. However, as the Urban League moderated its public statements about compensatory treatment, so did Pitney-Bowes clarify its policy, stating that while

17. "A Statement Urging a Crash Program of Special Effort to Close the Gap Between the Conditions of Negro and White Citizens," Working Draft No. 3, April 8, 1963, "Proposed 'Marshall Plan,'" July 19, 1963, in NUL Papers, II-I-A-38; Young, *To Be Equal,* 22, 29, 61, 65; Sterling Tucker, "The Role of Civil Rights Organizations: A 'Marshall Plan' Approach," *Boston College Industrial and Commercial Law Review,* VII (1966), 617–23; Graham, *Civil Rights,* 111–12; Charles E. Silberman, *Crisis in Black and White* (New York, 1964), 235–48.

special efforts would be taken to recruit and train Negroes, no preference based on race was being given. Both President Kennedy and Governor Rockefeller of New York made statements in 1963 against the use of racial quotas in an antidiscrimination program. Even the groups most willing to take up the program of preferential treatment advanced their ideas carefully, paying deference to the traditional understanding of civil rights and equal opportunity while they tried to change it.[18]

While national civil rights groups were cautious in their proposals for national programs, local organizations revived the use of boycotting and picketing for employment quotas seen in the 1930s. The revival began in the late 1950s in St. Louis, where voluntary agreements led to the hiring of some black workers. The *Hughes* decision limited the privilege of picketing for illegal purposes, and in many states FEPC laws made quota hiring contrary to public policy. The law in most states in 1960s was even more hostile to direct action for employment quotas than it had been in the 1930s.[19]

The Fair Share Organization in Indiana began picketing local retailers in 1959. The state courts enjoined it, and noted that Justice Roger Traynor's dissenting opinion in *Hughes* defending the right to picket for employment quotas did not apply in a state such as Indiana which had an antidiscrimination law. The U.S. Supreme Court declined to review the Indiana cases. Similarly, CORE efforts to compel racial hiring in St. Louis were thwarted, with state and federal courts noting that the demands made violated the state law against discrimination in employment. The federal court noted that "the whole tenor of their demand was one of discrimination." The Washington, D.C., branch of CORE was stopped from petitioning

18. Young, *To Be Equal,* 67; New York *Times,* September 30, 1963, p. 30, December 4, 1963, p. 37, December 13, 1963, p. 28; Hentoff, *New Equality,* 110–11; *Wall Street Journal,* August 12, 1963, p. 1; Graham, *Civil Rights,* 106–108.

19. Meier and Rudwick, *CORE,* 93; Gelber, *Black Men and Businessmen,* 150–56; "The Common-Law and Constitutional Status of Antidiscrimination Boycotts," *Yale Law Journal,* LXVI (1957), 397–412; Sanford Jay Rosen, "The Law and Racial Discrimination in Employment," *California Law Review,* LIII (1965), 729–99; Harold M. Weiner, "Negro Picketing for Employment Equality," *Howard Law Journal,* XIII (1967), 271–302.

the Potomac Electric Power Company for jobs by what a federal judge called "a minor form of sabotage" that went beyond the peaceful New Negro Alliance picketing of the 1930s. The New York courts enforced an injunction against an NAACP effort to compel Harlem liquor retailers to buy from black wholesalers, and the judge said of the NAACP effort, "Their active or even tacit approval of this anathematized intolerance, racial discrimination in connection with employment is beyond understanding." In states with fair employment laws, however, picketing which did not demand a specific quota, but merely protested discrimination, was protected, and civil rights groups successfully used boycotting, which did not involve the legal problems of picketing, to win jobs.[20]

Direct action was not only legally difficult, but achieved only local, small-scale results and required popular discipline. Most civil rights activists believed fair employment agencies could be more effective in ameliorating the complex problem of employment discrimination because of their scope, administrative flexibility, and ability to innovate. Nine states and the District of Columbia added fair employment laws in the years 1964–1965, and sixteen states extended or reinforced their statutes. If most of the obvious, blatant expressions of racial discrimination in employment had effectively been ended, subtler forms of discrimination remained, and many civil rights activists agreed with Whitney Young that there was no way of dealing with these short of resorting to racial preference.[21]

The New York SCAD responded to the crescendo of calls for more vigorous enforcement and adoption of new techniques. In 1960 the

20. *Fair Share Organization v. Philip Nagdeman & Sons*, 9 R.R.L.R. 1375 (1963); 193 N.E.2d 257 (1963); *cert. den.*, 379 U.S. 818 (1964); *Fair Share Organization v. Mitnick*, 188 N.E.2d 840 (1963); 191 N.E.2d 100 (1963); 198 N.E.2d 765 (1964); *cert. den.* 379 U.S. 843 (1964); *In Re Curtis' Petition*, 227 F.Supp. 438 (1964); *Curtis v. Boeger*, 331 F.2d 675 (1964); *Curtis v. Tozer*, 374 S.W.2d 557 (1964); *In Re Curtis' Petition*, 240 F.Supp. 475 (1965); *Ford v. Boeger*, 53 L.C. 51510 (1966); *PEPCO v. Washington Chapter of CORE*, 209 F.Supp. 559 (1962); 210 F.Supp. 418 (1962); *Levine v. Dempsey*, 47 L.R.R.M. 2606 (1961); *In Re Young*, 211 N.Y.S.2d 621 (1961); *Centennial Laundry Company v. West Side Organization*, 51 L.C. 51286 (1965); 53 L.C. 9013 (1966); *Wall Street Journal*, January 8, 1963, p. 1; "Philadelphia's Black List," *The Economist*, CCVIII (1963), 437–38; "Quotas on the Job?" *The Economist*, CCVIII (1963), 510–12.

21. Bonfield, "Origin and Development," 1087.

commission admitted that "it has become increasingly apparent over the years that there are substantial areas in the field of employment in which equal opportunity without reference to race, creed, color, or national origin cannot be assured by sole or even major reliance upon the individual complaint case process." Individuals could not provide an order of priorities and the basis for a systematic approach to the overall problem. The commission saw the need to anticipate and regulate discrimination, reflected in the legislature's 1962 re-naming of the SCAD as the New York State Commission for Human Rights (SCHR). The legislature also enacted a law prohibiting discrimination in apprenticeship, job training or retraining, which, along with seniority, had long been an elusive problem in employment discrimination. The commission quickly took action against the sheet metal workers and plumbers apprenticeship programs. In 1963 the commission noted "the intense acceleration during 1963 of the demand for significant and observable content to the concept of civil rights." The commission wanted to keep up with civil rights groups, who were turning to extra-legal means to achieve equality, and Congress, which was again considering a national FEP law.[22]

In the fall of 1963 Stanley Lowell, chairman of the New York City Commission on Human Rights, proposed that racial preference in employment be used as a method to compensate for the legacy of discrimination against blacks. Lowell regarded this effort as an extension of color-conscious integration efforts in public housing and education. He said, "One hundred, three hundred years of color consciousness, of deliberate discrimination based upon color, have kept the Negro at the bottom. It cannot be so unfathomable to people of good will who believe in equality, if we now use that same color to give him a leg up." Lowell denied, however, that this meant violating the LAD or that quotas would be filled by unqualified blacks.[23]

22. SCAD, 1961 *Annual Report,* 55; State Commission for Human Rights (SCHR), 1962 *Annual Report,* 2–3, 1963 *Annual Report,* 15.

23. [New York] City Commission on Human Rights, "Policy Statement on the State of the Negro Today," October 23, 1963, in Bayard Rustin Papers, Reel 5, Library of Congress; New York *Times,* October 28, 1963, p. 1; Gerald Benjamin, *Race Relations and the New York City Commission on Human Rights* (Ithaca, N.Y., 1974), 177–78; Stanley H. Lowell, "Equality in Our Time—A Restatement of Policy by the Chairman of the City Commission on Human Rights on 'The State of the Negro Today,'" November 17, 1963, in NUL Papers, II-5-38.

The chairman and vice-chairman of the SCHR disagreed with one another about the legality of Lowell's proposal, with Vice-Chairman Bernard Katzen saying that "the concept of preferential treatment to compensate for the sins of the past is utterly inconsistent with equality of opportunity and is utterly illegal," and Chairman George Fowler arguing that the difference between fair employment and preferential treatment was largely semantic. "Promotion of equal opportunity for nonwhites," Fowler concluded, "does not in and of itself deny equal opportunities to whites." The New York Civil Liberties Union opposed the proposal, as did the New York *Times*, which condemned the race-consciousness of white supremacists and black separatists alike and called for "a true blindness to the color of men's skin." The American Jewish Committee was ambivalent, condemning the principle of group rights as pernicious regardless of intent, but concerned that the specter of "quotas" would sidetrack legitimate efforts to assist Negroes.[24]

While eschewing preferential treatment and quota policies, the SCHR responded to the atmosphere of urgency with what Chairman Fowler called "creative interpretation of the law." Demonstrations against racial exclusion in the construction trades in the summer of 1963 prompted the commission to address one of the bastions of blatant racial exclusion in the early 1960s—the local building trades unions. The Sheet Metal Workers of the AFL had formally excluded Negroes until 1946, and for the next twenty years no Negro became a member of Local 28 in New York City. Admission to the union was through the apprenticeship program, administered by the union and the local employer associations. Admission to the apprenticeship program, in turn, almost always required

24. New York *Times*, October 29, 1963, p. 1, October 29, 1963, p. 34, November 5, 1963; Confidential Memo on Preferential Hiring, [November 27, 1963], in NAACP Papers, III-A-185; "Draft Statement for WDL," October 31, 1963, in Rustin Papers, Reel 1; American Jewish Committee, "Draft Statement on Quotas and Race Relations," October 16, 1963, in Series 10994–89, Records of the New York State Commission for Human Rights, NYSDHR Library; Leo Pfeffer, "A Suggested Program for a Lawful Revolution—Part I," American Jewish Congress, Commission on Law and Social Action Information Bulletin, October 15, 1963, in Rustin Papers, Reel 5.

sponsorship by union members, who usually sponsored their relatives. No longer excluded by the union constitution, blacks were excluded by this system of apprenticeship nepotism.[25]

Civil rights groups hoped that apprenticeship would increase the numbers of blacks qualified for jobs that equal treatment, fair employment laws had opened. Moreover, the construction trades provided high incomes for non-high school graduates, and could help make up for the loss in unskilled manufacturing jobs. At the same time, the construction trades posed particular problems for antidiscrimination efforts. Unions kept the number of jobs strictly limited in order to keep incomes up, and would feel threatened by the efforts of anyone to open the trades up. "Sometimes being non-Italian or non-Irish is almost as sufficient cause for exclusion as being Negro," it was observed. In addition to this common problem in labor union discrimination, the building trades shared a particular culture that made them especially resistant to social experimentation. These white ethnic tradesmen were proud, clannish, and independent, and would resist any outside influence in the economic niche they had carved out. The campaign to integrate the construction trades was among the most protracted and bitter in any industry.[26]

After an investigation and public hearing, the commission found the Joint Apprenticeship Committee (JAC) guilty of discrimination. It prohibited the use of the union's existing waiting list of applicants for apprenticeship training; abolished the sponsorship requirement; and ordered the union to adopt minimum qualifications for applicants based on objective standards, tests, and requirements approved by the state industrial commissioner.

When the JAC did not comply, the SCHR sued for enforcement of its order in New York State Supreme Court in 1964. Justice Jacob Markowitz expressed the emerging idea that discrimination did not

25. New York *Times*, April 3, 1964, p. 23; New York State Commission for Human Rights (NYSCHR), 1963 *Report of Progress*, 74; NYSCHR, 1964 *Report of Progress*, 47; George Strauss and Sidney Ingerman, "Public Policy and Discrimination in Apprenticeship," *Hastings Law Journal*, XVI (1965), 285–331; Herbert Hill, "Racial Discrimination in the Nation's Apprenticeship Programs," *Phylon*, XXIII (1962), 215–24.

26. Strauss and Ingerman, "Public Policy and Discrimination in Apprenticeship," 297, 302.

consist of discrete actions by individuals, but instead was rooted in social structures, patterns of behavior, and "forces" that were not clearly separable or identifiable. As a result, he amended the commission's order punishing individual members of the JAC—since there were no individual acts or victims of discrimination, there likewise were no individual perpetrators. His judgment relied as much on sociological as on legal premises. Markowitz encouraged the commission and the JAC to devise a mutually satisfactory agreement, urging conciliation and cooperation rather than legal sanction. The centerpiece of Markowitz's order was a new set of "objective standards" to determine eligibility for entry into the apprentice program. Drawn up by the JAC and the SCHR, these qualifications replaced the old system of sponsorship by a union member. The order called for testing to be done by the New York University Testing and Advisement Center, and limited the amount of discretion exercised by the JAC in the interview process. Markowitz accepted the plan "because it is enlightened, progressive, and in accord with the principles of nondiscrimination, equality of opportunity and on the basis of qualification alone under objective standards."[27]

The SCHR sought a broad order beyond the individual complaint that would make a public impression. It released details of the case prior to the issue of a formal order, breaking its tradition of confidentiality in order to impress the legislature. Some observers believed that the commission had probably stretched the meaning of racial discrimination too far in this case. The commission's attack on the system of nepotism removed the need to show discriminatory intent. Nepotism was a preference for family members, not racial members. It was the effect of Negro exclusion prior to 1946, not nepotism since then, that was the problem. As one scholar pointed out, "there is a sense in which a Negro suffers from racial discrimination whenever he is disqualified by a nonracial standard that he cannot meet because of past discrimination. No antidiscrimination law can possibly apply to all such cases without widespread disruption." Opening labor unions to minorities would be

27. *SCHR* v. *Farrell*, 252 N.Y.S.2d 649 (1964); Sovern, *Legal Restraints*, 180–92; Higbee, *Development and Administration*, 277.

less effective than an effort to lower barriers to entry for construction trade jobs. Antidiscrimination law could thus make employment decisions less arbitrary and create a freer market in labor, one more rational, efficient, and conducive to equal opportunity for all. Organized labor's interest was to limit the number of apprentices, and simply accept a proportion of minority group members. If antidiscrimination law did not expand opportunity generally, rather than a minority group's share of existing jobs, it would be unable to deal with the "underclass" problem which was driving the new antidiscrimination efforts. Yet civil rights groups hoped to gain a share of labor union monopoly rather than to open the monopoly to all.[28]

The Sheet Metal Workers case marked a new departure for antidiscrimination practice in the 1960s: aggressive and publicized suits, a shift from the individual intention and to a structural theory of discrimination, and an attempt to compensate for the present effects of past discrimination. Simultaneously the Illinois FEPC began to deal with the present effects of past discrimination. While the New York commission had done so by striking at one of the more obvious cases of nepotistic racial exclusion, Illinois took on the complex one of employment testing qualifications.

Leon Myart was rejected for an entry-level job as a phaser and analyzer with the Motorola company because of his performance on General Ability Test Number Ten, a test of basic reasoning and verbal ability used by the company for entry-level jobs since 1949. Myart brought a complaint to the Illinois FEPC in July, 1963, claiming that racial discrimination was the real cause for his denial. In February, 1964, Robert F. Bryant, the investigating commissioner for the FEPC, determined that the ability test was obsolete and discriminatory against persons from culturally disadvantaged backgrounds, because its norm had been "derived from standardization on advantaged groups." "In the light of current circumstances and the objectives of the spirit as well as the letter of the law," he said,

28. Sovern, *Legal Restraints*, 180–81; Higbee, *Development and Administration*, 213; Winter, "Improving the Economic Status of Negroes," 817–55; Harold Demsetz, "Minorities in the Market Place," *University of North Carolina Law Review*, XLIII (1965), 271–97; Orley Ashenfelter, "Discrimination and Trade Unions," in *Discrimination in Labor Markets*, eds. Orley Ashenfelter and Albert Rees (Princeton, 1973), 112.

"this test does not lend itself to equal opportunity to qualify for the hitherto culturally deprived and the disadvantaged groups." Bryant determined that the law required that employers make special efforts to accommodate workers heretofore discriminated against, and ordered Motorola to give Myart the job and to discontinue the use of the test.[29]

Motorola appealed Bryant's decision to the full Illinois FEPC. The appeal was heard during the summer of 1964, but the Illinois FEPC did not rule until November, 1964. (The case was closely followed in Congress, then considering the Civil Rights Act of 1964, and led to important amendments to the bill's FEP title.) The commission held that Motorola had violated the state's antidiscrimination law, but did not base its decision on the cultural bias of the aptitude test. In fact, the FEPC did not even consider this allegation, the source of most of the controversy. Instead the commission determined that Myart had passed the test, and that Motorola had recorded a failing grade in order to reject him. Lacking any direct evidence of this violation, the commission based its decision on circumstantial evidence, including the fact that Motorola had no blacks in its civilian production line jobs at the time of Myart's application. Myart had taken another job by the time of the FEPC's ruling, so Motorola was not ordered to hire him. Instead, the company was ordered to pay a one-thousand-dollar fine as punishment.

Although the controversial test-ban order had been overturned, Motorola appealed the FEPC's punitive judgment to the Cook County Circuit Court. In March, 1965, a judge upheld the commission's finding that Myart had passed the test. The judge noted that if the question had been brought before him in trial, he would not have reached this conclusion, but that he was bound to defer to the administrative body as to matters of fact. There was enough circumstantial evidence to justify the FEPC's decision. The commission had exceeded its authority in imposing the fine, and the judge reversed that part of the order.[30]

When Motorola appealed to the Illinois Supreme Court in March, 1966, Justice Walter Schaefer set aside the FEPC's finding of

29. Bryant's decision reprinted in *Congressional Record*, 110 (March 19, 1964), 5662–64.

30. *Motorola v. Illinois FEPC*, 51 L.C. 323 (1965).

fact that Myart had passed the exam, dismantling the remainder of the commission's ruling. Such a conclusion, he said, was not supported by a preponderance of the evidence. Although the allegation of cultural bias in the aptitude test had been abandoned long before, the court made it clear that this would not have withstood scrutiny. If Myart had failed the test, Schaefer concluded, "he would have been refused employment for a reason applicable to all who fared as he did on the examination." The court also found no direct evidence to substantiate the commission's finding that Negroes had been excluded from production line jobs. Previous discriminatory practices could be taken into account along with other evidence, but was not itself sufficient to justify the commission's findings. Motorola was completely vindicated.[31]

Like the New York SCHR in the Sheet Metal Workers case, the Illinois FEPC sought to demonstrate its zeal and meet the demands of civil rights activists. The Motorola case was more innovative than the Sheet Metal Workers case, and attracted more public attention, but its dubious complainant and administrative overreach set back efforts to expand the scope of fair employment laws. The Illinois FEPC's assault on occupational testing implied that there were no objective standards that employers could set, whereas objective standards were precisely what Judge Markowitz was attempting so sedulously to compose in New York. The incident prompted an important amendment to the Civil Rights Act of 1964, and led the Illinois Senate to remove the chairman of the FEPC in 1965. But despite adverse reactions in many circles, these actions were more successful than they at first appeared. They revealed the wave of the future in fair employment law, especially in the inferences they drew from the disparate racial effects of testing or labor union practices.[32]

Civil rights groups were not satisfied with the innovations reflected in these cases. Critics believed that the federal government must

31. *Motorola* v. *Illinois FEPC*, 215 N.E.2d 286 (1966); New York *Times*, March 25, 1966, p. 29.

32. Irving Kovarsky, "The Harlequinesque Motorola Decision and Its Implications," *Boston College Industrial and Commercial Law Review*, VII (1966), 535–47; Joseph Minsky, "FEPC in Illinois: Four Stormy Years," *Notre Dame Lawyer*, XL (1965), 152–81.

take over the task of antidiscrimination enforcement from the states, begin to compensate for the effects of past discrimination, and use enforcement instead of conciliation. The color-blind standard should be made more flexible, and private employers, not bound by fair employment strictures, should use racial preferences, even if they did not admit to it.[33]

The clearest rejection of the state FEPCs came from Herbert Hill, labor secretary of the NAACP. "Given the significant developments in the American economy during the last twenty years together with the current status of the Negro wage-earner in the states with FEPC laws we must conclude on the basis of the evidence that state FEP laws have failed," he argued. The statutes themselves were sound, but lax enforcement, using conciliation rather than enforcement, focusing on individual complaints rather than industry-wide investigations, rendered them useless. Efforts like the Sheet Metal Workers action came at least ten years too late, Hill argued. The rise of direct action and urban riots reflected the failure of the FEPC effort, and the state agencies could only salvage themselves if they followed the militants and attacked broad patterns of historic exclusion. Despite their recent steps in this direction, Hill regarded the state FEPC effort as a failure.[34]

Hill's critique of the state FEPCs was echoed in a study of the New Jersey FEPC by labor lawyer Alfred W. Blumrosen, who would be one of the major architects of affirmative action after 1965. He set out to explain why black Americans had not closed the economic gap between themselves and white Americans since World War II, despite the existence of laws against discrimination. He blamed the policy of waiting for a specific complaint before proceeding against an employer. Such an approach assumed that black victims of discrimination shared middle-class white attitudes about using government agencies for social services, and that poor blacks had the

33. Clarence Clyde Ferguson, "The Federal Interest in Employment Discrimination," *Buffalo Law Review*, XIV (1965), 1–15; John G. Field, "Hindsight and Foresight About FEPC," *ibid.*, 16–21; Sol Rabkin, "Enforcement of Laws Against Discrimination in Employment," *ibid.*, 110–13; George W. Culbertson, "Comment," *ibid.*, 170–74.

34. Hill, "Twenty Years of State FEPCs," 22–69; Duane Lockard, *Toward Equal Opportunity: A Study of State and Local Antidiscrimination Laws* (New York, 1968).

time and money to follow through on an individual complaint. The legalistic FEPCs had ignored the sociological reality of ghetto life and lost the confidence of the community they were supposed to serve. The procedural insistence on relying on a verified complaint was in fact a substantive decision not to enforce the law, Blumrosen concluded.[35]

The critics of state FEPCs proposed to measure the success of anti-discrimination laws by reference to "a fair share of resources and opportunities" for minority groups. The proportional standard for success implied that proportionalism as a means to that end could not be far behind. But defenders of traditional state FEPC techniques argued that it was impossible to measure their effectiveness by the same quantitative standards as those used to measure unemployment and incomes. Collecting data from employers on the ethnic composition of their work forces could encourage discrimination, tokenism, and quota systems. A departure from the individual-based conciliation and education techniques in favor of aggressive, group-focused enforcement would encourage quota hiring. It was increasingly apparent, however, that many civil rights activists were willing to take that risk.[36]

The willingness of civil rights activists to break with many of the principles that had guided their work since Reconstruction was increasingly evident by the mid-1960s. The idea of overtly race-conscious preferential treatment for minorities had been considered a line which could not be safely crossed. The awkwardness of the "benevolent housing quota" discussion, the retreat of Stanley Lowell, and the caution of Whitney Young showed that activists did not think that the time for a public discussion of these ideas had arrived. Their inhibitions were eroding by mid-decade, however, as calls emerged for fair employment tactics that risked encouraging preferential treatment and quotas. These consisted of aggressive legal

35. Alfred W. Blumrosen, "Antidiscrimination Laws in Action in New Jersey: A Law-Sociology Study," *Rutgers Law Review*, XIX (1965), 187–287; Blumrosen, *Black Employment*, vii, 3, 25; Blumrosen, *Modern Law*, 42.

36. Henry Spitz, "Tailoring the Techniques to Eliminate Employment Discrimination," *Buffalo Law Review*, XIV (1965), 79–99; Mayhew, *Law and Equal Opportunity*, 72; Couser, "The California FEPC," 187–212.

enforcement, pattern-centered approaches, and statistically determined proof of discrimination. While many still denied that these methods would in fact result in preferential treatment or quota hiring, more remarkable was the appearance not just of the willingness to risk, but the advocacy of, preferential treatment.[37]

More observers called for Americans to disenthrall themselves from the ideas of individual rights and color-blindness that had guided them since Reconstruction and embrace "positive discrimination" and group rights. Denying that any substantial improvement in the economic position of blacks had occurred since emancipation, Loren Miller, formerly an NAACP lawyer and now a Los Angeles judge, drew the analogy to preferential policy for the handicapped—black skin could be a worse obstacle than a physical disability. Others compared preferential treatment for blacks to child and female labor protection. Positive discrimination could compensate for the effects of years of negative discrimination, reversing the historic preference in favor of whites. The policy had to be open and widespread, and could not be sidetracked by objections to "reverse discrimination." "Only rigid and ruthless pursuit of such a policy can undo decades of a similar, but concealed, policy of favoritism for whites."[38]

The tendency toward color-consciousness, group rights, and equal outcomes through social engineering suggested in *Brown* were now being fleshed out. The analogy of black Americans to women, children, or the handicapped showed that the emerging sociological understanding of employment discrimination encompassed a paternalistic system of social engineering. The bifurcated nature of antidiscrimination law, involving both individual right and intergroup relations, allowed policy makers to shift from equal treatment as an individual right that one exercised for oneself, to equal outcomes as a group entitlement secured by government.[39]

The revived theory of color-consciousness and group rights contradicted the ideas that inspired fair employment laws after World

37. Lockard, *Toward Equality Opportunity*, 98–99.

38. Loren Miller in Abrams, *et al.*, *Equality*, 3–39; Harold Cruse, *The Crisis of the Negro Intellectual* (New York, 1967), 220.

39. Blumrosen, *Black Employment*, 48; Harvey Mansfield, *America's Constitutional Soul* (Baltimore, 1991), 74–75.

War II. The framers of these laws argued that they would promote equal treatment without regard to race, not that the law was a racial counterweight against previous racial bias. The laws did not protect any particular race as did legislation referring to women, children, veterans, or the handicapped. Age, sex, veteran's status, or disability could be defended as relevant differences which the law should recognize, while civil rights groups had long pressed the idea that race, unlike those categories, was irrelevant.

In particular, the new civil rights movement began to reject the goal of merit employment as an undesirable barrier to racial preference. There were no objective standards that could be used to determine ability of prospective employees, except perhaps in the most highly skilled technical jobs. In most other jobs, some minimal level of competence was all that was required for entry and the rest was acquired on the job. Therefore, a wide variety of means to expand the minority presence in the work force could be used. Antidiscrimination officers should enforce the law by pattern-centered suits, and should use the PWA-era definition of discrimination. "The absence or token presence of Negroes in various businesses, concerns, in apprentices, and on-the-job training, should constitute a prima facie case of discrimination, which can be rebutted by a showing that Negroes are not present because of factors having no relation to discrimination," NAACP General Counsel Robert L. Carter concluded. The definition of discrimination seen in the 1930s, largely abandoned after the *Hughes* decision in 1950 and rejected by the state FEPCs, had always been implicit in many calls for a more aggressive enforcement of state fair employment laws. By the mid-1960s it became explicit.

Civil rights advocates concluded that the state FEPCs and the disparate-treatment approach to discrimination had failed. It is important to recognize, however, that the state FEPCs were being called to a new task in their second decade. The disparate-treatment standard had been effective in the first decade of state FEPC operation, helping qualified minorities who aspired to middle-class status, and unskilled entrants into northern and western industrial centers in a generally expanding economy. After the mid-1950s, when the state FEPCs were called on to address the problem of the stagnation of the urban "underclass," guarantees against disparate treatment were inadequate. "Because of its individual emphasis, the implementation of the equal treatment standard fails to uproot the collective and structural sources of unequal participation," one analysis of a state FEPC noted, and this led to "fair share" or quota demands. The attractiveness of the "fair share" formula was that it was simple and promised to change the black economic situation quickly. This appeal, however, could lead to an exaggeration of the failure of the traditional antidiscrimination formula and a magnification of the difficulty of equal treatment.[40]

The principal problem with the "fair share" approach was its departure from the traditional definition of equal treatment, which was deeply rooted in American political philosophy. Civil rights groups thus sometimes couched their demands for equal outcomes in traditional language of equal opportunity. Above all, they avoided calls for specific quotas, reinforcing the lesson of the picketing cases of the 1930s and 1940s. Demands for hiring quotas in California were met by the California attorney general, who held that "if discriminatory practices in hiring exist, all lawful means may be used to bring an end to such practices and a protest or demand to end such practice may, of necessity, include a request or demand to hire members of the classes discriminated against." But, he pointed out, if the demand were for a fixed number, it would violate the state FEPC law. "The existence of a work force of one color or race is prima facie discriminatory," the attorney general explained, but "while we find a 'quota' to be invidious, we do not necessarily find a 'reasonable racial balance' to be unlawful. Or, while a demand to hire a specific number of a specified race solely on the basis of race is illegal, a demand that 'some' of a race be hired would not necessarily be improper." One observer called the distinction "totally unworkable. . . . One man's 'reasonable balance' . . . is another man's 'quota.'" Advocates of quotas believed there was room within the standard definition to experiment with compensatory programs.[41]

40. Lockard, *Toward Equal Opportunity,* 13; Mayhew, *Law and Equal Opportunity,* 263–66.

41. California Attorney General Opinion 63/148, April 30, 1964, 9 R.R.L.R. (1964), 1051; Weiner, "Negro Picketing for Employment Equality," 293; Michael C. Tobringer, "California FEPC," *Hastings Law Journal,* XVIII (1965), 333–49.

There are several questions to ask when evaluating the effectiveness of the state FEPCs. What was the proper measure of their effectiveness? While in the first period the state FEPCs pointed to the new industries that were opened to minority workers, in the second decade the call was for overall statistics of relative minority economic improvement. The first decade satisfied both of these definitions while the second decade did not. What was the proper relationship between the agencies and the minority community? Elmer Carter insisted that disadvantaged groups must avail themselves of the opportunities available, while Blumrosen argued that government agencies must solicit the support and participation of minority group members. Finally, how effective were the state FEPCs in operating on an equal-treatment basis? This is perhaps the most important question of all.[42]

Even if their record was at best mixed, it is clear that the state FEPCs had not earned the opprobrium to which civil rights groups subjected them in the late 1960s. But regardless of how effective the state FEPCs had been at their original task, they were clearly overwhelmed by demands that they do something about the unskilled, unemployed minority population of northern and western cities. More important, the enactment of the federal Civil Rights Act of 1964 preempted the operation of state FEPCs, despite its language of deferring to them. Employment discrimination law shifted decisively from the state to the federal level, and from administrative to legislative and judicial forums.[43]

42. New York was regarded as having the most effective FEPC in the country. See, for example, Norgren and Hill, *Toward Fair Employment,* 102. It is also important to note that New York was the only large state with an FEPC in the first decade, when fair employment laws were limited to the Northeast (Massachusetts, Connecticut, and Rhode Island) and the far West (New Mexico, Oregon, and Washington). Pennsylvania and Michigan did not enact FEP statutes until 1955, Ohio and California until 1959, and Illinois until 1961, although major municipalities in these states had local FEP ordinances.

43. "Employment Discrimination and Title VII of the Civil Rights Act of 1964," *Harvard Law Review,* LXXXIV (1971), 1210.

The Federal Government and Fair Employment, 1944–1964

The "Don't Buy Where You Can't Work" campaigns, New Deal agencies, the President's Committee on Fair Employment Practices, and federal and state courts provided different articulations of a fair employment policy. States promulgated nondiscrimination orders during the war and enacted fair employment practice statutes soon after the war. Congress made repeated attempts to enact a fair employment statute between 1944 and 1954, but its failure left executive and judicial action as the only expression of a federal antidiscrimination effort.

Efforts to enact a permanent FEPC under statutory authority began soon after Franklin D. Roosevelt created the President's Committee on Fair Employment Practice by executive order in 1941. New York Representative Vito Marcantonio introduced a bill in 1942 that would have given the FEPC congressional authorization and enforcement powers, but it was never reported out of the House Judiciary Committee. Democratic Senator Dennis Chavez of New Mexico and Democratic Representative Mary Norton of New Jersey sponsored the first bills to gain serious attention in the Seventy-eighth Congress in 1944. Modeled on the New York State Law Against Discrimination, the two bills established the pattern for every fair employment practice bill introduced in Congress from 1944 to 1954. Congress justified legislation to prohibit discrimination in employment by declaring that racial, religious, and ethnic discrimination caused domestic unrest, deprived the nation of the efficient use of manpower and resources in national defense, and obstructed commerce. It declared the right to equal employment opportunity without discrimination to be an immunity of United States citizenship under the Fourteenth Amendment that could not be abridged by any state or local government. This was apparently the first time that Congress had attempted to define this long-neglected provision of the Fourteenth Amendment.[1] The bills defined unfair employment practices to be the refusal to hire, or to discharge, or to discriminate in compensation or other terms of employment against any person because of his race, creed, color, national origin or ancestry. This was the standard definition of unfair employment practice, used by the president's committee and written into subsequent state FEP laws.[2] The legislation applied to employers of five or more persons engaged in interstate commerce or doing business with the federal government, although Congress raised the base of five employees in later bills to fifty to assuage small employers' fears. This scope was potentially quite broad, especially under a liberal construction of "interstate commerce." The bills also prohibited labor unions from placing racial, religious, or ethnic limitations on membership.

The bills created an FEPC with enforcement authority, to consist of a chairman and six members chosen by the president with the advice and consent of the Senate, to serve seven-year terms. The number and terms of the commissioners varied slightly in later bills, but the fundamental structure of commission enforcement persisted. The commission could promulgate rules and regulations to carry out the provisions of the act, with congressional oversight.

1. Ruchames, *Race, Jobs, and Politics,* 199–213; Will Maslow, "FEPC—A Case in Parliamentary Maneuver," *University of Chicago Law Review,* XIII (1946), 407–44; "Note—EEOC Charge," *Michigan Law Review,* XCI (1992), 128–34; the Marcantonio bill, H.R. 7412, appears in *Congressional Record* (hereafter cited as *CR*), 92 (February 8, 1946), 1147; Paul Burstein and Margo MacLeod, "Prohibiting Employment Discrimination: Ideas and Politics in the Congressional Debate Over Equal Employment Opportunity Legislation," *American Journal of Sociology,* LXXXVI (1980), 512–33; Felix S. Cohen, "The People vs. Discrimination," *Commentary,* I (1946), 17–22.

2. Like the New York State Law Against Discrimination, none of the bills proposed in Congress in the postwar years declared it an illegal employment practice to "refuse or *fail* to hire." This language, perhaps implying a wider employer obligation of affirmative action, began to appear in the early 1960s.

Upon a complaint of an unfair employment practice, the commission would serve notice to the respondent employer or labor union, and hear the respondent's answer and gather other evidence. The commission could subpoena witnesses and evidence, and then issue a cease-and-desist order if the complaint was sustained. In the eyes of fair employment advocates, this cease-and-desist power made congressional FEPC proposals superior to the president's committee. In addition to cease-and-desist orders, the commission could order an employer or union to take "affirmative action"—to hire, reinstate, or promote an employee, with or without back pay. The FEPC and the respondent both had recourse to the federal courts— the commission for enforcement of its orders and the respondent for appeal of the order. In such cases the federal courts were instructed to conduct further proceedings according to the procedures established by law governing petitions for enforcement of the orders of the National Labor Relations Board.

The administrative model for these bills was the National Labor Relations Act. Just as the local boycott and picket groups of the 1930s and 1940s sought the same legal protections organized labor had gained, so Congress proposed to eliminate racial discrimination in employment by the same means used to prevent employer discrimination against labor unions. Discrimination based on race, creed, color, national origin or ancestry was not made a crime or a tort. An individual complainant had to rely entirely upon the discretion of the FEPC to obtain justice, and could not bring an action in federal court, nor appeal to the courts if dissatisfied with commission action.

The debate over an FEPC also echoed many of the arguments made about the NLRA and the Taft-Hartley Act in 1947. Robert Taft, as Senate minority leader and as a midwestern Republican, held a pivotal position in Congress and took a critical view of a national FEPC. The solid bloc of southern Democrats necessitated substantial Republican support for any FEPC measure. Many liberal northeastern Republicans were reliable FEPC supporters, so the balance of power in Congress lay with the midwestern Republicans. Taft and others had concerns about the administrative structure of the proposed FEPC, proposing to limit the act's application to employers of twenty-five or more, require "substantial evidence" as the standard for judicial review, and include more defendant protections. Wayne Morse of Oregon argued that this would not only help the bill pass, but would "set a good example to administrative law procedure." When the Republicans gained control of Congress in 1947, they modified the Chavez and Norton bills to emphasize conciliation and voluntary compliance as the main approaches to discrimination, with enforcement only as a last resort. The Republican bill, sponsored by Irving Ives, New York Republican and author of New York's LAD, narrowed the scope of the law to apply only to employers of fifty or more, and added procedural safeguards for defendants to avoid the abuses of the NLRA. The National Council for a Permanent FEPC, an umbrella organization of civil rights groups led by A. Philip Randolph, supported this revised version.[3]

In particular, the Republican FEP bill conformed to the rules of the Administrative Procedure Act (APA) rather than to those of the NLRA. The APA was an attempt to assure that individual rights were protected as fully by executive agencies as they were in courts. It was a response to the proliferation of executive bureaus under the New Deal, and especially the emergency bureaus set up during World War II. Senator Richard Russell capitalized on this sentiment in 1944 when, in order to kill the FEPC, he persuaded Congress to legislate a one-year time limit on any agency not operated under a specific legislative appropriation. While the Taft-Hartley Act was a particular response to the NLRB, the APA represented a general reaction, and after 1947 FEP bills adopted its reforms. Nevertheless, the failure to enact a permanent FEPC can be seen as another indication of congressional resistance to New Deal expansion of government.[4]

The justification for a permanent FEPC also evolved over time.

3. Northrup, "Progress Without Federal Compulsion," 206–11; CR 91 (December 21, 1945), 12502–12503 (January 29, 1946), 503; Senate, Prohibiting Discrimination in Employment Because of Race, Religion, Color, National Origin, or Ancestry, 80th Cong., 2nd sess., 1948, S. Rept. 951; Senate Committee on Labor and Public Welfare, Antidiscrimination in Employment: Hearings Before a Subcommittee of the Committee on Labor and Public Welfare, 80th Cong., 1st sess., 1947, pp. 30–33; Paul Sifton memorandum, January 20, 1947, in Roy Wilkins Papers, Box 24, Manuscript Division, LC.

4. Kelly, Harbison, and Belz, The American Constitution, II, 644; James O. Freedman, Crisis and Legitimacy: The Administrative Process and American Government (Cambridge, Mass., 1978), 26; Graham, Civil Rights, 13.

Initially many pointed to the need to carry on the successful work of the wartime FEPC, and to deal with demobilization problems. The most urgent problem in 1944–1945 appeared to be possible race riots, such as had occurred after World War I, or during the summer of 1943 in Detroit. The Reverend Aron Gilmartin predicted "a wave of violence and terrorism against the Negro, the Mexican, and so forth, many times worse than that of 1919" in the absence of an FEP Act. FEPC chairman Malcolm Ross believed that violence, while not inevitable, was more likely now than it had been after World War I. Joseph Kovner of the ACLU supported FEPC legislation because it would extend to employers the antidiscrimination requirements that labor unions were required to follow as a result of the Supreme Court's *Steele* and *Tunstall* decisions. The Court regarded labor union discrimination as a form of "state action," while most employer discrimination was private. Organized labor was divided on the issue of a permanent FEPC, with the CIO supporting it while the AFL turned from opposition to lukewarm support by 1945. Roy Wilkins of the NAACP stressed the national economic benefits nondiscrimination would bring by boosting the purchasing power of minority groups. Henry Epstein of the National Community Relations Advisory Council emphasized that an FEPC was preferable to picketing and other minority group direct action tactics as a solution to employment discrimination.[5]

America's world power responsibilities also provided an argument in favor of a permanent FEPC. Supporters often noted that employment discrimination revealed the gap between American principles and practice, undermining the nation's claim to world leadership. In 1947 Senator Dennis Chavez noted that an FEPC would help fulfill the nation's obligations under the United Nations charter. The mistreatment of minority groups in America provided a propaganda target for the Soviets, who could charge the United States with hypocrisy in its claim to democratic leadership of the free world. The impression that racial discrimination made upon Third World dignitaries was also frequently cited as one of the harmful diplomatic effects of American race relations.

5. Senate Committee on Education and Labor, *Fair Employment Practices Act: Hearings Before a Subcommittee of the Committee on Education and Labor,* 78th Cong., 2nd sess., 1944, pp. 93–95, 104–105, 186; Kesselman, *Social Politics of FEPC,* 143–54.

As the Cold War intensified and rearmament commenced in 1950, national leaders stressed the concept developed in World War II that fair employment maximized the nation's resources for defense. In 1952 Minnesota senator Hubert H. Humphrey called the treatment of minorities and the defense of civil rights the most important part of our foreign policy. "Our foreign policy is not vulnerable because of lack of money, troops, or armament," he said. "It is vulnerable because we have not yet declared by public law and public policy not only our desire for equality of opportunity but our willingness fully to practice it." Humphrey presided over congressional hearings that he described as an inventory of the nation's manpower resources and a proceeding to prevent discrimination from impeding efficient manpower utilization against Soviet aggression. Large segments of the American work force were serving in the armed forces or in defense-related work, and their optimum employment was essential to the Cold War effort.[6]

The argument that there were practical and international reasons to adopt antidiscrimination legislation persisted into the 1960s when they were superseded by domestic considerations. While many segregationists denounced a permanent FEPC as communist-inspired, Humphrey and other liberals used the Cold War to alter the rhetoric of fair employment legislation. They believed it would be easier to persuade public opinion to support "full utilization of manpower resources" than "fair employment." As Humphrey noted, "I have heard everyone say that they want to do everything to lick the communists. I am interested in that, too, but sometimes I think it would be refreshing in this Nation's Capital if we did something because it was the right thing to do." But there is no reason to believe that Humphrey was merely being expedient. The marriage of domestic liberalism and internationalism was genuine, and it added urgency to the pursuit of civil rights legislation.[7]

6. Senate Committee, *Discrimination and Full Utilization of Manpower Resources;* Senate, *Federal Equality of Opportunity in Employment Act,* 82d Cong., 2nd sess., 1952, S. Rept. 2080; Donald R. McCoy and Richard T. Ruetten, *Quest and Response: Minority Rights and the Truman Administration* (Lawrence, Kan., 1973), 180, 199.

7. Senate Committee, *Discrimination and Full Utilization of Manpower Resources,* 251; Carl Brauer, *John F. Kennedy and the Second Reconstruction* (New York, 1977), 76; Gelber, *Black Men and Businessmen,* 89.

The chief obstacles to passage of civil rights legislation were the bloc of twenty-two southern senators and Senate Rule 22, requiring a two-thirds vote in the Senate to invoke cloture and limit debate. In the House of Representatives, the Rules Committee was dominated by southerners, and refused to allow FEPC bills to come to the floor for debate. In 1944 Representative Mary Norton, New Jersey Democrat and chair of the House Committee on Labor, was unable to convince the Rules Committee to bring her FEP bill to the floor, the Rules Committee dividing six to six on the question. When the Senate Committee on Education and Labor reported an FEP bill in 1945, southerners led a filibuster from January 18 to February 10, 1946, and a vote on cloture failed, 48 to 36, to gain the necessary two-thirds majority. Twenty-five Republicans and twenty-two Democrats voted for cloture, while twenty-eight Democrats and eight Republicans opposed it, and twelve did not vote. Civil rights groups blamed both these half-hearted supporters, and President Truman for his weak leadership. Minority leader Robert Taft, who opposed the bill but voted for cloture, criticized the civil rights groups for demanding the administrative features of the Chavez bill.[8]

The Eightieth Congress, controlled by Republicans, proved no better in FEPC terms. The southern Democrats saw the FEPC as the first step toward the end of segregation. Senator Allen Ellender, Louisiana Democrat, noted that the wartime FEPC had attacked segregated plant facilities in St. Louis and Baltimore. Although the FEPC had in fact exhibited an ambivalence about whether segregation was compatible with fair employment, and notwithstanding the assurances of New York Democrat Adam Clayton Powell that the legislation did not concern social relations, Ellender insisted that the bill would threaten segregation. During Senate hearings held by the Committee on Labor and Public Welfare, he asked almost every witness about segregation, and concluded that equal employment would lead to social equality, racial intermarriage, and the "mongrelization" of states like his with substantial black popu-

8. House Committee, *To Prohibit Discrimination in Employment Because of Race, Creed, Color, National Origin or Ancestry;* CR 92 (February 10, 1946), 1219; Ruchames, *Race, Jobs, and Politics,* 203–206; Robert Taft to Harry E. Davis, January 24, 1946, in Robert A. Taft Papers, Box 874, Manuscript Division, LC.

lations. Ellender vented his racial hatred in his contemptuous treatment of witness A. Philip Randolph, whom he refused to address as "Mr." Randolph, and he and other southern Democrats predicted violence if FEP legislation passed. Frequently referring to the FEPC bill as the most dangerous legislation ever introduced in Congress, they agreed with Louisiana Democrat Otto Passman that it would lead to "more bloodshed than did the Civil War."[9]

Yet cracks were beginning to show in the southern defense of segregation. Senator Lister Hill of Alabama moderated the southern Democrats' objections to an FEPC. Hill took Hugo Black's Senate seat in Alabama in 1938 as a supporter of the New Deal, defeated a primary challenger who accused him of supporting the Birmingham CIO's egalitarian racial policies, and voted in favor of extending the FEPC in 1944. Ralph Bunche considered Hill "mildly liberal," and the Birmingham NAACP considered him a potential supporter of a permanent FEPC. While Hill turned out to be an opponent of civil rights legislation, he eschewed Ellender's racism in the committee hearings, stressing instead the damage that the bill would do to free enterprise, the rights of employers to hire, and the rights of labor unions to set membership standards. It was on these points that the southern Democrats and the midwestern Republicans shared some common ground.[10]

The 1944 Republican platform endorsed a permanent FEPC, and Robert Taft had supported the Democratic FEPC bill in 1944 and ran for re-election supporting it. Taft offered to sponsor the National Council for a Permanent FEPC's bill, but the organization rebuffed him. In 1945, however, Taft introduced a substitute version that omitted the enforcement powers of the Democratic bill. He argued that the provisions of the Democratic bill, modeled on those of the NLRA, were more extensive than most people realized. Anyone could bring an action alleging discrimination based on racial, religious, or ethnic identification. "Such motives are always possible to

9. Senate Committee, *Antidiscrimination in Employment,* 124; *CR* 96 (February 22, 1950), 2215.

10. Nelson, "Organized Labor," 985; Kesselman, *Social Politics of FEPC,* 169; Bunche, *Political Status of the Negro,* 40; Emory O. Jackson to Lister Hill, May 30, 1945, June 4, 1945, in NAACP Papers, II-A-250.

allege, and the question is left for decision to a board which is bound by no rules of evidence, and practically not subject to court review." Suits by millions of employees would go even further than the NLRA toward regimentation of employers. Taft saw the need to alter the NLRB, not to create new agencies in its image. A. Philip Randolph, often seen as intransigent, yielded to other civil rights groups after initially indicating support for Taft's compromise bill.[11]

Although he had praised Firestone Rubber Company for adopting a race-based proportional layoff system in the 1930s, Taft opposed the Democrats' FEPC bill because it would result in a racial, religious, and ethnic quota system. Taking his cue from journalist Merlo Pusey, Taft argued that the problem with enforceable antidiscrimination laws lay in the "impossibility of determining whether racial or religious discrimination exists." Every rejected minority applicant was likely to feel that he had been discriminated against. "As I see it," Taft said, "the compulsory act, if duplicated in every state as its proponents plan, will finally force every employer to choose his employees approximately in proportion to the division of races and religions in his district, because that will be his best defense against harassing suits." Taft endorsed a gradual, voluntary, educational approach without compulsory enforcement. The Democratic bill would necessarily lead employers to resort to racial, religious, and ethnic quotas.[12]

The issues of proving discrimination and quota hiring continued to undermine the FEPC effort. Shad Polier of the American Jewish Congress asserted that discrimination on the basis of race, creed, or color could be proved in the same way that discrimination on the basis of labor union membership was proved. William Hastie, now dean of the Howard Law School, described the fear of proportional hiring based on race, religion, or ethnicity as nothing more than a "bad dream." No commission appointed by the president or confirmed by the Senate, Hastie said, would be so uninformed or arbitrary as to believe that discrimination could be measured in percent-

11. Kesselman, *Social Politics of FEPC,* 32–39; "Statement of Robert Taft in Connection with the Introduction of a Bill to Establish a Fair Employment Practice Commission," March 7, 1945, in Taft Papers, Box 726.

12. *CR* 84 (March 13, 1939), A950; Washington *Post,* March 20, 1945.

age terms. Moreover, courts would not accept such an interpretation. Federal courts had ruled in jury selection cases that the proportion of whites and Negroes on juries was of no moment. The complainant would have to prove discrimination, Hastie noted. The wartime FEPC had never even suggested that an employer utilize minorities in its population ratio. Hastie had coordinated the successful picketing-for-jobs campaign of the New Negro Alliance during the 1930s. The alliance had in fact attempted to prove discrimination by proportional comparisons, but had been careful to avoid making proportional or quota demands. Hastie's experience with this issue perhaps alerted him to the need to repudiate the idea of quota hiring.[13]

During hearings on FEPC legislation in 1947, Republican Forrest C. Donnell of Missouri apparently expected an FEPC to require quota hiring, and asked Julius Thomas of the New York Urban League what would happen to white workers when black workers "step up and claim their proportion of the jobs." Thomas assured him that the law would not operate in such a way, and cited the New York State Commission Against Discrimination as an example. "We do not use percentages in our discussions of employment practices in our organization because we do not think they are a very accurate yardstick by which to measure this whole business," Thomas said. The chairmen of the New Jersey and Boston FEPCs likewise attested that their commissions did not permit employers to use racial quotas to prove conformity with the law. A manufacturer pointed out that if an employer's work force contained no members of a particular race, it would be difficult to defend against charges of discrimination. "If we can judge by the interpretation that has been put on it by the NLRB and various other government agencies that have recently been set up, you would find it very difficult to refute that charge," he said. When New York Republican Senator Irving Ives answered that New York had satisfactorily dealt with that problem, the manufacturer pointed out that the cost of defending oneself against such charges increased the cost of doing business. A rep-

13. Senate Committee on Education and Labor, *Fair Employment Practice Act: Hearings Before a Subcommittee of the Committee on Education and Labor*, 79th Cong., 1st sess., 1945, pp. 39, 172–73.

resentative of the Southern States Industrial Council predicted that the FEPC would soon be overwhelmed with complaints. "Instead of having a backlog of 5,000 cases as the NLRB, you would have a backlog of 500,000 cases," he said. "It looks like as a practical proposition the Commission would be driven to the industry-by-industry practice. What you would have up for hearing would not be an individual but an industry, and you would arrive at some sort of quota system."[14]

The southern opponents of FEP legislation also pointed to the problem of the proof of discrimination, arguing that "claims of discrimination rest on intangible factors." If the experience of the NLRB were duplicated, the burden of proof would quickly shift to the employer, and race-consciousness would create antagonism among workers. In their view the small number of complaints in state commissions did not mean that the law was working well without harassing employers, but rather that the laws were dead letters. Ironically, this was a charge that civil rights groups frequently made in private in the 1940s and publicly in later years. While the segregationist aspect of this objection did not have wide appeal, the southern argument had merit insofar as it called attention to the complicated, subtle nature of discrimination and the difficulty of proof. It actually adumbrated the arguments of civil rights groups twenty years later.[15]

The strong Democratic platform on civil rights in 1948 and Democratic control of the new Congress indicated an improved chance for enactment of FEPC legislation, but Congress again failed. Recalcitrant southern opposition, weak presidential and congressional leadership, and a no-compromise strategy on the part of civil rights groups foreclosed any chance for FEPC legislation. Adam Clayton Powell of New York led the House effort to adopt an FEPC bill in 1949–1950. In the years before World War II Powell had been a leading figure in the campaign of picketing for jobs in New York City. The New York LAD made such action no longer necessary, he said, and he wanted to extend that model to the nation. Powell stressed

14. Senate Committee, *Antidiscrimination in Employment,* 609, 745.
15. Senate Report, *Prohibiting Discrimination in Employment.*

that the bill was limited to employment discrimination, and would not address social equality. He even went so far as to state that the wartime FEPC's action against segregated work places in St. Louis and Baltimore had been wrong.[16]

There were again repeated assurances that the law would not require racially balanced work forces. Following an argument often made by Mississippi Representative John Rankin, Michigan Representative Clare Hoffman testified that the proportion of Negroes on the wartime FEPC's staff (almost 60 percent) showed that it had discriminated in favor of Negroes. Powell answered, "I do not think that the preponderant percentage of a minority indicates discrimination. . . . Percentages do not prove pro or con the question of discrimination, and the bill does not mention that in any way." Democrat Charles Howell of New Jersey, who had sponsored state FEP legislation, desired to clear up this misunderstanding about the law. It did not require anyone to hire a specific number of minorities. One only had to hire minorities if they were eminently qualified and if an employer had positions open, and then only if they were as qualified as others under consideration. Charles Hamilton Houston again pointed to the jury discrimination cases. "The absence of a Negro from a jury does not mean and raises no presumption of unfairness," the Supreme Court had held. Such a discrimination had to be proved, and Houston believed that "you would not have any more difficulty in running the organization of industry on the question of discrimination on the ground of color than you have in running a jury system in your courts on the ground of race or color." When asked how an employer could disprove a charge of prejudice if his one-hundred-man work force was all white, Houston replied, "All he was to prove here would be very simple." If two people of different races applied and one man was better qualified, the employer need only show that it chose the more qualified one.[17]

After the southern-dominated Rules Committee refused to allow

16. Ruchames, *Race, Jobs, and Politics,* 206–13; Northrup, "Progress without Federal Compulsion," 206–11; McCoy and Ruetten, *Quest and Response,* chap. 8; House Committee, *Federal Fair Employment Practice Act,* 256, 507.

17. House Committee, *Federal Fair Employment Practice Act,* 20, 36, 272.

Powell's bill to be debated, FEPC proponents used a "Calendar Wednesday" procedure to force the committee to report it up in February, 1950. However, Samuel K. McConnell, Pennsylvania Republican and ranking member of the House Education and Labor Committee, had prepared a substitute measure that removed most of the enforcement powers from the Powell bill. McConnell's bill was not entirely "voluntary," however. It authorized an FEPC to investigate, gather evidence under a subpoena power, and study the problem of discrimination. If any employer resisted its investigations, he was liable to fines and imprisonment.[18] McConnell argued that only this kind of bill stood a chance of passing the House and making it through the Senate. If the voluntary bill did not work out, he said, it could be amended in the future.[19]

Civil rights groups and their congressional allies castigated the McConnell bill as a sham FEPC. Vito Marcantonio of New York, who admitted that he supported the FEPC because it would end segregation in the South, insisted that the bill was a subterfuge to defeat the FEPC, and would be supported only by its enemies. Powell did not go quite so far. He was disappointed that McConnell, who had sponsored enforceable FEPC legislation in previous congresses, now advocated this largely voluntary version. He concluded that "if it is true that those who are against any kind of FEPC will substitute the gentleman's amendment, then it is obvious that it is nothing but a subterfuge to kill FEPC."[20]

The southerners did not support McConnell's bill, but attempted to introduce a substitute FEPC with even less power. Representative Brooks Hays, Arkansas Democrat, introduced a substitute which also stressed conciliation, but which omitted the investigatory and subpoena powers of the McConnell bill. Even this, he said, was a long step for a southern Democrat to take. In answer to the problem of the proof of discrimination, the Hays bill, as amended, provided

18. Originally, the McConnell bill prescribed up to $5,000 in fines and one year in jail for anyone who "willfully" interfered in the FEPC's investigations. A later version dropped the prison penalty altogether, and lowered the fine to $500 for "forcible" interference.

19. New York *Times,* February 21, 1950.

20. *CR* 96 (February 22, 1950), 2221.

that any employer who employed one individual of any minority group would be presumed not to have discriminated against that particular group—that is, token hiring would be adequate defense against discrimination charges. This substitute was finally set aside and the only contest was between the Powell and McConnell bills.[21]

Southerners attempted to amend the McConnell bill in order to make it unpalatable to the House. Dwight Rogers of Florida added "sex" as a basis of nondiscrimination under the bill, as Howard Smith of Virginia had attempted in 1945 in order to kill the Norton bill, and would do again in 1964.[22] Charles E. Bennett of Florida won approval of an amendment that forbade discrimination on the basis of "physical disability," also to make the bill harder to pass. Marcantonio remarked that "the McConnell amendment started out as a bill to nullify FEPC. If there were any doubts of it, these amendments that have been added definitely nullify the very objectives of FEPC."[23]

Civil rights groups considered Marcantonio himself one of the major obstacles to FEPC, however. A. Philip Randolph's National Council for a Permanent FEPC was eager to dissociate its support for the legislation from that of Marcantonio, a longtime follower of the Communist party line. They knew Marcantonio's support would make it easy for segregationists to paint an FEPC as a communist measure and alienate undecided moderates. While Randolph was criticized for his visceral anti-communism, it was prudent of him to distance FEPC support from the Communist party.[24]

Along with the sex and physical disability amendments, the McConnell bill also provided that "the absence of individuals of a particular race, religion, color, national origin, or ancestry in the em-

21. *Ibid.*, 2230. The bill, H.R. 6668, was introduced by Hays, but offered as a substitute to the McConnell substitute by Tom Steed, Democrat of Oklahoma.

22. Graham, *Civil Rights*, 135, suggests that Smith himself may have been sincere when he proposed a similar amendment in 1964.

23. *CR* 96 (February 22, 1950), 2247–48.

24. Memorandum of A. Philip Randolph and Allen Knight Chalmers, March 13, 1948, in Meany Archives, Collection 25, Box 1; Kesselman, *Social Politics of FEPC*, 36–39; William A. Nolan, *Communism Versus the Negro* (Chicago, 1951), 181.

ploy of any person shall not be evidence of discrimination against individuals of such race, religion, color, national origin or ancestry." The Hays bill made token representation prima facie evidence of nondiscrimination; the McConnell bill provided that racial imbalance would not constitute prima facie evidence of discrimination. Congress for the first time had begun to address the problem of the standards of proof of discrimination.

The House voted, 222–178, to substitute the McConnell bill for the Powell bill. The southern Democrats did vote for the substitute, but the next day, on the vote for the bill as amended, the southern Democrats voted with Marcantonio, Powell, and other liberals against the bill, 240–177. The enemies of an FEPC did not support the McConnell substitute, but voted with Randolph's National Council for a Permanent FEPC. The Senate never took up the bill, nor a bill reported without recommendation by an evenly divided Committee on Labor and Public Welfare, and filibustered by southern Democrats in 1950. Robert Taft thought the Senate ought to give the voluntary version of an FEPC passed by the House a trial, but he regretted that civil rights groups remained opposed to it, preventing any FEPC legislation at all. Other midwestern senators were hostile not to an FEPC, but to cloture.[25]

The failure of the Eighty-first Congress to pass a permanent, enforceable FEPC was largely due to the southern irreconcilables who held filibuster power in the Senate and controlled the Rules Committee in the House. Public opinion was generally favorable to the idea of fair employment, but there was little coherent public opinion about specific legislation. In the face of the contumacious southern minority, most congressmen regarded public support for FEPC legislation as too uncertain to justify extraordinary efforts on its behalf. The administrative structure of enforcement favored by the Democratic leadership and civil rights groups also repelled many northern and western representatives of both parties. Even

25. *CR* 96 (February 22, 1950), 2162–2254 (February 23, 1950), 2301; Senate, *National Act Against Discrimination in Employment,* 81st Cong., 2nd sess., 1950, S. Rept. 1539; Thurman L. Dawson to Robert Taft, May 13, 1950, Taft to Dawson, 1950, in Taft Papers, Box 917; Gerald W. Johnson, "The Foes of FEPC—Not All Bigots," *The Reporter,* August 15, 1950.

after FEPC sponsors narrowed the scope of legislation, provided for conciliation before enforcement, and added procedural safeguards, the suspicion of Washington bureaucrats interfering in business decision making was the source of strong opposition. Finally, the maladroit organization of the FEPC campaign, particularly the mercurial leadership of A. Philip Randolph and the heavy-handed lobbying of the CIO, bears a share of responsibility for the failure of the legislative effort.[26]

The McConnell bill might have provided the opportunity to convince the public of the benefits of a fair employment policy through the operation of a voluntary law. Too many congressmen continued to believe, however, that there was no way to determine objectively whether discrimination had taken place, and that an antidiscrimination law would create an incentive for quota hiring, if it did not give an agency the power to order it. In addition to rules which gave southern obstructionists disproportionate influence, congressional efforts had run aground on the dilemma of the proof of discrimination and the possibility of quotas, and more generally on the anti-bureaucratic reaction to the New Deal expansion of government.[27]

The last important fair employment efforts of the postwar period came in the Republican-controlled Eighty-third Congress, elected with Dwight D. Eisenhower in 1952. The president, however, was on record against an enforceable FEPC, and Congress took no action on the bills sponsored by Minnesota Democrat Hubert H. Humphrey and New York Republican Irving Ives. Thus federal policy against discrimination in employment was left to the executive branch committees, descendants of the wartime FEPC.

Congress' failure to enact a permanent FEPC left the executive branch as the focus of government fair employment efforts. Truman may have fought for his civil rights program in fits and starts,

26. Burstein, *Discrimination, Jobs, and Politics,* 118–20; Kesselman, *Social Politics of FEPC,* 36–39, 153.

27. Northrup, "Progress Without Federal Compulsion," 206–11; Francis de Sales to Robert Taft, January 11, 1953, Taft to de Sales, January 24, 1953, in Taft Papers, Box 1220.

but he was the first president to have any coherent civil rights program at all. He was on record favoring a permanent, enforceable FEPC, and his 1948 campaign platform on civil rights drove the southern segregationists to form a separate party. Dwight D. Eisenhower, while more favorable to civil rights than historians have previously thought, differed little from his 1952 party challenger Robert Taft in advocating a voluntary, educational, fair employment effort, or from his Democratic opponent, Adlai E. Stevenson, who also opposed an enforceable federal FEP act. Eisenhower did, however, expand the steps that Truman had taken by executive order since World War II.[28]

In 1948 President Truman issued two executive orders on civil rights. Executive Order 9980 desegregated the military. Armed forces desegregation had been one of A. Philip Randolph's unmet demands in the 1941 March on Washington confrontation with Roosevelt, prompted by Randolph's threat to call for draft avoidance by black men. At the same time Truman issued Executive Order 9981, establishing a Fair Employment Board in the Civil Service Commission. The Fair Employment Board served to synchronize the fair employment efforts of each executive agency, and to review complaints of discrimination. It had no enforcement powers, but could appeal to the president. Unlike the overt segregation and quota systems used by the Army, discrimination in government agencies was more difficult to uncover and prove. The board had to deal with scores of agency heads without adequate staff or resources. At most it was able to provide some machinery for a fair employment policy for another administration to carry on. Like the FEPC, the Board may have improved employment policies by its mere existence, but such accomplishments are not quantifiable.[29]

When the Korean War broke out, President Truman was under pressure to create an FEPC, as Roosevelt had in the World War II

28. McCoy and Ruetten, *Quest and Response,* 316, 352; Clarence Mitchell, "Civil Rights Under the Eisenhower Administration, 1953–54," in NAACP Papers, II-A-591.

29. CFR 3 (1944–48), 720; McCoy and Ruetten, *Quest and Response,* 251–66; Paula F. Pfeffer, *A. Philip Randolph, Pioneer of the Civil Rights Movement* (Baton Rouge, 1990), chap. 4; William C. Berman, *The Politics of Civil Rights in the Truman Administration* (Columbus, 1970), 116; Graham, *Civil Rights,* 14.

emergency. Truman refused to do so, but in 1951, in Executive Order 10308, he created the Government Contract Compliance Committee (GCCC). Although it had no enforcement powers and no budget, and in the first six months of its existence it took no action, the committee's thinking indicates that it might have taken a different approach to fair employment than Roosevelt's FEPC or the state commissions, alert to race-conscious alternatives to the color-blind fair employment formula. The committee was aware of the programs of the Bureau of Employment Security and the Housing and Home Finance Agency (HHFA, which evolved out of the Public Works Administration in the 1930s) that endorsed special attention to defined minority groups, including the HHFA quota system. The committee noted that programs like the HHFA quota system might "plant basic ideas which will blossom in later deliberations of this staff." State FEPC officers advised the GCCC that it need not observe the strict, disparate-treatment definition of discrimination laid down by state FEP statutes. The GCCC, operating without a statutory definition of discrimination, could infer discrimination from statistical racial imbalance, revise seniority systems that perpetuated past discrimination, and take other measures unavailable to state FEPCs, even following the HHFA system of minority group quotas in government contracts. Committee members also considered the analogy of blacks with women, children, and the handicapped as needing special attention, although alerted to the potential psychological harm of this imputation. While it is impressive how aware this early effort was of color-conscious options, it continued to work with the definition of discrimination as disparate treatment. The GCCC focused on the future, aware of its limitations in a lame-duck administration. It heard over three hundred complaints, and through exhortation and conciliation opened some employment opportunities to minority group workers. Like the World War II FEPC, its mere existence may have prompted voluntary compliance.[30]

30. Bureau of Employment Security, Instructor's Guide, "Service to Minority Groups," December, 1951, Employment Service Manual, August 1, 1947, Summary of Staff Interviews, July 11, 1952, Final Report, Box 2, Transcript of the Conference on Training, September 10, 1952, Box 1, Notes to the Revised Clause for the Use of

In the summer of 1953 Eisenhower issued Executive Order 10479 establishing the President's Committee on Government Contracts (PCGC). The order declared fair and equitable treatment in employment, regardless of race, creed, color, or national origin, to be federal policy, and made the head of each government contracting agency responsible for equal employment opportunity policies. The committee, composed of fourteen members—some cabinet members and others appointed by the president—would receive complaints and refer them to the contracting agency for investigation. The committee would review agency performance, develop educational programs, and cooperate with voluntary groups and state and local antidiscrimination agencies. Vice-President Richard Nixon chaired the committee. Secretary of Labor James P. Mitchell served as vice-chairman, and the committee operated out of the Labor Department for eight years. While Nixon's views on fair employment approximated those of Eisenhower, Mitchell continued to call for Congress to enact an enforceable FEP statute.[31]

The PCGC set out to define fair employment and discrimination. Civil rights groups urged the committee to devise a clear standard to which contractors could be held, and one that would not be satisfied by tokenism. Although the HHFA quota system continued until at least 1958, and the committee was aware of it, in its early years the PCGC held a color-blind and individual rights position. The committee was aware of the problem of tokenism, and believed that it could, like the state FEPCs, find discrimination despite it.[32]

Executive Director Jacob Seidenberg was not so eager to define

the Committee, "'Discrimination' as a Legally Operative Concept," September 3, 1952, Final Report, Box 1, in Records of the President's Committee on Government Contracts Compliance, RG 325, NA; Stenographic Transcript of the Proceedings Before the PCGCC, Washington, D.C., July 15, 1952, pp. 178–82, July 16, 1952, pp. 347, 369, in Meany Archives, Collection 25, Box 7; McCoy and Ruetten, *Quest and Response*, 266–81.

31. CFR 3 (1949–53), 961; Statement by the president, December 3, 1951, in NUL Papers, IV-A-15; James P. Mitchell to Alexander H. Smith, February 18, 1954, Mitchell Press Conference, March 3, 1954, in Subject Files of Secretary James P. Mitchell, Box 50, RG 174, NA.

32. Thomas Augustine to Julian Thomas, November 23, 1953, Thomas to Executive and Industrial Secretaries, December 29, 1953, in NUL Papers, IV-A-16; Minutes of Meeting of Government Contracts Committee, July 20, 1954, Box 67, in Records

discrimination. He believed that an imprecise understanding could be an advantage rather than a hindrance to the fair employment effort. Presidential committees operated with more discretion than state FEPCs because they lacked statutory authority. While often regarded as a weakness, this lack of legislative mandate enabled them to apply methods that were not available to the state commissions. When pressed by lawyers, though, Seidenberg defined discrimination as "difference in treatment without regard to qualification. . . . I defy them to improve on that, this difference of treatment."[33]

To help define the antidiscrimination order, Eisenhower issued another executive order on September 2, 1954. The order applied the nondiscrimination clause to "employment, upgrading, demotion or transfer, recruitment or recruitment advertising, layoff or termination, rates of pay or other forms of compensation, and selection for training, including apprenticeship," and required the posting of notices of the order in contractor facilities. Contractors were surveyed for compliance, with absence of minorities as an indicator, but not conclusive proof, of discrimination. But the committee's definition of discrimination did not require an intent to discriminate—only discriminatory effect need be shown. Since the PCGC was an administrative and not a judicial body, legal standards of proof were not required. In its first years the committee thus adopted a disparate-treatment formula but, in its self-conscious flexibility, one that left room for disparate impact.[34]

---

of the Department of Labor, RG 174, NA; Albert M. Cole to Richard Nixon, December 18, 1953, General Subject Files (GSF), Box 33; HHFA Report on Compliance, July 20, 1956, Correspondence with Agency Contractors, Box 1, Norman P. Mason to Richard Nixon, July 30, 1959, Correspondence with Agency Contractors, Box 2, Alvin M. Rucker to Jacob Seidenberg, November 30, 1953, GSF, Box 6, Address of James C. Worthy, October 18, 1954, GSF, Box 60, Proceedings of the Sixth Annual Conference of Commissioners Against Discrimination, June 2–4, 1954, GSF, Box 41, Report on Conference with National and Private Agencies, Box 18, in PCGC Records, RG 220.

33. Second Army Labor Conference, November 18–19, 1954, GSF, Box 42, in PCGC Records, RG 220.

34. A Review for Discussion of Essential Aspects of Programs Designed to Implement Executive Order 10479, September 1, 1954, in Records of the Department of Labor, Box 66, RG 174; Interview, *U.S. News and World Report,* December 17, 1954; Nixon statement [1954] in Meany Archives, Collection 25, Box 2.

After two years, there remained profound doubts as to the effectiveness of the committee's work. It appeared that contractors did not take the nondiscrimination clause seriously, and that investigators accepted tokenism or any employer explanation as a satisfactory excuse for racial imbalance. Civil rights groups continued to urge statistic-based and industry-wide approaches, and more vigorous enforcement. While Secretary of Labor Mitchell was despondent, others in the administration close to the president counseled caution and patience.[35]

To improve compliance, in 1955 the PCGC prepared a guidance manual for investigators that would facilitate the determination of discriminatory employment practices. Gathering information on the numbers and kinds of employment of minority group members was an important first step, along with eliciting from the contractor an explanation for the absence of minority group members in the work force. Investigators were told that they "should not accept 'token' employment of minority groups as evidence of compliance," but were not told what level of minority group employees exceeded tokenism. If they found a complete absence or a disproportionately small number of minorities at work, a case could be made only if jobs were available, and if qualified minorities were in the area and applied for jobs. In many cases, however, qualifications were so basic that "time should produce an integrated employment pattern, in the absence of any artificial barriers." If such integration had not resulted, there was a strong presumption of discrimination. Chance distribution might result in a wide variance between the racial compositions of population and work force, but if the sample were large enough, discrimination was certainly the reason for it. Nevertheless, the investigator could never say for certain what the racial composition of the work force *should* be, so in the end each case remained a matter of individual judgment.[36]

35. Executive Director's Report, January 18–February 14, 1955, Minutes of the Meeting of the Government Contract Committee, February 15, 1955, March 15, 1955, Washington Urban League to President's Committee on Government Employment Policy [1955], in NUL Papers, IV-A-16; Notes for Mr. Lazarus and Mr. Sibert, GSF, Box 44, PCGC Records, RG 220.

36. "A Manual for the Guidance of Personnel Engaged in Obtaining Compliance with the National Equal Job Opportunity Program . . . [1955]," Box 111, Records of the Department of Labor, RG 174.

The committee faced both old and new problems as it looked for fresh approaches. Recessions at the beginning and end of the Eisenhower administration exacerbated the problem of discriminatory seniority systems and layoffs. Moreover, unskilled high-wage manufacturing jobs were no longer the most rapidly expanding part of the work force. In short, the PCGC faced the same complications of economic changes of the mid-1950s that the state commissions did.

The committee also faced problems inherent in regulating government contractors. As the customer, in effect, the government could use its leverage to influence the contractor-supplier, who did not want to risk losing a lucrative contract. At the same time, nobody wanted to interfere with the provision of vital defense-related goods and services, even for the sake of fair employment. This was the problem that the FEPC faced during World War II. A related problem was that of the government contractor as a monopolist. Since contractors were awarded cost-plus contracts, guaranteeing them profits, they could indulge in discrimination without regard to the economic cost to them. If discrimination was "bad business" and costly to those who engaged in it, as fair employment advocates often argued, then government contracting was the least likely place to combat it.[37]

In addition, by mid-decade the antidiscrimination effort ran into the problem of qualifications among minority group workers. Resistant employers frequently used the dearth of qualified minorities as a pretext to discriminate, but there were also many cases in which the claim was valid. The committee maintained that the nondiscrimination order protected only qualified individuals. Even some of the most conscientious employers lamented that skill and education levels made them unable to do more. Successful breaches in the color barrier at hiring left the problem of upgrading.[38]

37. John F. Cushman, "Mediation and Education for Equal Economic Opportunity," in *Aspects of Liberty: Essays Presented to Robert E. Cushman,* eds. Milton R. Konvitz and Clinton Rossiter (Ithaca, 1958), 124; Perkins McGuire to Jacob Seidenberg, December 17, 1957, GSF, Box 20, Margaret Garrity to Jacob Seidenberg, March 18, 1959, GSF, Box 1, in PCGC Records, RG 220; U.S. Commission on Civil Rights, *1961 Report, Part III, Employment,* 69; Thomas Sowell, "Ethnicity in a Changing America," *Daedelus,* CVII (1978), 213–37; Williams, *The State Against Blacks.*

38. Procedures for Investigation of Complaints of Discrimination, April 17, 1956, Jacob Seidenberg to Committee, May 11, 1956, GSF, Box 19, Seidenberg Speech,

In addition, most large government contractors had highly organized work forces. The PCGC had disavowed any authority to interfere with the membership practices of labor unions who worked for government contractors. While some of the committee's most successful efforts, like the integration of work in the Gulf Coast oil industry, involved labor unions, this policy, the direct result of the federal government's support for organized labor, gave every contractor a wide loophole to avoid the requirements of the nondiscrimination clause and put significant limits on the PCGC's program.[39]

Civil rights became a more pressing issue in Eisenhower's second term. The *Brown* decision had raised both the expectations of black Americans and the resistance of white southerners. Eisenhower had to face these conflicting pressures in the Little Rock Central High School integration crisis of 1957, as Congress did in the enactment of the Civil Rights Acts of 1957 and 1960, which were concerned mainly with voting rights. The Civil Rights Act of 1957 also created a new President's Committee on Civil Rights. Increased racial tension in the South had a serious impact on the PCGC's ability to integrate work forces.[40]

Civil rights groups demanded more action by the committee and intensified their criticism of it. As it had done with the New York SCAD, the NAACP sought to play a more direct role as broker between government and the black community. While concerned about the lack of confidence in its efforts, the PCGC also believed that it was misrepresented by civil rights groups. The committee agreed on the need for firmer compliance, but wanted to retain its

---

May 9, 1956, GSF, Box 45, Compliance Officers Seminar, December 15–16, 1958, GSF, Box 2, in PCGC Records, RG 220; Gelber, *Black Men and Businessmen,* 58, 130.

39. Roy Wilkins to Jacob Seidenberg, November 2, 1956, in NAACP Papers, III-A-192; Suggested Remarks for Mr. Willis, April 30, 1957, GSF, Box 19, Jacob Seidenberg Memo for Files, GSF, Box 6, Sub-Committee on Oil Industry, July 11, 1955, GSF, Box 30, in PCGC Records, RG 220; Lawrence Stessin, "Labor's Color Line," *Forbes,* February 15, 1955.

40. John Minor Wisdom to John A. Howard, October 24, 1956, GSF, Box 18, Memo to Files, December 15, 1958, Records of the Executive Vice-President, Box 5, in PCGC Records, RG 220.

methods of conciliation, and recognized the legal problems of administrative enforcement.[41]

In the second half of President Eisenhower's second term, the PCGC undertook a more aggressive enforcement policy. The committee had always condemned proportional demands and quota systems, but was turning toward proportionalism as a standard of compliance that signaled a significant change in basic philosophy. Executive Director Jacob Seidenberg noted late in 1957 that "the occupational breakdown of the work force by race probably is the most important information to be gathered during the survey. This is the yardstick by which the contractor's compliance . . . is measured." This proposed standard drew opposition from some compliance officers. While considering such new procedures, the committee was still trying to convince major southern contractors that compliance with the order did not, as many thought, require proportional goals.[42]

Clearly by the late 1950s the executive antidiscrimination effort was moving toward the affirmative action requirements that are

41. "Editorial Comment, News Treatment, Individual Observations, Five Years of Progress, 1953–58: A Report to President Eisenhower by the PCGC," Box 250; Jacob Seidenberg to Perkins McGuire, November 20, 1957, Seidenberg to Richard Nixon, July 23, 1958, Box 251, in Department of Labor Records, RG 174; Memorandum of Herbert Hill, January 13, 1958, in NAACP Papers, III-A-192; "Industry Integration," *Wall Street Journal*, September 29, 1958; Margaret Garrity to Jacob Seidenberg, October 5, 1957, Seidenberg to Files, June 9, 1958, GSF, Box 1, Minutes of PCGC Meeting, April 16, 1958, Report on the Subcommittee on Review, April 15, 1958, GSF, Box 21, Cornelius Ryan to Boris Shishkin, July 21, 1958, Records of the Executive Vice-President, Joseph R. Houchins to Seidenberg, July 25, 1958, GSF, Box 6, Minutes of PCGC Meeting, January 8, 1957, GSF, Box 19, Report of Meeting with Compliance Officers, May 1, 1957, GSF, Box 53, in PCGC Records, RG 220.

42. Seidenberg speech, May 9, 1956, GSF, Box 45, Minutes of PCGC Meeting, December 14, 1955, October 25, 1955, GSF, Box 61, Draft—General Instructions to Compliance Officers, November 27, 1957, T. M. Baldauf to Seidenberg, December 9, 1957, Records of the Director of Compliance, Box 10, in PCGC Records, RG 220; Jacob Seidenberg to All Committee Members, May 11, 1956, in Box 159, Summary, Conference on Equal Job Opportunity Sponsored by PCGC, October 25, 1955, in Box 111, John A. Howard to John Minor Wisdom, July 5, 1956, in Box 158, Department of Labor Records, RG 174; "Drive on Bias Moves into Spotlight," *Business Week*, October 29, 1955.

usually associated with the next administration. The committee had always had the power to negotiate "affirmative action," such as recruitment from black vocational schools or advertising in black newspapers, as a term of compliance, even if it implied "reverse discrimination." The committee believed it could order affirmative action as a remedy in cases of racial imbalance, regardless of intent to discriminate. Executive Vice-Chairman Irving Ferman recommended that the committee begin to insist on numbers as its measure of success, using statistical, industry-wide surveys. The PCGC now regarded integration as the "affirmative duty to make specific commitments. These are specific only when they spell out the fact that a definite number of qualified Negroes will be employed within a given period of time." By 1960 a program involving such goals and timetables was taking shape, but the committee began to run into problems in states with fair employment practice laws, because they made racial data collection illegal. Employers like the Ford Motor Company resisted what they felt were imputations of discrimination based on racial imbalance and illegal pressure to meet quotas.[43]

Congress refused the administration's recommendation to give the committee statutory authority in the Civil Rights Act of 1960. The committee then attempted to change its methods within the confines of its existing power, and increased its pressure on contractors to hire more minority workers. The committee hoped it could use prime contractors to persuade all-white craft unions to open their membership to Negroes by the threat of hiring non-union minority group workers. It declared that "the total absence of minority groups from the skilled or better-paying jobs is treated as a prima facie case of discrimination with the burden on the con-

43. Review of Case No. 53, September 17, 1958, GSF, Box 21, Joseph Houchins to Irving Ferman, September 15, 1959, GSF, Box 83, Minutes of PCGC Meeting, September 29, 1959, Irving Ferman and Jacob Seidenberg to Committee, September 24, 1959, GSF, Box 22, Speech, n. d., GSF, Box 86, K. D. Cassidy to Margaret Garrity, June 16, 1960, GSF, Box 74, Meeting of Compliance Officers, August 14, 1957, GSF, Box 60, Report on the Compliance Survey Program, November 14, 1958, GSF, Box 53, Percy H. Williams to Margaret Garrity, March 6, 1961, GSF, Box 2, in PCGC Records, RG 220.

tractor to demonstrate that his employment policy conforms to national policy." In March, 1960, the PCGC decided to institute a program requiring government contractors to furnish monthly data on their racial hiring practices and future hiring plans. In April it delayed this plan, although it was applied to contractors in the District of Columbia who hired through the all-white International Brotherhood of Electrical Workers (IBEW). Instead of using its ultimate sanction of contract cancellation, which might prove legally complicated, the committee encouraged employers to hire Negroes on a "limited preferential basis." If equally qualified black and white applicants presented themselves, the contractor would give preference to the Negro. While some objected, many contractors were willing to adopt such a policy. The policy of preferential treatment arose out of the realization that, due to limited opportunities to become qualified in the past, even a perfect nondiscrimination policy would not result in a large increase in minority employment. As one observer pointed out, although employers, unions, and most government agencies condemned the idea, preferential treatment was an increasingly common approach to the discrimination problem. Even so, the results were often no more than "token" minority representation.[44]

The problems that the PCGC faced by the end of Eisenhower's administration were largely beyond its control within the limits of its operations. The situation in southern industry showed that segregation was not compatible with fair employment. The free rein given to labor unions to discriminate was another obvious obstacle to progress. By the late 1950s it was more apparent than ever that the main barrier to black economic progress was not at the initial hiring stage but in promotion and upgrading. Here employers faced the problem of finding qualified minority group members to move beyond entry-level jobs. The problem was compounded where the work force was not all white but minorities were fewer than their population ratio. An employer who wanted to discriminate could

44. *Engineering News-Record*, March 24, 1960, p. 330, April 21, 1960, p. 145; U.S. Commission on Civil Rights, *1961 Report, Part III*, 68; Cushman, "Mediation and Education," 123; Ray Marshall, "Equal Employment Opportunities: Problems and Prospects," *Labor Law Journal*, XVI (1965), 464; Belz, *Equality Transformed*, 15.

devise his own quota system to limit the number of minorities. Since the PCGC had not devised a clear definition of employment discrimination, such quota systems would be almost undetectable by a committee which had a difficult enough time identifying blatant discrimination.[45] White-collar and service jobs continued to replace blue-collar manufacturing jobs, with qualification requirements that fewer minorities could meet. The committee was limited to government contractors, and lack of economic competition in the public sector made it easier for employers to discriminate than in the private sector. Labor unions, likewise protected from competition, were beyond its reach. Finally, the economic recessions of the mid-to-late 1950s showed that economic duress increased the number of complaints of discrimination. The PCGC showed itself willing to adopt race-conscious proportionalist methods, and civil rights groups moderated their criticism of the Eisenhower administration because of its efforts in employment.[46]

The Democratic administration of President John F. Kennedy in 1961 brought a new approach to the employment discrimination problem. Kennedy was reluctant to pursue civil rights legislation because of his dependence on southern Democrats in Congress. In lieu of congressional enactment of a fair employment practice law, President Kennedy issued Executive Order 10925 on March 6, 1961. The order created a new agency, the President's Committee on Equal Employment Opportunity (PCEEO), and imposed more explicit and stringent requirements on government contractors. It provided for a compliance reporting system, a fuller version of PCGC surveys that looked toward a statistical profile of the nation's

45. As late as 1959 in a workshop for religious leaders, the same questions of the relationship between numbers of minority group employees and the existence of discrimination were being asked, and still no clear answer, or alternative to this way of thinking about the problem of discrimination, was given by the committee; see "Transcript, PCGC, Religious Leaders Conference," May 11, 1959, in Department of Labor Records, Box 288, RG 174.

46. Meier and Bracey, "The NAACP as a Reform Movement," 26; Jesse Thomas Moore, Jr., *A Search for Equality: The National Urban League, 1910–61* (University Park, Penn., 1981), 185; Robert Fredrick Burk, *The Eisenhower Administration and Black Civil Rights* (Knoxville, 1984), 107.

racial employment pattern. The order provided explicit sanctions for government contractors who violated the order, apart from the threat of contract termination. The PCEEO was empowered to initiate its own investigations into discriminatory employment practices without waiting for an individual complaint. Despite the order's new emphasis on enforcement, it did not provide any new standards for proving discrimination, and this lack had always been the problem in making fair employment requirements "enforceable." Instead it provided that contractors not only cease discrimination, but also take "affirmative action" to ensure equal employment opportunity.[47]

The content of the phrase "affirmative action" was amorphous at this time. The term originated in the National Labor Relations Act of 1935, under which the NLRB had the power to order employers and labor unions to cease and desist from unfair labor practices, and also order them to hire, reinstate, promote, or take other appropriate affirmative action to conform to the act. State antidiscrimination commissions had the power to order "affirmative action," and the PCGC had negotiated cases involving it. The administration likely meant it to mean more aggressive recruitment, training, and encouragement for minority group advancement, to build on the gains made in the 1950s in hiring and to extend the steps taken in this direction by the PCGC. While "affirmative action" eventually became the symbol of a radical departure from the color-blind, individual-rights, procedural model of antidiscrimination, this potential was not altogether apparent in 1961. This does not mean, however, as one historian has argued, that "nowhere in the liberal establishment circa 1960 was affirmative action interpreted to mean a special preference or compensatory treatment for minorities that would not be equally available to all citizens." Most historians share the assumption that antidiscrimination advocates maintained the traditional, color-blind, individual-rights, procedural model until after the passage of the Civil Rights Act of 1964 and the civil rights movement had been superseded by the black power movement. However, the willingness of civil rights and asso-

47. CFR 3 (1959–64), 448.

ciated liberal groups to endorse the idea of special treatment for minority groups was evident as far back as the 1930s, receiving its fullest expression in the *Hughes* case of 1950. Rejected by the Supreme Court, the idea of preferential treatment appeared to lose favor in the 1950s. But in actuality it was still very much available for revival by civil rights groups in the 1960s and was present in later PCGC efforts. The idea that affirmative action began as a color-blind, individual-rights policy which was superseded by race-conscious measures only after the Civil Rights Act of 1964 ignores the extent to which racial preference was an objective of liberal equal employment opportunity policy throughout the 1960s.[48]

In its first year of operation President Kennedy's Committee met resistance from federal bureaucrats who believed it advocated preferential treatment. PCEEO Executive Director John G. Field responded that a committed attempt to increase the proportion of minority group employees was not necessarily unfair. While he did not endorse specific quotas he did recommend an energetic and resourceful recruitment and training program. But it is difficult to see how the PCEEO could improve upon the performance of the PCGC without resorting to some program of preferential treatment. The PCEEO observed most of the same limitations of the PCGC. The new committee would not impair the national defense program by mass cancellation of contracts to combat discrimination, nor would it confront exclusionary labor unions, nor could it produce large numbers of minorities qualified for technical and supervisory positions. A new approach, one less cautious about the difficulty of proving individual acts of discrimination at law, would be needed to achieve a dramatic change in minority employment status.[49]

The most visible sign of a new approach to employment discrimination by the PCEEO was the Plans for Progress program, which

48. Graham, *Civil Rights,* 34; Belz, *Equality Transformed,* 18; Jacob Seidenberg, "The President's Committee on Government Contracts: 1953–60—An Appraisal" (Columbia University School of Law, 1961, photocopy).

49. George Meany to Lyndon B. Johnson, August 15, 1961, D. Otis Beasley to Arthur J. Goldberg, April 18, 1961, "Conference on Equal Employment Opportunity," October 19, 1961, in General Subject Files of Secretary Arthur J. Goldberg, Box 44, RG 174.

sought to induce prominent government contractors to devise their own plans for increasing minority group hiring and upgrading. Using statistical profiles of the work force, it did not devise any new definition of discrimination or identify particular discriminatory policies of employers. It was concerned only with an increase in the number and level of minority group employment. It implied preferential treatment based on race, although it prescribed no openly preferential policies or quotas. The PCEEO depended on voluntary compliance, since it did not devise a standard of fair employment that could meet legal scrutiny. In order to achieve results, it sponsored a program of voluntary racial preference. In 1963 the National Urban League's Whitney Young, who advocated preferential treatment and compensatory treatment for blacks, praised Plans for Progress employers for engaging in such preferential hiring.[50]

After a year of operation the PCEEO drew fire from a number of quarters. Within the agency there was a dispute between moderates like Robert Troutman, engineer of the voluntary Plans for Progress effort, and activists like John G. Field, who favored enforcement rather than voluntarism. In Congress, Alabama Senator Lister Hill objected to the interference of the PCEEO in private enterprise. He regarded the executive order as a usurpation of congressional authority, because the PCEEO was nowhere by law permitted to take the action it did. Congress had many good reasons for not acting in this field, Hill wrote to the committee. Congress recognized "the very real, very difficult problem of defining, in an acceptable way and with any precision, exactly what constitutes unlawful discrimination in employment because of race, creed, color, or national origin." Neither Executive Order 10925 nor the committee had addressed this problem. As a result, despite committee denial, Hill remonstrated, its whole purpose was to force employers to hire and promote minorities.[51]

On the other side, civil rights activists took an increasingly critical view of the PCEEO. NAACP Labor Secretary Herbert Hill noted

50. Belz, *Equality Transformed,* 17–22; Graham, *Civil Rights,* 50–59; New York *Times,* September 30, 1963, p. 30.

51. New York *Times,* June 18, 1962, p. 1; Lister Hill to PCEEO, July 12, 1961, in Department of Labor Records, Box 44, RG 174.

that Executive Order 10925 was potentially a vast improvement over Eisenhower's orders in its call for affirmative action, compliance reporting, and sanctions. However, fear of southern conservatives in Congress had turned the order into a virtual replica of its predecessors.[52] Robert Troutman's Plans for Progress was a feckless public relations scheme which drained off resources that were needed for a real, systematic enforcement effort. Hill's appraisal did not represent the opinion of all civil rights activists, and NAACP Executive Secretary Roy Wilkins upbraided Hill for providing ammunition for opponents of equal employment opportunity. The Reverend Martin Luther King, Jr., of the Southern Christian Leadership Conference, thought Hill's observations were on target, indicating the impatience of the newer, more militant civil rights groups.[53]

In 1962 Vice-President Lyndon Johnson, chairman of the PCEEO, brought in Theodore Kheel as an outside consultant to monitor the PCEEO's work. Kheel had been a labor consultant for the National Urban League and a critic of the voluntary, conciliatory approach to equal employment opportunity. He assumed that the "affirmative action" provision meant that the PCEEO would go beyond cases of overt discrimination. Discrimination in the past, Kheel argued, had made such a lasting impression on minority group workers that it was necessary to "encourage employers to seek out Negroes who will be able to qualify" for employment and upgrading. The lack of qualified minority group members should no longer excuse an employer's lack of minority group employees. He urged the PCEEO to add more enforcement power to its conciliation and voluntary compliance program. Finally, Kheel recommended a pattern-centered rather than an individual-complaint procedure. The committee might just as well discard the entire individual complaint process, he said. In the past civil rights groups evinced concern for

52. In fact, Kennedy's caution on civil rights was for fear of offending *moderate* southerners like Lister Hill, lest he alienate them from the rest of his legislative program; see Brauer, *John F. Kennedy and the Second Reconstruction,* 62.

53. Graham, *Civil Rights,* 50–53; "The NAACP Appraises the First Year of the PCEEO," April 6, 1962, in NAACP Papers, III-A-186; Roy Wilkins to Herbert Hill, April 6, 1962, Martin Luther King, Jr., to Hill, April 30, 1962, in NAACP Papers, III-A-192; Whitney Young to Editor, New York *Times,* June 21, 1962, in NUL Papers, I-A-42.

the relief of individual victims of discrimination as well as a regard for a wider, systematic approach to the problem of discrimination. Frustration with the individual or disparate-treatment approach had by the 1960s led to calls for primary reliance on the systematic or disparate-impact theory. Behind this shift lurked the assumption that proportionalism was normal, and imbalance the mark of discrimination.[54]

Like New York's FEPC, the PCEEO applied new methods to the apprenticeship problem. Equal employment opportunity advocates targeted apprenticeship programs in the 1960s because they regarded them as a key to the problem of training and upgrading. Apprentice programs gave skills to unskilled workers, and since they were usually operated jointly by employers and labor unions, they provided a way of altering union practices through government contractors. Finally, apprentice programs in the skilled construction trades, with their tradition of nepotistic selection, were among the most obviously discriminatory of all aspects of employment. The PCEEO apprenticeship effort was also prompted by the protest activity of the early 1960s. Students at Howard University protested the exclusionary practices of the Washington, D.C., building trades that worked on the construction of a gymnasium. PCEEO investigation revealed no specific acts of discrimination, but "this is due in large part to the fact that segregation in these trades is so complete and has continued for so long in D.C. that few Negroes apply." Unable to affect this particular project, PCEEO Special Counsel N. Thompson Powers set out to devise regulations for the future, to be administered by the Bureau of Apprenticeship and Training (BAT) in the Department of Labor. An affirmative action program in apprenticeship would consist of two things: an announcement that qualified minority group members would be encouraged to apply, and, as an earnest of good intention, "the selection of a significant number of minority group apprentices." Secretary of Labor Willard W. Wirtz recommended leaving the measure of "a significant number" vague

54. Graham, *Civil Rights*, 57; "Report of Theodore W. Kheel to Vice-President Lyndon Johnson on the Structure and Operations of the PCEEO," [1962], in NUL Papers, I-A-42; Brauer, *John F. Kennedy and the Second Reconstruction*, 148; New York *Times*, April 17, 1962, p. 21.

enough to allow for flexibility in different trades and different areas. The only definition agreed upon was that it be "more than a token." The federal government did not want to impose quotas, but it would accept an arrangement whereby an apprenticeship program set aside a significant number of positions for minority group applicants.[55]

Such a provision would be controversial, Powers realized, but he believed that "only such a positive step will generate the necessary interest in applying for apprenticeship on the part of qualified Negroes." Mere statements of nondiscriminatory policy were not enough. If contractors chose apprentices on the basis of merit alone, he said, the PCEEO could probably not require anything more, "although I believe such an arrangement would still be regarded with suspicion by Negroes and would result in few additional Negroes being selected." The set-aside method was appropriate in a system where numbers of places were already set aside for members' relatives and friends. It would accommodate the trade's desire to preserve family ties at the same time that it met obligations to provide equal employment opportunity. Legal challenges by contractors would again raise the problem of legal proof of discrimination, Powers warned, underscoring the fact that proof of discrimination was the *sine qua non* of any enforceable antidiscrimination policy.[56]

The BAT decided on a program that allowed contractors to choose to select apprentices on the basis of merit alone or, in exchange for the privilege of nepotism, to use a "system which gives preference for a significant number of positions to minority group applicants." Powers noted that the bureau did not require reduced standards to admit minority group members. He came closer to defining "a significant number" as between a third and a half of a proposed apprentice class. He told Wirtz that the only evidence re-

55. Strauss and Ingerman, "Public Policy and Discrimination in Apprenticeship," 285–331; Hill, "Racial Discrimination," 215–24; Thompson Powers, "Memorandum on Construction Industry, Washington, D.C.," April 29, 1963, Powers to Willard W. Wirtz, "Status Report," May 4, 1963, in General Subject Files of Secretary Willard W. Wirtz, Box 66, RG 174; Brauer, *John F. Kennedy and the Second Reconstruction,* 82.

56. Powers, "Memorandum on Construction Industry," RG 174.

quired as proof that a contractor had not fulfilled affirmative action requirements was "evidence that there are no or only a token number of minority group members employed in a particular industry in a particular area."[57]

When the Labor Department promulgated these standards in July, 1963, it scrupulously avoided the language of preference. It allowed contractors to select by merit alone, or, if they continued to use nepotism, to take "whatever steps are necessary, in acting upon application lists developed prior to this time, to offset the effects of previous practices under which discriminatory patterns of employment have resulted." The new standards abolished established waiting lists that were based on racially exclusive policies. Although this would displace white applicants who were not themselves discriminating, Secretary Wirtz hoped that enlarging the number of applicants accepted would minimize the number of displaced whites. This implied preferential treatment for minority group members as compensation for the effects of past discrimination.[58]

The ideas of the Labor Department were a fair replication of the ideas that led to the Interior Department's construction industry quota system of thirty years earlier. The Interior Department had proceeded on the assumption that, because it was impossible to define compliance with the nondiscrimination clause of government contracts, a certain percentage of payroll to black labor should be regarded as prima facie evidence of compliance. In a similar way, Powers noted that even if contractors followed a perfect merit selection policy, civil rights groups would remain suspicious and substantial gains by minority group workers would not necessarily follow. Contractors were permitted to discriminate as much as they liked beyond a certain point—the nepotistic system was not only preserved, but served as a sort of model for the Labor Department.

57. Powers to Wirtz, "Status Report," RG 174.

58. House Committee on Education and Labor, Wirtz testimony, June 6, 1963, *Equal Employment Opportunity: Hearings Before the General Subcommittee on Labor*, 88th Cong., 1st sess., 1963, pp. 453–55 (hereafter cited as 1963 House EEO Hearings); Powers to Wirtz, "Status Report on Howard Gymnasium," Wirtz to Gino J. Sinni and others, June 5, 1963, U.S. Department of Labor, Circular 64–7, July 17, 1963, in Department of Labor Records, Box 67, RG 174; New York *Times*, July 27, 1963, p. 1.

Contractors could give preference based on race just as they gave preference based on family relationship.

The Labor Department retreated slightly from its July, 1963, proposed regulation in the face of contractor and public opposition. Local AFL building tradesmen were a tight-knit group and unusually sensitive to outside interference in their organizations. The department claimed that its standards did not impose quotas, but that contractor reluctance to abide by merit standards required another means of demonstrating equal employment opportunity. "Anyone who is offended by this alternative can avoid it by following the merit selection system," they noted. The Defense Department expressed concern about "minimum standards," but realized the necessity for some objective standards. In November, Secretary of Labor Wirtz told an Urban League audience that he was opposed to quotas because they assumed a zero-sum competition between racial groups. "The victims of preference would be individual human beings, and more likely than not today, persons who are themselves opposed to discrimination," he noted. At the same time, Wirtz repeated his commitment to special measures to make up for the effects of past discrimination. With regard to education he stated that "'more than equality' is not justified but is required so far as preparation for opportunity is concerned. There is no unfair hurting of someone else if preference in education is accorded to those who have been previously disadvantaged. Here there is only the necessary compensation for the ravages of a century of unfairness." When the final version of the proposed regulation was issued in the December, 1963, *Federal Register*, language suggesting redistribution rather than special recruitment efforts had been deleted. To defuse the quota issue, the regulations held that "nothing in this part shall be construed to require any program sponsor or employer to select or employ apprentices in the proportion which their race, color, religion, or national origin bears to the total population."[59]

59. Floyd Feeney to John Donovan, July 24, 1963, Norman S. Paul to Wirtz, October 22, 1963, in Box 67, "Address by Willard W. Wirtz at the Washington Urban League's Equal Opportunity Day Committee's 1963 Observance," November 18, 1963, in Box 113, *Federal Register*, December 18, 1963, Title 29—Labor, Subtitle A— Office of the Secretary of Labor—Nondiscrimination in Apprenticeship, Box 154,

Trying to avoid the difficult task of devising a standard of proof of discrimination that would make a color-blind antidiscrimination policy legally enforceable, the PCEEO attempted to encourage voluntary racial preference for minority group members. It is unlikely that in the absence of preferential treatment nonwhite, blue-collar employment by government contractors would have increased, while total blue-collar employment was declining. The BAT program tried to combine preferential treatment with enforcement. This effort quickly ran into the thicket of racial quotas, and the administration retreated from it. It appeared again that voluntarism did not achieve results, and that enforcement could not avoid quota hiring.[60]

Despite its best efforts, the PCEEO failed to satisfy the demands and expectations of civil rights advocates in the early 1960s. It achieved more visible results than its PCGC predecessor, opened more doors for minority workers, and prepared businessmen for affirmative action—including counting by race and preferential treatment if necessary. Yet it achieved only "token" results, as any program limited to government employment probably would. In important respects the Kennedy PCEEO continued the policies and foundered on the same rocks as the Eisenhower committee. Its choice of voluntarism in Plans for Progress and its reluctance to resort to sanctions reflected the fact that the PCEEO had no more satisfactory formula for proof of discrimination than the PCGC. Without legally satisfactory proof, no enforcement effort could survive a court challenge.[61]

The PCEEO had to fear reaction in Congress as well as failure in the courts. John F. Kennedy chose to take up the issue of employment discrimination through executive order, rather than through legislation, in order to pursue other parts of his domestic agenda

---

RG 174; New York *Times*, October 20, 1963, p. 1; December 18, 1963; "Federal Apprenticeship Rules Stand," *Engineering News-Record*, August 15, 1963; "Bias Drive Breeds Anger and Frustration," *Engineering News-Record*, August 29, 1963.

60. Marshall, "Equal Employment Opportunities," 453–68; Ray Marshall, "Prospects for Equal Employment Opportunity: Conflicting Portents," *Monthly Labor Review*, LXXXVIII (June, 1965), 650–53.

61. Gelber, *Black Men and Businessmen*, 142.

without offending southern Democrats. The civil rights movement of the early 1960s, beginning with the Greensboro sit-ins and proceeding through Birmingham and the March on Washington, expressed the aspirations and impatience of black Americans, and eventually forced Kennedy to call for a comprehensive civil rights act in 1963. Even then he called first for a general program of full employment and job training, followed by a strengthened, statutory PCEEO. Kennedy renewed his support for pending FEPC legislation without elaborating on the specifics of that legislation. The executive branch had reached the limits of its own antidiscrimination efforts, and Congress again became the principal theater of policy making.[62]

62. House, *Civil Rights Message from the President of the United States*, 88th Cong., 1st sess., 1963, H. Doc. 124.

8   The Civil Rights Act of 1964

The civil rights movement gained irresistible momentum between 1960, when the Greensboro sit-ins occurred, and 1963, when the crisis of direct-action protest in Birmingham, Alabama, made civil rights a national political issue. Popular calls for Congress to act against segregation provided an opportunity to enact national fair employment legislation. After keeping a low profile on civil rights for two years, President John F. Kennedy at last called for civil rights legislation in June, 1963. His proposal did not include a fair employment practice title, but rather asked Congress to give statutory authority for the President's Committee on Equal Employment Opportunity. Congress had considered FEP legislation in 1961 and 1963, however, and chose to deal with the problem of employment discrimination in what became Title VII of the Civil Rights Act of 1964.

The House Education and Labor Committee held hearings and reported FEP bills in 1961 and 1963. Chaired by Representative James Roosevelt of California, these hearings revealed that the debate over fair employment had changed considerably in the nine years since Congress had last considered such legislation. Supporters of the legislation argued repeatedly that the major challenge for minority group workers was no longer in hiring, but in training, upgrading, and promotion in the skilled, professional, and managerial areas. The principal problem lay in the area of minority "qualifications." Civil rights groups now argued that the problem of discrimination in employment was more complicated, deeply rooted, and structural than it had appeared in the 1940s and 1950s. Minorities were the victims not so much of blatant exclusion, but of business practices that reinforced the effects of past exclusion.

The changed outlook in the field of employment discrimination was evident in the 1961 hearings on equal employment legislation. Arnold Maremont, a Chicago manufacturer who regarded himself as a fair employer, impatiently asked, "I don't see why those who oppose fair employment practices don't stand up and admit what they are really fighting for. They want discrimination." Yet Maremont found himself under scrutiny when the committee discovered that, although he employed some twelve hundred Negroes and had promoted many of them, he had no black executives in a work force of eight thousand. Maremont's explanation that he could find no Negro qualified for an executive position, and that his Japanese-American financial officer was proof that he did not discriminate, was unavailing. Illinois Democrat Roman C. Pucinski said that if the committee accepted Maremont's explanation, it would "place a very serious cloud on this legislation." If a self-consciously fair employer like Maremont could not find a qualified Negro for an executive position, it was highly doubtful that the broad reach of employers could do any better. The committee impressed upon Maremont the importance of seeking out and taking affirmative action to qualify a Negro for such a position.[1]

Pucinski also wondered how legislation could reach the problem of "tokenism," referring to an employer who hired a small number of minorities in his work force to give the appearance of compliance with the requirements of a fair employment law. It was clear that this was one of the consequences of fair employment laws in the northern states. Minorities were admitted into occupations formerly closed to them, but the door had only been opened slightly. The fair employment process seemed to be stalled. Although this problem was on the mind of some committee members and witnesses, nothing in the legislation specifically addressed this problem.[2]

1. House Committee on Education and Labor, *Equal Employment Opportunity: Hearings Before the Special Subcommittee on Labor of the Committee on Education and Labor,* 87th Cong., 1st sess., 1962, pp. 92–101; hereafter cited as 1961 House EEO Hearings.
2. *Ibid.,* 163, 305.

Representatives of civil rights groups were now more willing to make exceptions to the color-blind rule that they once had regarded as the standard of fair employment. The issue was repeatedly brought up with reference to the usefulness of compiling racial statistics on an employer's work force. Before the late 1950s, civil rights groups had insisted that employers be prohibited from classifying their workers by race. In several states fair employment rules prohibited pre-employment inquiries into or reference to an applicant's race, creed, color, national origin or ancestry, and many employers had dispensed with all racial record keeping. By the 1960s, however, it appeared that the absence of racial information hindered monitoring of compliance with fair employment laws. Discriminatory employers were able to claim ignorance of the racial composition of their work forces. Edwin C. Berry of the Urban League regretted this development. "I must confess," he said, "that in the early 1940s, when the great drive was to get race off the records, I was one of the leaders in it. I was hollering the loudest, and now I apologize for having done it because I think it was a mistake." Others agreed with Berry that in order to monitor properly the extent of the problem and the progress of compliance, it was now necessary to become positively color-conscious. Stanley Lowell of the New York City Human Rights Commission stated, "I feel very strongly that the whole doctrine of color blind is outmoded, and that the doctrine should be color conscious." Lowell noted that New York City had already rejected the color-blind doctrine in public school and public housing integration.[3]

The related issue of preferential treatment for minority group members was also addressed by some civil rights advocates. Walter B. Lewis and Samuel E. Harris of the Washington, D.C., Urban League argued that job qualifications might have to be relaxed in order for minorities to qualify. This was necessary to overcome the effects of past discrimination, something that simple color-blind merit policies did not do. Lewis couched his argument in terms of compensatory treatment, saying, "Don't kid ourselves and think we are not being fair because we have given preference to whites for an awful long time in the very denial of the opportunities for Ne-

3. *Ibid.*, 190, 322, 601.

groes." Representative Augustus Hawkins of California was careful to deny that the proposed legislation envisioned preferential treatment, saying, "I certainly think the record should be very clear that the proposed legislation certainly does not imply that employment or its benefits will be distributed on a racial basis. Actually it seeks to achieve just the opposite. I would certainly think that under the proposed legislation it would be illegal to actually select individuals on a preferential basis even though we may for expedience think that should be done." Likewise when Cernoria Johnson of the Urban League brought up the concept of compensatory activity, Hawkins induced Johnson to make explicit that this did not consist of special favors. Compensatory treatment meant "accelerated machinery to guarantee the conferring of justice only on the basis of qualifications and merit." Preferential treatment, she said, was analogous to slavery and white paternalism.[4]

Secretary of Labor Willard Wirtz discussed the issue of preferential treatment with regard to the Bureau of Apprenticeship and Training's new regulations for admission to training programs.[5] Old waiting lists for apprenticeship positions would have to be abolished if they were drawn up on a racially discriminatory basis. Although this would displace white applicants who were not themselves guilty of discrimination, Wirtz said, these lists could not be allowed to perpetuate the discrimination of the past. He hoped that an expansion of the applicant pool would minimize the number of displaced whites. Thomas E. Harris, associate general counsel of the AFL-CIO, discussed the issue in the context of seniority. Even if all labor unions admitted minorities into full membership, they would still be liable to the "last hired, first fired" rule of seniority. Since the number of Negroes employed had been rising in industries where overall numbers were falling, this would be an acute problem. Harris rejected the idea of superseniority for members of minority groups who had been the victims of discrimination in the past.[6]

Whereas before 1953 FEPC advocates held up the state FEPCs as models for federal action and proof that the FEPC concept worked

4. 1963 House EEO Hearings, 56, 230–33.
5. See chap. seven.
6. 1961 House EEO Hearings, 83, 453–55.

effectively and without harming business, they cast a somewhat different light on the state efforts in the early 1960s. In 1961, Roman Pucinski was more impressed by the testimony of witnesses from groups that were critical of the state FEPCs' record than by that of Elmer Carter of the New York SCAD. Pucinski was inclined to fault the administration of the law rather than the law itself. Shirley Siegel, assistant attorney general for civil rights in New York, vigorously defended the SCAD's work, saying that "for the benefit of a national congressional committee it would perhaps be more appropriate to lay emphasis on the enormous progress that has been made in the last fifteen years." Likewise Senator Jacob Javitz of New York said that the New York law was deficient neither in itself nor in its administration. "I believe the defects are in our society," Javitz concluded. Nobody suggested, however, that the problem was too deeply rooted for any law to be effective against it.[7]

The question of the effectiveness of the state FEPCs persisted, with Roman Pucinski insisting that New York's antidiscrimination law was "bordering on mockery." Herbert Hill, NAACP labor secretary and scourge of the state FEPCs, noted that "with one or two exceptions, state and municipal FEPCs are drastically limited in their effectiveness by inadequate funds and inadequate staff." Representative Thomas P. Gill of Hawaii was the only one to ask why a federal FEPC law modeled after the New York state statute would be any more effective. Hill answered that a federal FEPC should emphasize affirmative action, have the power to investigate without an individual complaint, and focus on entire industries and patterns of employment. For Hill and other FEP advocates, the state FEPCs had provided models to avoid.[8]

The Equal Employment Opportunity bill of 1962 declared that discrimination on the basis of race, religion, color, national origin, ancestry or age was "contrary to the American principles of liberty and equality of opportunity," as well as economically wasteful and damaging to the nation's foreign interests. Based on Congress' constitutional power to regulate interstate commerce, it prohibited dis-

7. *Ibid.,* 633, 650, 881.
8. 1963 House EEO Hearings, 35, 143.

crimination by employers and labor unions of twenty-five or more, excluding government workers and tax-exempt membership clubs.[9] The bill established a five-member Equal Employment Opportunity Commission (EEOC) for enforcement. The commission could initiate its own investigations, but could not issue cease-and-desist orders. Instead, it could bring suit in federal court if it found discrimination. An individual could also bring suit under the bill if the Commission did not, and if any member of the commission gave permission.

The mode of FEP enforcement had been a key issue in the postwar debate, and choice of administrative or judicial enforcement of antidiscrimination orders was the principal issue animating FEP debate after 1960. Although the Equal Employment Opportunity bills of 1962 and 1963 were largely modeled along the classic FEPC lines established by the New York Law Against Discrimination of 1945, they differed in method of enforcement and administration. The 1962 bill moved away from the NLRB cease-and-desist enforcement mechanism. State FEPC experience had shown that conciliation was the most effective method of securing compliance with the law, and that enforcement orders against recalcitrant offenders were seldom necessary. The House committee deemed it potentially more effective in hard cases if the EEOC brought suit immediately in federal court. Subcommittee chairman James Roosevelt was the chief advocate for judicial enforcement. It appealed to conservatives, who preferred the safeguards of jury trials in federal court.

Conservatives were not pleased, however, at the innovation of the 1962 bill allowing commission investigation absent a specific verified complaint. This initiation or "self-starting" provision, though possessed by some state FEPCs, remained controversial. Opponents feared that this power would invite abuse of the law, permitting the EEOC to engage in "fishing expeditions" that would badger and ha-

9. Previous FEP bills made it unlawful to "refuse to hire," or "to discriminate against" individuals on the basis of race. H.R. 10144 was apparently the first bill that made it unlawful "to *fail* or refuse to hire" on this basis. All subsequent bills, and Title VII of the Civil Rights Act of 1964 used this language, although neither supporters nor opponents remarked on the evolution of language. Alfred W. Blumrosen, "The Duty of Fair Recruitment Under the Civil Rights Act of 1964," *Rutgers Law Review*, XXII (1968), 474.

rass employers. Republican members of the committee who otherwise approved of the bill expressed their disapproval of this section.[10]

The EEO bill of 1963 abjured the novel administrative provisions of the 1962 bill. Following the NLRB model, it returned to a cease-and-desist administrative model and required a verified individual complaint to proceed. However, the 1963 proposal made the EEOC a dual body. It provided for a single EEO administrator, responsible directly to the president, who would conduct investigations and issue orders. Respondents could appeal these orders to an EEO board, which would review the record of the case and sustain the administrator's ruling if accompanied by a preponderance of evidence. The federal courts could review commission decisions based only on substantial evidence. Because it rejected judicial enforcement and jury trial safeguards, this bill, which followed the NLRB model more closely, provoked more opposition than the 1962 bill had.[11]

The Senate followed the line of development in the 1963 House bill. Minnesota Democrat Hubert H. Humphrey introduced a bill, S. 1937, that was the most original departure from traditional FEPC bills yet. Humphrey cited economic statistics that detailed the vast gap between whites and nonwhites in America. This gap was in fact widening, Humphrey argued, due to basic changes in the national economy. The "second industrial revolution" was destroying jobs in agriculture and older production industries that used unskilled minority labor. It was creating jobs in areas of the economy for which minorities were not adequately prepared. A fair employment program for the 1960s, Humphrey said, would have to address itself to an economy that was vastly different from the one existing in the late 1940s when the initial state FEPCs were created.[12]

10. House, *Equal Employment Opportunity Act of 1962*, 87th Cong., 2nd sess., 1962, H Rept. 1370.

11. House, *Equal Employment Opportunity Act of 1963*, 88th Cong., 1st sess., 1963, H. Rept. 570; Andrew J. Biemiller to Boris Shishkin, February 9, 1962, in Meany Archives, Collection 25, Box 6.

12. *CR* 109 (July 24, 1963), 13244; Senate Committee on Labor and Public Welfare, *Equal Employment Opportunity: Hearings Before the Subcommittee on Employment and Manpower*, 88th Cong., 1st sess., 1963, pp. 137–44 (hereafter cited as Senate 1963 EEO Hearings).

Humphrey's bill proceeded from the assumption that the fair employment approach of the state FEPCs had proved inadequate. The individual, complaint-centered approach had to be replaced by a self-starting, pattern-centered, industry-wide one. The kind of willful, intentional, disparate-treatment discrimination that state FEPCs dealt with remained a problem, but it was mixed with impersonal, institutional processes that affected the availability of jobs for nonwhites. "Therefore," Humphrey said, "this legislation departs from the traditional concept of enforcing nondiscrimination in employment and seeks to establish the broader and more comprehensive obligation of promoting equal employment opportunities." While not departing radically from previous FEPC language, Humphrey left room for a more aggressive approach to the employment discrimination problem.[13]

The statement of findings and declaration of policy with which Humphrey introduced his bill indicated that a larger conception of employment discrimination was taking shape. Congress declared, "because of the accumulated impact of prior discrimination and related disadvantages in employment, education, housing, and other areas, a nationwide effort is urged to secure equal opportunity by the affirmative and conscious efforts of government, employers, unions, and others." This was the first mention of an attempt to take into account, or compensate for the effects of previous discrimination. The bill covered employers of one person or more, the broadest coverage ever proposed. The EEO administration was divided between an administrator and a board, as in the 1963 House bill. Humphrey placed the office of Equal Employment Opportunity administrator in the Department of Labor, in order to use the

---

13. Hubert H. Humphrey to NAACP, August 1, 1963, in NAACP Papers, III-A-147. Michael Evan Gold describes S. 1937's "equal employment opportunity" as a combination of traditional FEP antidiscrimination with the new requirement of affirmative action. While S. 1937 was a departure from traditional FEP bills, Humphrey had coined the term "equal employment opportunity" in the early 1950s with Irving Ives, to avoid the "compulsory" epithet with which many detractors tarred postwar FEP bills. Michael Evan Gold, "*Griggs'* Folly: An Essay on the Theory, Problems, and Origin of the Adverse Impact Definition of Discrimination and a Recommendation for Reform," *Industrial Relations Law Journal*, VII (1985), 429–598.

professional resources of this department. The administrator had the power to promulgate regulations and requirements to enforce compliance with the law as necessary. He had the power to initiate investigations, "including inspections regularly made under his authority to assure general compliance" with the law. This provision worried those who feared bureaucratic "fishing expeditions." The administrator was able to issue cease-and-desist orders, revisable by the EEO board. The board was a five-man independent agency in the executive branch which heard appeals from the administrator, but had no policy making or operating functions. Above the board, the limited right of appeal to a federal circuit court of appeals remained as in the 1963 House bill.[14]

Humphrey's bill raised the fear that the requirement of promoting equal employment opportunities, rather than the old prescription of fair employment practices based on the non-discrimination principle, would compel employers to resort to quota systems or preferential treatment for minority group members. Representatives of civil rights groups repeatedly testified that they did not want S. 1937 to impose a quota system on employers. New York Senator Jacob Javitz and George Meany of the AFL-CIO wanted to make certain that no one interpreted the bill as requiring redress of racial imbalance or preferential treatment based on race. Roy Wilkins of the NAACP noted that his organization had never supported quotas. All qualifications being equal, however, and in the face of a notorious historic exclusion of Negroes, Wilkins advocated minority preference. James Farmer of CORE said his organization opposed arbitrary quotas. "We do say, however, that we want to see Negroes working on a job, not in a quota, not 10% or 25% or 50%, but want to see a representative number of Negroes working in various categories." Farmer advocated "some sort of compensatory action to be taken in employment to wipe out the disadvantages of the past 100 or indeed the past 350 years." The distinction between "affirmative action" and racial preference was looming as an issue when Congress finally debated and adopted civil rights legislation.[15]

---

14. *CR* 109 (July 24, 1963), 13246–48; Senate 1963 EEO Hearings, 72–93.
15. Senate 1963 EEO Hearings, 164, 204, 224.

Senator Joseph S. Clark of Pennsylvania, for the Senate Committee on Labor and Public Welfare, reported Humphrey's bill with several amendments on February 4, 1964. The most important alterations narrowed the scope of the bill and weakened the EEO administrator's office. The reported version of S. 1937 covered employers of eight or more persons. The administrator could no longer issue orders (cease-and-desist, back pay, disqualification from federal contracts) on his own authority prior to appeal to the EEO board. Instead, the administrator was to attempt to persuade, conciliate, and, if unsuccessful, complain to the board for enforcement. Moreover, while the administrator could still promulgate regulations for compliance with the bill, the board could veto them. The reported bill also allowed employers to make a "good faith" defense, allowing efforts to comply with administrator regulations to serve as an adequate defense before the board.[16]

Clark stressed the voluntarist rather than the coercive nature of the bill. Its purpose, he said, was "to assure, through conciliation, mediation, and the orderly processes of law, the removal of all racial, color, religious, and nationality restrictions on employment opportunity." Clark based the bill on the same need that Humphrey cited, the deteriorating economic position of nonwhites, particularly Negroes. "Today after years of effort to obtain for these persons a fair share in the opportunities for employment, the economic status of the nonwhite relative to the white remains largely unchanged [since 1942]." State efforts since the war were laudable but insufficient. Taking the unemployment rate as a gauge, Clark noted that it was no better in states with FEPCs than in states without them. There was a particular urgency in securing equal employment opportunity, Clark said. "It is generally accepted that the Negro's century-old acceptance of his second-class status is at an end, and that a rising tide of discontent in protest of this condition now threatens the public safety."

Humphrey's bill, as amended by Clark's committee, had all of the best features of recently considered equal opportunity bills, Clark

16. Senate, *The Equal Employment Opportunity Act,* 88th Cong., 2nd sess., 1964, S. Rept. 867.

said. It exercised broad coverage under the interstate commerce power of Congress; it provided for strict separation of prosecution and adjudication; and it contained a self-starting provision. Clark also aimed at the structural and institutional "patterns" of discrimination. "This bill is designed specifically to reach into all the institutionalized areas and recesses of discrimination including the so-called built-in practices preserved through form, habit, or inertia." Finally, Clark claimed that quotas—reverse discrimination rather than "token" quotas—were prohibited by the bill. "Included in the broad prohibitions are practices with respect to quotas or percentages based upon any of the proscribed considerations. Exclusion of whites in order to fill the quota of non-whites operates to the disadvantage of the white in precisely the same manner as the reverse discrimination."

The possibility that the provisions of the bill would lead to racial quotas provoked strong opposition from three committee members. Republican Barry Goldwater, later the Republican presidential candidate, objected first to the additional power the bill would give to the federal government and the additional burden of record keeping it would impose on businessmen. It would be impossible for employers to record all of the subjective factors that went into every personnel decision they made, and the ultimate result would be the establishment of a racial or religious quota system. Employers would do this not because the law required it, but to avoid trouble and have a defense against charges of discrimination. The fact that the bill prohibited quotas made no difference, Goldwater argued, because "where no overt and obvious manifestations of discrimination can be shown, the existence of such a quota system would make it virtually impossible to prove a discriminatory motive in any particular personnel decision." Discrimination against the majority would be as difficult to prove as discrimination against minority groups. "A more disastrous effect upon sound race relations can scarcely be imagined," Goldwater concluded. He counseled Congress to attack discrimination in places where federal privileges coddled it, as in labor unions, and recommended Robert A. Taft's 1950 voluntary federal FEP proposal.

Lister Hill of Alabama, chairman of the committee, noted that no federal fair employment legislation had been considered by his committee since 1952, "because of the threats such legislation posed to the rights and property of the people of this nation and to our constitutional system of government." Hill denied that racial hiring quotas might be an unintended consequence of the legislation, as Goldwater suggested. Rather, he argued, quotas were precisely what the law intended. The bill sought "to force all employers . . . to give preferential treatment to any person of a racial or religious minority in order to avoid any charge of so-called discrimination against an applicant or employee." The great innovation of its sponsors, the ability to initiate investigations, Hill said, "would lead to intimidation, whether or not the bureau intended that result." The bill, in its belief that economic liberty was incompatible with personal liberty and its disdain for individual freedom and initiative, sought to substitute the decision of a federal agency for that of the employer. "The regulations of the Equal Employment Administrator would be an entering wedge for authority to invade and possibly destroy fundamental rights of employers and employees alike if they fail to conform to the Equal Employment Administrator's particular concept of equality." Employers would throw the merit system overboard in order to avoid trouble, Hill argued. The inducement of racial preference was only the beginning, as Hill saw it, of centralized bureaucratic control of the economy.

These independent House and Senate bills on equal employment opportunity foreshadowed the issues at stake in the debate over Title VII of the Civil Rights Act of 1964. These included questions of individual or group focus, of administrative or judicial enforcement, of minority preferences, racial balance, and quotas, as well as technical questions of qualifications and labor union seniority systems. What Senator Humphrey called the new requirement of providing equal employment opportunities, rather than mere nondiscrimination, was not part of the final version of the act, however, which appeared *weaker* than most state FEP statutes.

Blacks and white liberals, dissatisfied with the slow pace of progress in the first half of President Kennedy's term, increasingly challenged the president, culminating in the Birmingham crisis of 1963.

President Kennedy, responding to the crisis, did not recommend a fair employment title in his civil rights legislative proposal of June 19, 1963. Instead, he asked for a commission on equal employment opportunity, which would give a statutory foundation to his PCEEO to combat discrimination among government contractors. Kennedy did, however, renew his support for pending federal fair employment legislation, applicable to both employers and unions. Representative Emmanuel Celler of New York, chairman of the House Judiciary Committee, immediately introduced the administration's civil rights bill, H.R. 7152, and opened subcommittee hearings on June 26. After twenty-two days of testimony and one hundred witnesses, the subcommittee recommend a bill to the full Judiciary Committee. Celler responded to civil rights groups who were critical of the administration's employment proposals by adding a thirty-page amendment to it, the 1963 EEO bill in its entirety.[17]

In the full Judiciary Committee the civil rights bill was amended in accordance with an understanding worked out among the administration, Representative Celler, and the House Republican leadership. The administration wanted a civil rights bill that could pass Congress, and feared that excessively strong provisions might alienate moderate Democrats and Republicans. The House Republicans did not want to appear responsible for gutting a strong civil rights bill, thus handing the Democrats the mantle of champions of civil rights. Any bill that passed had to appear to be bipartisan. Responding to these concerns, the Judiciary Committee version of the bill allowed the five-member EEOC to investigate on its own initiative and conciliate, but not to issue enforceable orders. Instead of NLRB–type cease-and-desist power, the full committee adopted the

17. Branch, *Parting the Waters,* 807–25; Graham, *Civil Rights,* 74; Brauer, *John F. Kennedy and the Second Reconstruction,* 210; House, *Civil Rights Message of the President;* Charles Whalen and Barbara Whalen, *The Longest Debate: A Legislative History of the Civil Rights Act of 1964* (Cabin John, Md., 1985), 1–35; Francis J. Vaas, "Title VII: Legislative History," *Boston College Industrial and Commercial Law Review,* VII (1966), 431–35; United States Equal Employment Opportunity Commission, *Legislative History of Title VII and Title XI of the Civil Rights Act of 1964* (Washington, D.C., 1968); Richard K. Berg, "Equal Employment Opportunity Under the Civil Rights Act of 1964," *Brooklyn Law Review,* XXXI (1964), 62–97.

form of the EEO bill of 1962, permitting the EEOC to bring suit in federal district court after conciliation failed. The individual complainant could bring suit, if the EEOC granted permission. The federal district court would hear the case *de novo*, and could appoint a special master to determine questions of fact. The suit would be an equity proceeding, so the trial would not include a jury.

Liberals were unhappy with the revisions of the Judiciary Committee. Representative Robert W. Kastenmeier of Wisconsin said the revised administrative procedure for the EEOC was slower and more cumbersome, with "all the disadvantages of a slow and costly court action in which a person denied employment because of his race may have to wait as long as two years for relief." He supported the bill although it was not as strong as he would like. Republicans on the committee disputed Kastenmeier's charge that the changes weakened the bill. Echoing the 1962 House EEO bill, they maintained that judicial enforcement would settle complaints more rapidly and frequently than cease-and-desist orders. Since orders could be resisted, the ultimate arbiter in either system would be a United States court, and the committee bill brought the case to that forum sooner. In addition, the Republicans favored the protection that this procedure gave to innocent respondents, who would have the benefit of a trial *de novo* and a preponderance-of-evidence requirement, if not a jury trial. In effect, the bill recognized a legal rather than an administrative definition of discrimination, as state fair employment acts had.[18]

The Judiciary Committee reported the bill on November 20, 1963; days later the president's assassination gave special urgency to the enactment of civil rights legislation. The House Rules Committee, chaired by Howard Smith of Virginia, had long been the graveyard of civil rights legislation. In 1964, however, there were enough young representatives on the committee and enough public support for civil rights to force Smith to hold hearings on a rule for H.R. 7152. Smith reported the bill without amendment on January 30, 1964, with House debate limited to ten hours.[19]

18. House, *Civil Rights Act of 1963*, 88th Cong., 1st sess., 1963, H. Rept. 914; U.S. EEOC, *Legislative History*, 2001–53; Whalen and Whalen, *Longest Debate*, 38–63; Vaas, "Title VII," 435–37.

19. Whalen and Whalen, *Longest Debate*, 100–23; Vaas, "Title VII," 437–43.

Title VII, the employment discrimination section of the civil rights bill introduced as H.R. 405, was debated on February 8 and 10, 1964, and emerged with only one major amendment. On the House floor, Smith offered an amendment to forbid employers to discriminate on the basis of sex. The apparent motive of Smith and other opponents of civil rights legislation was to expand the scope of the act enough to make its enactment unpalatable to moderates. Others feared that employers would grant preferential treatment to black women and discriminate against white Christian women. Despite the opposition of the bill's managers, the Smith amendment passed by a comfortable 168–133 margin.[20]

The most important amendment to be defeated was one offered by John Bell Williams of Mississippi. It would have made "race" a bona fide occupational qualification, giving employers an exception from the law that they had in cases of religion or national origin. (The commonly cited examples, expected to be rare, were a salesman of religious literature or a chef in a French restaurant.) Without such a provision, its supporters argued, employers would have no defense against legal requirements to have a racially balanced work force. Representative Charles Goodell of New York defended the bill against this charge. Nothing in it, he said, required racial balance or quotas. Labor unions would not have to suspend their waiting lists even if they excluded members of one race; employers could use any standard they wanted except race, creed, color, or national origin; and the burden of proof of discrimination would always remain on the complainant. Nevertheless, Representative August Johansen of Michigan predicted that the pressures for a quota system would mount and eventually force Congress to make explicit provision for them. Williams' amendment was defeated, and the House passed the entire civil rights bill on February 10, 1964, by a 290–130 vote. It then went on to the Senate, where it faced the daunting challenge of a southern filibuster.[21]

Despite the hope of Hubert Humphrey and others that the federal law would depart from the ineffective state FEP–type of law, nothing in the civil rights bill, except for the sex provision, distin-

---

20. *CR* 110 (February 8, 1964), 2577–84; Graham, *Civil Rights,* 134–39.
21. *CR* 110 (February 8, 1964), 2557–60.

guished it from standard state FEP acts. Indeed, Humphrey and Clark lamented the fact that H.R. 405 rather than S. 1937 was the act's fair employment title, substituting judicial for administrative enforcement. Further significant changes were made in the Senate. Despite the assurances of the bill's supporters that it contemplated no race-conscious preferences, racial balancing, or quotas, Senate Republicans demanded and received explicit safeguards for labor union seniority systems, employer ability tests, and a prohibition on racial preference.

Senate majority leader Mike Mansfield feared that the bill would never make it out of James O. Eastland's Judiciary Committee, and so for strategic reasons did not refer the civil rights bill to a committee for hearings. Mansfield's move was opposed not only by southerners, but by Oregon's liberal Republican Wayne Morse. Morse called for hearings to provide "a historic document to which we can point as a basis for evidence on point after point that will be raised in the hearings." Mansfield prevailed. As a result, the legislative history of Title VII of the Civil Rights Act of 1964 depends mostly on debate on the Senate floor. There it went through seventeen days of debate on procedural questions, a fifty-eight day filibuster, and eight days of debate subsequent to cloture.[22]

Senator John Stennis of Mississippi attacked Title VII along the lines laid down by Lister Hill's minority report on S. 1937. "It is idle and more than a little unfair to argue that this title would not, in fact, force the hiring, promotion, and retention of minority group members," Stennis said. It was clearly the design and purpose of the act to induce employers to hire minority group workers that they would not employ without government coercion. Congress had repeatedly voted down FEP legislation, Stennis argued, and the chief reason for doing so was "the very real, very practical, and very difficult problem of defining, in a realistic and precise fashion, exactly what constitutes unlawful discrimination in employment on the basis of race, color, religion, sex, or national origin." The bill gave only vague and imprecise definitions. Moreover, Stennis added, the pressure for a federal act revealed the failure of the state FEPCs of

---

22. Whalen and Whalen, *Longest Debate*, 134; Vaas, "Title VII," 445.

the North. Stennis asked, "Why should we compound and enlarge the error by expanding such a law to all States?"[23]

Stennis was an irreconcilable segregationist, and his argument was typical of the southern opposition. The general hostility of southern senators to civil rights, especially to the simpler provisions on voting and public accommodations in other titles of the bill, obscures the fact that they offered valid criticism of the more complex fair employment title. It is doubtful that the unarticulated intention of the sponsors of Title VII was to foster racial preference in employment, for they denied this accusation almost as often as it was made. But it is apparent that the employment prospects of black Americans by 1964 had reached a point which required something beyond color-blind nondiscriminatory merit policies. Indeed, civil rights groups and some state and local fair employment officers had come to accept preferential treatment as necessary. As Representative Gill had asked, if the disparate-treatment approach had reached a dead end in the northern FEP states by 1964, how much more effective could it be if applied by federal statute in the South? Stennis' charge that the state FEPCs were a failure accorded with the views of most militant civil rights activists. Congressional testimony about the state FEPCs, uniformly positive in the early postwar period, was now ambivalent. Stennis' astute reference to the problem of legally defining "discrimination based on race" as the underlying intellectual problem of fair employment had been raised previously by proponents of fair employment. It is also true that none of Title VII's proponents offered a more satisfactory standard of discrimination than had been applied by the state FEPCs or the executive committees. Yet the ability of Stennis or any of the other segregationists to proffer constructive criticism of Title VII was negated by their general opposition to civil rights, and by the fact that many were the same congressmen who had defeated fair employment legislation twenty years earlier, not by the persuasiveness of their arguments, but by filibuster.

Southern critics continued to raise the prospect of preferential treatment and racial quotas. Senator Harry F. Byrd of Virginia asked,

---

23. *CR* 110 (March 20, 1964), 5810–20.

"If . . . an employer does business in a community having fifteen percent Negro population, is a prima facie assumption to be established that he is discriminating if fewer than fifteen percent of his employees are Negro? If so, then fifteen percent of which employees?" Byrd questioned the effect of Title VII on union seniority systems and its interference in the necessarily subjective aspects of employment decisions. The NLRB routinely accepted flimsy evidence as establishing discrimination against union members and, on the basis of this experience, Byrd predicted that "the problem of finding discrimination and the correction of discrimination will carry the practice of law into strange areas." A. Willis Robertson of Virginia also suggested that Title VII called for racial quotas. "The bill does not say so, but its backers in the House gave no assurance in this respect, even when alarmed opponents cited the 'quota system' as a certainty."[24]

Robertson's charge was not accurate. The House Republicans in their report on H.R. 7152 advised the EEOC to "confine its activities to correcting abuse, not promoting equality with mathematical certainty." The bill gave nobody the right to demand employment, said the Republican minority, and warned that "the Commission will only jeopardize its continued existence if it seeks to impose forced racial balance upon employers or labor unions." Representative Goodell had also defended the act on the House floor against southern charges of quota systems. In the Senate, Thomas H. Kuchel, Republican floor manager of H.R. 7152, denied that federal bureaucrats would dictate to labor unions the racial composition of their membership, job classifications, and seniority systems. The powers of the EEOC were quite limited, Kuchel argued. Even a federal court, he said, "in response to the scare charges which have been widely circulated to local unions throughout America, . . . cannot order preferential hiring or promotion considerations for any particular race, religion, or other group." Hubert Humphrey likewise dismissed fears of racial quotas as a bugbear of civil rights opponents.[25] Nevertheless, the fears provoked by opponents of Title VII were sub-

24. *CR* 110 (March 23, 1964), 5933, (March 21, 1964), 5877.
25. House, *Civil Rights Act of 1963; CR* 110 (February 8, 1964), 2557–60, (March 30, 1964), 6563, 6549.

stantial enough to prompt the Senate managers of Title VII, Pennsylvania Democrat Joseph Clark and New Jersey Republican Clifford Case, to circulate a detailed memorandum on Title VII which addressed the problem.

The Clark-Case memorandum is one of the central documents in the legislative history of Title VII. It appeared on April 8, 1964, while the Senate was still considering the House-passed version of H.R. 7152. The memorandum defended the bill against the charge that the concept of discrimination was vague. "In fact, it is clear and simple, and has no hidden meanings. To discriminate is to make a distinction, to make a difference in treatment or favor . . . based on any five of the forbidden criteria. . . . Any other criterion or qualification for employment is not affected by this title. . . . Discrimination is a word which has been used in the State FEPC statutes for at least twenty years, and has been used in Federal statutes . . . for an even longer period." Presenting the definition of discrimination as unproblematic, the memorandum assumed that the fair employment definition of discrimination would continue to operate in the federal statute.

As to the question of the effectiveness of the state FEPCs, the memorandum insisted that "much progress has been made under State FEPC laws but they cover less than half of the Negro working population." The federal law would provide remedies in twenty-five states that had no FEP laws and would supplement states that did. In asserting that the problem with the state FEPCs was their extent rather than their effectiveness, the Senate managers of Title VII indicated that the course of state FEPCs would continue in the federal act. The memorandum made it clear that Title VII was intended to apply the northern definition of discrimination to the South, rather than to apply a new standard of fair employment.[26]

As to the question of racial data collection and racial balance, the memorandum again abjured any intention to foster racial quotas. Racial balancing, it argued, "would involve a violation of Title VII because maintaining such a balance would require an employer to

26. *CR* 110 (April 8, 1964), 7212–18; Hill, *Black Labor and the American Legal System*, 50.

hire or refuse to hire on the basis of race." It emphasized that the right to equal employment opportunity was an individual right. In what was standard fair employment language it noted that "while the presence of other members of the same minority group in the work force may be a relevant factor in determining if in a given case a decision to hire or refuse to hire was based on race, color, etc., it is only one factor, and the question in each case would be whether that individual was discriminated against." At the same time, state laws that prohibited employers from referring to race on employment application forms would have to yield to the federal law, "since it is necessary to have this data to determine if a pattern of discrimination exists." This statement indicated that racial imbalance might be more important as a probative factor when the EEOC pursued "patterns" of discrimination. Humphrey and Clark had recommended the "pattern-centered" approach in S.R. 1937, but it appeared nowhere in the text of H.R. 7152. The memorandum suggests that it might have been implicit in the bill, and later Senate amendments would elaborate on the "pattern" aspect of discrimination. Finally, the memo briefly addressed a nettlesome question by Senate minority leader Everett M. Dirksen: "If an employer is directed to abolish his employment list because of discrimination what happens to seniority?" The Senate managers responded that the bill was not retroactive, and would not require an employer to change existing seniority lists.

The southern Democrats continued to hammer away at Title VII based on the quota issue. Lister Hill brought up the meaning of "affirmative action" in light of James Farmer's call for preferential treatment before the Senate Committee on Labor and Public Welfare in 1963 and the recent Motorola case in Illinois. Senator Humphrey, however, pointed out that Hill's objection was not to any specific provision of Title VII, but to the entire act. Indeed, Hill made it clear that he objected to the most fundamental prohibitions on discrimination promulgated by the New York SCAD in the 1940s. The next day Stennis and John J. Sparkman of Alabama together agreed that Title VII might not require quota hiring, but that employers would adopt it to keep out of trouble with the EEOC. They cited the tendency toward racial preferences in the federal bureaucracy. Finally, on May 4, 1964, Senator Gordon Allott, Colorado Republican, proposed an amendment that would put the issue to rest by forbidding any federal court from requiring race-based hiring as a remedy to racial imbalance in the work force. Allott did not believe Title VII required or permitted quotas, but he wanted this amendment to take the issue away from opponents. The Senate leadership considered these and other issues when they put together a substitute amendment for H.R. 7152.[27]

Republican leader Everett M. Dirksen was indispensable in passing the Civil Rights act in the Senate. Midwestern Republicans held the balance of power in the Senate between the northern and western liberals of both parties and the southern Democrats. The same situation obtained in the postwar years when Robert A. Taft was the crucial midwestern Republican leader in the FEPC debate. In 1945 Dirksen, a young Illinois representative, had himself introduced an enforceable FEPC bill identical to the ones offered by northeastern liberals. On May 26, 1964, he introduced a substitute for H.R. 7152 that had the approval of the Senate Democratic leaders and, crucially, of House Republican William McCulloch.[28] Dirksen's main concerns were the power of the EEOC, the fate of the state FEPCs under a federal act, employer record keeping, and EEOC investigations. The revised version of H.R. 7152, known as the Mansfield-Dirksen substitute, contained many new features.[29]

The most important change appeared to be the removal of the EEOC's power to bring suit in federal court on behalf of complainants against employers who would not conciliate. To supporters of a strong antidiscrimination law, it appeared that the EEOC, first shorn of its power to issue cease-and-desist orders, was now

27. *CR* 110 (April 20, 1964), 8441–46, (April 21, 1964), 8617–19, (May 4, 1964), 9881–82.

28. McCulloch guaranteed House Republican support for the bill only if all Senate amendments had his prior approval. The object was to avoid a House-Senate conference and another filibuster. McCulloch's support would guarantee immediate House approval of the bill that passed the Senate.

29. *CR* 110 (May 5, 1964), 12811–17 shows the changes in H.R. 7152 by the Senate substitute amendment; U.S. EEOC, *Legislative History*, 3049–59; Berg, "Equal Employment Opportunity," 66–68.

weakened irreparably. However, individuals could still bring suit on their own, without the permission of the EEOC. More important, the Senate substitute provided broad new powers for the attorney general to bring antidiscrimination actions. The attorney general could bring suit in federal court if he had "reasonable cause to believe that any person or group of persons is engaged in a pattern or practice of resistance to the full enjoyment of any rights secured by this title," the statute stated. This new provision appeared to contemplate the broad, industry-wide, pattern-centered approach recommended by Humphrey and Clark. The substitute also protected state and local FEPCs by giving them original and exclusive jurisdiction for sixty days after the filing of a charge. Provisions were also added to prevent unnecessary duplication of record keeping requirements under the federal act, Executive Order 10925, and state statutes. A further safeguard appeared in the requirement that court orders be issued only if the respondent was found to have *intentionally* violated Title VII. The substitute also made more explicit references to unlawful labor union practices in hiring halls and apprenticeship systems.

The Mansfield-Dirksen substitute added the explicit provision recommended by Gordon Allott. Section 703 (j) held:

> Nothing contained in this title shall be interpreted to require any employer . . . to grant preferential treatment to any individual or to any group because of the race, color, religion, sex, or national origin of such individual or group on account of an imbalance which may exist with respect to the total number or percentage of persons of any race . . . employed by an employer . . . in comparison with the total number or percentage of persons of such race . . . in any community, state, section, or other area, or in the available work force of any community, state, section, or other area.

The question remained whether this section, which held that racial balancing could not be required by public officials, also prohibited it if undertaken by private employers.[30]

The Mansfield-Dirksen substitute also added a section to reassure union workers that Title VII would not disturb their seniority rights. The idea that Title VII would require racial balance in membership, job classifications, and promotions, received expression in late

30. Marshall, "Prospects for Equal Employment," 651.

1963, in the minority House Judiciary Committee report on H.R. 7152. "Under the power granted in this bill," the minority members argued, "if a carpenters' hiring hall, say, had twenty men awaiting call, the first ten in seniority being white carpenters, the union could be forced to pass them over in favor of carpenters beneath them in seniority, but of the stipulated race." The minority added that if there were not enough union members of the stipulated race, unions might be forced to find them in order to racially balance the job. Lister Hill reiterated these arguments in a Senate speech on January 15, 1964, which reportedly was distributed to thirty thousand local unions.[31]

The AFL-CIO vigorously denied that Title VII would hurt organized labor, and regretted Lister Hill's argument to that effect in the Senate, because Hill had been a friend of organized labor. The AFL-CIO believed that the act helped organized labor by applying the same rule of nondiscrimination that bound unions through the "fair representation" doctrine to non-union employees. They believed the act would not disturb seniority rights already acquired, even if they had been acquired during a pre–Title VII practice of racial exclusion. It was apparent, as one senator put it, "that if all racial discrimination in employment were to cease tomorrow, the legacy of past discrimination as reflected in inadequate training, economic and cultural deprivation, as well as the seniority rights of the present work force, will be felt for at least a generation." Nevertheless, the AFL-CIO stated its belief that ancient wrongs could not be righted by new ones. "It does not believe that white workers who possess hard-earned seniority should be discriminated against in the future because Negroes were discriminated against in the past." The act did not require this, nor could the EEOC infer such a requirement from the language of the act, they said.[32]

31. House, *Civil Rights Act of 1963;* "Civil Rights Bill Destroys Union Seniority," Box E-5, "Discussion of Sattersfield Comments on Civil Rights Bill," Box E-7, in Leadership Conference on Civil Rights (LCCR) Papers, Manuscript Division, Library of Congress.

32. AFL-CIO Legal Department, "Comments on Senator Lister Hill's Criticism of Civil Rights Bill," January 31, 1964, Box E-7, in LCCR Papers; J. Albert Woll, "Labor Looks at Equal Rights in Employment," *Federal Bar Journal,* XXIV (1964), 93–101; *CR* 110 (April 9, 1964), 7386; Walter Reuther to Lister Hill, in *CR* 110 (April 8, 1964), 7206.

Notwithstanding the explanation of organized labor's leadership, the Mansfield-Dirksen substitute included a section declaring that it was not unlawful for an employer to discriminate "pursuant to a bona fide seniority or merit system, or a system which measures earnings by quantity or quality or production or to employees who work in different locations, provided that such differences are not the result of an intention to discriminate because of race."[33] The terms "bona fide" and "result of an intention" invited judicial interpretation, as did section 703 (j). Federal courts would also test the AFL-CIO's assumption that the act did not regard "past discrimination" such as that built into seniority systems. Although the AFL-CIO explanation carried no force of its own, it informed Congress on these issues and shed light on the legislators' intent.

Hubert H. Humphrey, floor manager of the whole civil rights bill, was willing to accept the Mansfield-Dirksen substitute. Although he regretted the loss of power by the EEOC, the specific additions only made explicit and clarified what he believed had always been the plain meaning of the bill. Clark and Case, Title VII captains in the Senate, were less happy. "The compromise set forth in the substitute bill constitutes a further softening of the enforcement provisions," Clark said, "although the new powers given to the Attorney General do compensate to some extent for its weakening." Although it appeared that "the federal FEPC has had its teeth pulled," the attorney general's power might have provided a net gain. The political nature of the attorney general's office, however, made the long-run prospects less hopeful.[34]

The pressures on Congress to pass the civil rights bill mounted in mid-1964. President Johnson, who as Senate majority leader had

33. Herbert Hill argues that "The AFL-CIO, as a condition of its support, insisted upon the inclusion of section 703 (h) in Title VII, which they believed would protect the racial status quo of seniority systems at least for a generation," but provides no evidence to support this claim; see "Black Workers, Organized Labor, and Title VII of the Civil Rights Act of 1964: Legislative History and Litigation Record," in *Race in America: The Struggle for Equality*, eds. Herbert Hill and James E. Jones, Jr. (Madison, 1993), 270.

34. *CR* 110 (June 4, 1964), 12721–25, (June 3, 1964), 12595–99; U.S. EEOC, *Legislative History*, 3003–15.

managed the Civil Rights acts of 1957 and 1960, wanted the Senate to act, even if it meant wearing down the old southern senators by continuous session. Since no compromise could satisfy the southerners and since no compromise was possible without the consent of House Republican leader McCulloch, senate managers entreated minority leader Dirksen to invoke cloture. By June, Dirksen approved, and the Republicans secured a cloture vote on June 10, 1964, limiting debate and assuring a vote on the Civil Rights Act. Southerners called up some twenty-three amendments which the Senate rejected. Among them were proposals by Sam Ervin of North Carolina to delete Title VII from the act, John Tower of Texas to make Title VII the exclusive remedy for unlawful employment acts, and John McClellan of Arkansas to allow employers to refer to an applicant's race, color, religion, sex, or national origin if they believed it would benefit their business. All of these proposals received about thirty supporting votes. McClellan's amendment to make racial discrimination illegal only if it was the "sole" reason for rejection was defeated, 39–50. McClellan sought to restrict the interpretation of discrimination available to the EEOC and courts, to prevent a "dragnet." Warren Manguson of Washington explained that "a legal interpretation or a court interpretation of the word 'solely' would so limit this section as probably to negate the entire purpose of what we are trying to do."[35]

The Senate adopted eight amendments to Title VII, the most important of which was the Tower amendment regarding ability testing. The amendment grew out of the Illinois FEPC's decision in the Motorola case, in which an Illinois FEP commissioner ordered Motorola to discontinue the use of a standard ability test because such tests were inherently discriminatory against culturally deprived minority groups.[36] Dirksen and John Tower of Texas repeatedly brought up the case as an example of the sort of decision that might be made by the EEOC under Title VII. Tower, referring to the Labor Department's apprenticeship rules and the trend he saw in recent judicial decisions, believed that racial balance was likely to follow

35. Whalen and Whalen, *Longest Debate*, 152–88; *CR* 110 (June 9, 1964), 13073–85, (June 12, 1964), 13650–52, (June 15, 1964), 13825–26, 13837–38.

36. See chap. six.

under Title VII. Clifford Case defended the act, saying that Title VII and the Illinois statute were so fundamentally different that such a result could never occur under the federal act. First, unlike the Illinois agency, the EEOC had no enforcement powers. Second, no federal court could issue an order similar to the Illinois FEPC's because, while the Illinois commission sought to provide equal opportunity to Negroes, whether or not as well qualified as white applicants, the federal law had no such purpose. Case maintained that, "under Title VII, even a federal court could not order an employer to lower or change job qualifications simply because proportionately fewer Negroes than whites are able to meet them."[37]

The Senate leadership believed that the Mansfield-Dirksen amendment which protected seniority and merit systems would prevent a Motorola-type decision on testing. Case called the persistent criticism of Title VII based on the Motorola case a "red herring," and Senator John Sherman Cooper believed that an interpretation of Title VII based on the language and legislative history would be enough to prevent the "extreme" interpretation suggested by Tower and others.[38] Tower introduced an amendment that would allow employers to use professionally developed ability tests, if such tests were given to all applicants for a particular job regardless of race, and if the test were designed to predict the performance of the applicant for the job in question. Failure to adopt such an amendment, Tower said, would invite the EEOC to "invalidate tests of various kinds of employees by both private business and Government to determine the professional competence or ability or trainability or suitability of a person to do a job." Humphrey and Case maintained that the amendment was unnecessary because the law already allowed nondiscriminatory testing. They condemned the conclusion reached by the hearing examiner in the Illinois case and promised that nothing like it could occur under Title VII. "Such tests are considered to be legal; there is no denial of that," Humphrey said. Tower's amendment was rejected on June 11 by a 38–49 vote.[39]

37. John Tower, "FEPC—Some Practical Considerations," *Federal Bar Journal,* XXIV (1964), 87–92; *CR* 110 (March 13, 1964), 5244, (March 19, 1964), 5662–64, (March 26, 1964), 6415–16, (April 8, 1964), 7246–47, (April 24, 1964), 9024–25.

38. *CR* 110 (June 9, 1964), 13081, 13078, (June 11, 1964), 13504.

39. *CR* 110 (June 11, 1964), 13492–13505.

Two days later, however, the Senate leadership agreed to a modified version of the Tower amendment. It added to section 703 (h) language stating that it was not an unlawful employment practice "for an employer to give and to act upon the results of any professionally developed ability test provided that such test, its administration or action upon the results is not designed, intended, or used to discriminate because of race, color, religion, sex, or national origin." This was the final important amendment to Title VII, and the entire Civil Rights Act passed the Senate on June 19 by a vote of 73 to 27. When the bill returned to the House, the leadership kept it out of the hands of the Rules Committee and avoided a conference with the Senate. On July 2, 1964, the House approved the version of the bill passed by the Senate, and, with President Lyndon Johnson's signature, the Civil Rights Act of 1964 became law. Title VII of the act took effect on July 2, 1965, almost twenty years to the day after the enactment of the New York State Law Against Discrimination.[40]

As enacted, Title VII of the Civil Rights Act of 1964 prohibited discrimination on the basis of race, color, religion, national origin, and sex. It applied to employers of twenty-five or more, in three phases: employers of one hundred or more as of July 2, 1965; employers of fifty or more one year later; and employers of twenty-five or more as of July 2, 1967. All labor unions and employment agencies were also prohibited from discriminating on the grounds of race, religion, color, national origin, or sex. The coverage of employers was somewhat less full than that of the state FEPCs (New York's 1945 act covered employers of six or more), but its prohibition on the basis of sex made it wider than any state law. The administrative structure of the law showed the legislative compromises that went into Title VII. The EEOC, denied the power to issue cease-and-desist orders or to sue in federal court, was primarily an investigatory body which would combat discrimination by conciliation, persuasion, and education, and assist individual complainants who could themselves sue in federal court to enforce the act. The addition of attorney general suits in "pattern or practice" situations, however, held vast potential for the kind of pattern-centered, industry-wide actions favored by civil rights groups. The act con-

40. *CR* 110 (June 13, 1964), 13724.

tained three provisos (703 [h], 703 [j], and 706 [g]) intended to prevent preferential treatment and racial proportionalism as proof of discrimination or a remedy. While the Supreme Court had never held the Constitution to require strictly color-blind legislation, the text of Title VII, enacted under the interstate commerce power, was pristinely color-blind.

The conjunction of a number of forces led to the enactment of a federal fair employment statute in 1964, after twenty years of unsuccessful attempts. The most important long-range factor was the steady rise of public opinion behind the idea, combined with the immediate, dramatic events of the civil rights movement and the Kennedy assassination. If A. Philip Randolph's 1941 March on Washington threat, which created the wartime FEPC, was generally regarded as a bluff, the nation saw a real march on Washington in 1963. In addition, Randolph's National Council for a Permanent FEPC had been replaced by a more effective lobbying effort by Clarence Mitchell and the Leadership Conference on Civil Rights, and the association of fair employment with communism had largely disappeared by then. Organized labor, the most powerful interest group on Capitol Hill in the 1960s, was squarely behind the effort. Above all, the compromises that went into Title VII, to reassure those who feared that an enforceable fair employment act would result in proportionalism, made its enactment possible.

Reactions to the fair employment title of the Civil Rights Act of 1964 were mixed. The vanguard of the civil rights movement was the most disappointed. Carl Rachlin, CORE general counsel, regretted that Congress made no requirement to hire minority group members to compensate for past discrimination. It required only nondiscrimination regarding new, qualified applicants. "In other words," Rachlin said, "preferential treatment to right past wrongs is not required." Moreover, opening traditionally black jobs to white competition threatened black security in these jobs, "some of which have now achieved a fair earning power." Labor arbitrator Charles Schmidt, Jr., thought the compromises that went into Title VII revealed the inadequacy of democratic lawmaking, even as the black revolution threatened its foundations. Congress had failed to address the problems of the Negro in particular, and had written a statute in broad terms of equal opportunity. Schmidt warned, "The problem in civil rights is the *Negro*, . . . the one internal national force that threatens to extinguish this nation is the *Negro, and extinguish he will* unless his demands for jobs, employment, and training are fulfilled immediately—without question, without debate, and without qualification." Others took a calmer view, noting that "even a comprehensive federal law, and even the most effective implementation of such a law, could bring about only a rather modest improvement in the Negro's occupational status in the near future."[41]

Most observers were particularly disappointed with the weakened EEOC. They had envisioned an administrative agency that could prosecute and adjudicate like the NLRB. Many believed that the NLRB would be a more effective forum to combat discrimination in employment. Some recognized that the EEOC might play an important role as the interpreter of Title VII. Title VII might be most useful in the South, but in the North the NLRB and state FEPCs, which were stronger on paper than Title VII, would be more effective. Indeed, insofar as the Dirksen amendments provided an incentive for states to enforce FEP laws, they improved the title, allowing for decentralized administration that could bolster the moral force of the law and build a political consensus behind it.[42]

---

41. Carl Rachlin, "The 1964 Civil Rights Law: A Hard Look," *Law in Transition Quarterly*, II (1965), 80–84; Rachlin, "Title VII: Limitations and Qualifications," *Boston College Industrial and Commercial Law Review*, VII (1966), 473–94; Charles T. Schmidt, Jr., "Title VII: Coverage and Comments," *Boston College Industrial and Commercial Law Review*, VII (1966), 459–72; Norgren and Hill, *Toward Fair Employment*, 278.

42. Sanford Jay Rosen, "Division of Authority Under Title VII of the Civil Rights Act of 1964: A Preliminary Study in Federal-State Interagency Relations," *George Washington University Law Review*, XXXIV (1966), 846–92; Robert L. Carter, "The National Labor Relations Board and Racial Discrimination," *Law in Transition Quarterly*, II (1965), 87–95; Herbert Hill, "The Role of Law in Securing Equal Employment Opportunity: Legal Powers and Social Change," *Boston College Industrial and Commercial Law Review*, VII (1966), 625–52; Berg, "Equal Employment Opportunity"; Marshall, "Equal Employment Opportunities"; Sovern, *Legal Restraints*, 92; "Enforcement of Fair Employment Under the Civil Rights Act of 1964," *University of Chicago Law Review*, XXXII (1965), 430–70.

Among the concerns of fair employment advocates was the appearance that Title VII had transformed fair employment from a public to a private right. Driven by individual complaints and geared toward the vindication of individual rights, the act seemed to eschew the broad, pattern-centered, industry-wide mode of enforcement. The key question in this regard was whether Title VII permitted class actions. Most observers recognized that the unique enforcement provisions of section 707 provided a promising avenue for wider remedies. Legal scholar Michael Sovern believed that the Justice Department would have to interpret its powers broadly, exercise them vigorously, and persuade the courts to support it. The lack of any one of these elements would render Title VII a failure. Ralph K. Winter, Jr., replying to Sovern in the *University of Chicago Law Review,* saw section 707 as a blank check for the Justice Department to pursue quota hiring within entire labor markets.[43]

Winter believed that the only way to improve the economic status of black Americans through fair employment laws was by racial quotas. Doubting that discrimination was the primary reason for the economic problems of black Americans, and approaching the subject from a free market perspective, Winter blamed government restrictions on the labor market, principally the privileges granted to labor unions. Advocates of fair employment laws argued that they would improve the economic position of Negroes through application of the color-blind principle, but, Winter countered, these goals clashed with rather than complemented one another. The rational business decision for employers would be to resort to quota systems, which were simple and relatively inexpensive to administer, as insurance against antidiscrimination suits. Government coercion leading to such preferential treatment based on race would undermine the moral claim of the antidiscrimination effort.[44]

Most observers did not share Winter's assumptions, and wondered whether Title VII required, encouraged, or permitted preferential treatment. Many agreed that Title VII did not require, but did

43. Berg, "Equal Employment Opportunity"; "Enforcement of Fair Employment"; Rosen, "Division of Authority"; Sovern, *Legal Restraints,* 80; Winter, "Improving the Economic Status of Negroes," 817–55.

44. Winter, "Improving the Economic Status of Negroes."

permit, preferential treatment to redress racial imbalance, so long as it did not violate the rights of white workers. Since the conduct proscribed by the act was vaguely defined, discrimination might be inferred from statistical evidence, with employment policies judged by their results, rather than intent. The intent to discriminate required in section 706(g) could be inferred by racial outcomes: if an employer's policy resulted in racial imbalance, it was fair to assume that the employer anticipated its discriminatory consequences. Thus established seniority systems, apparently protected by section 703(h), could be overturned because they had the result of perpetuating past discrimination. Likewise, ability tests that had the result of disqualifying minority group members could be struck down as inherently discriminatory.[45]

Other commentators believed that Title VII prohibited such methods to combat the effects of past discrimination. "To violate Title VII one must treat differently because of race itself and not merely because [of] an applicant's lack of qualification which he was prevented from acquiring because of his race," wrote Michael Sovern. The best hope, he argued, lay in persuading employers to abandon tests that disqualified minority group members. The technical question of seniority systems, he said, would have to be decided in the courts. The law seemed to bar all race-based preferential treatment, and the best hope for effective administration lay in some balancing of the burden of proof: if an applicant could prove that he was qualified for the job and the work force exhibited a racial imbalance, the burden of proof should shift to the defendant. Richard Berg of the Justice Department noted that the restriction of section 703(j) on racial preference as a requirement to remedy racial imbalance did not "add to or detract from the probative force which evidence of racial imbalance may have in any given case." This fact, he said, "touches on a grain of truth in the racial quota argument." Employers would want to avoid the semblance of racial discrimination that such imbalance indicated. "The law, therefore, places some psychological pressure on the employer to attain a racial balance in his work force. This pressure is based on what is an

45. Rachlin, "Title VII"; Marshall, "Equal Employment Opportunities."

undoubtedly exaggerated notion of the probative force of evidence of racial imbalance."[46]

The impact of Title VII of the Civil Rights Act of 1964 would depend on how the EEOC and the Justice Department defined their roles under the statute and how the courts received that definition. Civil rights groups feared that the statute protected individual rather than group rights, outlawed only discriminatory acts committed after its enactment, prohibited preferential treatment, and protected discriminatory seniority systems and ability tests. Their next step after the enactment of the statute was to convince the EEOC and the Justice Department that the statute was not as restrictive as it appeared. The state fair employment practice commissions had done everything possible to keep out of court, but the structure of Title VII assured that the federal courts would be the principal interpreters of the act. Civil rights advocates would have to meet the legal challenge of defining discrimination and its remedies.

46. Sovern, *Legal Restraints*, 71, 73, 191; "Enforcement of Fair Employment"; Berg, "Equal Employment Opportunity."

9   Past Discrimination: Title VII Development, 1965–1971

The Civil Rights Act of 1964 took effect on July 2, 1965, one year after its enactment. This one year of lead time allowed the EEOC to establish itself and for businesses and labor unions to begin compliance. Civil rights groups had little confidence in the commission to begin with, as it lacked enforcement powers, was designed to deal with individual complaints, and had to defer to state FEPCs. They hoped for more from the Justice Department in "pattern or practice" suits, the President's Committee on Equal Employment Opportunity, and the NLRB. Indeed, the main interest of civil rights groups was to show that the legislative design of the EEOC was unworkable and to have it amended. The commission, unhappy about the civil rights groups' strategy, accepted it and concentrated on the stronger cases. Ironically, the weakness of the EEOC as an administrative body turned out to be a source of strength. Title VII allowed civil rights groups to seek enforcement of the statute over the head of the administrative agency, in the courts. This strategy was not possible under state FEP laws which, like the National Labor Relations Act, provided for no individual right apart from administrative discretion. Most important, administrators within the EEOC redefined the agency's legislative mandate and worked with individual plaintiffs, their civil rights advocates, and other executive agencies in redefining Title VII in the courts.[1]

1. Graham, *Civil Rights,* 177–90; "The EEOC During the Administration of Lyndon B. Johnson," Vol. I, Administrative History, November 1, 1968, in U.S. Equal Employment Opportunity Records, EEOC Library, Washington, D.C.; NAACP Press Release, April 29, 1965, NAACP Papers.

A White House Conference on Equal Employment Opportunity in August, 1965, began to explore some of the questions of Title VII enforcement. Justice Department representatives said they planned to proceed along the lines laid down in voting rights cases, including class actions and statistical proof of discrimination. The department had been undefeated in uncovering and correcting even the subtlest methods of discrimination in voting rights cases, and believed that employment discrimination would be easier to detect because it had not been illegal in many states and employers often engaged in overt discrimination. Assistant Attorney General John Doar was especially heartened by the recent U.S. Supreme Court voting rights decision in *U.S.* v. *Louisiana,* which held that the courts had the duty not only to "eliminate current and future discrimination but also had an affirmative duty to correct the effects of past discrimination." Doar also explained that the department, following the encouraging lead of the Fifth Circuit Court of Appeals in the South, would impress upon the courts the danger of testing and other qualifications that had the effect of "freezing" Negroes in the places they occupied due to past discrimination. Although the nature of the voting and employment cases differed—principally that employment discrimination had not been illegal in many places before Title VII—the department would attempt to persuade the courts that the effects of past discrimination should not continue into the future. The old problem of labor union seniority systems was the most obvious place to start.[2]

Early EEOC conciliation action showed that the commission could be a more forceful and successful advocate than civil rights groups expected. The fledgling agency strove to depart from its individual complaint-and-conciliation legislative mandate from the outset, drawing up a "zero list" of large government contractors with no minority employees. The PCEEO, which had jurisdiction over gov-

2. White House Conference on Equal Employment Opportunity, August 19, 1965, Panel 1, First Session, 1–39, Third Session, 3–30, EEOC Records; Memo of St. John Barrett, June 30, 1964, in U.S. Department of Justice, Records of Assistant Attorney General John Doar, Box 2, RG 60, NA; Jack Bass, *Unlikely Heroes* (New York, 1981), 269.

ernment contractors, balked at this proposal, and the EEOC dropped it when President Johnson sided with the PCEEO. Nevertheless, the EEOC was committed to accomplishing more than the "cosmetic compliance" of the previous twenty years.[3]

The commission's first important conciliation agreement came with the Newport News Shipbuilding and Dry Dock Company in 1966. The architect of the agreement was Alfred W. Blumrosen, EEOC chief of conciliation. A labor relations lawyer and law professor at Rutgers University, Blumrosen was an exceptionally creative thinker in the field of employment discrimination, and saw that the EEOC's unique administrative structure did not necessarily render it ineffective. Indeed, the provisions for court enforcement instead of cease-and-desist power made it stronger. Creative administrators could interpret the enabling legislation in such a way as to achieve the chief purpose of the law, minority group economic advancement.

Newport News was in many ways a perfect target. The largest employer in the state of Virginia, it did not segregate its Negro employees in the lowest occupational categories as many southern employers did. As was often the case, employers with better employment practices were frequently the first targets of FEP laws, having minority group workers who were qualified for promotion. The company did not maintain a formal seniority system, avoiding a particularly nettlesome point of contention between white and black workers. Most important, Newport News derived the vast majority of its business from government contracts, making it vulnerable to pressure from the Justice and Labor Departments. Likelihood of a Justice Department pattern-or-practice suit and the loss of government contracts overcame the company's initial reluctance to admit that it had violated the law and brought it to negotiate with the EEOC.[4]

The conciliation agreement provided for the immediate promo-

3. Blumrosen, *Modern Law,* 57–58; Graham, *Civil Rights,* 194–95.

4. Blumrosen, *Black Employment,* chap. 8; Franklin D. Roosevelt, Jr., to Willard W. Wirtz, "Weekly Activities Report," March 7–11, 1966, March 21–25, 1966, EEOC News Release, April 4, 1966, in U.S. Department of Labor, Records of Secretary Willard W. Wirtz, Box 341, RG 174, NA.

tion of several blacks into supervisory positions and the retention of an outside industrial relations expert, approved by the EEOC and paid by Newport News, to review the company's promotion policy. Nearly four thousand Negroes were promoted within the first year of the agreement. The company also agreed to file detailed reports with the EEOC for two years after the agreement. The company agreed to maintain an "affirmative action file" of Negro employees who were qualified or qualifiable for promotion in the future, and these employees were to be given priority in promotions and training. Although there was some disagreement in the EEOC about measures providing preferential treatment as a remedy for past discrimination rather than equal treatment henceforth, the commission went forward with the plan. Blumrosen considered it a model conciliation agreement, in which the government acted "with one voice" and avoided cumbersome legal proceedings. It was, however, the last agreement of its kind.

Most employers were either unwilling or unable to agree to conciliation terms such as those of Newport News. The EEOC's demands for affirmative action, remedying the effects of past discrimination by preferential treatment, and control of personnel decisions by industrial relations experts seemed to go far beyond the antidiscrimination mandate of the 1964 Civil Rights Act. Moreover, a preferential promotion policy would violate most of the labor union seniority agreements which bound many employers, most of which were not as vulnerable as Newport News. Even if it were approved by the government, it would create dissension in the work force— the Newport News shipyard had the first strike in its history shortly after the EEOC agreement. As Blumrosen later put it, "The Newport News agreement sent shivers down the spine of the industrial relations community because of its specificity." Faced with the prospect of such terms, most employers would take their chances in court. Thus the EEOC's main enforcement activity shifted from conciliation to plaintiff advocacy in the private suits under Title VII.[5]

Like state fair employment acts, Title VII exhibited a tension between its concern for individual rights and the public interest in

5. Blumrosen, *Modern Law*, 88; *Congressional Record* 113 (August 22, 1967), 23513–19, (September 18, 1967), 25820–22.

nondiscrimination. It appeared that the Justice Department's prosecution of "pattern or practice" cases under section 707 protected the public interest, while the EEOC guided private interests with individual resort to the federal courts under section 706. The Justice Department was slow in bringing section 707 suits, and the EEOC succeeded in turning section 706 private suits into wider, class actions. The EEOC transformed Title VII from an individual, complaint-centered, conciliatory antidiscrimination program into a group-centered enforcement of affirmative action.

The first step was taken in the 1966 case of *Hall* v. *Werthan Bag Corp.*, decided during the Newport News negotiations. A federal district court in Tennessee ruled that Title VII suits could be brought as class actions on behalf of minority group members who were similarly situated. Insofar as injunctive relief was concerned, the court held that "racial discrimination is by definition class discrimination. If it exists, it applies throughout the class." Only one member of the class need pursue relief through the EEOC before bringing suit, and all others could join the suit without passing through the EEOC. These intervenors, however, were not entitled to remedial relief (reinstatement, promotions, or back pay) since the effects of class discrimination were not felt equally throughout the class. Judge Frank Gray, Jr., regarded his decision as a reasonable solution to the problems that resulted from the "ambiguous structure of the enforcement provisions of Title VII resulting from its somewhat chaotic legislative history." A private class action suit, he said, was "unique in its adaptability to Title VII's split personality," thus turning a potential weakness of the statute into a strength.[6]

In March, 1967, a federal district court in Alabama ruled that the EEOC must make some attempt, however minimal, at conciliation before a complainant could sue in federal court. The EEOC could extend the sixty-day period during which individuals could file suit in order to do so. Other district courts agreed, one pointing out that the plain language of the statute made conciliation a prerequisite to suit, and that "statutes creative of remedies not known to the common law are to be strictly construed." The New York LAD contained an explicit provision that courts should construe the statute broadly,

6. 53 L.C. 9014 (1966); Franklin D. Roosevelt, Jr., to Willard W. Wirtz, "Weekly Activities Report," March 7–11, 1966, Box 341, RG 174.

while Title VII contained no such instruction to the courts. In addition, Title VII sought to guarantee employers against frivolous charges and demands. The EEOC took the position that delay would subvert Congress' desire for prompt adjudication of individual claims, here stressing the individual rights nature of Title VII. The EEOC pushed this interpretation and prevailed in other district courts, arguing that "all they have to do under the Act is to show that voluntary compliance has not been accomplished within the sixty-day period." In upholding the commission's interpretation the courts pointed to the confusion of the legislative history.[7]

The EEOC was vindicated in 1968 when the Fifth Circuit Court of Appeals applied the principle from a recent Supreme Court decision in a Title II (public accommodations) case that a private plaintiff who acts against segregation "does so not for himself alone, but also as a 'private attorney general,' vindicating a policy that Congress considered of the highest priority." Without much discussion, the Fifth Circuit held that "clearly the same logic applies to Title VII of the Act." The Seventh Circuit followed, and the Fifth Circuit reaffirmed this decision, overturning the district courts that had dismissed cases for lack of conciliation efforts.[8]

Similarly, the EEOC prevailed in cases where the individual complainant's grievance had been settled (by hiring, reinstatement, or promotion) and the respondent claimed that this satisfaction rendered the case moot. The EEOC claimed that it had an interest in acting against broad patterns of discrimination, despite having been denied cease-and-desist and pattern-centered power in Title VII. Although the attorney general was authorized to bring pattern or practice suits, he could not bring all such suits. If the satisfaction of the individual claim mooted the case and the court did not reach the broader discriminatory practices, the EEOC argued, discrimina-

7. *Dent* v. *St. Louis–San Francisco Railway Co.*, 55 L.C. 9047 (1967); *Mickel* v. *South Carolina State Employment Agency,* 55 L.C. 9057 (1967); *Choate* v. *Caterpillar Tractor Co.*, 56 L.C. 9086 (1967); Blumrosen, *Modern Law,* 102; Brief for EEOC in *Dent* v. *St. Louis–San Francisco Ry. Co.,* EEOC Appellate Court Briefs, 1967–68, EEOC Records; *Evenson* v. *Northwest Airlines,* 55 L.C. 9053 (1967); *Quarles* v. *Philip Morris,* 271 F.Supp. 842 (1967); *Moody* v. *Albemarle Paper Co.,* 56 L.C. 9070 (1967); *Mondy* v. *Crown-Zellerbach Corp.* 56 L.C. 9082 (1967).

8. *Oatis* v. *Crown-Zellerbach Corp.,* 58 L.C. 9140 (1968); *Choate* v. *Caterpillar Co.,* 58 L.C. 9162 (1968); *Dent* v. *Saint Louis–San Francisco Railway Co.,* 59 L.C. 9189 (1969).

tors would refuse to conciliate in the broad terms contemplated under the statute, and "the Commission's role in the prevention and elimination of unlawful employment practices by voluntary compliance would be seriously undermined." This claim was at least partly disingenuous, as the commission's conciliation efforts had been overwhelmed by complaints and because it had opted for pattern-centered enforcement in lieu of conciliation. It was asking the court not to help restore voluntary compliance through conciliation, but to facilitate pattern-centered enforcement. Although district courts disagreed, the Fifth Circuit again endorsed the EEOC position.[9]

The commission also helped complainants with technical procedural matters under Title VII. It accepted charges that were not made under oath, automatically deferred prematurely filed charges to state FEPCs, and interpreted time limits liberally. Along with maintaining class actions and making conciliation a formality, these procedural rules indicated clear goals. As critics of the state FEPCs had charged that the procedural choice to rely on the verified individual complaint was a substantive decision not to enforce the law, likewise EEOC positions on the procedural questions of Title VII were in fact substantive decisions to make Title VII a group-centered, pattern-based enforcement statute. The courts followed the EEOC's argument and affirmed that the procedural rules of Title VII were of great importance. The Fifth Circuit Court of Appeals, in a 1969 case addressing class action, time limits, conciliation prerequisites, and other technical issues, gave a ringing endorsement of the EEOC's position. Although the case appeared to address only technical statutory provisions, the court held that "beneath the legal facade a faint hope is discernible rising like a distant star over a swamp of uncertainty and perhaps despair." The liberal construction of Title VII's enforcement provisions, the court added, would help those who otherwise might be relegated to toil without hope of recognition and reward.[10]

9. *Parham* v. *Southwestern Bell Telephone Co.*, 58 L.C. 9147 (1968); *Jenkins* v. *United Gas Corp.*, 55 L.C. 9045 (1966), 58 L.C. 9154 (1968); EEOC Brief in *Jenkins*, EEOC Appellate Court Briefs, 1967–68, EEOC Records.

10. Blumrosen, "Antidiscrimination Laws in Action"; *Miller* v. *International Paper Co.*, 59 L.C. 9211 (1969).

The EEOC's methods indicated that it would administer Title VII essentially as a plaintiff's attorney. The Fifth Circuit Court of Appeals, which was determined not to allow the "deliberate speed" of southern school desegregation to repeat itself in employment, helped it, applying the more demanding principles of its recent voting rights decisions to employment cases. The Justice Department was concerned about EEOC advocacy. They wanted the government to "speak with one voice," but EEOC lawyers "tend to take a strict advocate position even when they are participating as amicus." The Justice Department wanted to maintain its reputation for fairness in the courts. Moreover, the department complained, "Even where EEOC has participated in private suits, . . . allegedly on the procedural issues, there has been a strong tendency by lawyers in the EEOC to drift off into substantive issues." This tendency was clearly exhibited in the development of Title VII law on the seniority system issues of past discrimination, testing, and preferential treatment. [11]

By the mid-1950s state fair employment officers and civil rights advocates had decided that the principal problem in minority-group employment was no longer in hiring, but in promotion. The effects of discrimination, especially of segregated and inferior education and housing, prevented many black workers from advancing beyond the lowest occupational categories in many enterprises. As the EEOC noted, "It is a sobering thought that if tomorrow employers and trade unions opened their doors and extended a genuine welcome to all minorities, large numbers of persons would be unable to take advantage of the opportunities." In the South this pattern was often overt and formal, relegating black workers to the lowest occupation categories, while in the North blacks were more often entirely absent.[12]

The seniority system aggravated this condition of black segregation and exclusion. The principle of seniority was not itself dis-

11. Bass, *Unlikely Heroes;* Blumrosen, *Modern Law,* 95; Stephen Pollack Memorandum, December 14, 1967, in U.S. Dept. of Justice, Files of St. John Barrett, Box 1, RG 60; Belz, *Equality Transformed,* 43–45.

12. U.S. EEOC, *First Annual Report* (Washington, D.C., 1966).

criminatory. Both labor unions and management valued it—labor because it reduced the discretion of management in personnel decisions, management because it provided a system of orderly progression into related jobs that built and husbanded a skilled work force. In times of economic contraction, however, the seniority principle of "last hired, first fired" often meant that black workers were the least secure. The dynamics of this problem were seen at the end of World War II, where the seniority system eroded some of the advancement made by black workers during the wartime full employment economy and fair employment national policy. By the mid-1950s the seniority system revealed another characteristic detrimental to black workers. Those who had gained seniority in their segregated jobs risked losing that security if jobs were integrated. They would be able to advance into previously white lines only at the risk of surrendering the seniority they had accumulated in the previously all-black departments.

The simplest means of preventing this situation was to allow black workers who desired to transfer into white departments credit for the seniority which they had accumulated in black departments—that is, allow black workers to transfer based on "plant" rather than "departmental" seniority. The AFL and the CIO had both rejected the policy of giving recently hired black workers "superseniority" to prevent postwar layoffs, and they opposed this method of allowing black workers to carry plant seniority into white departments. So when labor unions desegregated unions, or plants desegregated job lines, black workers had to begin at the bottom of the seniority lists in previously all-white departments. Moreover, if there were white workers who had been laid off, or were on waiting lists for apprenticeship and training programs based on seniority, black workers had to get in line behind them.

The unfairness of the system was manifest. Past discrimination made black workers less secure competing in a desegregated work force. Indeed, the initial effects of integration might impose penalties on black workers. Seniority systems acted as a grandfather clause in employment for white workers who entered the system before integration. On the other hand, white workers did not feel personally responsible for the system of employment discrimination, and giving black workers preferential treatment to compensate for the discrimination of the past did not appear fair to them. The issue of integrating seniority systems posed a dilemma for civil rights and labor organizations, and proved to be the most contentious issue of Title VII law.

The system of integrating seniority systems without giving black workers credit for seniority accumulated in their segregated jobs was common in the postwar period. The New York SCAD did not compel labor unions to compensate black workers for seniority in previously segregated departments, but it did work informally to persuade unions to give them some special consideration, and often achieved this by conciliation.[13] Some black workers did challenge collective bargaining agreements that merged seniority systems without consideration for time spent in previously segregated departments. The law in this area was governed by the principle of "fair representation," developed in the 1944 case of *Steele* under the Railway Labor Act and later extended to the National Labor Relations Act. According to the fair representation doctrine, labor unions did not have to extend full membership privileges to all applicants, but they did have to represent excluded minority workers fairly if they bargained for them. In 1954 a white railroad clerk sued his union for altering its seniority system in the course of integrating black workers. He claimed such an alteration of the collective bargaining agreement was made solely for the benefit of black clerks and amounted to discrimination against whites. The Fifth Circuit Court of Appeals denied his claim, stating that the agreement "merely rectified an existing discrimination against the colored employees." The next year the Shell Oil Company in Texas, at the behest of the President's Committee on Government Contracts, integrated its work force and included some plant seniority and preferential promotion opportunities for its black workers, which a Texas federal district court regarded as "a valid compromise and set-

13. Stenographic Transcript of the Proceedings Before the President's Committee on Government Contract Compliance, July 15, 1952, Meany Archives; compare SCAD Pennsylvania Railroad and the Brewery cases, chap. 5, above; "Title VII, Seniority Discrimination, and the Incumbent Negro," *Harvard Law Review*, LXXX (1967), 1260–83.

tlement of issues involved." Thus the conversion of departmental seniority into plant seniority was already established as an option in fair employment.[14]

The leading case on this subject came in 1959 in *Whitfield* v. *United Steelworkers*. In this case the Armco Steel Company of Texas abolished its system of segregating black workers into a separate, unskilled line of progression. Black workers were given the exclusive opportunity to bid for skilled jobs previously reserved for whites, provided they passed a qualifying test. The company imposed this test in lieu of its previous screening and probation system for skilled workers. Black steelworkers sued, claiming that the new system was unfair to them, requiring them to take qualifying tests that white incumbents were not required to take. Fifth Circuit Court of Appeals Judge John Minor Wisdom dismissed the complaint, holding that if the new requirements had a discriminatory effect on black employees, these effects were the result of relevant business considerations and not racial animus. Indeed, Wisdom held, "If there is racial discrimination under the new contract, it is discrimination in favor of negroes." The preference given to black employees to bid for the skilled jobs was balanced by the qualifying test for the sake of efficient management and orderly promotion, of interest to all employees. Wisdom stated that this sort of problem was bound to arise whenever a company substituted equal opportunity for racial discrimination. "In such cases it is impossible to place negro incumbents holding certain jobs, especially unskilled jobs, on an absolutely equal footing with white incumbents in skilled jobs. In this situation time and tolerance, patience and forbearance, compromise and accommodation are needed in solving a problem rooted deeply in custom." The company and the union had made a good faith attempt to provide for equal opportunity in the future. Although the agreement was not perfect, Wisdom said, "Angels could do no more." There was no doubt that black workers in the unskilled line were at a disadvantage, but, Wisdom said, "This is a product of the past. We cannot turn back the clock." Wis-

14. *Pellicer v. Brotherhood of Railway Clerks*, 35 L.R.R.M. 2209 (1954); *Holt v. Oil Workers Union*, 36 L.R.R.M. 2703 (1955).

dom concluded, "Unfair treatment . . . in the past gives the plaintiffs no claim now to be paid back by unfair treatment in their favor."[15]

The Supreme Court denied certiorari to the case in 1959, and *Whitfield* remained the statement of the law under the NLRA requirement of "fair representation." The NLRB continued to approve of union desegregation along these lines. NAACP Labor Secretary Herbert Hill was advised that it was useless to bring charges of discrimination against labor unions if their interdepartmental transfer policy was accompanied by the loss of seniority, although "someday we hope to change the law on this point." Wisdom's decision remained the fullest expression of what came to be known as the "status quo" approach to labor union integration: it was enough to allow blacks and whites to compete on the same terms in the future, without giving blacks preferential treatment to compensate for the effects of past discrimination.[16]

Whitfield applied under the National Labor Relations Act, but it was unclear what Title VII would do to the seniority problem. As one judge said in a Title VII sex discrimination case, Title VII was "a statutory embodiment of constitutional rights that all persons are entitled to enjoy, while the [NLRA] has as its primary purpose the maintenance of peace between labor and management." Although it appeared that section 703 (h)'s exception for "bona fide seniority systems" required no more than the *Whitfield* "status quo" desegregation of seniority systems, no one in Congress directly addressed the specific problem of departmental seniority. The early EEOC seemed to demand no more than *Whitfield,* and negotiations with the Crown-Zellerbach Corporation's paper plant in Bogalusa, Louisiana, provided for the retention of the departmental seniority system as well as personnel tests for interdepartmental transfers. This led to the first private suit on the issue, by a Crown-Zellerbach employee who was not satisfied with the EEOC's 1965 terms.[17]

Crown-Zellerbach was a San Francisco firm with a liberal reputa-

15. *Whitfield* v. *United Steelworkers,* 156 F.Supp 430 (1957), 263 F.2d 546 (1959).

16. 360 U.S. 902 (1959); NLRB News Release, April 9, 1963, Atlantic Steel case, Marie L. Marcus to Herbert Hill, May 8, 1963, in NAACP Papers, III-A-309.

17. *Bowe* v. *Colgate-Palmolive,* 56 L.C. 9069 (1967); *Mondy* v. *Crown-Zellerbach,* 56 L.C. 9082.

tion on racial employment policy, but faced a bitter racial situation in its Bogalusa plant. The company faced not only private suits by black employees unhappy with the EEOC terms, but pressure by the Office of Federal Contract Compliance (OFCC) to substitute a combination plant-departmental seniority system in its place. Crown was unable to induce its two unions, the United Papermakers and Paperworkers Locals 189 and 189-A, to accept the joint plant-departmental system proposed by the OFCC. The white local, 189, thought the combination system went too far, while the black local, 189-A, did not think it went far enough. Crown was faced with the prospect of a white Papermakers strike if it imposed the OFCC terms (the black Papermakers were willing to accept the combination system as a step in the right direction), or a cutoff of vital government contracts if it did not. The company got a reprieve on January 2, 1968, when District of Columbia district court judge John Sirica enjoined the OFCC cancellation of Crown-Zellerbach contracts pending administrative hearing or private suit resolution of the seniority issue.[18]

Legal writers were meanwhile fashioning new approaches to the problem of discriminatory seniority systems. While the "status quo" position did not seem to do enough to compensate for past discrimination, an alternative "freedom now" position seemed to do too much. Such a position would give black workers, or even the black unemployed, the right to displace incumbent white workers, assuming that these white workers had only gained their positions at the expense of black workers—or even the black unemployed. This position stretched the connection between past discrimination and its present effects and had far-reaching potential. Like the direct-action pickets of the 1930s, civil rights advocates of the 1960s abjured any intention to displace incumbent white workers lest it provoke a political reaction against the entire EEO program. Most commentators favored what was called the "rightful place" doctrine, whereby incumbent black workers would gain the seniority they would have had absent past discrimination. These writers agreed that Congress

18. Gelber, *Black Men and Businessmen*, 78; *Crown-Zellerbach Corp.* v. *Wirtz* and *United Papermakers and Paperworkers* v. *Crown-Zellerbach*, 57 L.C. 9104 (1968); *U.S.* v. *Local 189, United Papermakers and Paperworkers and Crown-Zellerbach Corp.*, 282 F.2d 980 (1969).

had not addressed the problem directly, and that the legislative history left room for maneuver on this issue. Although the question of qualifications and testing remained, the "rightful place" doctrine would preserve the business and labor interest in seniority systems, and would be the best way to achieve the purpose of the 1964 Civil Rights Act—the improvement of minority economic status—without undue cost or disruption.[19]

The "rightful place" theory received a favorable judicial decision in the 1968 case of *Quarles* v. *Philip Morris,* decided two days after Judge Sirica's injunction in the Crown-Zellerbach case. The Philip Morris company had desegregated its tobacco processing plant in Richmond, Virginia, after the enactment of Title VII, but maintained a departmental progression system based on the previously segregated departments. The company allowed a limited number of interdepartmental transfers which had the effect of integrating the departments. Two black workers complained of continued discrimination in pay rates, promotion into supervisory positions, and the departmental seniority system. The judge found no evidence for most of the charges of current discrimination, but went on to explore the problem of past discrimination's current effects.[20]

While Judge John Decker Butzner, Jr., noted that departmental organization served many legitimate management functions, he saw that the company's nondiscriminatory employment policy since January, 1966, had only partly eliminated the disadvantage that black employees suffered due to past segregation.[21] The company claimed that the present effects of past discrimination lay outside the coverage of Title VII, as demonstrated by the legislative history. Butzner held, however, that Congress had made no express statement about departmental seniority, and that discriminatory systems enacted before the act could not be continued after it took effect. He concluded that "Congress did not intend to require 'reverse discrimination'; that is, the act does not require that Negroes

19. "Title VII, Seniority Discrimination, and the Incumbent Negro"; William B. Gould, "Employment Security, Seniority, and Race: The Role of Title VII of the Civil Rights Act of 1964, *Howard Law Journal,* XIII (1967), 1–50; Blumrosen, *Modern Law,* 76.

20. *Quarles* v. *Philip Morris Co.,* 279 F.Supp. 505 (1968).

21. Butzner was a Fourth Circuit Court of Appeals judge, designated by the circuit to sit on the district court for this case.

be preferred over white employees who possess employment seniority," disposing of the "freedom now" theory. "It is also apparent that Congress did not intend to freeze an entire generation of Negro employees into discriminatory patterns that existed before the act," he concluded, discarding the "status quo" theory and embracing the Justice Department's voting rights analogy.

Butzner did not reject *Whitfield* entirely, but confined it to supervisory personnel, where lack of qualifications kept out most black employees. The departmental seniority system was unacceptable only when it kept otherwise qualified employees from promotion. *Whitfield's* condemnation of "reverse discrimination" implied that employers did not have to take affirmative action to provide minority victims of past discrimination with special training to make them promotable. Recognizing that the Civil Rights Act intended to promote minority economic interests within the limits of color-blindness, Butzner also saw that Congress intended to promote economic efficiency and merit employment. *Quarles* implied strict judicial scrutiny of seniority systems that were unrelated to qualifications. As one critic of Title VII put it, seniority was, rather than a racially neutral standard like productivity, "merely an arbitrary standard which allocates economic benefits on a preferential basis unrelated to qualifications or ability. . . . Seniority is itself a preferential system unrelated to productivity; to condition continued use upon its not being employed to perpetuate the effect of racial prejudice is not the kind of preferential treatment for Negroes we ought to avoid." This adoption of the "rightful place" theory would only slightly alter the disparate-treatment approach to discrimination. Indeed, some supporters of affirmative action thought that while *Quarles* appeared to be a step in the right direction, recognizing the present effects of past discrimination, it might do as much harm as good. Insofar as it considered the rights of incumbent non-minority workers and valued economic efficiency, this interpretation of Title VII would not bring substantial immediate relief to minority group members.[22]

22. "Employment Discrimination and Title VII," 1109–1316; Winter, "Improving the Economic Status of Negroes," 817–55; William B. Gould, "Seniority and the Black Worker: Reflections on *Quarles* and Its Implications," *Texas Law Review,* XLVII (1969), 1039–74.

Quarles indicated that Title VII could be applied to pre–Civil Rights Act discrimination. Title VII would at least prevent seniority systems and waiting lists for apprenticeship and training programs devised before 1965, or after 1965 in violation of the law, from depriving otherwise qualified minority workers of advancement. The principal question in the Title VII cases of 1968 and 1969 involved the issue of qualifications, and especially of the use of tests.

The EEOC stated its position on qualifications and testing in its 1966 *Guidelines on Employment Testing Procedures.*[23] The commission interpreted a "professionally developed ability test" permitted by section 703 (h) as "a test which fairly measures the knowledge or skills required by the particular job or class of jobs which the applicant seeks, or which fairly affords the employer a chance to measure the applicant's ability to perform a particular job or class of jobs." The commission argued that tests could have as much discriminatory impact as an overt policy of racial exclusion. The commission recommended affirmative action—special efforts to seek out minority group members who might be "qualifiable." If employers used tests, they should not rely on them exclusively, and should guard against cultural biases that would disqualify otherwise competent minorities. The tests should also possess a demonstrable connection between performance on the test and performance on the job, or "criterion-related validity." When the test was given to a sample group in order to derive a standard or norm, that group should include minority group members. Title VII did not empower the EEOC to issue substantive rules and regulations. Section 713 (a) of the act stated that "the Commission shall have authority from time to time to issue, amend, or rescind suitable procedural regulations to carry out the provisions of this title."[24] The commission thus called its testing position a "guideline," and its authority would be

23. U.S. Equal Employment Opportunity Commission, *Guidelines on Employment Testing Procedures* (Washington, D.C., 1966).

24. This was not a weakening of the *original* version of Title VII, H.R. 405, but it was a weakening of the House-passed version by the Senate, which restored the word "procedural." Humphrey's S.R. 1937, however, had permitted the EEO administrator to issue "rules and regulations," presumably substantive ones.

determined in section 706 private suits in which the EEOC served as *amicus*.

While the EEOC worked through private suits under section 706, the Justice Department shaped Title VII law in its pattern-or-practice suits against construction trade unions and contractors. Its first important efforts were made in New Orleans and St. Louis. The department had to deal with the question of apprenticeship nepotism, which was cherished by the union members, and of skills and qualifications, of concern to the contractors. The department believed that once the unions had resigned themselves to accepting Negroes into membership, "it will make little difference to the union whether or not the Negro is a skilled craftsman," but in the meantime the contractors would insist on some kind of qualification test to prevent Negroes from entering. "The fact is that because of past discrimination in the industry and because of inferior educational opportunities, there are very few Negroes presently qualified as craftsmen in the building trades," the department noted. The key was to get "qualifiable" minorities admitted.[25]

The Justice Department was initially very successful in its craft union cases. In 1966 the Missouri district upheld most of the attorney general's procedural claims in its suit against the St. Louis building trades. In 1967 a U.S. district court found the New Orleans heat and frost insulators union guilty of violating Title VII through its limitation on membership size and its admission requirement of familial relationship to or recommendation by a union member. In previously all-white unions, the judge held, such requirements effectively denied to Negroes the opportunity to join the union without regard to race. While nepotism and limitation served interests of union members and were not inherently or primarily devices of racial exclusion, racial exclusion was their effect.[26]

25. Memorandum to William F. McCabe, December 1, 1966, "A Review of the Activities of the Department of Justice in Civil Rights, 1966," in U.S. Dept. of Justice, Records of John Doar, Box 1, RG 60.

26. *U.S. v. Building and Construction Trades Council of St. Louis*, 62 L.C. 9412, 9413 (1966); *Vogler v. McCarty* and *U.S. v. International Association of Heat and Frost Insulators and Asbestos Workers, Local 53*, 55 L.C. 9063 (1967).

The Justice Department did not prevail in its actions against the St. Louis sheet metal workers and the Cincinnati electrical workers unions, with courts rejecting the department's argument that the statistical disparity between Negroes in the union and in the population showed discrimination. Denying the model of voting rights cases proffered by the department in the St. Louis *Sheet Metal Workers* case, Judge James Hargrove Meredith held, "Mere absence of Negroes in a particular group does not constitute proof of pattern or practice of discrimination." The union now applied objective standards to all applicants and applied them without regard to race, the judge noted, and their disproportionate racial impact did not make them illegal. Title VII prohibited only "intentional" discrimination, the court held, and these effects were incidental rather than intentional. The act also applied prospectively; forcing the union to atone for its past discrimination would be an improper retrospective application. Finally, the suspension of the qualifications, urged by the attorney general, would constitute preferential treatment prohibited by section 703 (j).[27]

Judge Timothy S. Hogan in the Cincinnati *Dobbins* case faced more complicated circumstances and rendered a subtler decision. He was willing to consider facts of the union's behavior prior to 1965, but only because this conduct might offer clues as to the "intent" of post-act policies which appeared neutral but might be pretexts for discrimination. The judge also noted that labor union discrimination had been illegal since the *Steele* decision of 1944. Most judges and commentators did not emphasize this point—that while some employment discrimination was not illegal prior to 1965, labor union discrimination was illegal, and thus more comparable to voting or jury exclusion. Such an approach might have made the seniority cases easier to prove and at the same time limited the doctrine of the "present effects of past discrimination." The court's requirement of "intent" made the government's case harder to prove. Moreover, the court dismissed the government's argument that Title VII required an all-white union to take affirmative action to re-

27. *U.S. v. Sheet Metal Workers International Association, Local 36*, 280 F.Supp. 719 (1968).

lieve the present effects of past discrimination. Such action would constitute preferential treatment. The government could not assume in employment cases that a significant number of potential craftsmen existed as it did in voting rights cases when it assumed that a significant number of potential voters existed. Employment, especially in a field like electrical work, depended on skills, and the court was convinced that a large number of qualified Negro electricians did not exist in the Cincinnati area. Thus, *Quarles* did not apply. The court insisted that evidence of disparate treatment of white and black workers with equal qualifications be shown. The court did not attach any weight to the EEOC testing guidelines, noting that the commission had power to issue procedural regulations only.[28]

In *U.S.* v. *Hayes International Corporation* the Justice Department similarly lost a suit against an Alabama aircraft plant which desegregated its lines of progression and gave its black employees special transfer rights. Judge Seybourn Harris Lynne interpreted *Quarles* as holding that "the *Whitfield* case was applicable under Title VII with respect to transfer to jobs which required skills and training." If black workers chose not to avail themselves of these opportunities, for fear of losing their seniority in their former jobs, this proved no violation of the law. The court argued that the act "contemplates and requires a triangular adjustment of the rights of minority group employees, the rights of other employees, and the interest of management and labor." The case of *Griggs* v. *Duke Power Company* tied together the issues of testing, seniority, and the application of Title VII to past discrimination. Private plaintiffs sued a North Carolina power company because interdepartmental transfer depended on either a high school diploma or passing qualifying exams. In what was to become the leading Title VII case when appealed to the U.S. Supreme Court, Judge Eugene Andrew Gordon disputed *Quarles,* denying that Title VII applied to the present consequences of past discrimination. "In providing for prospective application only, Congress faced the cold hard fact of past discrimination and the resulting inequities. Congress also realized the impossibility of eradicat-

---

28. *Dobbins* v. *Local 212, IBEW,* and *US* v. *IBEW Local 212,* 292 F.Supp. 413 (1968).

ing all the consequences of past discrimination," the court held. The judge also dismissed the EEOC's testing guidelines, declaring that "employers may set the qualities that they desire of employees without regard to performance of the job, and may use any test which validly and accurately measures those qualities."[29]

While the Justice Department compiled a mixed record in pattern-or-practice suits in the district courts, the government's most significant victory concerning issues of seniority came in the Papermakers case of 1968. Combined EEOC and OFCC action against the Crown-Zellerbach Bogalusa paper mill reached a judicial determination in March, 1968. The Justice Department now endorsed the black workers' desire for complete dismantlement of the departmental seniority system and its replacement with a plantwide system. The combination system originally designed by the OFCC guarded black job security by allowing bump-back rights, so that in case of layoffs black workers could return to the previously all-black departments. These rights applied to laid-off white workers, too, so that laid-off whites had recall rights ahead of blacks when positions opened in the previously all-white departments. A full plantwide seniority system would allow black workers to be promoted ahead of these white workers who had longer departmental seniority but less plant seniority. It appears that the EEOC, which in 1965 had advised Crown-Zellerbach that the integration of seniority lines should proceed according to *Whitfield,* had moved beyond the OFCC's combination proposal toward a full adoption of the "rightful place" theory. The commission advocated "not just an increase in the Negroes' opportunities, but an equalization of present opportunity." While this seemed to imply a substitution of equality of result for equality of opportunity, the EEOC still spoke of giving Negro workers positions according to past seniority, but "within the confines of skill and training."[30]

29. *U.S.* v. *Hayes International Corp.,* 58 L.C. 9224 (1968); *Griggs* v. *Duke Power Co.,* 58 L.C. 9163 (1968).

30. *U.S.* v. *Local 189, United Papermakers and Paperworkers and Crown-Zellerbach Corp.,* 282 F.Supp. 39 (1968); EEOC Decision and Addendum, August 25, 1967, Meany Archives, Collection 36, Box 1.

Judge Frederick Jacob Regan Heebe accepted the Justice Department's argument that any seniority system that was based substantially on departmental seniority discriminated against black workers. The court denied that departmental seniority was necessary for any relevant business purpose such as safety or efficiency, and that plant seniority could easily be substituted for it. Departmental seniority was not inherently discriminatory, but in this case it perpetuated the effects of past discrimination. The company retained "the right to require that the competing employees have the fundamental qualifications necessary to fill the vacant position." Indeed, if the company or union could devise a system other than plant seniority which did not perpetuate the effects of past discrimination, the court would consider it.

The Papermakers case stood out as a victory for the OFCC and EEOC in 1968, when most district court decisions had gone against them. The decision was essentially a restatement of *Quarles*, with a clearer rationale and a more sweeping remedy. As in *Quarles*, which involved cigarette manufacturing, the Papermakers' work was not highly skilled, so the departmental systems served no clear business purpose. The government was unable to win the cases in which departmental seniority or union membership depended on skills demonstrated by experience or testing.

The EEOC noted that while Crown-Zellerbach had made good faith efforts to eliminate the gross discrimination that existed before 1966, stopping obvious, disparate treatment would not be enough to solve the problem of the economic condition of black Americans. This was apparent in the northern FEP states by the mid-1950s. Applying Title VII to the present effects of past discrimination in the labor union seniority systems was a reasonable application of the statute along disparate-treatment lines especially when, as in *Quarles*, it promoted merit employment. But the present effect of past discrimination, if more broadly defined, was probably the explanation for minority underemployment: segregated and inferior education and housing in addition to previous exclusion from promotion and training. Employer qualifications and tests merely revealed the accumulated impact of past discrimination. It was the strategy of the

EEOC, OFCC, and civil rights groups to deal with the problem of qualifications by forcing employers to qualify minority group members. As Alfred W. Blumrosen put it, tests were "carriers" of discrimination from the larger society into the workplace and permitted employers to "skim the cream" of the work force and blame other institutions of society for the rest.[31]

This was the practical meaning of the theory of "institutional discrimination," that it was unfair to apply equal treatment to victims of past discrimination, and that all black Americans were victims of past discrimination. The "present effects" doctrine condemned the application of neutral standards to those who were victims of discrimination at an earlier time—in the seniority cases, a recent and proximate past. Limiting relief to members of a particular class, as in *Quarles*, ensured that employers would not be responsible for "training the world." The connection between past discrimination and present disadvantage was easily discernible in the seniority system cases; to overcome the problem of qualifications and testing, that connection would have to be attenuated, further back in time and to other areas of society. State EEO officials could thus make employers bear more of the burden of the discrimination of other institutions. Employer responsibility also kept white and black labor from falling out over seniority rights, and helped to keep the labor–civil rights political coalition together. The great achievement of EEOC litigation was to expand "present effects" from its technical and limited application to seniority systems into a general theory of discrimination that would support race-conscious, result-oriented remedies.[32]

The way around the qualifications problem was to apply the EEOC guidelines strictly: force employers to justify any test or standard that had an adverse impact on minority group members. This interpretation would replicate the Motorola decision that Congress had hoped to avoid through section 703 (h). As one law review noted, "it is possible to read the Guidelines so strictly as to make testing virtually impossible." If the educational or skill standard

---

31. Blumrosen, "Duty of Fair Recruitment," 503.

32. "Employment Discrimination and Title VII"; Blumrosen, "Duty of Fair Recruitment"; Alfred W. Blumrosen, "Seniority and Equal Employment Opportunity: A Glimmer of Hope," *Rutgers Law Review,* XXIII (1969), 268–317.

had a disparate impact on minority group members, as almost all standards would, the employer would have to justify it in terms of "business necessity." It would then fall upon the employer to provide the training necessary to make up for the adverse racial impact. Blumrosen wrote, "The failure to establish such programs for entry level jobs may be discrimination where the skills in question are not adequately developed in both majority and minority groups."[33]

The "business necessity" idea had wide appeal. The argument that tests should have some relationship to the job in question was consistent with the underlying goal of the Civil Rights Act to make American business more rational and efficient. This had been a large part of the 1950s FEP "manpower utilization" justification, stressing the cost of discrimination in terms of GNP. Proponents of free-market economic policies criticized excessive qualifications in employment as barriers to full employment. Title VII thus would promote American economic growth and competitiveness while furthering social justice.[34]

As lawyers and judges expounded the idea of business necessity, however, it became apparent that Title VII enforcement might work against economic efficiency. Advocates suggested that antidiscrimination laws might create more jobs in the long run, but in the short run they necessarily involved the restriction of white employment opportunities. As long as testing or other qualifications did not have a disparate impact on minority group members, they would not violate Title VII, regardless of their irrelevance. As two Title VII litigators put it, "If an employer hired every fifth applicant on a random basis, his selection procedure would be arbitrary and might not relate well to job performance, but it would not deny equal employment opportunity." The economic atmosphere of the mid-1960s helped ease this transition. While affirmative action might impose some costs to the economy, the economy was growing at such a rate as to make that cost affordable. Rather than resort to random hiring, employers could use tests in which all racial and

---

33. "Employment Discrimination and Title VII"; Blumrosen, "Duty of Fair Recruitment."

34. Thomas Sowell, *Race and Economics* (New York, 1975), 153; Banfield, *Unheavenly City,* 115.

ethnic groups scored equally.[35] The task for employers would not be to find a valid test, but one that qualified the right proportion of minorities, they concluded. "If, whatever his standards, the employer's performance is measured by the extent to which he has acquired substantial numbers of minority employees, the civil rights interest is satisfied and the 'affirmative duty' is met." Statistics would prove the success of employers' efforts. "I suggest that the objective criterion to which the civil rights interest is moving is the number of minorities employed in various job classifications," Blumrosen wrote. This did not necessarily mean quotas; but employers must find non-quota systems which satisfied this test. The goal of color-blind equal treatment, even if applied with consideration for the effects of discernible past discrimination, was giving way to one of strict numerical equal outcome without any real regard for business necessity or any of the Civil Rights Act's goals other than minority group employment.[36]

The crucial question, then, was to what extent "business necessity" could excuse personnel selection devices which had a disparate impact. Some EEOC officials and legal commentators now urged that no amount of business necessity could justify a seniority system which had a disparate impact, and that a concentration of blacks in lower-level grades sufficed as proof of discrimination. In the construction union cases, the measure of discrimination would be the disparity between the percentage of black members and the percentage of blacks in the general population. Racial proportionalism was the yardstick.[37]

In 1968 and 1969 the Justice Department brought more section 707 pattern-or-practice suits and asked the courts for remedies that

35. George Cooper and Richard Sobol, "Seniority and Testing Under Fair Employment Laws: A General Approach to Objective Criteria of Hiring and Promotion," *Harvard Law Review*, LXXXII (1969), 1660. The impact of this article, written by two Title VII plaintiff attorneys, cannot be overstated. Judges in Title VII cases adopted it almost whole.

36. Blumrosen, "Duty of Fair Recruitment," 504.

37. See "Employment Discrimination and Title VII"; Gould, "Seniority and the Black Worker"; "Title VII of the Civil Rights Act of 1964 and Minority Group Entry into the Building Trade Unions," *University of Chicago Law Review*, XXXVII (1969), 328–58.

went beyond the removal of the immediate "present effects of past discrimination." It lost two of these cases where the departmental seniority system or trade union referral and apprenticeship system was based on relevant skills and "business necessity." The first case was against the H. K. Porter Company's steel plant in Birmingham, Alabama. District court judge Clarence William Allgood wrote a detailed opinion that dismissed most of the attorney general's claims, insisting that judgments in Title VII cases must hew closely to the facts and circumstances of each individual case. The company manufactured steel bars, angles, and shapes with the elaborate departmental progression system common in the steel industry. It had maintained separate lines of progression for black and white workers until 1962, when the PCEEO induced it to merge lines. Although the president's committee judged the company to be complying with equal employment opportunity requirements, the attorney general and the court agreed that the old committee's interpretation did not necessarily satisfy the requirements of Title VII. The company argued that compliance with the executive order exceeded the requirements of compliance with Title VII. The attorney general contended, and the court agreed, that H. K. Porter's new employment practices did not demonstrate full compliance with the statute.[38]

The court did find that the company and union had made special transfer opportunities available to black employees in its latest collective bargaining agreement. While relevant, "The fact that a procedure which has been adopted for the benefit of Negro employees is unique is certainly a long way from proving compliance with the law," the court noted. The attorney general argued, as in the Papermakers case, for the abolition of the departmental seniority system and institution of a plantwide system. "This result is necessary, in the Attorney General's view, to compensate the Negro employees for the segregation which existed prior to October of 1962 and to achieve a more proportionate racial balance in the departments."

Allgood regarded the matter of the retrospective application of Title VII as an open question. While the attorney general pressed *Quarles* and *Papermakers*, the company appealed to the *Sheet Metal Workers, Dobbins,* and *Griggs* decisions. The court denied that it

---

38. *U.S. v. H. K. Porter Co.*, 59 L.C. 9204.

must apply either theory mechanically, but should consult the particular facts of each case. Allgood had no quarrel with *Quarles* or *Papermakers,* but denied that these cases were apposite to the case at hand. Black workers were not "locked in" as in these cases; many had availed themselves of the special transfer opportunities. The ones who had not had "voluntarily frozen themselves," the court held. This fact considerably weakened the attorney general's contention that only plantwide seniority could remedy the effects of past discrimination.

The court held that the departmental system fulfilled legitimate business purposes, was based on substantial job-related criteria, and was not contrived to subordinate black workers. Moreover, the judge applied a disparate-treatment analysis and found that departmental standards had been applied equally to black and white workers. Allgood dismissed the attorney general's jury and voting analogies, saying that "while it is one thing to assume that a significant number of a group have the qualifications for schooling or voting or jury service, it cannot be assumed without evidence that they have the qualifications to perform a given trade." Moreover, not all trades were equivalent. Manufacturing paper or cigarettes was not equivalent to manufacturing steel. Thus, "the position urged by the Attorney General is entirely inappropriate to the factual setting of this case." Under these circumstances, the relief demanded by the attorney general amounted to preferential treatment contrary to congressional intent. Allgood endorsed John Minor Wisdom's *Whitfield* statement that "fairness is not achieved by treating white incumbents unfairly."

The attorney general also argued that the tests used by H. K. Porter to qualify for transfer were not covered by section 703 (h) because they had not been validated. Again Allgood would accept neither this proposition, that all tests must be validated, nor the company's argument that any professionally developed test was legitimate under Title VII. The court agreed "in principle with the proposition that the aptitudes which are measured by a test should be relevant to the aptitudes which are involved in the performance of jobs." Although not professionally validated, H. K. Porter administered the tests with adequate care and attention to the jobs in question. Instead of proving discrimination, the racial disparity in test results, he noted, could as easily be evidence that the aptitudes of the persons tested differed, and that the test fulfilled its intended purpose. The court denied the argument that "the use of aptitude tests without validation necessarily equals discrimination." The suggestion of differential validation or race-norming, the court held, would itself constitute prohibited discrimination. An industrial psychologist testifying on behalf of the government noted that if this were so, the laws should be changed. "This may ultimately be the answer," Allgood remarked, "but it will have to be the Congress and not the courts which change the law to reach this result."

While the judge found certain of the company's practices to be discriminatory, particularly the assignment of temporary workers in the general labor pool, the court did not find a "pattern or practice." "To the contrary," the court noted, "it would be more accurate to say that the company and the union are engaged in a pattern of compliance and implementation of equal opportunities in employment." While rejecting almost all of the attorney general's contentions, the court did not reject the attorney general's broad propositions in general. "They may be applicable to the facts of other cases, but the point is that they are not applicable to the facts of this case."

The Cleveland International Brotherhood of Electrical Workers was another target of a Justice Department section 707 suit. The IBEW had engaged in exclusion of Negro workers through their nepotistic admission process. When the Civil Rights Act of 1964 took effect, the union altered its selection procedure and substituted objective standards for admission. It maintained its limited total membership, and insisted that applicants for membership have electrical work experience or go through apprenticeship. Priorities in referrals went to union members. These limitations acted like a seniority system, giving an advantage to members of long standing, regardless of the fact that black workers had been excluded prior to 1965. The attorney general argued that these practices perpetuated the effects of past discrimination and must be discontinued and replaced by an affirmative action program.[39]

39. *U.S.* v. *IBEW Local 38,* 59 L.C. 9226 (1969).

While the district court found that the union had practiced discrimination in referrals after 1965, it rejected most of the other government arguments. Judge Ben Charles Green rejected the attorney general's demand that the union change its objective standards, referral system, and apprenticeship system in order to redress the racial imbalance in the union. Such an attempt to achieve racial balance would constitute preferential treatment in violation of the act. Past discrimination's effects were properly considered, but affirmative action relief for it was limited by section 703 (j). Gross statistical imbalance was not in itself a prima facie proof of discrimination, but would be if coupled with specific acts of discrimination, meaning "a showing of differentiation in treatment." Again, the voting cases presented by the attorney general were of little specific relevance. The court insisted that "intent," not just statistical correlation, be shown.

The court denied the government's assertion that Title VII carried a duty of affirmative action. Title VII "should not be considered as a panacea for the effects of lifetimes of deprivation nor applied in a vindictive manner against those who have inherited problems originating in another era." The union had no duty to seek out qualified minority group electrical workers. "It appears to the court that the only way in which the defendant union could improve its statistical record with regard to Negro referrals would be to solicit Negro electricians for employment, which the Civil Rights Act does not require, or to grant preferential treatment to Negro referral applicants, which the Civil Rights Act does not permit."

In apprentice selection, the court determined that the union's tests were administered in good faith. While not completely objective and validated, they allowed room for subjective consideration of the special cultural problems of minority group members. While the court eschewed preferential treatment, it indicated that treating minority status as a "plus" would not violate the law.

The government consistently lost disparate-treatment cases in district courts in 1968. The next year, however, the circuit courts of appeal reversed many of these decisions and encouraged a new and more aggressive application of disparate-impact standards by the

EEOC and Justice Department. Ruling on several Title VII cases in 1969, the Fifth Circuit affirmed and extended the EEOC interpretation of the substance of the statute, as it had on procedural issues in its initial decisions. In January, 1969, it upheld the district court decision in *Vogler* v. *McCarty*, striking down the Asbestos Workers' nepotistic selection system. The court, citing district court decisions in *Quarles* and *Papermakers*, noted that the trial court "was fully empowered to eliminate the present effects of past discrimination." Moreover, it upheld the district court's order that the union make referrals on a one-to-one, black-white ratio, as "affirmative action" relief and not "preferential treatment." This was the first quota ordered by a federal court under the Civil Rights Act.[40]

In July, 1969, the Fifth Circuit upheld the *Papermakers* decision. John Minor Wisdom, author of the *Whitfield* opinion ten years earlier, announced broad support for affirmative action principles. His decision used a loose definition of the "intent" to discriminate under Title VII. Wisdom noted that "the statute, read literally, requires only that the defendant meant to do what he did, that is, his employment practice was not accidental." Such a definition eased the burden of proof on Title VII plaintiffs and helped the transition toward result-oriented affirmative action. The court also endorsed the "present effects" doctrine. Wisdom noted, "In this case we deal with one of the most perplexing issues troubling the courts under Title VII: how to reconcile equal employment opportunity *today* with seniority expectations based on *yesterday's* built-in racial discrimination." It was obviously unfair for Crown-Zellerbach to deny Negroes opportunities to advance because they lacked what the company had not allowed them to obtain before 1965. "The crux of the problem is how far the employer must go to undo the effects of past discrimination." Although there was some business necessity in Crown-Zellerbach's progression system, the court affirmed that it was not essential to the plant's safety or efficiency. Although the court accepted that qualifications with a disparate impact on minority group members could withstand judicial scrutiny, the test of

40. *Local 53, International Association of Heat and Frost Insulators and Asbestos Workers* v. *Vogler,* 59 L.C. 9195 (1969).

business purpose as "essential" meant that tests and qualifications would be harder for employers to defend.[41]

In August the Fifth Circuit overruled the district court in the *Hayes* case. First, the court held that "the employment statistics discussed amply demonstrated a preliminary showing that the company hiring practices violated Title VII." The appellate court found Hayes's limited transfer program inadequate. It did not open all jobs in the plant to black transfers, applied a time limit, and provided only one chance to take advantage of it. Since the company had unlimited discretion over transfers, the court saw the limits as the result of discriminatory intent. Recall rights for white laid-off employees ahead of transferring blacks also perpetuated the effects of past discrimination. The company would have to go further to eradicate the effects of past discrimination. These more stringent requirements, stretching the "present effects" idea, allowed the EEOC and Justice Department to demand affirmative action and qualification reform.[42]

In September, 1969, the Eighth Circuit Court of Appeals overruled the district court in the Saint Louis Sheet Metal Workers and IBEW cases. The opening of union membership and referrals on a nondiscriminatory basis was not adequate compliance with the law, since these new standards required experience that Negroes had been prevented from gaining prior to 1965. It was not necessary to demonstrate that any black craftsman had in fact been denied membership or referral, as in other Title VII cases. Judge Gerald William Heaney ordered that the requirement of previous experience under a local collective bargaining agreement be modified and the black workers be given greater options to demonstrate their ability. Tests would be objective and older black workers beyond apprenticeship age would be given opportunities for referral work. The union was required to publicize its new standards. The court concluded, "In requiring the modifications, we impose no quotas, we grant no preferences." As in the *Papermakers* case, the court insisted that qualified Negroes not be held back by artificial standards.[43]

41. *Local 189 United Papermakers and Paperworkers* v. *U.S.* 416 F.2d 980 (1969).
42. *U.S.* v. *Hayes International Corp.*, 60 L.C. 9303 (1969).
43. *U.S.* v. *Sheet Metal Workers International Association, Local 36*, 416 F.2d 123 (1969).

The first appellate interpretations of the substantive issues of the statute reversed district court decisions that construed Title VII narrowly, and extended the obligations of affirmative action to remedy the effects of past discrimination, even to the point, in *Vogler*, of approving outright quotas. Perhaps most revealing, the appellate courts regarded the improvement of minority group employment as the only concern of the Civil Rights Act, without the balancing of competing rights and interests in lower court decisions and in the *Quarles* decision. It accepted the EEOC's interpretation of Title VII completely, taking advantage of malleable statutory language when it could and ignoring or refashioning clear legislative instruction when necessary. The EEOC gained more power than anyone expected through the courts, turning what its supporters saw as its main weakness into a considerable strength. Following the model of the voting rights and school desegregation cases, both the agencies and the Fifth Circuit were concerned above all with results, and cleared away any procedural impediments to the hiring and promotion of minority workers.

The PCEEO, along with the EEOC, helped fashion a stronger antidiscrimination policy. The president's committee operated in the executive branch under the executive order that explicitly obliged government contractors to take affirmative action, not as a remedy to proved discrimination, but as a prerequisite to doing business with the government. The value of government contracts to businesses made equal employment opportunity easier to enforce—indeed, the most successful EEOC–Justice Department efforts involved government contracts, as in Newport News. An increasingly large part of the economy had some connection to government work and the executive orders covered a potentially vast portion of the nation's work force.

In September, 1965, President Johnson issued Executive Order 11246, abolishing the old PCEEO and establishing the Office of Federal Contract Compliance in the Department of Labor.[44] As seen in the Crown-Zellerbach negotiations, the early OFCC sometimes

44. Executive Order 11114 of 1963 extended PCEEO oversight to government construction contractors as well as over government procurement.

took a more forceful position than the EEOC, but by 1968 the two agencies pursued common tactics. The OFCC turned its attention to the areas where the EEOC and Justice Department had failed, and where civil rights efforts had been typically frustrated, against local building trades unions. The PWA quota system of the 1930s showed the potential for forceful government enforcement of antidiscrimination provisions. The first OFCC efforts were in Cleveland, where the government attempted to compel contractors to employ minority labor in terms to be negotiated after a contract was awarded. The comptroller general and others objected to this scheme as a violation of the rules of competitive bidding. As a result, in Philadelphia the OFCC set more specific conditions before contracts were bid upon, requiring contractors to state the numbers of minorities they would employ in various trades and the schedule on which they would reach these numbers. Construction contractors challenged the "goals and timetables" in the courts, claiming that they were quota systems which compelled violation of Title VII.[45]

State and federal courts upheld both the Cleveland and the Philadelphia plans. In the summer of 1968 a building contractor lost a bid for a Cuyahoga Community College project partially funded with federal money because his bid did not include a satisfactory manning table. The contractor submitted a manning table which contained the caveat that the contractor's obligation depended on availability of minority group workers in the local unions. The local unions had none or few minority group members, virtually nullifying the contractor's promise. The contractor failed to persuade the Ohio Court of Common Pleas that goals and timetables violated the rules of competitive bidding or constituted a preferential quota system in violation of Title VII. The court found that the college, in awarding the contract to a second low bidder who submitted an unconditional manning table, had not violated Title VII or abused its discretion in contract awards. This decision was upheld by a divided Ohio Supreme Court a year later, and the United States Supreme Court declined to review it.[46]

45. Graham, *Civil Rights*, 278–97, 322–45; Belz, *Equality Transformed*, 29–41, 89–93; Blumrosen, *Modern Law*, 128–31.
46. *Weiner* v. *Cuyahoga Community College District*, 58 L.C. 9164 (1968), 60 L.C. 9288 (1969).

The OFCC issued a revised Philadelphia Plan in June, 1969, in response to congressional objections that its goals and timetables constituted a quota system. The revised plan was not substantially different from the 1968 plan, and the objections of the comptroller general and Congress continued. Attorney General John Mitchell successfully answered these political objections, and the Nixon administration Department of Labor extended the Philadelphia Plan to other cities, and ultimately to all major government contractors. Federal contractors were no more successful than those in Ohio in challenging the plans in court.

The contractors bound by the Philadelphia Plan sued the Labor Department in 1969. A federal district court rejected their claims in the spring of 1970, supporting the Ohio courts in favor of the plan. "The Plan does not require the contractors to hire a definite percentage of a minority group," but asked only for a good faith effort defensible in court. Judge Charles R. Weiner noted that the union policy of racial exclusion was "repugnant, unworthy, and contrary to present national policy. The Philadelphia Plan will provide an unpolluted breath of fresh air to ventilate this unpalatable situation."[47]

The Third Circuit Court of Appeals offered a more elaborate justification for the plan when it denied the contractors' appeal a year later. Judge John J. Gibbons noted that the Philadelphia Plan was merely a more specific version of the affirmative action obligations in effect since 1961. The federal government had a legitimate interest in equal employment opportunity because it would provide for a wider potential work force, increased efficiency, more effective utilization of manpower and lower cost to taxpayers. It was significant, the court noted, that the OFCC did not impose a social policy on the states wholesale. "Rather, they acted in one area in which discrimination in employment was most likely to affect the cost and the progress of projects in which the federal government had both financial and completion interests." The Philadelphia Plan thus served to stem the disruption of construction site activity by civil rights demonstrations. The court had to assume that the Philadelphia Plan did not violate congressional intent as Congress took no ac-

47. *Contractors Association of Eastern Pennsylvania* v. *Shultz*, 62 L.C. 9421 (1970).

tion to curtail or cancel the program. The plan imposed no quotas, nor did it require a work force proportional to Philadelphia's racial composition, and section 703 (j) referred to Title VII, not Title VI, enforcement. The minority group recruitment could be increased without displacing any white workers, the court noted. The court cited Title VII cases which held that Congress did not intend to "freeze" minority group employment in pre-act patterns. "Clearly the Philadelphia Plan is color-conscious," the court noted, arguing that color-consciousness was inherent in the affirmative action concept of equal employment opportunity. The court denied, however, that conscious efforts to improve minority group employment were inconsistent with obligations not to discriminate on the basis of race. "This is pure sophistry," it held. Because the construction industry labor force was transitory and usually fell far short of industry demand, normal attrition and an expanded work force would enable contractors to expand minority group opportunities without limiting non-minority ones.[48]

Several of the assumptions on which the courts based their Philadelphia Plan decisions were dubious. The plan quickly became not just a program for a few trades in the construction industry of Philadelphia, but the model for all government contractors. It was unlikely that the plans would make government projects more efficient and save taxpayer money. The OFCC, like the EEOC and Justice Department, was concerned exclusively with minority group employment. The construction unions had more of an interest in keeping their numbers down and wages up than in expanding their numbers in order to preserve white employment opportunities. Moreover, the economic downturn that began just as these cases were litigated intensified conflict, demonstrating that minority group economic opportunities might not be improveable by affirmative action without at least the appearance of denial of majority group opportunities. The inherent clash and contradiction of affirmative action and antidiscrimination was not "sophistry." Because the unions proved reluctant to change their admissions policies

48. *Contractors Association of Eastern Pennsylvania* v. *Shultz*, 3 E.P.D. 8180 (1971). One of the three judges hearing the case was William Hastie, legal architect of the New Negro Alliance's picketing campaign in the 1930s.

and minority group entry into the construction trades did not rise considerably under the Philadelphia Plan and its progeny, exasperated courts resorted to strict quota policies to force them to admit minorities. Increased endorsement of race-conscious affirmative action in the late 1960s intensified this tendency. Indeed, by the late 1960s many civil rights activists believed that "goals and timetables" would not effectively change employment policies and that strict racial quotas were required. If Title VII prohibited quotas, then the title was an unconstitutional restriction of equal employment opportunity.[49]

The idea that policy made by administrators and courts was valid unless Congress legislated against it had vast implications for antidiscrimination law. The redefinition of the traditional understanding of discrimination undertaken by the federal bureaucracy and the courts was especially prominent in school desegregation cases. The Department of Health, Education, and Welfare (HEW), at the prodding of the U.S. Commission on Civil Rights, pressed for desegregation plans that went beyond the dismantlement of formal, state-imposed segregation toward a state obligation of integration. The Department of Justice pleaded HEW's case in the federal courts, and found favor in the Fifth Circuit Court of Appeals, with Judge John Minor Wisdom in particular. In the series of cases from 1966 to 1971 the federal courts replaced the prospective, color-blind obligation to end segregation with a color-conscious requirement to integrate in order to undo the effects of past discrimination. These decisions used racial statistics and racial balance as a measure of discrimination and desegregation, and required effective, statistically demonstrable integration immediately. They gave federal courts authority to use their equity powers to fashion remedies like busing. The school desegregation decisions could have enormous impact in employment, where the end of formal, overt discrimination achieved only limited immediate results. The EEOC and Justice Department routinely used education and voting rights cases in

49. Paul Marcus, "The Philadelphia Plan and Strict Racial Quotas on Federal Contracts," *UCLA Law Review,* XVII (1970), 817–36; Stanley R. Krakower, "The Constitutionality of 'Affirmative Action' to Integrate Construction Trades: The Philadelphia Plan," *Temple Law Quarterly,* XLIII (1970), 329–46.

Title VII litigation, and the redefinition of discrimination fashioned by the federal bureaucracy and Fifth Circuit expanded into the employment field, where it decided cases "based on the assumption that a black plaintiff in a Title VII action had probably been discriminated against."[50]

Employment discrimination law and policy had been radically transformed in the five years following the Civil Rights Act of 1964. The EEOC, Justice Department, and OFCC had advanced doctrines that made fair employment a group rather than an individual right, reached into the past to deal with the present effects of earlier discrimination, eliminated intent as part of discrimination, and brought any test or policy that had a disparate impact under suspicion. Thus racial proportionalism was in a practical sense the measure and remedy of discrimination, including preferential treatment and quotas. Some federal district and appellate courts followed, ratifying the agencies' clear departure from statutory language. Some differing interpretations remained by the end of the decade, and the Supreme Court had yet to rule on an employment discrimination case. The *Griggs* case would announce a clear ratification of the new understanding of fair employment.

50. Kull, *The Color-Blind Constitution,* 177–79; Wilkinson, *From "Brown" to "Bakke,"* 111–49; Ravitch, *Troubled Crusade,* 160–81; Graham, *Civil Rights,* 372–75, 382–86; Bass, *Unlikely Heroes,* 298–308; Alfred W. Blumrosen, "The Law Transmission System and the Southern Jurisprudence of Employment Discrimination," *Industrial Relations Law Journal* VI (1984), 333.

10   The *Griggs* Case

The movement toward adopting racial proportionalism as the standard in antidiscrimination law accelerated in 1970. The EEOC and the Justice Department further refined and advanced their positions on testing, disparate impact, and preferential treatment, and enjoyed more success in the courts than ever. A district court rendered final judgment requiring the Asbestos Workers Union to refer workers on a one-to-one racial ratio until the membership of the union itself reached this ratio. In the case of *Jones* v. *Lee Way Motor Freight,* the commission argued that a trucking company's previous policy of limiting black drivers to short-haul routes, combined with a no-transfer policy between short- and long-haul departments, constituted discrimination under Title VII. The district court accepted the company's policy as a bona fide departmental system justified by business purpose and, using *H. K. Porter,* denied that the company need grant preferential treatment to correct a racial imbalance in its work force. The Tenth Circuit Court of Appeals reversed the decision, urged by the EEOC that the gross statistical imbalance constituted a prima facie case of discrimination that should be remedied by the abolition of the no-transfer policy. "In racial discrimination cases," the court declared, "statistics often demonstrate more than the testimony of many witnesses, and they should be given proper effect by the courts." The Eighth Circuit had accepted such statistical inferences in the *Sheet Metal Workers* appeal, the EEOC noted, arguing that in that decision the court held "that statistics which showed an historically all-white union *required* the inference that Negroes were unlawfully excluded from membership." The defendant's answer that qualified Negroes were unavailable could not defeat the "staggering" statistical proof offered by the plaintiff.[1] The EEOC noted, "Federal courts have accepted the proposition advanced by the Commission that discrimination may be proved largely by statistics and have begun to develop meaningful remedies." Courts would consider defendants' arguments about the irrelevance of pre-act discrimination or the relevance of qualifications and business necessity only after statistics had shifted the burden of proof onto them. Federal courts in Massachusetts and California reinforced this tendency when they held that the Civil Rights Acts of 1870 prohibited tests for public employment which evinced a disparate impact on minorities.[2] In two other cases, the Eighth Circuit and a district court found violations of Title VII based on statistical evidence of racial imbalance alone, and applied the EEOC guidelines that prohibited qualifications with a disparate impact if not validated.[3]

The only case that went against the government was the North Carolina utility company decision, *Griggs* v. *Duke Power Company.* In January, 1970, the Fourth Circuit rendered a decision only partially in accord with EEOC principles. The Fourth Circuit reversed some of the restrictive interpretations of the district court with regard to the "present effects" doctrine, but refused to overturn qualifications that perpetuated past discrimination in a less direct fashion. Still, the discord between the Fourth Circuit and others, particularly the Fifth, finally required the Supreme Court to address Title VII.[4]

The Duke Power Company operated a power plant on the Dan

1. *Vogler* v. *McCarty,* 62 L.C. 9411 (1970); *Jones* v. *Lee Way Motor Freight,* 61 L.C. 9325 (1969); EEOC Appellate Court Briefs, October 20, 1969, EEOC Records; *Jones* v. *Lee Way Motor Freight,* 431 F.2d 245 (1970). To a large extent this decision anticipated the Supreme Court's decision in *Griggs.*

2. EEOC, *Fifth Annual Report,* 1970, p. 17; *Arrington* v. *Massachusetts Bay Transportation Authority,* 61 L.C. 9375 (1969); *Penn* v. *Stumpf,* 62 L.C. 9404 (1970).

3. *Parham* v. *Southwestern Bell Telephone Co.,* 3 E.P.D. 8021 (1970); *Hicks* v. *Crown-Zellerbach,* 3 E.P.D. 8037 (1970). These decisions were handed down while *Griggs* was being argued before the Supreme Court.

4. *Griggs* v. *Duke Power Co.,* 420 F.2d 1225 (1970).

River in western North Carolina. It segregated its labor force by race and permitted blacks to work only in the Labor Department, its lowest-paid department. In 1955 the company attempted to improve the quality of its work force by requiring a high school diploma for any workers hired into the more desirable "inside" operations jobs, or for workers transferring from the "outside" Coal Handling or Labor departments. After the enactment of the Civil Rights Act of 1964, the company allowed black workers from the Labor Department who met these qualifications to transfer into the all-white operating departments. When white coal handlers, an outside department similar to labor but paying more money, saw their black co-workers with high school diplomas promoted, they convinced the company to allow interdepartmental transfers if an employee passed two intelligence tests in lieu of a high school diploma. Black workers hired before 1955 sued the company, arguing that they were subject to requirements for promotion which white workers hired before 1955 were not. Black workers hired between 1955 and 1963 also sued, claiming that the high school and testing requirements had a disparate impact on minority group members and bore no relation to job performance.

The district court rejected both groups of black workers' claims, but the appellate court granted relief to the black workers hired prior to 1955, while denying it to those hired after that date. The court applied the *Quarles* principle that arbitrary qualifications could not perpetuate the effects of past discrimination, which the district court had rejected. Thus Duke Power must waive the high school testing requirements for the six black workers hired before 1955 and consider them for promotion based on their plantwide seniority. The court based this conclusion on the fact that white workers in the operating departments hired prior to 1955 never had these requirements applied to them. After 1955, however, the high school requirement covered all applicants, regardless of race.

The court upheld the high school requirement, despite the fact that neither it nor the tests used in lieu of it had been professionally validated for the jobs in question, denying that the EEOC regulations which required validation were binding on employers or the courts. The court determined that Duke did not use the requirements of the diploma or tests as a pretext for discrimination, but to develop a promotable work force. Nothing in the legislative history of section 703 (h) required validation for tests to be considered lawful under Title VII.

Circuit Judge Simon Sobeloff dissented, arguing that the majority decision would render Title VII nugatory, and that it conflicted with the Fifth Circuit's opinions. He urged the court to apply the models of school, voting, and jury cases to Title VII, seeing through what appeared to be neutral standards and ferreting out subtle discrimination. Sobeloff contended that the subjective intent of the employer was irrelevant, and that the majority's faith in Duke's motives in 1955 was of no moment. "Intent" under Title VII was the mere knowledge that certain practices would have certain discriminatory effects. Sobeloff argued that Title VII was "unambiguous" in its prohibition of discriminatory practices. "Thus it has become well settled that 'objective' or 'neutral' standards that favor whites but do not serve business needs are indubitably unlawful employment practices." This was a distortion of the development of Title VII in the courts, where judges had been able to expand the statute in procedural decisions and in developing the "present effects" doctrine because it was ambiguous. Sobeloff argued that the courts should accept the EEOC testing guidelines. Sobeloff believed that the majority's rejection of them would amount to a "built-in invitation to evade the mandate of the statute." This ignored the standard of intent that the majority applied—tests might be professionally developed but still be seen as a pretext to discriminate.

The U.S. Supreme Court heard the black workers' appeal of *Griggs* in December, 1970, the first Title VII case to reach the Supreme Court. While the Fourth Circuit had overturned the restrictive interpretation of Title VII given in the district court, its decision still stood contrary to other recent circuit rulings, particularly those of the Fifth Circuit, in 1969 and 1970. *Griggs* allowed the Supreme Court to clarify the question of qualifications and testing for the lower courts. The Supreme Court could either uphold *Griggs* and the disparate-treatment standard it attempted to use, or overrule it and encourage the EEOC–Justice Department interpretation along disparate-impact lines. The Court chose to overrule the Fourth Circuit, completely vindicating the government.

Griggs argued, in close cooperation with the EEOC and Justice Departments as *amici,* that the intelligence tests used by Duke were "potent tools for substantially reducing Negro opportunities," which operated as "thinly veiled racial discrimination."[5] Simply put, Griggs urged the EEOC guideline rule that if a test disqualified a disproportionate number of minority group members, it could not be used unless validated. The Fourth Circuit decision "was contrary to established principles calling for judicial deference to the contemporaneous interpretation of the agency charged with enforcement of a complex law, a principle that has particular applicability to the EEOC."[6]

It was true that Title VII was a complex law, but this was primarily because the EEOC had made it so. Most of the problems had been introduced by the EEOC, which had abandoned its statutory mandate of conciliation, and adopted an advocacy role in a series of *amicus* briefs on behalf of individuals or the Justice Department. Indeed, the commission had no enforcement power, as civil rights groups lamented in 1964, and was able to issue "procedural regulations" only. Griggs denied that the commission's unique administrative nature should make the courts less deferential to its interpretive authority. The Fourth Circuit's decision conflicted with decisions of other courts which applied the guidelines, and with analogous cases in voting, education, and jury service.

Duke pointed out that the courts below had never directly ruled on the applicability of the EEOC guidelines, let alone educational

5. The high school diploma requirement was not directly at issue under section 703 (h). The appellants argued that *all* qualifications which had a disparate impact without job-related validation were unlawful; the defendants assumed that a high school diploma requirement was not a test and in no way limited by Title VII. The argument centered on the tests and section 703 (h). It appears that, as the defendants argued, "If the company had merely gone along requiring a high school education, it is improbable that this action would have been instituted." Duke defended the test as a short-cut opportunity for all non–high school graduates to use, but in reality it was instituted at the behest of white coal handlers. This fact cast further doubt on Duke's bona fide intent; but intent, crucial to a disparate treatment case, was irrelevant to the government and the Court.

6. U.S. Supreme Court, Petition for Writ of Certiorari, April 9, 1970, *Transcript of Record and File Copies of Briefs, Griggs* v. *Duke Power Co., * vol. 124; hereafter cited as *Griggs, Transcript of Record.*

requirements.[7] But the Fourth Circuit had applied the seniority system cases to the six black workers hired before 1955. The facts of each case had to be decided by trial courts, and their factual determinations could not be overruled unless "clearly erroneous." Thus the Supreme Court would have to defer to the district court's decision that Duke did not intend to discriminate. Contrary to Judge Sobeloff's dissenting opinion, the Fourth Circuit decision "carefully guards against a broad approval of all educational and testing requirements and restricts its decision solely to the facts of this case."[8]

A crucial first question was thus one of intent. The EEOC and Justice Department had long maintained that intent could be inferred from results—if an employer was aware that qualifications or tests had a disparate impact on minorities, he intended to discriminate. Sections 706 (g) and 703 (h) guarded against only "accidental" discrimination. The disparate impact, therefore, was proof of intent to discriminate and could be justified only by business necessity. Duke's tests, the appellants argued, "are 'intended' to discriminate, and are being 'used' to discriminate even if not so intended." The commission feared that if employer intent had to be proved in each case by evidence outside of disparate impact, then Title VII would have to be enforced on a case-by-case basis, hindering the pattern-centered, "wholesale" approach which it desired.[9]

The Justice Department supported the EEOC. It argued that the Fourth Circuit had been misled by focusing on the employer's motive rather than his needs. "For the congressional purpose in enacting Title VII was—as its heading 'Equal Employment Opportunities' suggests—to accomplish economic results, not merely to influence motives or feelings." Here the government deftly translated equality of opportunity into equality of result, making intent irrelevant and statistical result the proof of discrimination. In their reply brief the petitioners urged the Supreme Court to reject the Fourth Cir-

7. The government relied principally on four precedents: *Dobbins* and *H. K. Porter* disallowed tests that had been used intentionally to discriminate; and *Arrington* and *Penn* were not Title VII cases, nor had they been tried on the merits.

8. Brief for Respondent in Opposition, May 7, 1970, *Griggs, Transcript of Record.*

9. Blumrosen, *Modern Law,* 165.

cuit's decision, which reduced Title VII "to dealing only with situations where there is a showing of racial animus." Impact and effect, not motive, mattered.[10]

The U.S. Chamber of Commerce submitted a brief on behalf of Duke, arguing that discriminatory motives, not business necessity, were the *sine qua non* of a permissible test. It argued that "independent evidence of discrimination" must accompany the statistical disparate impact to make out a prima facie case. Such evidence might consist of an intelligence test for menial work, the timing of the adoption of the test, the employer's general record in race relations, a test not being professionally developed or without any attempt at validation. "Even failure to undertake a comparison of the results of such tests with actual employee performance might be sufficient to infer a discriminatory effect." Although the Chamber of Commerce probably did not mean to do so, its list of independent evidence clearly indicated that Duke had intended to discriminate. The company had instituted its revised standards only after the Civil Rights Act of 1964 was passed, and made no attempt to give consideration to its incumbent black employees, resisting even a *Quarles*-type settlement until the Fourth Circuit ordered it. The first promotion of black workers out of the Labor Department did not occur until 1966, months after the EEOC brought charges. Tellingly, the company instituted tests as an option instead of the high school diploma at the behest of white coal handlers who saw black laborers with high school diplomas promoted inside. Finally, Duke never made *any* attempt to validate its qualifications. Duke should have lost a disparate-treatment case, but such a case was never brought. Instead *Griggs* turned on disparate-impact principles and their compatibility with the legislative history of section 703 (h), the Tower amendment.

Griggs and the government argued that ability tests were permissible under section 703 (h) only if validated, since "there is commonly little or no relationship between test scores and job performance." A high school graduation requirement was entitled to no

10. Brief for the United States as amicus curiae, September 4, 1970, Reply Brief for Petitioners, December 5, 1970, *Griggs, Transcript of Record.*

protection by 703 (h).[11] Duke Power's hope that these "quickie intelligence tests" served its purpose of improving its work force was "wishful thinking" or a "blind hope." Griggs agreed that Title VII did not guarantee a job to every black citizen, regardless of ability, but if ability tests had a disparate impact they must be validated. (The issue was not validation per se, for an unvalidated, irrelevant ability test was acceptable if it did not have a disparate impact. As the plaintiffs noted, "A requirement which does not result in a great preference for whites over blacks need be subjected to little, if any, examination under fair employment laws.") The Tower amendment meant to prevent situations like the Motorola case, where a test was invalidated because it exhibited a cultural bias. The EEOC did not advocate the Motorola situation in it guidelines, because the case did not consider the question of validation. The amendment protected culturally biased tests if the company could demonstrate business necessity—a purpose vital to the safety and efficiency of the business.

The EEOC's interpretation of the Tower amendment was doubtful. The strongest part of its argument was that Congress had never explicitly addressed the issue of validation. Ironically, the original version of the amendment did refer to tests which could "determine or predict whether . . . [an] individual is suitable or trainable with respect to his employment in the particular . . . enterprise." The Senate dropped this language from the final version of the act two days later. Almost every supporter of the EEOC position argued that the revised language was tighter, because the leadership desired to protect only validated tests. In fact, the revised language was looser, with no reference to validation appearing in the statute.[12]

Recent attempts to write the EEOC validation requirement into a revised Title VII figured in the arguments of both sides in *Griggs*. Congress failed to act on these EEO bills in 1968, and while *Griggs*

---

11. The tests involved exhibited a greater disparate impact than the high school graduation requirement. The disparate impact of test requirements was generally greater than the disparate impact of schooling requirements. Banfield, *Unheavenly City,* 115.

12. Ironically, only the brief of the attorney general of New York State, on behalf of the petitioners, made this point.

was being argued in 1970, a version had passed the full Senate and been reported out of the House Judiciary Committee. Ultimately this bill also failed to pass. The government argued that "this amendment [the 1970 version] is necessary to legislatively overrule the misinterpretation given the statute" by the Fourth Circuit. The defendants claimed that "the rejection of this amendment [the 1968 version] *requiring* that tests be job-related clearly demonstrates that Congress never intended to impose such a requirement in the first place." It was unclear what relevance congressional inaction had to the original act. In the OFCC Philadelphia Plan cases, the federal judiciary noted that congressional failure to cease funding the federal projects implied congressional approval of the Labor Department policy. Here the Justice Department did not maintain that congressional failure to approve the controversial EEOC guidelines implied its disapproval.

The defendants conceded that the high school or test requirements might not be perfectly suited to the company's business purposes, but that they were acceptable under Title VII. They argued that the discretion lay with the employer to define business necessity. "Once a private employer makes such a determination and the evidence supports that decision, his business reasons for doing so are legitimately established, absent any showing of intent to discriminate." As the Chamber of Commerce pointed out, test validation, while doubtlessly desirable, was often prohibitively expensive, difficult, and beyond the capacity of psychometric testing.[13] In the defendant's interpretation, business necessity was presumed, and plaintiffs must overcome it by showing both a disparate impact and evidence of disparate treatment.

Duke argued that Griggs depended on an EEOC interpretation (that disparate impact could only be justified by business necessity, and that disparate treatment was irrelevant) which was a pretense

13. The Chamber of Commerce noted that one of the Civil Rights Act's goals was to replace subjective standards with objective ones. However, civil rights activists had reconsidered this old premise of the 1950s when it became apparent that objective standards could disqualify minority applicants. In addition, subjective standards might allow room for preferential treatment by conscientious employers where objective standards did not.

of congressionally denied substantive rule making. If the petition-ers wanted the EEOC guidelines to apply, they argued, they should appeal to Congress rather than the courts. The Chamber of Com-merce noted that the EEOC's interpretations should be construed narrowly, since the commission had deliberately interpreted Title VII broadly in order to maximize its effectiveness without returning to ask Congress for a strengthened statute. Rather than construe the statute as framed, the plaintiffs sought "to turn back the clock and thereby gain preferential treatment in promotion and interdepart-mental transfers without regard to the qualifications the company has determined necessary to perform the higher skilled jobs."[14]

The Supreme Court handed down a unanimous decision on March 8, 1971. It decided every point in the plaintiff's favor, ac-cepting all of the EEOC's interpretations, usually without much ar-gument or exposition. It held that "Congress provided, in Title VII of the Civil Rights Act of 1964, for class actions for enforcement." Class actions under section 706 were not provided for in the statute, but lower courts had accepted the EEOC argument for them. Chief Justice Warren Burger's opinion noted that the district court and Fourth Circuit had not erred in examining employer intent. How-ever, "good intent or absence of discriminatory intent does not re-deem employment procedures or testing mechanisms that operate as 'built-in headwinds' for minority groups and are unrelated to measuring job ability." Congress aimed at the consequences of em-ployment decisions, not simply their motivation. "More than that," the Court noted, "Congress has placed on the employer the burden of showing that any given requirement must have a manifest relationship to the employment in question." The Court could point to no language in the statute which indicated this burden; it simply accepted the EEOC guidelines. "Since the Act and its legislative his-tory support the Commission's construction, this affords good reason to treat the guidelines as expressing the will of Congress."[15]

14. Quoting Alfred W. Blumrosen, "Administrative Creativity: The first Year of the EEOC," *George Washington Law Review*, XXXVIII (1970), 695–703.

15. *Griggs* v. *Duke Power Co.*, 401 U.S. 424 (1971). Justice William Brennan took no part in the case because he had worked for a law firm which had the Duke Power Company as a client.

The Court declared that in applying Title VII, "The touchstone is business necessity." As the crux of its opinion, however, the Court's appeal to legislative history was remarkably weak. It concluded that "from the sum of the legislative history relevant in this case, the conclusion is inescapable that the EEOC's construction of section 703 (h) to require that employment tests be job related comports with congressional intent." The conclusion was hardly "inescapable"; the legislative history surely weighed more heavily against the EEOC interpretation. The Court repeated the assertion that the Tower amendment had been revised due to its original "loose wording," when the original wording was the only wording anywhere in the debate that resembled a requirement of validation.[16]

The Court accepted the EEOC interpretation of Title VII which evaded the congressional requirements of individual rights, proof of an intent to discriminate, and the disparate-treatment definition of discrimination. While a similar result could have been achieved in the *Griggs* case under the disparate-treatment standard, that standard would leave too much discretion to district court judges in individual cases. Disparate impact permitted the Supreme Court to overturn the Fourth Circuit on an overarching principle rather than on the particular merits of the case.

The Court was at pains to point out the limits of its opinion, since its foundation in legislative text and history was so weak. It repeated the government's assurance that "Congress did not intend by Title VII, however, to guarantee a job to every person regardless of qualifications," and that "Congress has not commanded that the less qualified be preferred over the better qualified simply because of minority origins." Announcing simple adherence to congressional intent throughout, the Court had in fact effected a thorough transformation of Title VII along the lines laid down by the EEOC and the Justice Department. For the next twenty years, the development of Title VII law would be based not on what Congress meant in Title VII but on what the Court meant in *Griggs*.

The immediate impact of *Griggs* appeared to be quite small. The

16. Steven Wilson, "A Second Look at *Griggs* v. *Duke Power Company:* Restrictions on Job Testing, Discrimination, and the Role of the Federal Courts," *Virginia Law Review,* LVIII (1972), 844–74; Gold, *"Griggs'* Folly," 429–598.

relief won by incumbent black workers seemed to apply the *Quarles* "present effects" doctrine. However, the EEOC guidelines did not apply to incumbents held back by previous discriminatory seniority systems. They applied to all uses of tests and qualifications, in hiring as well as promotions. The Supreme Court had given the EEOC interpretations a new authority to apply the disparate-impact theory of discrimination. Alfred W. Blumrosen, a leading disparate-impact and affirmative action theorist, was so surprised and elated at the complete victory in *Griggs* that he entitled an article he wrote about the case, "Strangers in Paradise."[17]

Blumrosen noted that the Court had accepted almost every argument the EEOC lawyers had made since 1965. Discrimination was now defined in a completely new way. Although this definition did not fit the one used by Congress in enacting the Civil Rights Act, this was because Congress either ignored or did not understand the true nature of discrimination. "The legal concept of discrimination, which is itself a fundamental notion underlying all of the detailed matters of interpretation, was not seriously addressed by the Congress." Rather, it was a sociological-jurisprudential creation, not suited to political debate and compromise. As Blumrosen saw it, *Griggs* was an example of the "law transmission system," whereby the decisions of the centralized, bureaucratic state were disseminated to employers through court rulings. Congress enacted the general frame of legislation, but administrators and judges fleshed it out, using the ideas of social science.[18]

The new definition of discrimination rested on several premises. One was that fair employment was defined in terms of results, measured by statistics of minority group employment. This was related to the idea that motive or intent to discriminate was irrelevant. It held that employment practices which did not alleviate racial imbalance could only be justified by business necessity. Business necessity was to be strictly construed—it must be overriding or compelling, not merely convenient or rational. "To implement the concept that discrimination consists of conduct adversely affecting

17. "Strangers in Paradise: *Griggs* v. *Duke Power Co.* and the Concept of Employment Discrimination," *Michigan Law Review,* LXXI (1972), 59–110.

18. Blumrosen, "Law Transmission System," 313–52.

minorities," Blumrosen advised, "it is essential for courts to fashion a narrow and carefully limited test of business necessity." Finally, the burden of proof in discrimination cases was shifted to the defendant once the disparate-impact claim was made. This was of the utmost importance because the allocation of the burden of proof in any litigation is often dispositive.

The reallocation of the burdens of proof effected by *Griggs* was a means of forcing employers to grant preferential treatment to minority group members. As Michael H. Gottesman, an attorney for the United Steelworkers of America supporting Griggs, later put it, "Despite the Court's rhetoric, the disparate impact doctrine *is* a form of preferential treatment." He explained, "Peeling away the rhetorical fiction that the disparate impact doctrine merely requires employers to treat equally qualified candidates equally, the doctrine comes to this: Title VII requires employers to invest in increased search costs, which will not reflect themselves in increased profits, to overcome the disadvantage in discoverability that blacks suffer because of past discrimination." Disparate impact ensured that Title VII would not permit employers to lapse into token compliance that civil rights groups claimed marked pre-1964 fair employment law, but its mandate of preferential treatment ran the risk of encouraging racial proportionalism and quotas that fair employment advocates had assiduously avoided.[19]

Fair employment had now moved beyond the traditional understanding of discrimination. As a result, the specters that haunted the traditional understanding of antidiscrimination efforts—the fear that a vigorous antidiscrimination effort might lead to preferential treatment, quota systems, and racial proportionalism—no longer threatened, and these results were increasingly recognized as part of the affirmative action effort. While antidiscrimination advocates claimed that they preferred that employers not resort to quota systems, quotas were preferable to lax enforcement of the law and slow progress in minority employment. By 1970 preferential treatment and quotas were publicly defensible in ways unaccept-

19. Michael H. Gottesman, "Twelve Options to Consider Before Opting for Racial Quotas," *Georgetown Law Journal*, LXXIX (1991), 1750.

able only a decade earlier. Blumrosen advocated that employers be forced to employ marginally qualified minority group members over the best qualified nonminority at least until the headwinds against minorities dissipated. If employers resorted to quotas because qualifications which could pass the strict business necessity test were too costly or troublesome, wrote another, "Such quota systems are legal." This new definition of discrimination, with its tendency toward racial proportionalism, racial preference, and racial quotas, marked the end of the fair employment era.[20]

Griggs shaped employment discrimination law for the next twenty years, and the disparate-impact concept was deepened and strengthened in the 1970s. Proportionalism was not required, but any employment standard that resulted in racial imbalance was suspect and required stringent validation, so much so that a proportional quota system was the easiest way for employers to avoid trouble. Congress neither curbed the EEOC's power nor gave it all the powers it wanted in 1972 amendments to Title VII. The OFCC continued to require quota plans by executive order. Congress itself, in the Public Works Employment Act of 1977, required that government contractors set aside 10 percent of their funds for minority contractors, reviving the quota system used by the Public Works Administration in the 1930s. Later that decade the EEOC and the Office of Federal Contract Compliance Programs (the successor to the OFCC) explicitly adopted a "bottom line" standard: if an employer's policies resulted in 80 percent of a proportional goal, the agency would leave it alone. The Supreme Court also legitimized "voluntary" affirmative action plans that included quotas, protecting companies against individual claims of discrimination by blacks or whites. Individual victims of discrimination, black or white, had no claim if their racial group was adequately represented. Such a person might bring a disparate-treatment case, but he would get no help from the EEOC, and would face the old problem of proving discrimination at law. The problem of proving discrimination, which had been such a hindrance to fair employment efforts, was now an advantage to affirmative action policy.

20. Wilson, "A Second Look," 873.

The Reagan administration did little to alter this system, although its judicial appointments led the Supreme Court to revise the disparate-impact theory in 1988–1989. The Court attempted at once to expand disparate impact to "subjective" employment practices while shifting the burden of proof to guard against a corresponding expansion of quotas. After vetoing a bill that would have gone beyond the restoration of *Griggs*, President George Bush signed the Civil Rights Act of 1991, in which Congress for the first time gave legislative assent to the disparate-impact idea. Thus the disparate-impact system, engineered by legal scholars, federal bureaucrats, and ratified by the courts, in defiance of the statute under which they operated, in place for two decades by tacit consent of Congress and the president, at last gained explicit popular consent.

Still the act did not settle the fundamental issue of the nature of discrimination or the proper remedy for it. As Alfred W. Blumrosen noted, "an acceptable standard for assessing the state of minority employment opportunities has not been established in public consciousness or private opinion." The act struck a political balance on the issue of affirmative action, but "did not disturb the uncertainties concerning the issue. Because of the underlying tension between the need to provide meaningful opportunities to women and minorities and a legitimate concern about a drift toward proportional representation, the time for settled law on this issue has not arrived and might never come." Events in the twenty years following *Griggs* were consistent with the tensions, perhaps inherent in fair employment policy, seen in the forty years that led up to it.[21]

Racial discrimination in employment was part of the "American dilemma," the conflict of white Americans' profession of belief in individual rights and meritocracy with their long history of discrimination against black Americans. In 1943 Richard Sterner, in the economic section of the Carnegie-Myrdal study of *An American Dilemma*, asked the question, "What Should Be the Negro's Share?" He pointed out,

> There are several points of reference which seem relevant. . . . One is the living conditions of the white group. One standard of equality is that Negroes should share in economic opportunities and benefits in

21. Blumrosen, *Modern Law*, 287, 313.

proportion to their numbers in the population. This would imply that the average level of living for the Negro should correspond to that of the white population. There may also be ideologies, however, which do not have this implication but which nevertheless could be called equalitarian. One may accept the consequences of the fact that the average adult Negro, because of poorer educational opportunities and other environmental circumstances, is unable to compete for the more remunerative jobs in much the same way that one recognizes differences within the white group which likewise are due to different educational opportunities. Such an attitude can be coupled with a demand for equal economic chances for Negroes and whites who have the same abilities and qualities as workers, citizens, and consumers. Even those who believe that the Negro's lower average level of living is due not only to environmental factors but to some extent also to innate racial inferiority may accept a similar principle, but only if they admit variations in ability among Negroes and that many Negroes are as capable as many whites does this acceptance have any practical significance.

Sterner wrote just as the period of explicit, legally-sanctioned discrimination against black Americans began to decline before the "American Creed" of equal treatment. In the following twenty years, proportionalism did not result from equal treatment, in part because of the fear that the attempt to gain proportional outcomes would require violation of the principles that created the dilemma in the first place. With proportionalism as the means, the "American Creed" was once again abandoned.[22]

22. Richard Sterner, *The Negro's Share: A Study of Income, Consumption, Housing, and Public Assistance* (New York, 1943), 5; Gelber, *Black Men and Businessmen*, 217–18.

BIBLIOGRAPHY

Manuscript Collections

Abrams, Charles. Papers. Department of Archives and Manuscripts, John M. Olin Library, Cornell University, Ithaca, New York.

Frankfurter, Felix. Papers. Manuscript Division, Library of Congress.

Hastie, William. Papers. Manuscript Division, Library of Congress.

Ickes, Harold. Diary. Manuscript Division, Library of Congress.

Leadership Conference on Civil Rights. Papers. Manuscript Division, Library of Congress.

Meany, George B. Collections 25, 36. Meany Memorial Archives, Silver Spring, Maryland.

National Association for the Advancement of Colored People. Papers. Manuscript Division, Library of Congress.

National Negro Congress. Papers. Microfilm Collection. Manuscript Division, Library of Congress.

National Urban League. Papers. Manuscript Division, Library of Congress.

New Negro Alliance, Washington, D.C., Branch. Papers. Howard University, Washington, D.C.

New York State Commission Against Discrimination. Records. New York State Archives, Albany, New York.

New York State Commission Against Discrimination. Records. New York State Division for Human Rights Library, New York.

New York State War Council. Records. Series A-4301, New York State Archives, Albany, New York.

Oxley, Lawrence. Records. Record Group 183, National Archives.

President's Committee on Fair Employment Practice. Records. Record Group 228, National Archives.

President's Committee on Government Contract Compliance. Records. Record Group 325, National Archives.

President's Committee on Government Contracts. Records. Record Group 220, National Archives.

Rustin, Bayard. Papers. Microfilm Collection. Manuscript Division, Library of Congress.

Spingarn, Arthur B. Papers. Manuscript Division, Library of Congress.

Taft, Robert A. Papers. Manuscript Division, Library of Congress.

U.S. Department of Justice. Records. Record Group 60, National Archives.

U.S. Department of Labor. Records. Record Group 174, National Archives.

U.S. Department of the Interior. Records. Record Group 48, National Archives.

U.S. Equal Employment Opportunity Commission. Records. EEOC Library, Washington, D.C.

Wilkins, Roy. Papers. Manuscript Division, Library of Congress.

Works Progress Administration. Records. Record Group 69, National Archives.

Books

Abrams, Charles, *et al. Equality.* New York, 1965.

Ashenfelter, Orley, and Albert Rees, eds. *Discrimination in Labor Markets.* Princeton, 1973.

Banfield, Edward C. *The Unheavenly City Revisited.* Boston, 1974.

Bass, Jack. *Unlikely Heroes.* New York, 1981.

Becker, Gary S. *The Economics of Discrimination.* 2nd ed. Chicago, 1971.

Belz, Herman. *A New Birth of Freedom.* Westport, Conn., 1976.

———. *Equality Transformed: A Quarter-Century of Affirmative Action.* New Brunswick, 1991.

Benjamin, Gerald. *Race Relations and the New York City Commission on Human Rights.* Ithaca, N.Y., 1974.

Bentley, George R. *A History of the Freedmen's Bureau.* Philadelphia, 1955.

Berger, Morroe. *Equality by Statute: The Revolution in Civil Rights.* Rev. ed. New York, 1967.

Berman, William C. *The Politics of Civil Rights in the Truman Administration.* Columbus, 1970.

Bickel, Alexander M. *The Least Dangerous Branch: The Supreme Court at the Bar of Politics.* New Haven, 1962.

Bickel, Alexander M., and Benno C. Schmidt. *The Judiciary and Responsible Government, 1910–21.* New York, 1984.

Blood, Robert O., Jr. *Northern Breakthrough*. Belmont, 1968.

Blumrosen, Alfred W. *Black Employment and the Law*. New Brunswick, 1971.

———. *Modern Law: The Law Transmission System and Equal Employment Opportunity*. Madison, 1993.

Bracey, John H., Jr., August Meier, and Elliott Rudwick, eds. *Black Nationalism in America*. New York, 1970.

Bradley, Philip D., ed. *The Public Stake in Union Power*. Charlottesville, 1959.

Branch, Taylor. *Parting the Waters: America in the King Years, 1954–63*. New York, 1988.

Brauer, Carl M. *John F. Kennedy and the Second Reconstruction*. New York, 1977.

Broussard, Albert S. *Black San Francisco: The Struggle for Equality in the West, 1900–1954*. Lawrence, Kan., 1993.

Bullock, Paul. *Merit Employment: Nondiscrimination in Industry*. Los Angeles, 1960.

Bunche, Ralph. *The Political Status of the Negro in the Age of FDR*. Chicago, 1940.

Burk, Robert Fredrick. *The Eisenhower Administration and Black Civil Rights*. Knoxville, 1984.

Burstein, Paul. *Discrimination, Jobs, and Politics: The Struggle for Equal Employment Opportunity in the United States Since the New Deal*. Chicago, 1985.

Chase, Harold, *et al. Biographical Dictionary of the Federal Judiciary*. Detroit, 1976.

Clark, Kenneth B. *Dark Ghetto: Dilemmas of Social Power*. New York, 1965.

Cornwall, Richard R., and Phanindra V. Wunnava, eds. *New Approaches to Economic and Social Analyses of Discrimination*. New York, 1991.

Daniel, Clete. *Chicano Workers and the Politics of Fairness: The FEPC in the Southwest, 1941–45*. Austin, 1991.

Eastland, Terry, and William J. Bennett. *Counting By Race: Equality from the Founding Fathers to "Bakke."* New York, 1979.

Epstein, Richard. *Forbidden Grounds: The Case Against Antidiscrimination Laws*. Cambridge, 1992.

Fairman, Charles. *Reconstruction and Reunion, 1864–88: Part One*. New York, 1971.

Fiscus, Ronald J. *The Constitutional Logic of Affirmative Action*. Stephen L. Wasby, ed. Durham, 1992.

Frankfurter, Felix, and Nathan Green. *The Labor Injunction*. New York, 1930.

Franklin, Charles Lionel. *The Negro Labor Unionist of New York*. New York, 1936.

Freedman, James O. *Crisis and Legitimacy: The Administrative Process and American Government*. Cambridge, Mass., 1978.

Freeman, Joshua B. *In Transit: The Transit Workers Union in New York City, 1933–66.* New York, 1989.

Garfinkel, Herbert. *When Negroes March: The Organizational Politics of FEPC.* New York, 1969.

Gelber, Steven M. *Black Men and Businessmen: The Growing Awareness of a Social Responsibility.* Port Washington, N.Y., 1974.

Glazer, Nathan. *Affirmative Discrimination: Ethnic Inequality and Public Policy.* New York, 1975.

Graham, Hugh Davis. *The Civil Rights Era: Origins of a National Policy, 1960–72.* New York, 1990.

Grant, Nancy L. *TVA and Black Americans: Planning for the Status Quo.* Philadelphia, 1990.

Grantham, Dewey W. *Southern Progressivism: The Reconciliation of Progress and Tradition.* Knoxville, 1983.

Graves, W. Brooke. *Fair Employment Practice Legislation in the United States, Federal-State-Municipal.* Washington, D.C., 1951.

Greenberg, Cheryl Lynn. *"Or Does It Explode?" Black Harlem in the Great Depression.* New York, 1991.

Greenberg, Jack. *Race Relations and American Law.* New York, 1959.

Grodzins, Morton. *The Metropolitan Area as a Racial Problem.* Pittsburgh, 1958.

Hamilton, Charles V. *Adam Clayton Powell, Jr.* New York, 1992.

Hand, Samuel B. *Counsel and Advise: A Political Biography of Samuel I. Rosenman.* New York, 1979.

Harris, Abram L. *The Negro as Capitalist.* Philadelphia, 1936.

Hawley, Ellis. *The New Deal and the Problem of Monopoly: A Study in Economic Ambivalence.* Princeton, 1966.

Haws, Robert, ed. *The Age of Segregation: Race Relations in the South, 1890–1945.* Jackson, Miss., 1978.

Hentoff, Nat. *The New Equality.* New York, 1965.

Higbee, Jay Anders. *The Development and Administration of the New York Law Against Discrimination.* University, Ala., 1966.

Higgs, Robert. *Competition and Coercion: Blacks in the American Economy, 1865–1914.* Cambridge, Mass., 1977.

Hill, Herbert. *Black Labor and the American Legal System.* Washington, D.C., 1977.

Hill, Herbert, and James E. Jones, Jr., eds. *Race in America: The Struggle for Equality.* Madison, 1993.

Hoffer, Peter Charles. *The Law's Conscience: Equitable Constitutionalism in America.* Chapel Hill, 1990.

Horn, Robert A. *Groups and the Constitution.* Stanford, 1956.

Kelly, Alfred H., Winfred A. Harbison, and Herman Belz. *The American Constitution.* 2 vols. 7th ed. New York, 1992.

Kesselman, Louis C. *The Social Politics of FEPC: A Study in Reform Pressure Movements.* Chapel Hill, 1948.

King, Donald B., and Charles W. Quick, eds. *Legal Aspects of the Civil Rights Movement.* Detroit, 1965.

Kinzer, Robert H., and Edward Sagarin. *The Negro in American Business: The Conflict Between Separatism and Integration.* New York, 1950.

Kirby, John B. *Black Americans in the Roosevelt Era: Liberalism and Race.* Knoxville, 1980.

Konvitz, Milton R. *A Century of Civil Rights.* New York, 1961.

Krislov, Samuel. *The Negro in Federal Employment: The Quest for Equal Opportunity.* Minneapolis, 1967.

Kull, Andrew. *The Color-Blind Constitution.* Cambridge, Mass., 1992.

Lemann, Nicholas. *The Promised Land: The Great Migration and How It Changed America.* New York, 1991.

Lively, Donald E. *The Constitution and Race.* New York, 1992.

Lockard, Duane. *Toward Equal Opportunity: A Study of State and Local Antidiscrimination Laws.* New York, 1968.

Lofgren, Charles A. *The Plessy Case: A Legal-Historical Interpretation.* New York, 1987.

Lomax, Louis E. *The Negro Revolt.* New York, 1962.

MacIver, Robert Morrison. *The More Perfect Union: A Program for the Control of Inter-group Discrimination in the United States.* New York, 1948.

———, ed. *Discrimination and National Welfare.* Port Washington, N.Y., 1949.

Maltz, Earl. *Civil Rights, the Constitution, and Congress, 1863–69.* Lawrence, Kan., 1990.

Mandle, Jay R. *Not Slave, Not Free: The African American Economic Experience Since the Civil War.* Durham, 1992.

Mayhew, Leon. *Law and Equal Opportunity: A Study of the Massachusetts Commission Against Discrimination.* Cambridge, Mass., 1968.

McCoy, Donald R., and Richard T. Ruetten. *Quest and Response: Minority Rights and the Truman Administration.* Lawrence, Kan., 1973.

McKay, Claude. *Harlem: Negro Metropolis.* New York, 1940.

McNeil, Genna Rae. *Groundwork: Charles Hamilton Houston and the Struggle for Civil Rights.* Philadelphia, 1983.

Meier, August, and Elliot Rudwick. *Along the Color Line.* Urbana, 1976.

———. *CORE: A Study in the Civil Rights Movement, 1942–68.* New York, 1973.

Moore, Jesse Thomas, Jr. *A Search for Equality: The National Urban League, 1910–61.* University Park, Penn., 1981.

Murray, Charles. *Losing Ground: American Social Policy, 1950–80.* New York, 1984.

Myrdal, Gunnar. *An American Dilemma: The Negro Problem and Modern Democracy.* New York, 1944.

Naison, Mark. *Communists in Harlem During the Depression.* New York, 1983.

Nelson, William E. *The Fourteenth Amendment: From Political Principle to Judicial Doctrine.* Cambridge, Mass., 1988.

Nieman, Donald G. *To Set the Law in Motion.* Millwood, N.Y., 1979.

Norgren, Paul H., and Samuel E. Hill. *Toward Fair Employment.* New York, 1964.

Ottley, Roi. *New World A-Coming.* New York, 1943.

Peeks, Edward. *The Long Struggle for Black Power.* New York, 1971.

Pennock, J. Roland, and John W. Chapman, eds. *Equality.* New York, 1967.

Pfeffer, Paula F. *A. Philip Randolph, Pioneer of the Civil Rights Movement.* Baton Rouge, 1990.

Pole, J. R. *The Pursuit of Equality in American History.* Rev. ed. Berkeley, 1993.

Polenberg, Richard. *One Nation Divisible: Class, Race, and Ethnicity in the United States Since 1938.* New York, 1980.

Ravitch, Diane. *The Troubled Crusade: American Education, 1945–80.* New York, 1983.

Reed, Merl E. *Seedtime for the Modern Civil Rights Movement: The President's Committee on Fair Employment Practices, 1941–1946.* Baton Rouge, 1991.

Ross, Arthur M., and Herbert Hill, eds. *Employment, Race, and Poverty.* New York, 1967.

Ross, Malcolm. *All Manner of Men.* New York, 1948.

Ruchames, Louis. *Race, Jobs, and Politics: The Story of FEPC.* New York, 1952.

Schwartz, Joel. *The New York Approach: Robert Moses, Urban Liberals, and Redevelopment of the Inner City.* Columbus, 1993.

Shulman, Steven, and William Darity, Jr., eds. *The Question of Discrimination: Racial Inequality in the United States Labor Market.* Middletown, 1989.

Siegan, Bernard H. *Economic Liberties and the Constitution.* Chicago, 1980.

Simon, Arthur. *Stuyvesant Town, U.S.A.: Pattern for Two Americas.* New York, 1970.

Southall, Sara E. *Industry's Unfinished Business: Achieving Sound Industrial Relations and Fair Employment.* New York, 1950.

Sovern, Michael. *Legal Restraints on Racial Discrimination in Employment.* New York, 1966.

Sowell, Thomas. *Civil Rights: Rhetoric or Reality?* New York, 1984.

————. *Preferential Policies: An International Perspective.* New York, 1990.

————. *Race and Economics.* New York, 1975.

Sterner, Richard. *The Negro's Share: A Study of Income, Consumption, Housing, and Public Assistance.* New York, 1943.

Ware, Gilbert. *William Hastie: Grace Under Pressure.* New York, 1984.

Watson, Denton L. *Lion in the Lobby: A Biography of Clarence Mitchell.* New York, 1990.

Weaver, Robert C. *Negro Labor: A National Problem.* Port Washington, N.Y., 1946.

Weiss, Nancy J. *Farewell to the Party of Lincoln: Black Politics in the Age of FDR.* Princeton, 1983.

Whalen, Charles, and Barbara Whalen. *The Longest Debate: A Legislative History of the Civil Rights Act of 1964.* Cabin John, Md., 1985.

White, G. Edward. *The American Judicial Tradition.* New York, 1988.

Wilkinson, J. Harvie III. *From "Brown" to "Bakke": The Supreme Court and School Integration, 1954–78.* New York, 1979.

Williams, Walter. *The State Against Blacks.* New York, 1982.

Wilson, William Julius. *The Declining Significance of Race.* 2nd ed. Chicago, 1980.

Wolters, Raymond. *Negroes and the Great Depression.* Westport, 1970.

Woodward, C. Vann. *The Strange Career of Jim Crow.* 3rd ed. New York, 1974.

Wright, Gavin. *Old South, New South: Revolutions in the Southern Economy Since the Civil War.* New York 1986.

Young, Whitney, Jr. *To Be Equal.* New York, 1964.

Articles

Abrams, Charles. "Discrimination and the Struggle for Shelter." *New York Law Forum,* VI (1960), 3–12.

Affeldt, Richard J. "Title VII in the Federal Courts—Private or Public Law." *Villanova Law Review,* XIV (1969), 664–88.

Alexander, Cynthia L. "The Defeat of the Civil Rights Act of 1990: Wading Through the Rhetoric in Search of Compromise." *Vanderbilt Law Review,* XLIV (1991), 595–640.

"An American Legal Dilemma: Proof of Discrimination." *University of Chicago Law Review,* XIV (1949), 107–25.

Auerbach, Philip G., and Murray C. Goldman. "Racial Discrimination in Housing." *University of Pennsylvania Law Review,* CVII (1959), 515–50.

Avery, Dennis Stanton. "Title VII of the Civil Rights Act of 1964—A Prayer for Damages." *California Western Law Review,* V (1969), 252–65.

Avins, Alfred. "Anti-Discrimination Legislation as an Infringement on Freedom of Choice." *New York Law Forum,* VI (1960), 13–37.

Barnes, David W. "The Problem of Multiple Components or Divisions in Title VII Litigation: A Comment." *Law and Contemporary Problems,* XLVI (1983), 201–208.

Bates, Timothy. "Black Economic Well-Being Since the 1950s." *The Review of Black Political Economy,* XII (1984), 5–39.

Beller, Andrea. "The Economics of Enforcement of An Antidiscrimination Law: Title VII of the Civil Rights Act of 1964." *Journal of Law and Economics,* XXI (1978), 359–80.

Belton, Robert. "Title VII of the Civil Rights Act of 1964: A Decade of Private Enforcement and Judicial Developments." *St. Louis University Law Review,* XX (1976), 219–307.

Belz, Herman. "The Freedmen's Bureau Act of 1865 and the Principle of No Discrimination According to Color." *Civil War History,* XXI (1975), 197–217.

Benedict, Michael Les. "Laissez-Faire and Liberty: A Re-Evaluation of the Meaning and Origins of Laissez-Faire Constitutionalism." *Law and History Review,* III (1985), 293–331.

———. "Preserving Federalism: Reconstruction and the Waite Court." *Supreme Court Review* (1979), 39–79.

"Benign Quotas: A Plan for Integrated Private Housing." *Yale Law Journal,* LXX (1960), 126–34.

Berg, Richard K. "Equal Employment Opportunity Under the Civil Rights Act of 1964." *Brooklyn Law Review,* XXXI (1964), 62–97.

———. "Title VII: A Three Years' View." *Notre Dame Lawyer,* XLIV (1969), 311–44.

Berger, Morroe. "Fair Employment Practice Legislation." *Annals of the American Academy of Political and Social Sciences,* CCLXXV (1951), 34–40.

———. "The New York Law Against Discrimination: Operation and Administration." *Cornell Law Quarterly,* XXXV (1950), 747–96.

Bernhardt, Henry R. "The Right to a Job." *Cornell Law Quarterly,* XXX (1945), 292–317.

Berry, Mary Frances. "Reparations for the Freedmen, 1890–1916: Fraudulent Practices or Justice Deferred?" *Journal of Negro History,* LVII (1972), 219–30.

Bickel, Alexander. "The Original Understanding and the Segregation Decision." *Harvard Law Review,* LXIX (1955), 1–65.

Bittker, Boris I. "The Case of the Checker-Board Ordinance: An Experiment in Race Relations." *Yale Law Journal,* LXXI (1962), 1387–1423.

Blumrosen, Alfred W. "Administrative Creativity: The First Year of the EEOC." *George Washington Law Review,* XXXVIII (1970), 695–703.

———. "Antidiscrimination Laws in Action in New Jersey: A Law-Sociology Study." *Rutgers Law Review,* XIX (1965), 187–287.

———. "The Duty of Fair Recruitment Under the Civil Rights Act of 1964." *Rutgers Law Review,* XXII (1968), 465–536.

———. "The Group Interest Concept, Employment Discrimination, and Legislative Intent: The Fallacy of *Connecticut* v. *Teal.*" *Harvard Journal on Legislation,* XX (1983), 99–135.

———. "The Law Transmission System and the Southern Jurisprudence of Employment Discrimination." *Industrial Relations Law Journal,* VI (1984), 313–52.

———. "Seniority and Equal Employment Opportunity: A Glimmer of Hope." *Rutgers Law Review,* XXIII (1969), 268–317.

———. "Strangers in Paradise: *Griggs* v. *Duke Power Co.* and the Concept of Employment Discrimination." *Michigan Law Review,* LXXI (1972), 59–110.

Bonfield, Arthur Earl. "The Origin and Development of American Fair Employment Legislation." *Iowa Law Review,* LII (1967), 1043–92.

———. "The Substance of Fair Employment Legislation." *Northwestern University Law Review,* LXI (1967), 907–77.

Bryerton, Gary L. "Employment Discrimination, State Fair Employment Practice Laws and the Impact of Title VII of the Civil Rights Act of 1964," *Western Reserve Law Review,* XVI (1965), 608–59.

Bunche, Ralph. "A Critical Analysis of the Tactics and Programs of Minority Groups." *Journal of Negro Education,* IV (1935), 308–20.

———. "The Programs of Organizations Devoted to the Improvement of the Status of the American Negro." *Journal of Negro Education,* VIII (1939), 539–50.

Burstein, Paul, and Margo MacLeod. "Prohibiting Employment Discrimination: Ideas and Politics in the Congressional Debate Over Equal Employment Opportunity Legislation." *American Journal of Sociology,* LXXXVI (1980), 512–33.

Capeci, Dominic J., Jr. "From Harlem to Montgomery: The Bus Boycotts and Leadership of Adam Clayton Powell, Jr. and Martin Luther King, Jr." *Historian,* XLI (1979), 721–37.

Carpenter, Dale. "Bumping the Status Quo: Actual Relief for Actual Victims Under Title VII." *University of Chicago Law Review,* LVIII (1991), 703–32.

Carter, Elmer A. "Practical Considerations Under the New York Law Against Discrimination." *Cornell Law Quarterly,* XL (1954), 40–59.

———. "Policies and Practices of Discrimination Commissions." *Annals of the American Academy of Political and Social Sciences,* CCCIV (1956), 62–77.

Carter, Robert L. "The National Labor Relations Board and Racial Discrimination." *Law in Transition Quarterly,* II (1965), 87–95.

"The Civil Rights Act of 1991: The Business Necessity Standard." *Harvard Law Review,* CVI (1993), 896–913.

Cohen, Felix. "The People vs. Discrimination." *Commentary,* I (1946), 17–22.

Cohen, Oscar. "The Case for Benign Quotas in Housing." *Phylon,* XXI (1960), 20–29.

"The Common-Law and Constitutional Status of Antidiscrimination Boycotts." *Yale Law Journal,* LXVI (1957), 397–412.

Cooper, George, and Richard Sobol. "Seniority and Testing Under Fair Employment Laws: A General Approach to Objective Criteria of Hiring and Promotion." *Harvard Law Review,* LXXXII (1969), 1598–1679.

Couser, Richard B. "The California FEPC: Stepchild of the State Agencies." *Stanford Law Review,* XVIII (1966), 187–212.

Cowan, Thomas A. "Group Interests." *Virginia Law Review,* XLIV (1958), 331–46.

Creamer, George Louis. "Collective Bargaining and Racial Discrimination." *Rocky Mountain Law Review,* XVII (1945), 163–96.

Crowder, Ralph L. "'Don't Buy Where You Can't Work': An Investigation of the Political Forces and Social Conflict Within the Harlem Boycott of 1934." In *Afro-Americans in New York Life and History,* vol. 14, 7–44. New York, 1990.

Davis, John Aubrey. "We Win the Right to Fight for Jobs." *Opportunity,* XVI (1938), 230–37.

Demsetz, Harold. "Minorities in the Market Place." *University of North Carolina Law Review,* XLIII (1965), 271–97.

"Discrimination in Employment and Housing: Private Enforcement Provisions of the Civil Rights Acts of 1964 and 1968." *Harvard Law Review,* LXXXII (1969), 834–64.

Donohue, John J., III. "Is Title VII Efficient?" *University of Pennsylvania Law Review,* CXXXIV (1986), 1411–31.

Dudley, Earl C., Jr. "The Congress, the Court, and Jury Selection: A Critique of Titles I and II of the Civil Rights Bill of 1966." *Virginia Law Review,* LII (1966), 1069–1156.

Elden, Gary. "'Forty Acres and a Mule,' with Interest: The Constitutionality of Black Capitalism, Benign School Quotas, and Other Statutory Racial Classifications." *Journal of Urban Law,* XLVII (1969), 591–652.

Ely, John Hart. "The Constitutionality of Reverse Racial Discrimination." *University of Chicago Law Review,* XLI (1974), 723–41.

"Employment Discrimination and Title VII of the Civil Rights Act of 1964." *Harvard Law Review,* LXXXIV (1971), 1109–1316.

"Employment Opportunity: Class Membership for Title VII Action Not Restricted to Parties Previously Filing Charges with the EEOC." *Duke Law Journal* (1968), 1000–1007.

"Enforcement of Fair Employment Under the Civil Rights Act of 1964." *University of Chicago Law Review,* XXXII (1965), 430–70.

Ferguson, Clarence Clyde. "The Federal Interest in Employment Discrimination." *Buffalo Law Review,* XIV (1965), 1–15.

Field, John G. "Hindsight and Foresight About FEPC." *Buffalo Law Review,* XIV (1965), 16–21.

Fiss, Owen M. "A Theory of Fair Employment Laws." *University of Chicago Law Review,* XXXVIII (1971), 235–314.

———. "Groups and the Equal Protection Clause." *Philosophy and Public Affairs,* V (1976), 107–77.

Fleming, G. James. "Historical Roots of Fair Employment Practice." *Phylon,* VII (1946), 32–40.

Freeman, Alan. "Racism, Rights, and the Quest for Equality of Opportunity: A Critical Legal Essay." *Harvard Civil Rights–Civil Liberties Law Review,* XXIII (1988), 295–392.

Freeman, Richard B. "Changes in the Labor Market for Black Americans, 1948–72." *Brookings Papers on Economic Activity* (1973), 67–131.

"The Future of Civil Rights Law." *Harvard Journal of Law and Public Policy,* XIV (1991), 1–172.

Glenn, Norval D. "Some Changes in the Relative Status of American Nonwhites, 1940–60." *Phylon,* XXIV (1963), 109–22.

Gold, Michael Evan. "*Griggs'* Folly: An Essay on the Theory, Problems, and Origin of the Adverse Impact Definition of Discrimination and a Recommendation for Reform." *Industrial Relations Law Journal,* VII (1985), 429–598.

Gould, William B. "Employment Security, Seniority, and Race: The Role of Title VII of the Civil Rights Act of 1964." *Howard Law Journal,* XIII (1967), 1–50.

———. "Seniority and the Black Worker: Reflections on *Quarles* and Its Implications." *Texas Law Review,* XLVII (1969), 1039–74.

Greenberg, Jack. "Race Relations and Group Interests in the Law." *Rutgers Law Review,* XIII (1959), 503–10.

Grover, Isaac N., and David M. Helfeld. "Race Discrimination in Housing." *Yale Law Journal,* LVII (1948), 426–58.

Hellerstein, William E. "The Benign Quota, Equal Protection, and the Rule in Shelley's Case." *Rutgers Law Review,* VII (1963), 531–61.

Hill, Herbert. "Racial Discrimination in the Nation's Apprenticeship Programs." *Phylon,* XXIII (1962), 215–24.

———. "The Role of Law in Securing Equal Employment Opportunity: Legal Powers and Social Change." *Boston College Industrial and Commercial Law Review,* VII (1966), 625–52.

———. "Twenty Years of State FEPCs: A Critical Analysis with Recommendations." *Buffalo Law Review,* XIV (1965), 22–69.

Hill, T. Arnold. "Picketing for Jobs." *Opportunity,* VIII (1930), 216.

Holsey, Albon L. "A Harlem Shoe Store." *Southern Workman,* LX (1931), 395–97.

Hunt, A. Bruce. "The Proposed Fair Employment Practice Act: Facts and Fallacies." *Virginia Law Review,* XXXII (1945), 1–38.

Johnson, Gerald W. "The Foes of FEPC—Not All Bigots." *The Reporter,* August 15, 1950.

Kaplan, John. "Equal Justice in an Unequal World: Equality for the Negro—the Problem of Equal Treatment." *Northwestern University Law Review,* LXI (1966), 363–410.

Kelly, Alfred H. "Clio and the Court: An Illicit Love Affair." *Supreme Court Review* (1965), 119.

Keyser, Leo, III. "Tort Remedies for Employment Discrimination Under Title VII." *Virginia Law Review,* LIV (1968), 491–504.

Kizer, Marshall F. "Discrimination Against Persons Because of Race or Color." *The Notre Dame Lawyer,* V (1930), 322–36.

Kovarsky, Irving. "The Harlequinesque Motorola Decision and Its Implications." *Boston College Industrial and Commercial Law Review,* VII (1966), 535–47.

———. "A Review of State FEPC Laws." *Labor Law Journal,* IX (1958), 478–94.

———. "Some Social Aspects of Testing Under the Civil Rights Act." *Labor Law Journal,* XX (1969), 346–56.

———. "Testing and the Civil Rights Act." *Howard Law Journal,* XV (1969), 227–49.

Krakower, Stanley R. "The Constitutionality of 'Affirmative Action' to Integrate Construction Trades: The Philadelphia Plan." *Temple Law Quarterly,* XLIII (1970), 329–46.

Kruman, Marc W. "Quotas for Blacks: The PWA and the Black Construction Worker." *Labor History,* XVI (1975), 37–49.

"Labor Law—When a Dispute Exists Within the Meaning of the Norris-LaGuardia Act," *Michigan Law Review,* XXXVI (1938), 1146–76.

"Labor—Norris–La Guardia Act." *St. John's Law Review,* XIII (1938), 171.

"Labor Relations: Racially Discriminatory Seniority System Unjustified by Business Necessity Held to Violate Title VII of the Civil Rights Act of 1964." *Duke Law Journal* (1969), 1091–99.

Lamb, William H. "Proof of Discrimination at the Commission Level." *Temple Law Quarterly,* XXXIX (1966), 299–338.

Landes, William M. "The Economics of Fair Employment Laws." *Journal of Political Economy,* LXXVI (1968), 507–52.

"The Law and Economics of Racial Discrimination in Employment." *Georgetown Law Journal,* LXXIX (1991), 1619–1782.

Lichtman, Richard. "The Ethics of Compensatory Justice." *Law in Transition Quarterly,* I (1964), 76–103.

Lusky, Louis. "The Stereotype: Hard Core of Racism." *Buffalo Law Review,* XIII (1963), 450–61.

Mandel, Jeffrey I. "Civil Rights in the '90s: Are Quotas the Answer?" *Loyola Law Review,* XXXVI (1991), 1051–81.

Marcus, Paul. "The Philadelphia Plan and Strict Racial Quotas on Federal Contracts." *UCLA Law Review,* XVII (1970), 817–36.

Marshall, Ray. "Prospects for Equal Employment: Conflicting Portents." *Monthly Labor Review,* LXXXVIII (1965), 650–53.

Maslow, Will. "FEPC—A Case in Parliamentary Maneuver." *University of Chicago Law Review,* XIII (1946), 407–44.

Maslow, Will, and Joseph B. Robison. "Civil Rights Legislation and the Fight for Equality, 1863–1952." *University of Chicago Law Review,* XX (1953), 363–413.

McGuinn, Henry J. "Race, Cultural Groups, and Social Differentiation." *Social Forces,* XVIII (1939), 256–68.

Means, John E. "Fair Employment Practices Legislation and Enforcement in the United States." *International Labour Review,* XCIII (1964), 211–47.

Meier, August, and John H. Bracey, Jr. "The NAACP as a Reform Movement, 1909–1965: 'To Reach the Conscience of America.'" *Journal of Southern History,* LIX (1993), 3–30.

Minsky, Joseph. "FEPC in Illinois: Four Stormy Years." *Notre Dame Lawyer,* XL (1965), 152–81.

Morse, Stuart A. "The Scope of Judicial Relief Under Title VII of the Civil Rights Act of 1964." *Texas Law Review,* XLVI (1968), 516–31.

Mundlin, Albert. "The Designation of Race or Color on Forms." *Public Administration Review,* XXVI (1966), 110–18.

Muraskin, William. "The Harlem Boycott of 1934." *Labor History,* XIII (1972), 361–73.

Murray, Pauli. "The Right to Equal Opportunity in Employment." *California Law Review,* XXXIII (1945), 388–433.

Navasky, Victor. "The Benevolent Housing Quota." *Howard Law Journal,* VI (1960), 30–68.

Nelson, Bruce. "Organized Labor and the Struggle for Black Equality in Mobile During World War II." *Journal of American History,* LXXX (1993), 952–88.

"The New York State Commission Against Discrimination: A New Technique for an Old Problem." *Yale Law Journal,* LVI (1947), 836–63.

Northrup, Herbert R. "Progress without Federal Compulsion." *Commentary,* XIV (1952), 206–11.

Nuechterlein, James A. "The Politics of Civil Rights: The FEPC, 1941–46." *Prologue* (Fall, 1978), 171–91.

"The Operation of State FEPCs." *Harvard Law Review,* LXVIII (1955), 685–97.

"Overview: Civil Rights in the 1990s—Title VII and Employment Discrimination." *Yale Law and Policy Review,* VIII (1990), 197–365.

Paley, Robert S. "The Nondiscrimination Clause in Government Contracts." *Virginia Law Review,* XLIII (1957), 837–71.

Palmer, Robert C. "The Parameters of Constitutional Reconstruction: *Slaughter-House, Cruikshank,* and the Fourteenth Amendment." *University of Illinois Law Review* (1984), 739–70.

Posner, Richard A. "The Efficiency and the Efficacy of Title VII." *University of Pennsylvania Law Review,* CXXXVI (1987), 513–21.

Powers, N. Thompson. "Federal Procurement and Equal Employment Opportunity." *Law and Contemporary Problems,* XXIX (1964), 468–87.

Price, Hugh Douglas. "Picketing—A Legal Cinderella." *University of Florida Law Review,* VII (1954), 143–77.

Rabkin, Sol. "Enforcement of Laws Against Discrimination in Employment." *Buffalo Law Review,* XIV (1965), 110–13.

Rachlin, Carl. "The 1964 Civil Rights Law: A Hard Look." *Law in Transition Quarterly,* II (1965), 80–84.

———. "Title VII: Limitations and Qualifications." *Boston College Industrial and Commercial Law Review,* VII (1966), 473–94.

"The Right to Equal Treatment: Administrative Enforcement of Antidiscrimination Legislation." *Harvard Law Review,* LXXIV (1961), 526–89.

"The Right to a Jury Trial Under Title VII of the Civil Rights Act of 1964." *University of Chicago Law Review,* XXXVII (1969), 167–80.

Roback, Jennifer. "Racism as Rent Seeking." *Economic Inquiry,* XXVII (1989), 661–81.

———. "Southern Labor Law in the Jim Crow Era: Exploitative or Competitive?" *University of Chicago Law Review,* LI (1984), 1161–92.

Robison, Joseph B. "Giving Reality to the Promise of Job Equality." *Law in Transition Quarterly,* I (1964), 104–17.

Rorty, James. "FEPC in the States: A Progress Report." *Antioch Review,* XVIII (1958), 317–29.

Rosen, Sanford Jay. "Division of Authority Under Title VII of the Civil Rights Act of 1964: A Preliminary Study in Federal-State Interagency Relations." *George Washington University Law Review,* XXXIV (1966), 846–92.

––––––. "The Law and Racial Discrimination in Employment." *California Law Review,* LIII (1965), 729–99.

Rutherglen, George. "Disparate Impact Under Title VII: An Objective Theory of Discrimination." *Virginia Law Review,* LXXIII (1987), 1297–1345.

Schmidt, Charles T., Jr. "Title VII, Coverage and Comments." *Boston College Industrial and Commercial Law Review,* VII (1966), 459–72.

Schnapper, Eric. "Affirmative Action and the Legislative History of the Fourteenth Amendment." *Virginia Law Review,* LXXI (1985), 753–98.

Shirk, Elliot M. "Cases Are People: An Interpretation of the Pennsylvania Fair Employment Practice Law." *Dickinson Law Review,* LXII (1958), 289–305.

Smith, James P., and Finis Welch. "Black Economic Progress After Myrdal." *Journal of Economic Literature,* XXVII (1989), 519–64.

Sowell, Thomas. "Ethnicity in a Changing America." *Daedalus,* CVII (1978), 213–37.

––––––. "Ethnicity, Three Black Histories." *Wilson Quarterly,* III (1979), 96–106.

Spitz, Henry. "Tailoring the Techniques to Eliminate Employment Discrimination." *Buffalo Law Review,* XIV (1965), 79–99.

St. Antoine, Theodore J. "Color Blindness But Not Myopia: A New Look at State Action, Equal Protection, and 'Private' Racial Discrimination." *Michigan Law Review,* LIX (1961), 993–1016.

Strauss, George, and Sidney Ingerman. "Public Policy and Discrimination in Apprenticeship." *Hastings Law Journal,* XVI (1965), 285–331.

"Title VII of the Civil Rights Act of 1964 and Minority Group Entry into the Building Trade Unions." *University of Chicago Law Review,* XXXVII (1969), 328–58.

"Title VII, Seniority Discrimination, and the Incumbent Negro." *Harvard Law Review,* LXXX (1967), 1260–83.

Tobringer, Michael C. "California FEPC." *Hastings Law Journal,* XVIII (1965), 333–49.

Tower, John. "FEPC—Some Practical Considerations." *Federal Bar Journal,* XXIV (1964), 87–92.

Tribe, Laurence. "In What Vision of the Constitution Must the Law Be Color-Blind?" *John Marshall Law Review,* XX (1986), 201–207.

Tucker, Sterling. "The Role of Civil Rights Organizations: A 'Marshall Plan' Approach." *Boston College Industrial and Commercial Law Review,* VII (1966), 617–23.

Vaas, Francis J. "Title VII, Legislative History." *Boston College Industrial and Commercial Law Review,* VII (1966), 431–58.

Viera, Norman. "Racial Imbalance, Black Separatism, and Permissible Classification by Race." *Michigan Law Review,* LXVII (1969), 1553–1626.

Weaver, Robert C. "An Experiment in Negro Labor." *Opportunity,* XIV (1936), 295–98.

———. "Federal Aid, Local Control, and Negro Participation." *Journal of Negro Education,* XI (1942), 47–59.

———. "Racial Policy in Public Housing." *Phylon,* I (1940), 149–61.

———. "The Negro in a Program of Public Housing." *Opportunity,* XVI (1938), 198–203.

Weiner, Harold M. "Negro Picketing for Employment Equality." *Howard Law Journal,* XIII (1967), 271–302.

Wilson, Abraham. "The Proposed Legislative Death Knell of Private Discriminatory Employment Practices." *Virginia Law Review,* XXXI (1945), 798–810.

Wilson, Steven. "A Second Look at *Griggs* v. *Duke Power Company:* Restrictions on Job Testing, Discrimination, and the Role of the Federal Courts." *Virginia Law Review,* LVIII (1972), 844–74.

Winter, Ralph K., Jr. "Improving the Economic Status of Negroes Through Laws Against Discrimination: A Reply to Professor Sovern." *University of Chicago Law Review,* XXXIV (1967), 817–55.

Woll, J. Albert. "Labor Looks at Equal Rights in Employment." *Federal Bar Journal,* XXIV (1964), 93–101.

Wollenberg, Charles. "*James* v. *Marinship:* Trouble on the New Black Frontier." *California History,* LX (1981), 262–79.

Yellen, David N. "The Bottom Line Defense in Title VII Actions: Supreme Court Rejection in *Connecticut* v. *Teal* and a Modified Approach." *Cornell Law Review,* LXVIII (1983), 735–53.

Published Court Cases and Materials

A. S. Beck Shoe Corp. v. *Johnson.* 274 N.Y.S. 946 (1934).

Anora Amusement Corp. v. *Doe.* 12 N.Y.S.2d 400 (1939).

Arrington v. *Massachusetts Bay Transportation Authority.* 61 L.C. 9375 (1969).

Banks v. *Capitol Airlines.* 5 R.R.L.R. 263 (1960).

Banks v. *Housing Authority.* 260 P.2d 668 (1953).

Bowe v. *Colgate-Palmolive.* 56 L.C. 9069 (1967).

Centennial Laundry Company v. *West Side Organization.* 51 L.C. 51286 (1965).

Choate v. *Caterpillar Tractor Co.* 56 L.C. 9086 (1967).

Choate v. *Caterpillar Tractor Co.* 58 L.C. 9162 (1968).

The Civil Rights Cases. 109 U.S. 3 (1883).

Contractors Association of Eastern Pennsylvania v. *Shultz.* 3 E.P.D. 8180 (1971).

Contractors Association of Eastern Pennsylvania v. *Shultz.* 62 L.C. 9421 (1970).

Crown-Zellerbach Corp. v. *Wirtz.* 57 L.C. 9104 (1968).

Curtis v. *Boeger.* 331 F.2d 675 (1964).

Curtis v. *Tozer.* 374 S.W.2d 557 (1964).

Dent v. *St. Louis–San Francisco Railway Co.* 55 L.C. 9047 (1967).

Dent v. *St. Louis–San Francisco Railway Co.* 59 L.C. 9189 (1969).

Dobbins v. *Local 212, IBEW.* 292 F.Supp. 413 (1968).

Dorsey v. *Stuyvesant Town Corp.* 87 N.E.2d 541 (1949).

Draper v. *Clark Dairy.* 25 L.R.R.M. 79 (1950).

Evenson v. *Northwest Airlines.* 55 L.C. 9053 (1967).

F. W. Woolworth Co. 25 N.L.R.B. 1362 (1940).

Fair Share Organization v. *Mitnick.* 188 N.E.2d 840 (1963).

Fair Share Organization v. *Philip Nagdeman & Sons.* 9 R.R.L.R. 1375 (1963).

Favors v. *Randall.* 40 F.Supp. 743 (1941).

Ford v. *Boeger.* 53 L.C. 51510 (1966).

Green v. *Samuelson.* 99 A.L.R. 529 (1935).

Green v. *Samuelson.* Maryland Court of Appeals, *Records and Briefs,* vol. 574 (1935).

Griggs v. *Duke Power Co.* 58 L.C. 9163 (1968).

Griggs v. *Duke Power Co.* 401 U.S. 424 (1971).

Griggs v. *Duke Power Co.* 420 F.2d 1225 (1970).

Griggs v. *Duke Power Co.* U.S. Supreme Court. *Transcript of Record and File Copies of Briefs.* vol. 124 (1971).

Hall v. *Werthan Bag Corp.* 53 L.C. 9014 (1966).

Hicks v. *Crown-Zellerbach Corp.* 3 E.P.D. 8037 (1970).

Holt v. *Oil Workers Union.* 36 L.R.R.M. 2703 (1955).

Hughes v. *Superior Court.* 186 P.2d 756 (1947).

Hughes v. *Superior Court.* 198 P.2d 885 (1948).

Hughes v. *Superior Court.* 339 U.S. 460 (1950).

Hughes v. *Superior Court.* U.S. Supreme Court. *Transcript of Records and File Copies of Briefs,* vol. 35, no. 61 (1949).

In Re Curtis' Petition. 227 F.Supp. 438 (1964).

In Re Curtis' Petition. 240 F.Supp. 475 (1965).

In Re Young. 211 N.Y.S.2d 621 (1961).

James v. *Marinship Corp.* 155 P.2d 329 (1945).

Jenkins v. *United Gas Corp.* 55 L.C. 9045 (1966).

Jones v. *Lee Way Motor Freight.* 61 L.C. 9325 (1969).

Jones v. *Lee Way Motor Freight.* 431 F.2d 245 (1970).

Levine v. *Dempsey.* 47 L.R.R.M. 2606 (1961).

Lifschitz v. *Straughn.* 27 N.Y.S.2d 193 (1940).

Local 53, International Association of Heat and Frost Insulators and Asbestos Workers v. *Vogler.* 59 L.C. 9195 (1969).

Local 189 United Papermakers and Paperworkers v. *U.S.* 416 F.2d 980 (1969).

Mickel v. *South Carolina State Employment Agency.* 55 L.C. 9057 (1967).

Miller v. *International Paper Co.* 59 L.C. 9211 (1969).

Mondy v. *Crown-Zellerbach Corp.* 56 L.C. 9082 (1967).

Moody v. *Albemarle Paper Co.* 56 L.C. 9070 (1967).

Motorola v. *Illinois FEPC.* 51 L.C. 323 (1965).

Motorola v. *Illinois FEPC.* 215 N.E.2d 286 (1966).

New Negro Alliance v. *Kaufman, Inc.* U.S. Court of Appeals, District of Columbia, *Records and Briefs,* vol. 483, no. 6187 (1934).

New Negro Alliance v. *Sanitary Grocery Co.* 92 F.2d 510 (1937).

New Negro Alliance v. *Sanitary Grocery Co.* 303 U.S. 552 (1938).

New Negro Alliance v. *Sanitary Grocery Co.* U.S. Court of Appeals for the District of Columbia, *Records and Briefs,* vol. 549, no. 6836 (1936).

New Negro Alliance v. *Sanitary Grocery Co.* U.S. Supreme Court, *Transcripts of Records and File Copies of Briefs,* vol. 106, no. 511 (1937).

New York State Commission Against Discrimination v. *Pelham Hall Apartments.* 170 N.Y.S.2d 750 (1958).

Oatis v. *Crown-Zellerbach Corp.* 58 L.C. 9140 (1968).

Pappas v. *Straughn.* 7 L.R.R.M. 693 (1940).

Parham v. *Southwestern Bell Telephone Co.* 3 E.P.D. 8021 (1970).

Parham v. *Southwestern Bell Telephone Co.* 58 L.C. 9147 (1968).

Pellicer v. *Brotherhood of Railway Clerks.* 35 L.R.R.M. 2209 (1954).

Penn v. *Stumpf.* 62 L.C. 9404 (1970).

PEPCO v. *Washington Chapter of CORE.* 209 F.Supp. 559 (1962).

Plessy v. *Ferguson.* 163 U.S. 537 (1896).

Progress Development Corp. v. *Mitchell.* 182 F.Supp. 681 (1960).

Progress Development Corp. v. *Mitchell.* 286 F.2d 222 (1961).

Quarles v. *Philip Morris Co.* 271 F.Supp. 842 (1967).

Quarles v. *Philip Morris Co.* 279 F.Supp. 505 (1968).

Railway Mail Association v. *Corsi.* 326 U.S. 88 (1945).

Regents of California v. *Bakke.* 438 U.S. 265 (1978).

SCHR v. *Farrell.* 252 N.Y.S.2d 649 (1964).

Shelley v. *Kraemer.* 334 U.S. 1 (1948).

Siegall, et al. v. *Newark National Negro Congress.* 2 L.R.R.M. 859 (1938).

Steele v. *Louisville & Nashville Railroad.* 16 So.2d 416 (1944).

Steele v. *Louisville & Nashville Railroad.* 323 U.S. 192 (1944).

Stevens v. *West Philadelphia Youth Civic League.* 3 L.R.R.M. 792 (1939).

Stoller v. *Citizens Civic Affairs Committee.* 19 N.Y.S.2d 597 (1940).

Stolper v. *Straughn.* 23 N.Y.S.2d 604 (1940).

Strauder v. *West Virginia.* 100 U.S. 303 (1880).

Taylor v. *Leonard.* 103 A.2d 632 (1954).

Texas Motion Picture and Vitaphone Operators v. *Galveston Motion Picture Operators.* 132 S.W.2d 299 (1939).

Thompson v. *Erie Railroad.* 2 R.R.L.R. 237 (1957).

Truax v. *Raich.* 239 U.S. 33 (1915).

Tunstall v. *Brotherhood of Locomotive Firemen and Enginemen.* 140 F.2d 35 (1944).

Tunstall v. *Brotherhood of Locomotive Firemen and Enginemen.* 323 U.S. 210 (1944).

U.S. v. *Building and Construction Trades Council of St. Louis.* 62 L.C. 9412, 9413 (1966).

U.S. v. *H. K. Porter Co.* 59 L.C. 9204 (1968).

U.S. v. *Hayes International Corp.* 58 L.C. 9224 (1968).

U.S. v. *Hayes International Corp.* 60 L.C. 9303 (1969).

U.S. v. *IBEW Local 38.* 59 L.C. 9226 (1969).

U.S. v. *Local 189, United Papermakers and Paperworkers and Crown-Zellerbach Corp.* 282 F.Supp. 39 (1968).

U.S. v. *Local 189, United Papermakers and Paperworkers, and Crown-Zellerbach Corp.* 282 F.2d 980 (1969).

U.S. v. *Sheet Metal Workers International Association, Local 36.* 280 F.Supp. 719 (1968).

U.S. v. *Sheet Metal Workers International Association, Local 36.* 416 F.2d 123 (1969).

Virginia v. *Rives.* 100 U.S. 313 (1880).

Vogler v. *McCarty.* 55 L.C. 9063 (1967).

Vogler v. *McCarty.* 62 L.C. 9411 (1970).

Weiner v. *Cuyahoga Community College District.* 58 L.C. 9164 (1968).

Weiner v. *Cuyahoga Community College District.* 60 L.C. 9288 (1969).

Whitfield v. *United Steelworkers.* 156 F.Supp. 430 (1957).

Whitfield v. *United Steelworkers.* 263 F.2d 546 (1959).

Yick Wo v. *Hopkins.* 118 U.S. 356 (1886).

Unpublished Court Cases

A. S. Beck Shoe Corp. v. *Johnson.* New York County Supreme Court, Index No. 33–689, New York City Hall of Records, New York.

Hillary Theater v. *Straughn.* File no. 16694 (1940). Kings County Supreme Court, Brooklyn, New York.

Kaufman, Inc. v. *New Negro Alliance.* U.S. District Court for the District of Columbia, Equity No. 56586, Accession No. 64-A-379, Box 2563, National Federal Records Center, Suitland, Maryland.

Lifschitz v. *Straughn.* File no. 14917 (1940). Kings County Supreme Court, Brooklyn, New York.

Lucky Stores v. *Progressive Citizens of America.* California State Archives, Sacramento.

Parkshire Ridge Amusements v. *Miller.* File no. 15873 (1937). Kings County Supreme Court, Brooklyn, New York.

Samuelson v. *Green.* Baltimore City Circuit Court, Equity Papers, Boxes 3954–3955, Folder A-19400, Maryland State Archives, Hall of Records, Annapolis.

Sanitary Grocery Co. v. *New Negro Alliance.* Supreme Court of the District of Columbia, Equity No. 61165, Accession No. 64-A-379, Box 2652, National Federal Records Center, Suitland, Maryland.

Smith v. *Citizens Federation of Labor.* File no. 12729 (1941). Kings County Supreme Court, Brooklyn, N.Y.

Solomon v. *Straughn.* File no. 9705 (1940). Kings County Supreme Court, Brooklyn, New York.

Stoller v. *Citizens Civic Affairs Committee.* File no. 3858 (1940). Kings County Supreme Court, Brooklyn, New York.

Government Documents

Bureau of National Affairs. *The Equal Employment Opportunity Act of 1972.* Washington, D.C., 1973.

Congressional Record. Vols. 92–110, 1941–65.

New York State Commission Against Discrimination. *Annual Report.* 1945–70.

President's Committee on Government Contract Compliance. *Equal Employment Opportunity: A Report by the President's Committee on Government Contract Compliance.* Washington, D.C., 1953.

President's Committee on Government Contracts. *Annual Report.* 1953–61.

U.S. Commission on Civil Rights. *1961 Report.* Washington, D.C., 1961.

U.S. Committee on Fair Employment Practice. *Final Report.* Washington, D.C., 1947.

———. *First Report.* Washington, D.C., 1945.

U.S. Department of Commerce, Bureau of the Census. *Historical Statistics of the United States: Colonial Times to 1970.* Washington, D.C., 1975.

U.S. Equal Employment Opportunity Commission. *Annual Report.* 1966–72.

———. *EEOC Appellate Court Briefs.* EEOC Library, Washington, D.C.

———. *The EEOC During the Administration of Lyndon B. Johnson.* Washington, D.C., 1968.

———. *Guidelines on Employment Testing Procedures.* Washington, D.C., 1966.

———. *Legislative History of Title VII and Title XI of the Civil Rights Act of 1964.* Washington, D.C., 1968. EEOC Library.

U.S. House of Representatives. *Civil Rights Act of 1963.* 88th Cong., 1st sess., 1963. H. Rept. 914.

———. *Equal Employment Opportunity Act of 1962.* 87th Cong., 2nd sess., 1962. H. Rept 1370.

———. *Equal Employment Opportunity Act of 1963.* 88th Cong., 1st sess., 1963. H. Rept. 570.

———. Committee on Education and Labor. *Equal Employment Opportunity: Hearings Before the General Subcommittee on Labor.* 88th Cong., 1st sess., 1963.

———. Committee on Education and Labor. *Equal Employment Opportunity: Hearings Before the Special Subcommittee on Labor.* 87th Cong., 1st sess., 1961.

———. Committee on Education and Labor. *Federal Fair Employment Practice Act: Hearings Before a Special Subcommittee on Labor.* 81st Cong., 1st sess., 1949.

———. *Federal Fair Employment Practice Act.* 81st Cong., 1st sess., 1949. H. Rept. 1165.

———. *Prohibiting Discrimination in Employment Because of Race, Creed, Color, National Origin or Ancestry.* 78th Cong., 2nd sess., 1944. H. Rept. 2016.

———. *The Fair Employment Practice Act.* 79th Cong., 1st sess., 1945. H. Rept. 187.

———. Committee on Rules. *To Prohibit Discrimination in Employment Because of Race, Creed, Color, National Origin or Ancestry: Hearings Before the Committee on Rules.* 79th Cong., 1st sess., 1945.

———. Committee on Labor. *To Prohibit Discrimination in Employment: Hearings Before the Committee on Labor.* 78th Cong., 2nd sess., 1944.

U.S. Senate. Committee on Labor and Public Welfare. *Antidiscrimination in Employment: Hearings Before a Subcommittee of the Committee on Labor and Public Welfare.* 80th Cong., 1st sess., 1947.

———. Committee on Labor and Public Welfare. *Antidiscrimination in Employment: Hearings Before the Subcommittee on Civil Rights.* 83d Cong., 2nd sess., 1954.

———. Committee on the Judiciary. *Commission on Civil Rights: Hearings Before a Subcommittee of the Committee on the Judiciary.* 83d Cong., 2nd sess., 1954.

———. Committee on Labor and Public Welfare. *Discrimination and Full Utilization of Manpower Resources: Hearings Before the Subcommittee on Labor and Labor-Management Relations.* 82d Cong., 2nd sess., 1952.

———. Committee on Labor and Public Welfare. *Equal Employment Opportunity: Hearings Before the Subcommittee on Employment and Manpower.* 88th Cong., 1st sess., 1963.

———. Committee on Education and Labor. *Fair Employment Practices Act: Hearings Before a Subcommittee of the Committee on Education and Labor.* 78th Cong., 2nd sess., 1944.

———. Committee on Education and Labor. *Fair Employment Practice Act: Hearings Before a Subcommittee of the Committee on Education and Labor.* 79th Cong., 1st sess., 1945.

———. *Federal Equality of Opportunity Act.* 82d Cong., 2nd sess., 1952. S. Rept. 2080.

———. *Federal Equality of Opportunity in Employment Act.* 83rd Cong., 2nd sess., 1954. S. Rept. 1267.

———. *National Act Against Discrimination in Employment.* 81st Cong., 2nd sess., 1950. S. Rept. 1539.

———. *Prohibiting Discrimination in Employment Because of Race, Creed, Color, National Origin, or Ancestry.* 79th Cong., 1st sess., 1945. S. Rept. 290.

———. *Prohibiting Discrimination in Employment Because of Race, Creed, Color, National Origin, or Ancestry.* 78th Cong., 2nd sess., 1944. S. Rept. 1109.

———. *Prohibiting Discrimination in Employment Because of Race, Religion, Color, National Origin, or Ancestry.* 80th Cong., 2nd sess., 1948. S. Rept. 951.

———. Committee on Labor and Public Welfare. *State and Municipal Fair Employment Practices Legislation.* 82nd Cong., 2nd sess., 1952. Staff Report.

———. *The Equal Employment Opportunity Act.* 88th Cong., 2nd sess., 1964. S. Report 867.

Dissertations

Alford, Albert Lee. "FEPC, An Administrative Study of Selected State and Local Programs." Princeton University, 1953.

Cartwright, Marguerite. "Legislation Against Discrimination in Employment in New York State." New York University, 1948.

Gray, Gibson Hendrix. "The Lobbying Game: A Study of the 1953 Campaign of the State Council for a Pennsylvania FEPC." Columbia University, 1967.

Hunter, Gary Jerome. "'Don't Buy from Where You Can't Work': Black Urban Boycott Movements During the Depression, 1929–41." University of Michigan, 1977.

Kifer, Francis Allen. "The Negro Under the New Deal, 1933–41." University of Wisconsin, 1961.

Lloyd, Kent Murdock. "Solving an American Dilemma, The Role of the FEPC Official: A Comparative Study of Civil Rights Commissions." Stanford University, 1964.

Mayer, Michael S. "Eisenhower's Conditional Crusade: The Eisenhower Administration and Civil Rights, 1953–57." Princeton University, 1984.

Schlundt, Ronald Alan. "Civil Rights Policies in the Eisenhower Years." Rice University, 1973.

Skotnes, Andor D. "The Black Freedom Movement and the Workers' Movement in Baltimore, 1930–39." Rutgers University, 1991.

Timbers, Edwin. "Labor Unions and Fair Employment Practice Legislation." University of Michigan, 1954.

Weiss, Robert John. "'We Want Jobs': The History of Affirmative Action." New York University, 1985.

Williams, Alma Rene. "Robert C. Weaver: From the Black Cabinet to the President's Cabinet." Washington University, 1978.

INDEX